D0309516

Dorothy Whitehead
8 Orchard End
Rowledge, Farnham
Surrey, GU10 4EE

LET'S PRAISE!

Editor: David Peacock

Consultant: Graham Kendrick

Executive Editor: Michael Perry

Marshall Pickering
An Imprint of HarperCollins*Publishers*

First published in Great Britain in 1988
by Marshall Morgan & Scott Publications Ltd

Marshall Pickering is an imprint of HarperCollins*Religious*
Part of HarperCollins*Publishers*
77–85 Fulham Palace Road
London W6 8JB

9 8 7 6 5 4

Copyright © 1988 by David Peacock and Michael Perry

The editors assert the moral right to be
identified as the editors of this work

Music and text set by Barnes Music Engraving Ltd., East Sussex
Printed in Great Britain by HarperCollinsManufacturing, Glasgow

A catalogue record for this book is
available from the British Library

CONDITIONS OF SALE

This book is sold subject to the condition that it shall not, by way of trade or otherwise, be lent, re-sold, hired out or otherwise circulated without the publisher's prior consent in any form of binding or cover other than that in which it is published and without a similar condition including this condition being imposed on the subsequent purchaser.

Copyright details will be found with each item, and further information at the page 'Legal Information'. Every effort has been made to trace copyright holders and obtain permission; the publishers would welcome details of any error or omission, which will be corrected in future reprints.

ISBN 0 551 01658 2

Also available from Marshall Pickering
Let's Praise! Words Edition
Single copy ISBN 0 551 01696 5
Pack of 25 copies ISBN 0 551 01749 X
Lets Praise! 2 Music Edition ISBN 0 551 04007 6
Lets Praise! Combined Words Edition ISBN 0 551 04008 4

By the same Editors
in association with the Jubilate group

Carol Praise
Carolling (Carol Praise Selection)
Play Carol Praise
Come Rejoice!
The Dramatised Bible
The Wedding Book
Carols for Today
Carols for Today: Choir Supplement
Church Family Worship
Hymns for Today's Church

Jubilate agents in the USA

Hope Publishing Company
Carol Stream, Illinois 60188

CONTENTS

PREFACE TO LET'S PRAISE!

We have researched the songs young people are singing across the denominations and throughout the world, and we believe the result to be a magnificent collection of material, suitable for all occasions involving young people.

Styles and Sources

Let's Praise! songs range from soft to hard rock, from reggae to black gospel; from performance items to recently composed and previously unpublished material; from jazz to response-style psalms and hymns.

A good selection of music from Africa can be found in the book alongside material from, for example, Scandinavia, Germany, and South America. Previously unpublished rock worship songs from Australia are included in the collection. Taizé music, which has long been popular amongst thousands of European young people, is well represented.

All this, together with most of the popular and current worship songs from Britain and North America, make *Let's Praise!* a truly distinctive songbook for young people. All the Graham Kendrick *Make Way 1 – A Carnival of Praise* street procession songs are in the book (in march order) together with a good selection of songs from *Make Way 2 – Shine, Jesus, Shine.*

We believe that there is tremendous value in having hymns of deep spiritual content, which are also in a language understandable to today's generation, included in the *Let's Praise!* collection. This results in a songbook readily available for use in youth groups, colleges and universities, youth houseparties and conferences. It is the ideal songbook for youth services in churches – even as your church's basic songbook.

Finding your way around

All the items are arranged alphabetically where possible. The thematic indexes relate the songs to themes utilised at the *Baptist Youth World Conference* held in Scotland in July 1988 ('Jesus Christ Rules'). Within each of these all-embracing themes you will discover a variety of sub-themes suitable for most occasions. For example, songs of social and international concern are included in the section 'Jesus Christ rules the world'.

The extensive Bible index, the worship and stylistic indexes will further help you use *Let's Praise!* to the best possible advantage. Of special interest will be new words set to familiar melodies: this makes new texts immediately accessible to the singers. Other indexes relate the songs to vocal arrangements, styles of singing, and use of instruments.

Acknowledgements

We acknowledge the help given by leaders of youth activities both in Britain and throughout the world in the compilation of *Let's Praise!*

Bunty Grundy has, as ever, been untiring in clearing and administering the copyrights throughout the world. For this we are deeply grateful. We also thank Ann Darlington, Sylvia Bleasdale and Niki Coffey for their help in getting material ready for publication.

My personal thanks to Graham Kendrick for his help in the compilation of the core worship material, and for his own excellent contributions; to members of the 'Jubilate' team for their continuing help and advice; and especially to Michael Perry for his work and expertise in progressing the book towards publication.

We commend this songbook to the new generation of Christians around the world, praying it will enrich our worship and give expression to our concern for sharing the Christian gospel with a world in need.

David Peacock

FOREWORD TO LET'S PRAISE!

With the new generation of young Baptists from around the world gathering in Scotland for the 11th Baptist Youth World Conference, we asked David Peacock, together with Graham Kendrick, to collect music material from around the world, and enlisted Michael Perry as consultant editor. Youth groups and leaders have shared in this to create a truly international praise book.

The music we use in worship within God's global village varies considerably between continents and cultures. Yet we find a growth in the use of contemporary words and music alongside a new understanding of the great truths contained in more traditional items. We also find a greater sharing of music from different cultures – all helping us to discover that 'Jesus Christ rules.'

We shall use *Let's Praise!* to resource our praise and worship, and to confirm our commitment to mission and evangelism throughout our world.

Paul Montacute
Chairperson
Baptist World Alliance Youth Department
July 1988

1 Abba, Father

Words and music: Dave Bilbrough
Mark 14.36, Romans 8.15, Galatians 4.6
Music arranged David Peacock

Thoughtfully
G C D7 G
1 Ab - ba, Fa - ther, let me be
2 may my will for ev - er be,
3 Ab - ba, Fa - ther, let me be
1.
2.3.
C D7 G D D7
yours and yours a - lone;
ev - er - more your
yours and yours a -
G Fine B Em B
own.
lone!
Ne - ver let my heart grow
Em C Am7 D D7 D.C. al Fine
cold, ne - ver let me go:

Words and music: © 1977 Kingsway's Thankyou Music,
PO Box 75, Eastbourne, East Sussex BN23 6NW

2 All hail the power of Jesus' name

Miles Lane 8 6 8 6 (CM)

Words: after E Perronet (1725–1792)
and J Rippon (1751–1836)
in this version Jubilate Hymns
Isaiah 60.3, Revelation 14.14 and 19.6
Music: later form of melody
by W Shrubsole (c.1759–1806)
arranged David Peacock

Triumphantly

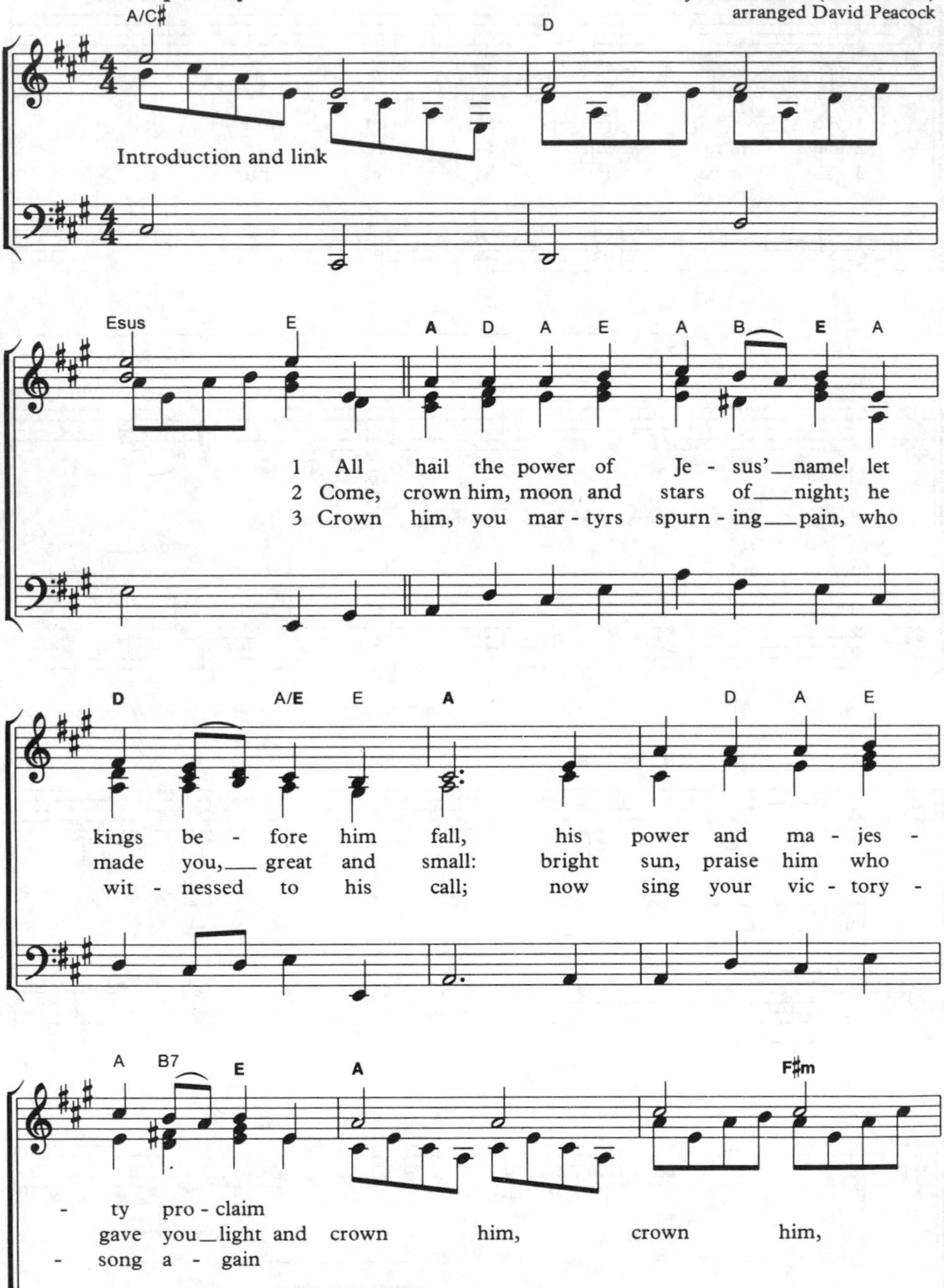
A/C♯ D
Introduction and link
Esus E A D A E A B E A
1 All hail the power of Je - sus' name! let
2 Come, crown him, moon and stars of night; he
3 Crown him, you mar - tyrs spurn - ing pain, who
D A/E E A D A E
kings be - fore him fall, his power and ma - jes -
made you, great and small: bright sun, praise him who
wit - nessed to his call; now sing your vic - tory -
A B7 E A F♯m
- ty pro - claim
gave you light and crown him, crown him,
- song a - gain

Music arrangement: © David Peacock / Jubilate Hymns †
Words: © in this version Jubilate Hymns †

4 Let all who trust in Christ exclaim
in wonder, to recall
the one who bore our sin and shame,
and crown him . . .

5 Then in that final judgement hour
when all rebellions fall,
we'll rise in his triumphant power
and crown him . . .

2A PRAISE SHOUT

LEADER Praise the Lord, O my soul;
ALL **praise the Lord!**

LEADER O Lord my God, how great you are;
ALL **robed in majesty and splendour.**

LEADER Praise the Lord, O my soul;
ALL **praise the Lord! Amen.**

From Psalm 104

3 All I am will sing out

Jag vill ge dig o Herre min lovsang

Capo 3(G)

Original words and music: Christer Hultgren
Words: Jeanne Harper
Music arranged Christopher Norton

With joyful abandon

Eb/Bb (C) Ebm/Bb (Cm) Bb (G) Bb7 (G7)
mf 1 All I am will sing out as a praise song – ev - ery
2 There is no - bo dy else who is wor - thy – to
mp 3 If at times through my si - lence I grieve you, if through
Eb/Bb (C) Ebm/Bb (Cm) Bb (G) Bb/A
note, ev - ery tone is for you; whe - ther
no - bo - dy else can I sing; and to
doubt, praise and wor - ship-ping cease; then, Lord,
Gm7 (Em7) C7 (A7) Fmaj7 (Dmaj7) Bbmaj7 (Gmaj7)
days will be hard or be ea - sy, I will
you will be all of the glo - ry in
o - pen my eyes that I see you, see in
Eb (C) Bb/D (G) Eb (C) Cm (Am) Fsus (Dsus) F (D) F7 (D7)
live ev - ery mo - ment for you.
heaven where my prais - es I'll bring. You have
you a - lone I have peace.
f

Words and music: © 1978 Forlaget Filadelfia Dagenhuset, 105 36 Stockholm Sweden

B♭ (G) F/A (D) E♭/G (C) Cm7 (Am7)
mp
all of the praise I can of - fer, for your
Dm/F (Bm) E♭maj7 (Cmaj7) B♭/D (G) Csus (Asus) C (A) F (D) F7 (D7)
love is to one who has no me - rit: here I
B♭ (G) F/A (D) E♭/G (C) Cm (Am)
f
am, take me Lord, and my wor - ship, for your
B♭/D (G) E♭ (C) B♭/F (G) Gm7 (Em7) Cm/E♭ (Am) F7 (D7) B♭ (G)
good - ness and grace have no li - mit.

4 Alleluia, praise the Lord

Words and music: Shimrit Orr
and Kobi Oshrat
Music arranged Christopher Norton

Capo 3(G)

With abandon
mf
B♭ (G)
Al - le - lu - ia, praise the Lord, Al - le -
Dm (Bm) Gm7 (Em7) Cm (Am7) F7 (D7) Dm7 (Bm7) D7 (B7) E♭ (C)
- lu - ia, in one ac - cord! When it seems there are no
C♯dim (B♭dim) B♭/F (G) Dm/F (Bm) F♯dim (E♭dim) Gm (Em)
words to say all the love I get from the Lord to - day, when my
C9 (A9) Cm7 (Am7) F7 (D7)
heart sings out with joy – Al - le - lu - ia. Al - le -
B♭ (G) Dm (Bm)
- lu - ia, is my song, al - le - lu - ia

Words and music: © 1979 Gogly Music / Intersong Music Ltd
Reproduced by permission of Chappell Music Ltd and International Music Publications

Gm (Em7) Cm (Am7) F7 (D7) Dm7 (Bm7) D7 (B7) E♭ (C)
the whole day long, al - le - lu - ia,
C♯dim (B♭dim) B♭/F (G) D7 (B7) Gm (Em) C7 (A7)
the hea - vens are ring - ing with ev - ery-one
1.
Cm7 (Am7) F7 (D7) B♭ (G) E♭/B♭ (C) B♭ (G)
sing - ing 'Al - le - lu - ia!' Al - le -
2.
B♭ (G) Dm7 (Bm7) D7 (B7) E♭ (C) C♯dim (B♭dim) B♭/F (G) D7 (B7) Gm (Em)
- Al - le - lu - ia, the hea - vens are ring - ing
C7 (A7) Cm7 (Am7) F7 (D7) B♭ (G) E♭/B♭ (C) B♭ (G)
with ev - ery-one sing - ing 'Al - le - lu - ia!'

5 Alleluia! We sing your praises

Haleluya! Pelo tsa rona

Words: African origin, collected and edited by Anders Nyberg
John 6.35 and 6.48
Music: African melody scored by Notman KB, Ljungsbro and Lars Parkman

Strong African rhythm

Am G C G D Am
Al - le - lu - ia! We sing your prais - es, all our hearts are filled with glad -
Ha - le - lu-ya! Pe - lo tsa ro - na, di tha - bi - le ka - o - fe -
Fine
G G7 Am G/D Em D7 G
- ness. Al - le - lu - ia! We sing your prais - es, all our hearts are filled with glad - ness:
- la: Ha - le - lu-ya! Pe - lo tsa ro - na, di tha - bi - le ka - o - fe - la:
Verses
Am G C G D7
1 Christ the Lord to us said, 'I am wine, I am
2 Now he sends us all out, strong in faith, free of
1 Ke Mo - re - na Je - so, ya re du - me - let -
2 O na na le bo mang? Le ba - ru - tu - wa
D.C. al Fine
G G7 Am G/D Em D7 G
bread'; 'I am wine, I am bread' – give to all who thirst and hun - ger.
doubt; strong in faith, free of doubt – tell the earth the joy - ful Gos - pel.
- seng, ya re du - me-let - seng, ho tsa - mai - sa e - van - ge - di.
ba hae: O na na le bo mang? Le ba - ru - tu - wa ba hae.

Words and music: © Wild Goose Publications / The Iona Community

6 Amazing grace

Words: J Newton (1725–1807)
in this version Jubilate Hymns
Matthew 18.14, Luke 15.6, John 9.25, Ephesians 2.5
Music: Southern Harmony (1835)
arranged David Peacock

Flowing
G G7 C G
1 A - maz - ing grace – how sweet the sound – that
(2) grace first taught my heart to fear, his
(3) ev - ery dan - ger, trial and snare I
Em A7 C/D D
saved a wretch like me! I
grace my fears re - lieved: how
have al - rea - dy come; for
Gmaj7 G7 C Bm E7
once was lost, but now am found; was
pre - cious did that grace ap - pear the
grace has brought me safe thus far, and
1-4. 5.
Am7 D7 C/G G G
blind, but now I see. 2 God's
hour I first be - lieved! 3 Through
grace will lead me home. 4 The

4 The Lord has promised good to me,
his word my hope secures;
my shield and stronghold he shall be
as long as life endures.

5 And when this earthly life is past,
and mortal cares shall cease,
I shall possess with Christ at last
eternal joy and peace.

Music arrangement: © David Peacock / Jubilate Hymns †

Words: © in this version Jubilate Hymns †

7 Almighty God

Words: from The Alternative Service Book 1980
Music: Chris Rolinson
arranged David Peacock

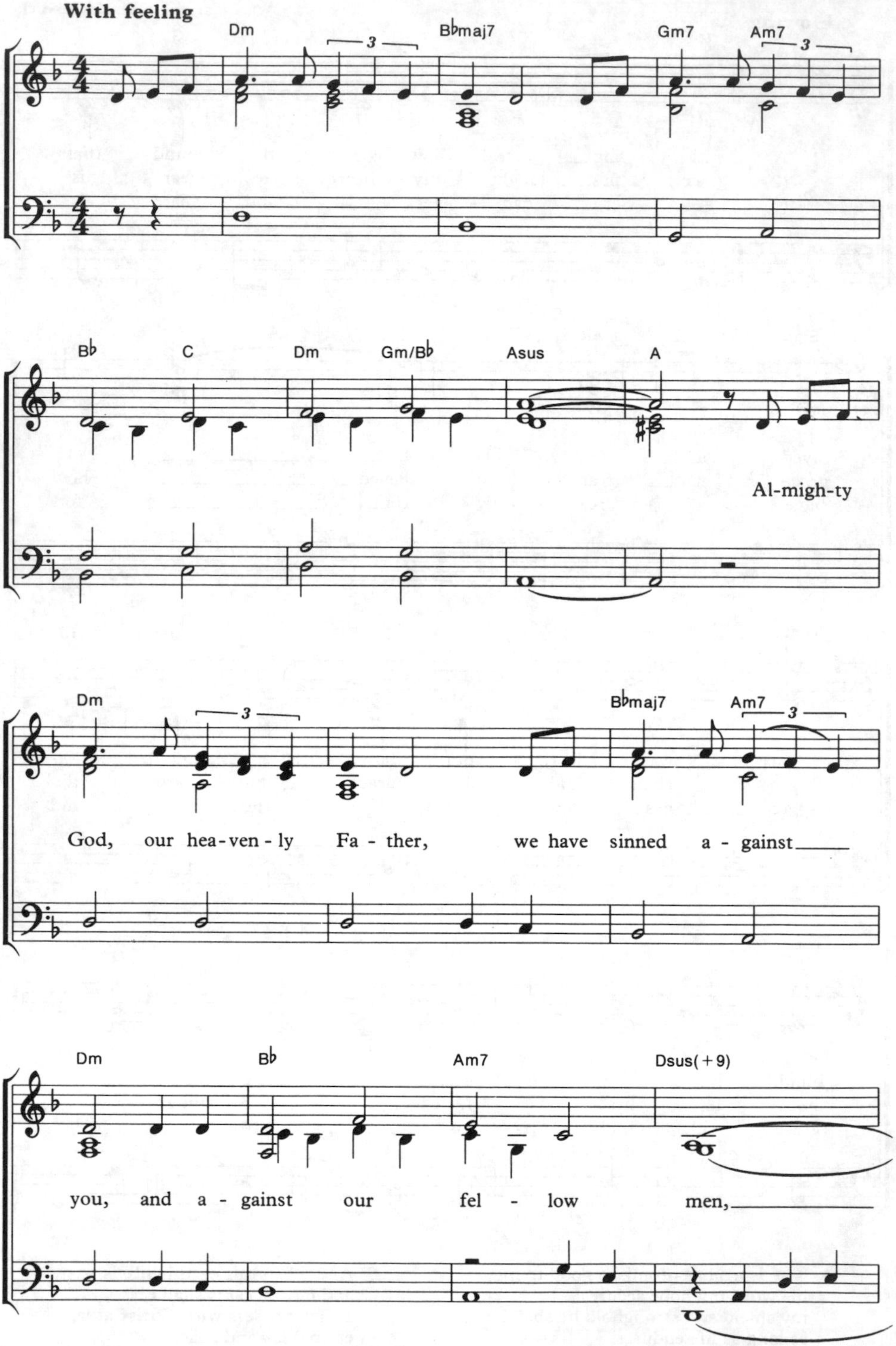
With feeling
Dm Bbmaj7 Gm7 Am7
Bb C Dm Gm/Bb Asus A
Al-migh-ty
Dm Bbmaj7 Am7
God, our hea-ven-ly Fa-ther, we have sinned a-gainst
Dm Bb Am7 Dsus(+9)
you, and a-gainst our fel-low men,

Music: © 1987 Kingsway's Thankyou Music, PO Box 75, Eastbourne, East Sussex BN23 6NW

Words: © 1980 Central Board of Finance of the Church of England. Used with permission

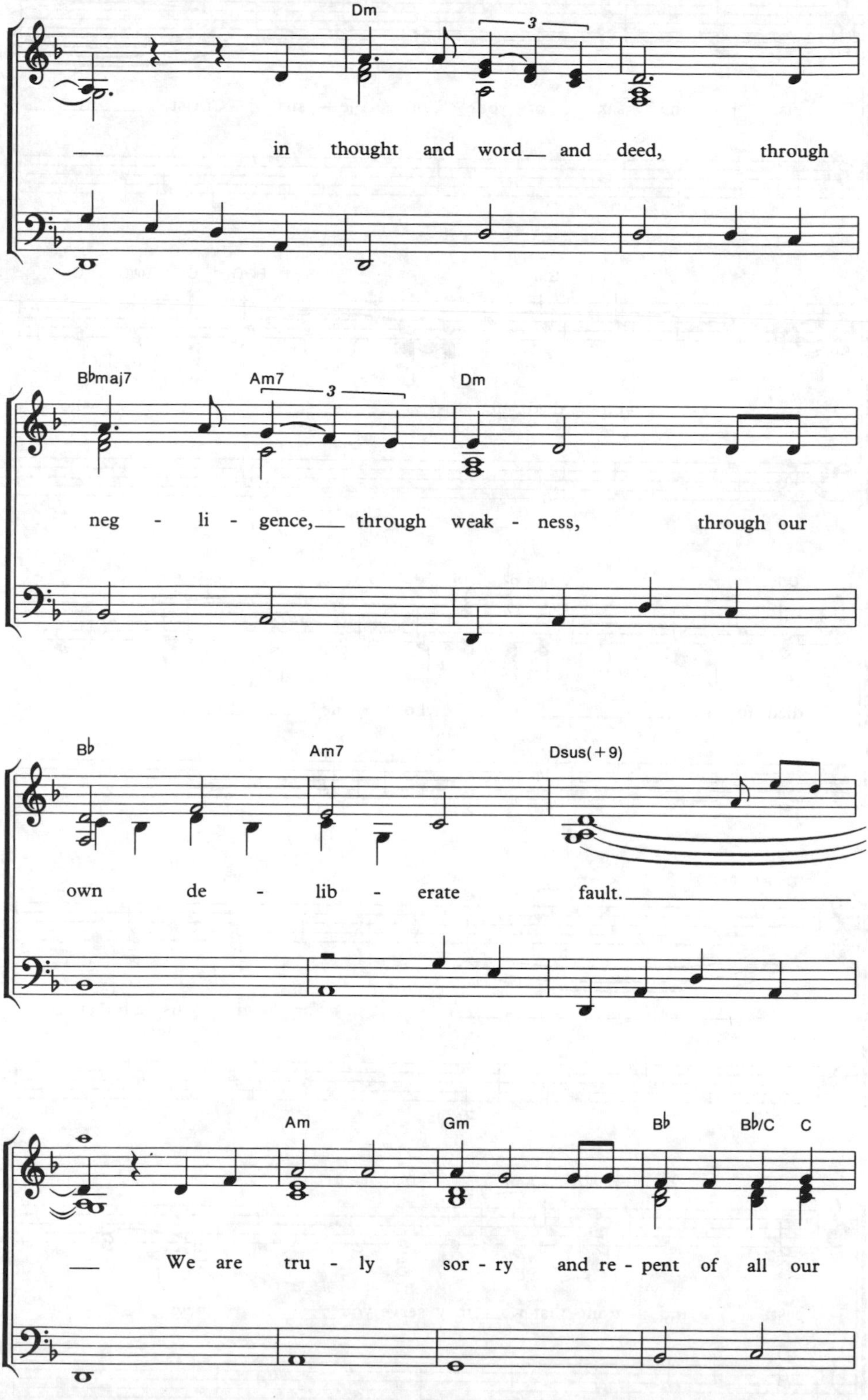
Dm
— in thought and word — and deed, through
B♭maj7 Am7 Dm
neg - li - gence, — through weak - ness, through our
B♭ Am7 Dsus(+9)
own de - lib - erate fault. —
Am Gm B♭ B♭/C C
— We are tru - ly sor - ry and re - pent of all our

F Dm Am7 Dsus(+9)
sins. For the sake of your Son, Je - sus Christ,
Gm B♭/C C B♭/C C
who died for us, who
C/F F C/B♭ B♭ C/B♭ B♭ Gm7 Am
died for us, who died for
Dsus(+9) Dm
us, for - give us all that is
B♭maj7 Am7 Dm B♭
past; and grant that we may serve you in new -

Am7 D
- ness of life MEN to the
Em7 G/A D/A D Bm Em7 G/A D/A
glo - ry of your name, WOMEN to the glo - ry of your
D Bm Em7 G/A D/A F♯m6 Bm7
name, MEN to the glo - ry of your name, WOMEN to the
Em7 G/A D/A D G D/F♯
glo - ry of your name, ALL to the glo - ry of your
Em7 G Asus A Dsus(+9)
name. A - men, a - men.

8 And can it be

Words: C Wesley (1707–1788)
Acts 12.6, Romans 8.1, 1 Corinthians 15.9
Music: T Campbell's 'Bouquet' 1825

Sagina 8 8 8 8 8 8 extended

G G/B G C D G
1 And can it be that I___ should__ gain
2 What mys - tery here! – the Im - mor - tal____ dies;
3 He left his Fa - ther's throne__ a - bove –
C D G D/A A7 D
an in - terest__ in the____ Sav - iour's blood?
who can____ ex - plore his____ strange de - sign?
so free,___ so_____ in - fi - nite his grace –
G/D D G D
Died he for me,______ who caused his pain;
In vain the first - born se - raph tries
emp - tied him - self________ of all but love,
C G/B Am7/C G/D D7 G
for me,____ who him____ to death pur - sued?
to sound__ the depths__ of love di - vine.
and bled____ for Ad - am's help - less race.

* Verse 4 may be omitted

D G C A7/C♯ D
A - ma - zing love! – how can it be
Such mer - cy this! – let earth a - dore;
What mer - cy this, im - mense and free,
G C D G
that you, my God, should die for me?
let an - gel minds en - quire no more.
for, O my God, it found out me!
D D7 G
A - ma - zing love! – how can it be that
Such mer - cy this! – let earth a - dore; let
What mer - cy this, im - mense and free, for,
A - ma - zing love! – how can it be
Such mer - cy this! – let earth a - dore;
What mer - cy this, im - mense and free,
C G Am/C G/D D7 G
you, my God, should die for me?
an - gel minds en - quire no more.
O my God, it found out me!
that you, my God, should die for me?
let an - gel minds en - quire no more.
for, O my God, it found out me!

4 Long my imprisoned spirit lay,
fast bound in sin and nature's night:
your sunrise turned that night to day;
I woke – the dungeon flamed with light.
My chains fell off, my heart was free;
I rose, went out to liberty!

5 No condemnation now I dread;
Jèsus, and all in him, is mine!
Alive in him, my living head,
and clothed in righteousness divine,
bold I approach the eternal throne
and claim the crown through Christ my own.

9 At the name of Jesus

Camberwell 6 5 6 5 D

Words: C M Noel (1817–1877)
in this version Jubilate Hymns
Philippians 2.10
Music: Michael Brierley

C Dm7 G7 C F G7
1 At the name of Je - sus ev - ery knee shall
2 At his voice cre - a - tion sprang at once to
3 Hum - bled for a sea - son, to re - ceive a
C Am Dm7/F C/E C♯dim
bow, ev - ery tongue con - fess him king of
sight, all the an - gel fa - ces, all the
name from the lips of sin - ners un - to
G/D D7 G G7 C Dm7 G7
glo - ry now; this the Fa - ther's
hosts of light; thrones and dom - in -
whom he came; faith - ful - ly he
C C7 F E7 Am
plea - sure, that we call him Lord,
- a - tions, stars up - on their way,
bore it spot - less to the last,

* Verses 2 and 6 may be omitted

Music: © 1960 Josef Weinberger,
12–14 Mortimer Street, London W1N 7RD

Words: © in this version Jubilate Hymns †

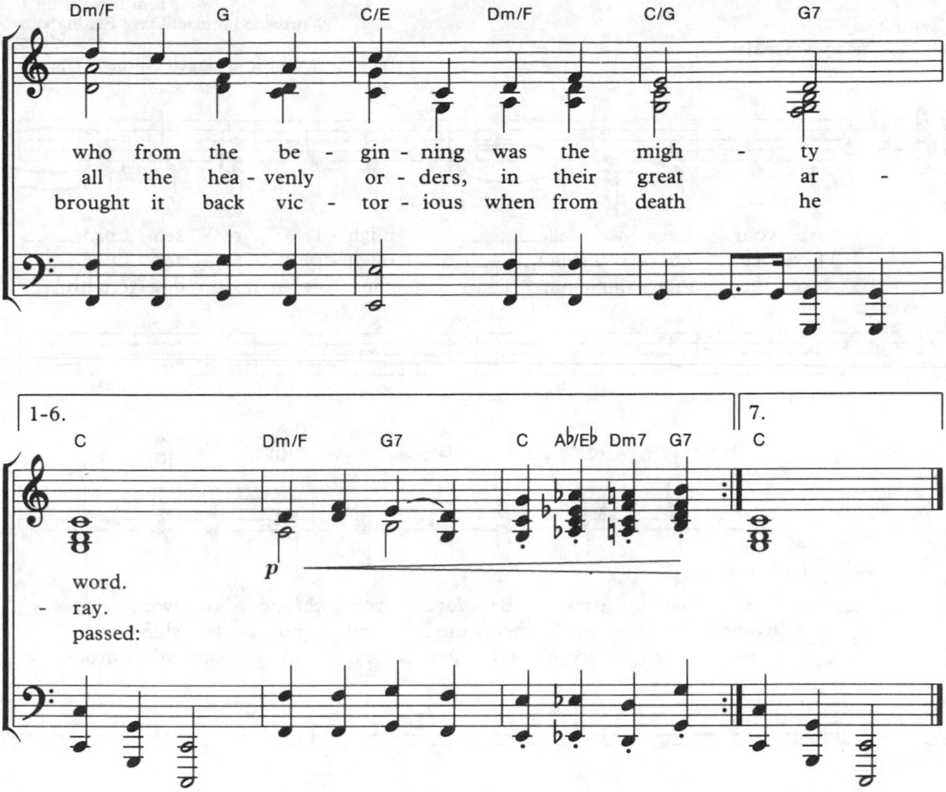
Dm/F G C/E Dm/F C/G G7
who from the be - gin - ning was the migh - ty
all the hea - venly or - ders, in their great ar -
brought it back vic - tor - ious when from death he
1-6.
C Dm/F G7 C A♭/E♭ Dm7 G7
7.
C
word.
- ray.
passed:
p

4 Bore it up triumphant
with its human light,
through all ranks of creatures
to the central height;
to the eternal Godhead,
to the Father's throne,
filled it to the glory
of his triumph won.

5 Name him, Christians, name him,
with love strong as death,
but with awe and wonder,
and with bated breath:
he is God the saviour,
he is Christ the Lord,
ever to be worshipped,
trusted and adored.

6 In your hearts enthrone him –
there let him subdue
all that is not holy,
all that is not true;
crown him as your captain
in temptation's hour,
let his will enfold you
in its light and power.

7 With his Father's glory
Jesus comes again,
angel hosts attend him
and announce his reign;
for all wreaths of empire
meet upon his brow,
and our hearts confess him
king of glory now.

10 At your feet we fall

From Revelation 1
Words and music: Dave Fellingham
Revelation 1.12 and 1.18
Music arranged Norman Warren

Capo 2(G)

Majestically

A (G)
1 At your feet we fall, mighty risen Lord,
2 There we see you stand, mighty risen Lord,
3 Like the shining sun in its noon-day strength,
D/A (C/G)
A (G)
D/A (C/G)
A (G)
as we come before your throne to worship
clothed in garments pure and holy, shining
we now see the glory of your wondrous
D (C)
F♯7 (E7)
Bm (Am)
F♯7 (E7)
Bm (Am)
F♯7 (E7)
you! By your Spirit's power
bright; eyes of flashing fire,
face: once that face was marred,
Bm (Am)
F♯7 (E7)
Bm (Am)
F♯7 (E7)
Bm (Am)
you now draw our hearts, and we
feet like burnished bronze, and the
but now you're glorified; and your

Words and music: © 1982 Kingsway's Thankyou Music,
PO Box 75, Eastbourne, East Sussex BN23 6NW

E7 (D7)
A (G) D (C) A (G)
hear your voice in tri - umph ring-ing clear:
sound of ma - ny wa - ters is your voice.
words, like a two-edged sword, have migh-ty power.
Chorus
F♯m (Em)
B7 (A7)
E (D)
'I am he that lives, that lives and was dead: be -
A (G) Em6/G (Dm6/F) D/F♯ (C/E) F7 (E♭7) A/E (G/D) E7 (D7) A (G)
- hold I am a - live – a - live ev - er - more!'
B♭ version for chorus

11 Be bold, be strong

Words and music: Morris Chapman
Joshua 1.9

Lively
F/G C C/E
Be bold, be strong, for the
F G
Lord your God is with you; be bold,
C C/E F
be strong, for the Lord your God is with
G F G Am
you! I am not a - fraid,

Words and music: © 1983 Word Music (UK)/CopyCare Ltd,
PO Box 77, Hailsham, East Sussex BN27 3EF

F G Am
I am not dis - mayed, be-cause I'm
F G Am
walk - ing in faith and vic - to - ry: come on and
F G Am F
walk in faith and vic - to - ry, for the Lord your
G G7 C
God is with you!

12 Bind us together, Lord

Words and music: Bob Gillman
Music arranged David Peacock

Capo 5(C)

With a lilt

F (C) Gm7 (Dm7) Am7 (Em7) Dm7 (Am7)
Bind us to - ge - ther, Lord, bind us to - ge - ther with
Gm (Dm) C7 (G7) F (C) B♭/C (F)
cords that can - not be bro - ken;
last time to Coda
F (C) Gm7 (Dm7) Am7 (Em7) Dm7 (Am7)
bind us to - ge - ther, Lord, bind us to - ge - ther, O
Gm (Dm) C7 (G7) F (C) B♭/C (F) F (C) Cm7 (Gm7)
bind us to - ge - ther in love!
1 There is on - ly one
2 We are the fam - ily of

Words and music: © 1977 Kingsway's Thankyou Music,
PO Box 75, Eastbourne, East Sussex BN23 6NW

F (C)
Cm7 (Gm7)
F (C)
Cm7 (Gm7)
God, there is on - ly one
God, joined by the Spi - rit a -
F (C)
Cm7 (Gm7)
F (C)
Gm7 (Dm7)
King, there is on - ly one
- bove, work - ing to - ge - ther with
Am (Em)
D7 (A7)
Gm7 (Dm7)
C7 (G7)
Bo - dy that is why we
Christ, grow - ing and build - ing in
F (C)
B♭/C (F)
D.C.
CODA
Gm (Dm)
C7 (G7)
F (C)
sing:
love.
bind us to - ge-ther in love!

13 Be still

Words and music: David Evans
Exodus 3.5, Psalm 46.10, Acts 7.33
Music arranged Geoff Baker

Unhurried
D F♯m7 Bm Em7 A9 A
1 Be still, for the pres-ence of the Lord, the ho - ly One, is here;
2 Be still, for the glo - ry of the Lord is shin-ing all a - round;
3 Be still, for the pow - er of the Lord is mov-ing in this place:
D F♯m7 Bm Em7 Asus A
come bow be - fore him now with re - ver-ence and fear:
he burns with ho - ly fire, with splen-dour he is crowned:
he comes to cleanse and heal, to min - is - ter his grace –
G A/G D/F♯ G A/G D/F♯
in him no sin is found – we stand on ho - ly ground.
how awe-some is the sight – our rad-iant king of light!
no work too hard for him. In faith re - ceive from him.
G A F♯m7 Bm Em7 Em7/A A D
Be still, for the pres-ence of the Lord, the ho - ly One, is here.
Be still, for the glo - ry of the Lord is shin-ing all a - round.
Be still, for the pow - er of the Lord is mov-ing in this place.

Words and music: © 1986 Kingsway's Thankyou Music,
PO Box 75, Eastbourne, East Sussex BN23 6NW

14 Bless the Lord, O my soul

From Psalm 103
Words and music: Unknown
Music arranged David Peacock

With majesty

G C E7 A
Bless the Lord, O my soul, bless the Lord, O my
last time to Coda
D G C Am G/D Dsus
soul, and all that is with - in me bless his ho - ly
1.
G C G/B D7/A
name; bless the
2.
G C D7 G C G C G
name; King of kings (for ev-er and ev-er),
A D A D A B Em B Em B
Lord of lords (for ev-er and ev-er) King of kings (for ev-er and ev-er),
D.S. al Coda
CODA
Am G/B Am/C C/E G/D D7 G C G/B D7/A G
King of kings and Lord of lords! Bless the name.

Music arrangement: © David Peacock / Jubilate Hymns †

15 Bless the Lord

Words: derived from the 'Daily Office'
of the Joint Liturgical Group
Music: Chris Rolinson
arranged by David Peacock

With a swing
D A/D G/D A/D D A/D G/D A
Introduction
SOLO/GROUP
1 Bless the
D G/A D D/F♯
Lord the God of our fa - thers:
(5) sits be - tween the che - ru - bim:
ALL
sing his
Em7 D/A G/A D
praise and ex - alt him for ev - er.
SOLO/GROUP
2 Bless his
6 Bless him
G/A D D/F♯ Em7 D/A G/A
ho - ly and glo - ri - ous name:
on the throne of his king - dom:
ALL
sing his praise and ex - alt him for ev -

Words and music: © 1987 Kingsway's Thankyou Music,
PO Box 75, Eastbourne, East Sussex BN23 6NW

Words: © Joint Liturgical Group

D D/F♯ G D/F♯
SOLO/GROUP
- er. 3 Bless him in his ho - ly and glo - ri - ous tem -
7 Bless him in the heights of hea -
2nd time to Coda
Em7 D/F♯ G D/F♯ Em7 D/F♯
- ple: ALL sing his praise and ex - alt him for ev - er. SOLO/GROUP 4 Bless
- ven: 8 Bless the
G A Bm Em7 D/A G/A
him who be - holds the depths: ALL sing his praise and ex - alt him for ev -
D
- er. SOLO/GROUP 5 Bless him who
CODA
G A Bm
Fa - ther, the Son and the Ho - ly
B♭ Em7 D/A G/A D
Spi - rit: ALL sing his praise and ex - alt him for ev - er.

16 Breathe on me, breath of God

Saints Alive
Capo 3(C)

Words: E Hatch (1835–1889)
in this version Jubilate Hymns
Genesis 2.7, Job 33.4, John 20.22
Music: Roger Jones

Thoughtfully
Eb (C) Fm7 (Dm7) Bb7 (G7) Eb (C)
1 Breathe on me,
3 Breathe on me,
Fm7 (Dm7) Bb7 (G7)
breath of God: fill me with
breath of God; ful - fil my
Eb (C) Ab (F)
life a - new, that as you
heart's de - sire, un - til this
Gm (Em) Eb (C) Cm (Am) F9 (D9) Bb7 (G7)
love, so I may love, and do what you would do.
earth-ly part of me glows with your hea-venly fire.

Music: © Roger Jones

Words: © in this version Jubilate Hymns †

G7 (E7) Cm (Am) A♭ (F) B♭7 (G7)
2 Breathe on me, breath of God, un - til my
4 Breathe on me, breath of God: so shall I
E♭ (C) A♭ (F)
heart is pure, un - til my
ne - ver die, but live with
Gm (Em) E♭ (C) Cm (Am) F9 (D9) B♭7 (G7)
will is one with yours to do and to en -
you the per - fect life of your e - ter - ni -
1. 2.
E♭ (C) Fm7 (Dm7) B♭7 (G7) E♭ (C)
- dure.
- ty.

17 Bring to the Lord a glad new song

Jerusalem 8 8 8 8 D (DLM)

Words: from Psalms 149 and 150
Michael Perry
Music: C H H Parry (1848–1918)

Slow but with animation
D Bm B7 Em B7 Em Bm G
D G/D G
Bring to the Lord a glad new
D G D Bm
song, chil - dren of grace, ex - tol your
G D Bm F♯m Bm F♯m
king; wor-ship and praise to God be - long– to in - stru -

Words: © Michael Perry / Jubilate Hymns †

Bm7 E7 A Em B7 Em Am
- ments of mu - sic, sing! Let those be warned who spurn his
Em G/D D7
name; na - tions and kings, at - tend his
poco cresc.
G Em A A7 D G
word – God's jus - tice shall bring ty - rants shame: let ev - ery
f ff poco rit.
D Gmaj7 A7 D Bm
crea - ture praise the Lord!
f a tempo

B7 Em Bm G D
Praise him with -
ff
mf
8va
G/D G D G
- in these hal - lowed walls, praise him be -
8va
D Bm G D Bm F♯m
- neath the dome of heaven; by cym-bals' sounds and trum-pets'
Bm F♯m Bm7 E7
calls let prais - es fit for God be

A Em B7 Em Am Em
given: with strings and brass and wind re- joice – then, join his
G/D D7 G
praise with full ac - cord all liv - ing
allargando
Em A A7 D G D Gmaj7 A7
things with breath and voice: let ev - ery crea - ture praise the
ff
rit.
D G/D G D
Lord!
ff
8va

18 Broken for me

Words and music: Janet Lunt
Matthew 26.26, Mark 14.22, Luke 22.19

Sensitively

E
Amaj7
F♯m
Bro-ken for me,
(for me)
bro-ken for
B7
E
Amaj7
you,
the bo-dy of Je - sus
F♯m
B7
E
bro-ken for you.
1 He of-fered his
2 Come to my
3 This is my
4 This is my
Amaj7
F♯m
B7
bo - dy, he poured out his soul,
ta - ble and with me dine,
bo - dy giv - en for you,
blood I shed for you,

Words and music: © 1978 Sovereign Lifestyle Music,
PO Box 356, Leighton Buzzard LU7 8WP. Used by permission.

E Amaj7 F♯m
Je - sus was bro - ken that we might be
eat of my bread and drink of my
eat it re - mem - bering I died for
for your for - give - ness, mak-ing you
1.2.3. B7 D.C.
whole:
wine:
you:
new:
4. E Amaj7
Bro - ken for me, (for
F♯m B7 E
bro-ken for you, the bo-dy of
me)
Amaj7 F♯m B7 E
Je - sus bro - ken for you.

19 By every nation, race and tongue

Easter Song 8 8 4 4 8 8 and Alleluias

Capo 3(C)

Words: H B George (1838–1910)
Revelation 5.9
Music: *Geistliche Kirchengesang* Cologne 1623
arranged Noël Tredinnick

1 By ev-ery na-tion, race and tongue, wor-
ship and praise be ev-er sung; praise the Fa-ther: Al-le-
lu - ia! For par-doned sin, death ov-er-

2 Saints who on earth have suf-fered long, for
Je-sus' sake en-dur-ing wrong, ev-er faith-ful: Al-le-
lu - ia! Where faith is lost in sight, re-

3 Let earth and air and sea u - nite to
ce-le-brate his glo-rious might, their cre-a-tor: Al-le-
lu - ia! Sun, moon and stars in end-less

Music arrangement: © Noël Tredinnick/Jubilate Hymns †

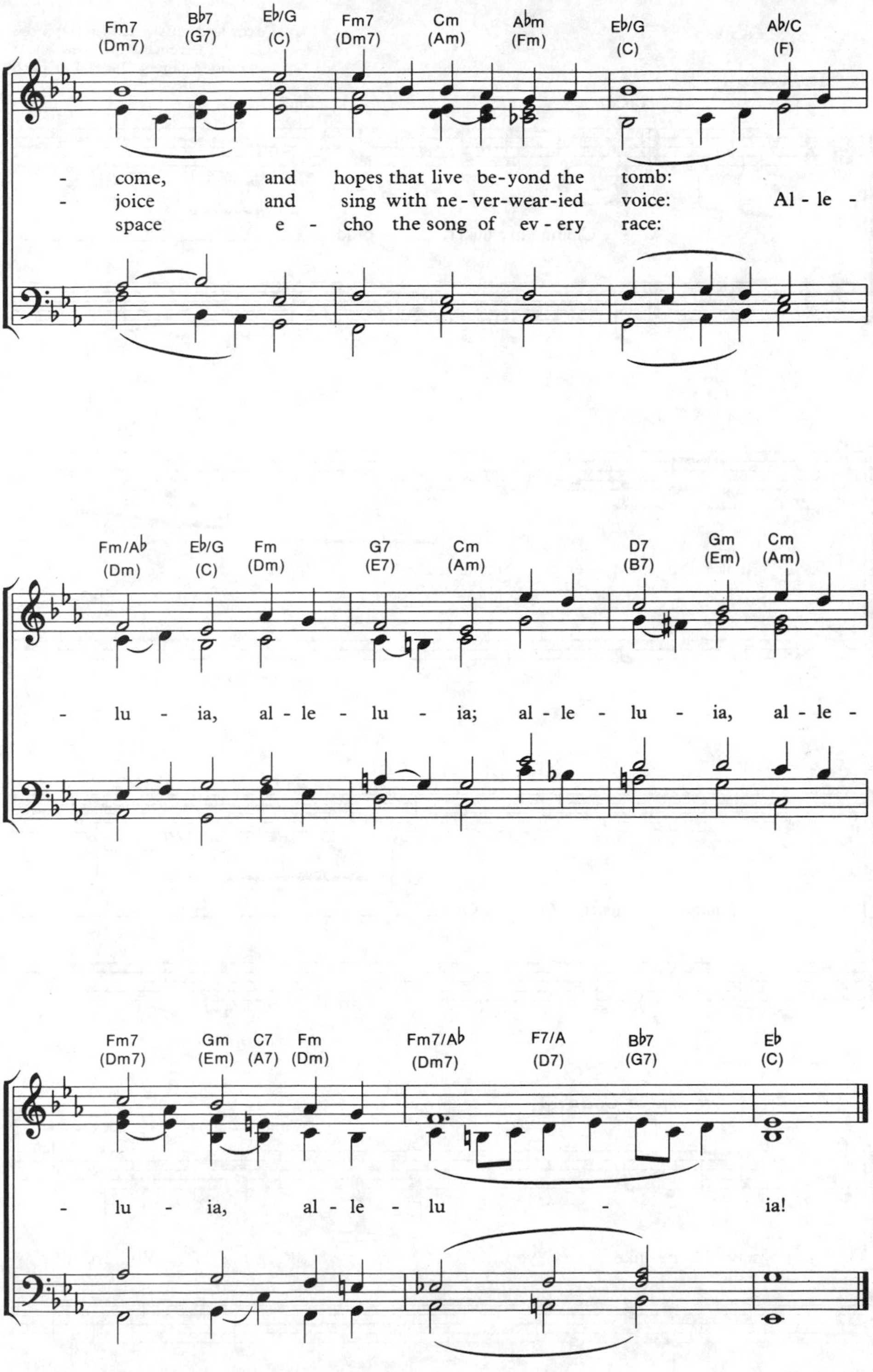
Fm7 (Dm7) B♭7 (G7) E♭/G (C) Fm7 (Dm7) Cm (Am) A♭m (Fm) E♭/G (C) A♭/C (F)
- come, and hopes that live be-yond the tomb:
- joice and sing with ne-ver-wear-ied voice: Al-le-
space e-cho the song of ev-ery race:
Fm/A♭ (Dm) E♭/G (C) Fm (Dm) G7 (E7) Cm (Am) D7 (B7) Gm (Em) Cm (Am)
- lu - ia, al - le - lu - ia; al - le - lu - ia, al - le -
Fm7 (Dm7) Gm (Em) C7 (A7) Fm (Dm) Fm7/A♭ (Dm7) F7/A (D7) B♭7 (G7) E♭ (C)
- lu - ia, al - le - lu - ia!

20 Change my heart, O God

Words and music: Eddie Espinosa
Jeremiah 18.5, Romans 9.21
arranged James Gabriel Stipech

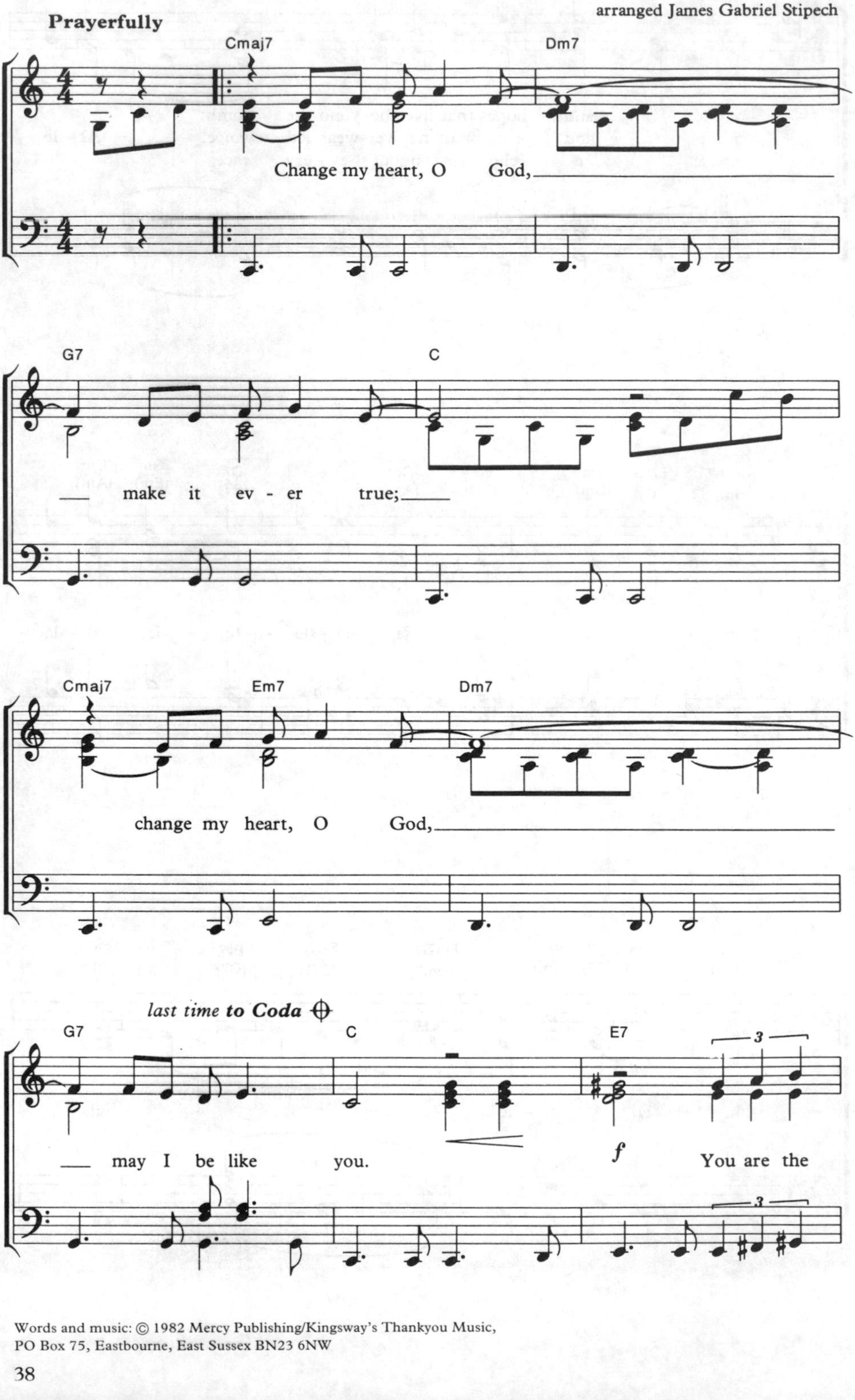
Prayerfully
Cmaj7
Dm7
Change my heart, O God,
G7
C
make it ev - er true;
Cmaj7
Em7
Dm7
change my heart, O God,
last time to Coda
G7
C
E7
may I be like you.
f
You are the
3

Words and music: © 1982 Mercy Publishing/Kingsway's Thankyou Music,
PO Box 75, Eastbourne, East Sussex BN23 6NW

Am Dm7 G7
pot - ter, I am the clay;
C E7 3 Am Am/G
mould me and make me,
1. D D7 G
this is what I pray.
2. D D7
this is what I
G
pray.
CODA slower
C F C/E Dm7 C
you.

21(i) Christ triumphant, ever reigning

(FIRST TUNE)

Christ triumphant 8 5 8 5 7 9

Capo 3(D)

Words: Michael Saward
Isaiah 53, John 1.14, Hebrews 8.1
Music: Michael Baughen
arranged Noël Tredinnick

Majestically

F (D) F7 (D7) Dm/F (Bm)
1 Christ tri - um - phant, ev - er reign - ing,
2 Word in - car - nate, truth re - vea - ling,
3 Suf - fering ser - vant, scorned, ill - trea - ted,
F/A (D) Dm (Bm) Gm7 (Em7) C7/F♯ (A7)
Sav - iour, Mas - ter, King!
Son of Man on earth!
vic - tim cru - ci - fied!
F (D) B♭ (G) Gm (Em)
Lord of heaven, our lives sus - tain - ing,
power and ma - jes - ty con - ceal - ing
death is through the cross de - fea - ted,
C (A) C7 (A7) F (D)
hear us as we sing:
by your hum - ble birth:
sin - ners jus - ti - fied:

Music: © Michael Baughen/Jubilate Hymns †
Music arrangement: © Noël Tredinnick/Jubilate Hymns †
Words: © Michael Saward / Jubilate Hymns †

4 Priestly king, enthroned for ever
high in heaven above!
sin and death and hell shall never
stifle hymns of love:
Yours the glory . . .

5 So, our hearts and voices raising
through the ages long,
ceaselessly upon you gazing,
this shall be our song:
Yours the glory . . .

21(ii) Christ triumphant, ever reigning

(SECOND TUNE)

Guiting Power 8 5 8 5 7 9
Capo 3(C)

Words: Michael Saward
Isaiah 53, John 1.14, Hebrews 8.1
Music: John Barnard

E♭ (C) Descant Cm (Am) A♭ (F) B♭ (G)
5 Our hearts and voi - ces rai - sing
1 Christ tri - um - phant, ev - er reign - ing,
2 Word in - car - nate, truth re - veal - ing,
3 Suf - fering ser - vant, scorned, ill - trea - ted,
4 Priest - ly king, en - throned for ev - er
5 So, our hearts and voi - ces rais - ing
E♭ (C) Fm (Dm) B♭ (G)
through the a - ges long,
Sav - iour, Ma - ster, King!
Son of Man on earth!
vic - tim cru - ci - fied!
high in heaven a - bove!
through the a - ges long,
E♭ (C) Cm (Am) Cm/A D (B)
up - on you gaz - ing,
Lord of heaven, our lives sus - tain - ing,
power and ma - jes - ty con - ceal - ing
death is through the cross de - fea - ted,
sin and death and hell shall ne - ver
cease - less - ly up - on you gaz - ing,
Org.

Music: © John Barnard / Jubilate Hymns †

Words: © Michael Saward / Jubilate Hymns †

Gm (Em) F7 (D7) Bb (G) Bb/Ab (G7)
this shall be our song: Yours the
hear us as we sing:
by your hum - ble birth:
sin - ners jus - ti - fied:
sti - fle hymns of love:
this shall be our song:
Gm (Em) Eb7 (C7) Ab (F) G7 (E7)
glo - ry and the crown, the high re -
Yours the glo - ry and the crown, the
Cm (Am) Gm (Em) Fm7 (Dm7) Bb (G) Eb (C)
- nown, the e - ter - nal name.
high re-nown, the e - ter - nal name.

22 Clear the road

Prepare the way

Words and music: Graham Kendrick
Isaiah 40.3, Mark 1.3

Capo 2(C)

Brightly ♩ = 133

D (C) Bm (Am) Em7 (Dm7) A7 (G7) D (C) D (C) F♯m (Em) G (F) Gsus (Asus) A (G)
MEN
1 Clear the road, make wide the way;
2 Raise your voice and join the song,
3 For all sin the price is paid,
4 At his feet, come, hum-bly bow,

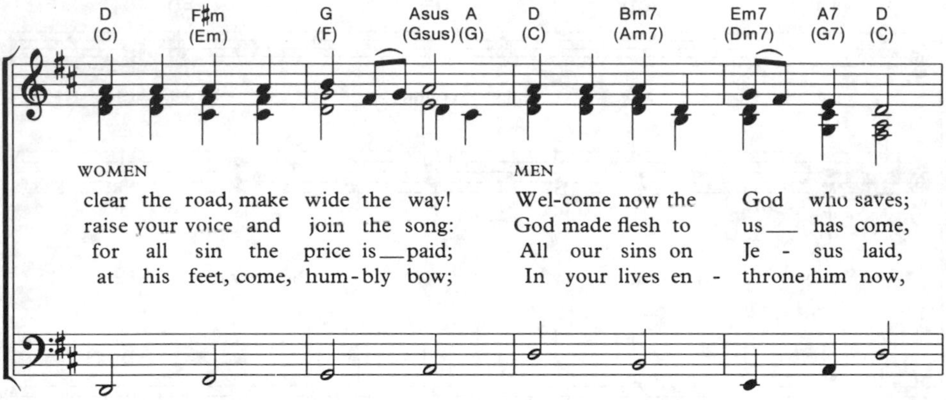
D (C) F♯m (Em) G (F) Asus (Gsus) A (G) D (C) Bm7 (Am7) Em7 (Dm7) A7 (G7) D (C)
WOMEN
clear the road, make wide the way!
raise your voice and join the song:
for all sin the price is paid;
at his feet, come, hum-bly bow;
MEN
Wel-come now the God who saves;
God made flesh to us has come,
All our sins on Je - sus laid,
In your lives en - throne him now,

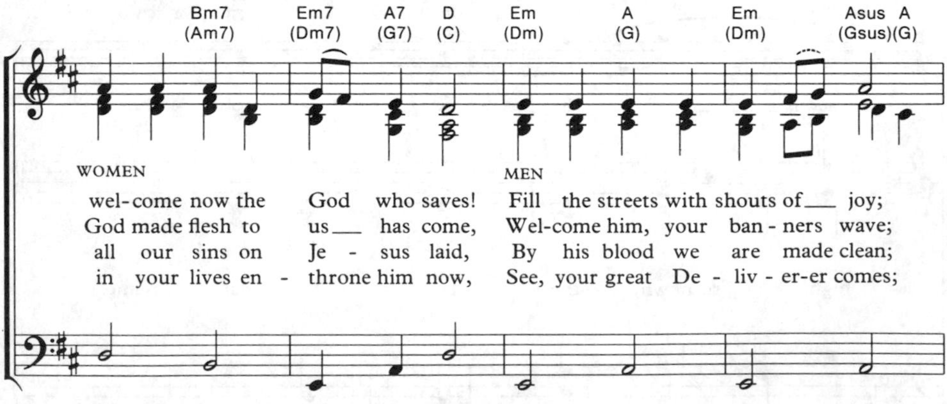
Bm7 (Am7) Em7 (Dm7) A7 (G7) D (C) Em (Dm) A (G) Em (Dm) Asus (Gsus) A (G)
WOMEN
wel-come now the God who saves!
God made flesh to us has come,
all our sins on Je - sus laid,
in your lives en - throne him now,
MEN
Fill the streets with shouts of joy;
Wel-come him, your ban-ners wave;
By his blood we are made clean;
See, your great De - liv - er-er comes;

Words and music: © 1988 Make Way Music,
PO Box 263, Croydon, Surrey CR9 5AP.
International copyright secured. All rights reserved. Used by permission.

Em (Dm) A (G) Em (Dm) Asus A (Gsus)(G) Gsus (Asus) A (G) Asus2 (Gsus2) A (G)
WOMEN
fill the streets with shouts of joy!
wel-come him, your ban-ners wave!
by his blood we are made clean.
see, your great De-liv-er-er comes!
(Cheers, etc.)
Bm (Am) A (G) Bm (Am) A (G)
WOMEN
Pre-pare the way of the
MEN
Pre-pare the way of the Lord,
Fine
4th time D.S.
Bm (Am) A (G) Bsus (Asus) B (A)
Lord; of the Lord!
pre-pare the way of the Lord!

23 Come to set us free

Advent Entrance Song

Words and music: Bernadette Farrell
John 1.5, Revelation 22.16

Brightly ♩ = 88+

Chorus

Dm Am Dm G A
Come to set us free, come to make us your own;
Dm Am Dm G A
come to show the way to your peo - ple, your cho - sen:
B♭ C Fmaj7 Dm Gm C Am
o - pen our lives to the light of your pro - mise.
(♭)

Words and music: © Bernadette Farrell. Published by OCP Publications.
Administered by Calamus, 30 North Terrace, Mildenhall, Suffolk IP28 7AB

last time to Coda
B♭ C Dm B♭
Come to our hearts with heal-ing, come to our minds with po-wer;
Dm Am Dm Am Dm
come to us and bring us your life.
1 You are
2 You are
3 You are
B♭ C F Gm7 C Dm
light which shines in dark-ness, Morn-ing Star which ne-ver sets:
hope which brings us cour-age, you are strength which ne-ver fails:
pro-mise of sal-va-tion, you are God in hu-man form:

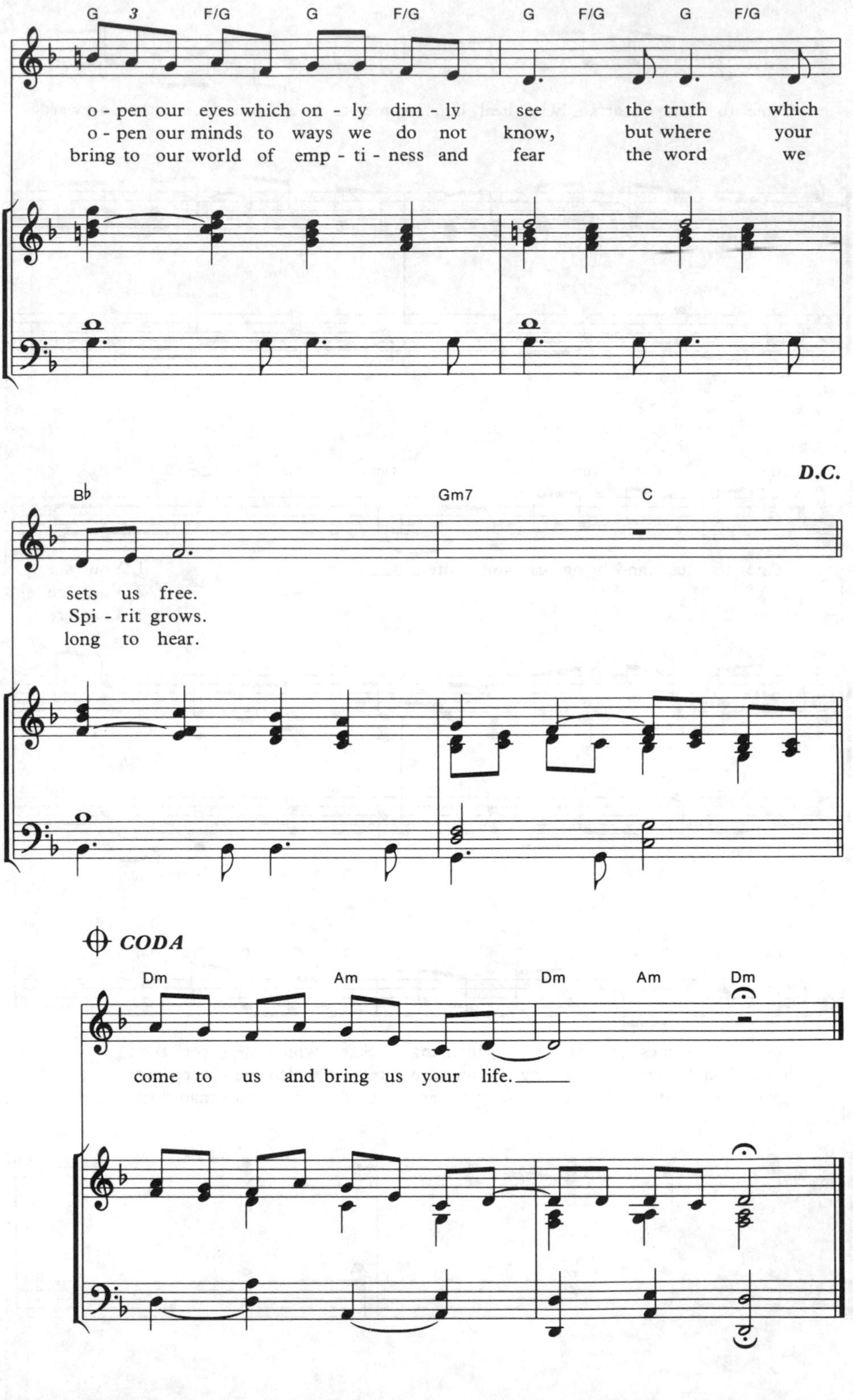
G 3 F/G G F/G G F/G G F/G
o - pen our eyes which on - ly dim - ly see the truth which
o - pen our minds to ways we do not know, but where your
bring to our world of emp - ti - ness and fear the word we
D.C.
B♭ Gm7 C
sets us free.
Spi - rit grows.
long to hear.
CODA
Dm Am Dm Am Dm
come to us and bring us your life.

24 Come, let us sing for joy

Lively

From Psalm 95
Words and music: Brent Chambers

Introduction
G
Come, let us sing for joy to the Lord,
come, let us sing for joy to the Lord,
come, let us sing for joy to the Lord,
come, let us sing for joy to the Lord!

Words and music: © 1985 Scripture in Song/CopyCare Ltd,
PO Box 77, Hailsham, East Sussex BN27 3EF

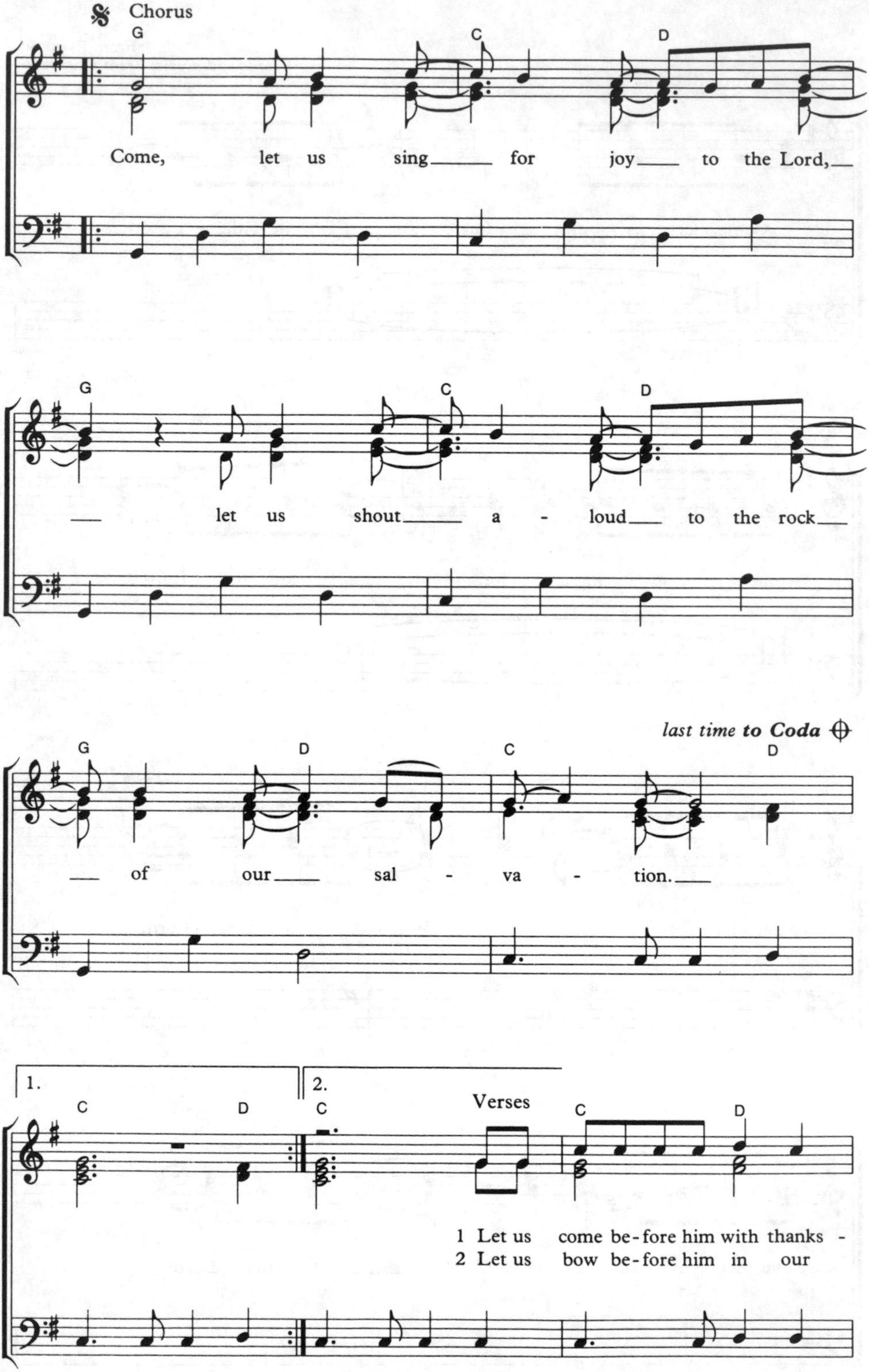
Chorus
G C D
Come, let us sing for joy to the Lord,
G C D
let us shout a - loud to the rock
last time to Coda
G D C D
of our sal - va - tion.
1.
C D
2.
C
Verses
C D
1 Let us come be-fore him with thanks -
2 Let us bow be-fore him in our

G
C
D
- giv - ing, and ex - tol him with mu - sic and
wor - ship, let us kneel be - fore God, our great
G
C/G
G
C
D
song: for the Lord, our Lord, is the
king; for he is our God, and
Verse 2
B
Em
Asus
A7
great God the great king a - bove all gods.
we are his peo - ple – that's why we shout and sing!
Dsus
D7
D.𝄋 al Coda
CODA
C
D
G

25 Come on and celebrate

Celebrate

Words and music: Patricia Morgan

Very lively

G
Come on and ce - le - brate! His gift of love we will
Bm
Em
C
ce - le - brate – the Son of God, who loved us
Am
Dsus
D
and gave us life: We'll shout your
G
Bm
praise, O King: you give us joy no-thing else can bring;

Words and music: © 1984 Kingsway's Thankyou Music,
PO Box 75, Eastbourne, East Sussex BN23 6NW

Em
Am7
D
we'll give to you our of - fer - ing in ce - le - bra - tion
G
C
praise. Come on and ce - le - brate,
Am
G
Em
ce - le - brate, ce - le - brate and sing,
1.
Am7
D
G
ce - le - brate and sing to the King:
2.
Am7
D
G
ce - le - brate and sing to the King!

26 Crown him with many crowns

Diademata 6 6 8 6 D (DSM)

Words: M Bridges (1800–1894) and
G Thring (1823–1903)
in this version Word & Music
Revelation 19.12
Music: G J Elvey (1816–1893)

Victoriously ♩ = 112

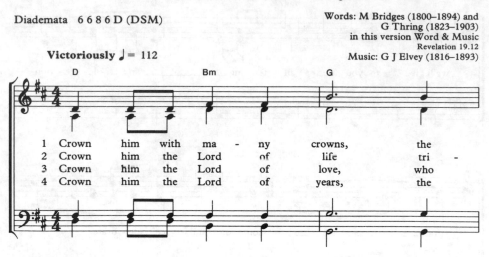

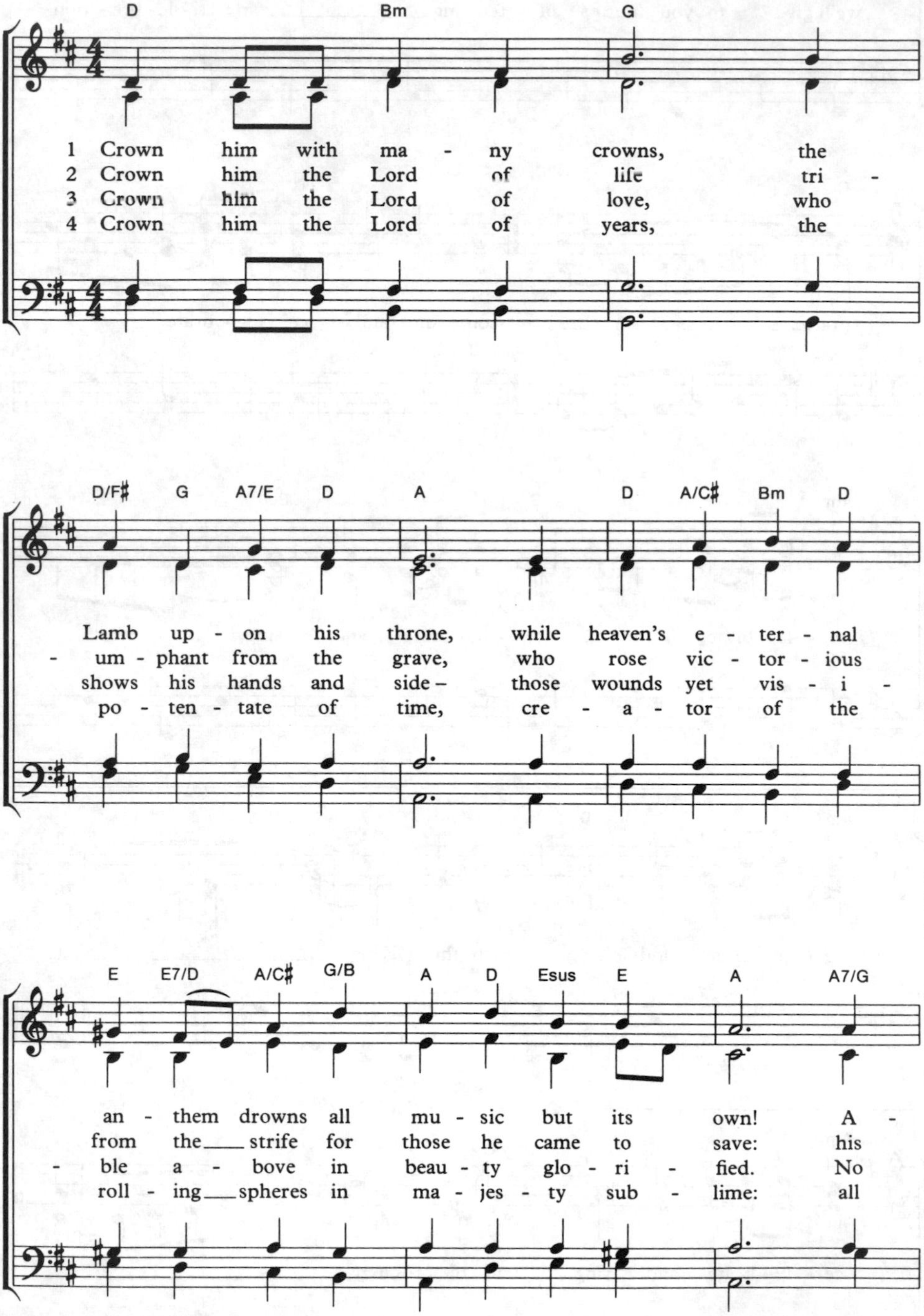

D Bm G
1 Crown him with ma - ny crowns, the
2 Crown him the Lord of life tri -
3 Crown him the Lord of love, who
4 Crown him the Lord of years, the
D/F♯ G A7/E D A D A/C♯ Bm D
Lamb up - on his throne, while heaven's e - ter - nal
- um - phant from the grave, who rose vic - tor - ious
shows his hands and side – those wounds yet vis - i -
po - ten - tate of time, cre - a - tor of the
E E7/D A/C♯ G/B A D Esus E A A7/G
an - them drowns all mu - sic but its own! A -
from the___ strife for those he came to save: his
- ble a - bove in beau - ty glo - ri - fied. No
roll - ing___ spheres in ma - jes - ty sub - lime: all

Words: © in this version Word & Music / Jubilate Hymns †

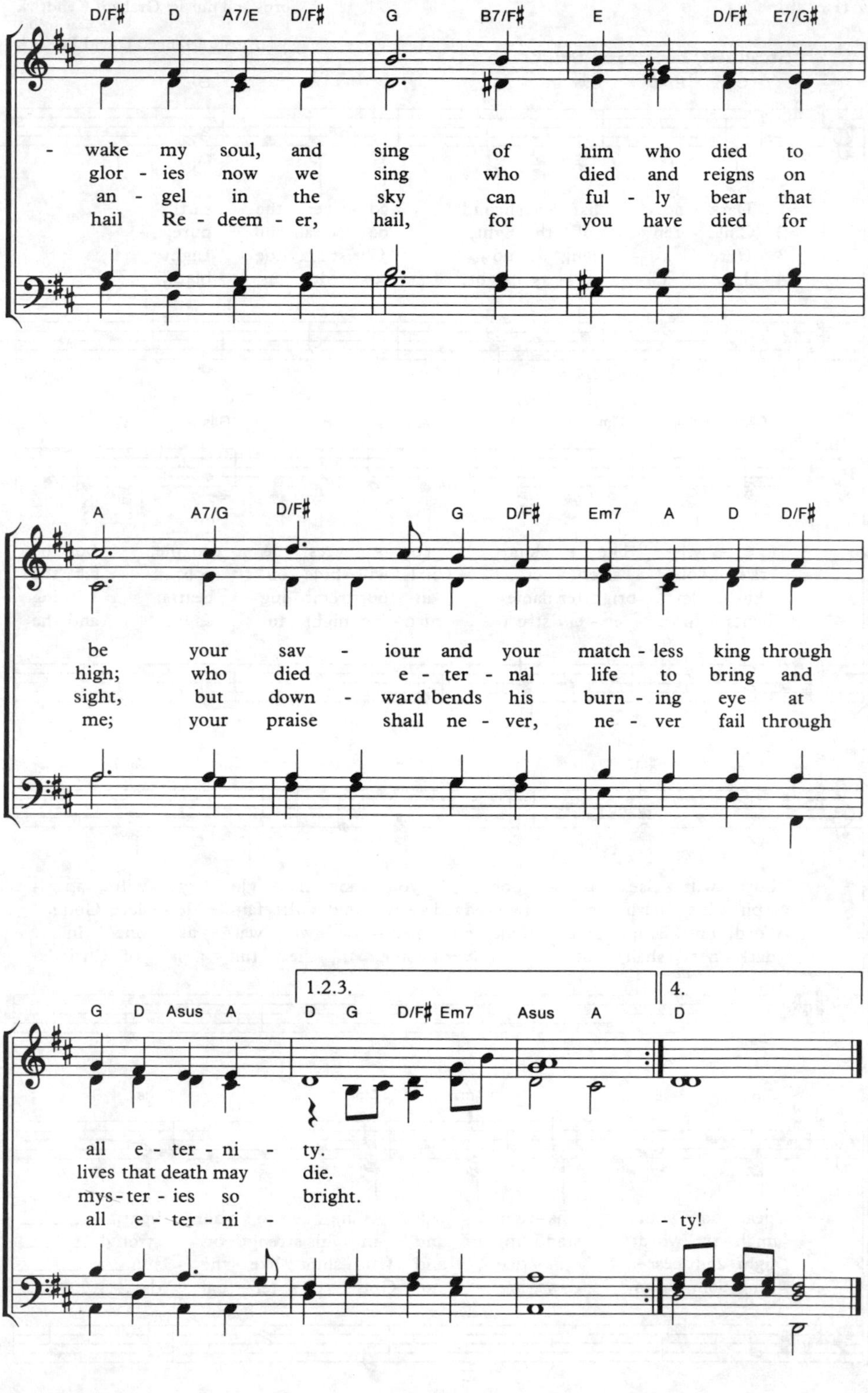
D/F♯ D A7/E D/F♯ G B7/F♯ E D/F♯ E7/G♯
- wake my soul, and sing of him who died to
glor - ies now we sing who died and reigns on
an - gel in the sky can ful - ly bear that
hail Re - deem - er, hail, for you have died for
A A7/G D/F♯ G D/F♯ Em7 A D D/F♯
be your sav - iour and your match - less king through
high; who died e - ter - nal life to bring and
sight, but down - ward bends his burn - ing eye at
me; your praise shall ne - ver, ne - ver fail through
1.2.3.
4.
G D Asus A D G D/F♯ Em7 Asus A D
all e - ter - ni - ty.
lives that death may die.
mys - ter - ies so bright.
all e - ter - ni - - ty!

27 Darkness like a shroud

Arise, shine

Words and music: Graham Kendrick
Isaiah 60.1
Music arranged David Peacock

Subdued, becoming bright

C♯m B/C♯ C♯m A B E
1 Dark - ness like a shroud co - vers the earth,
2 Child - ren of the light, be clean and pure;
3 Here a - mong us now, Christ__ the Light
4 Like a ci - ty bright, so let us blaze;
C♯m B/C♯ C♯m A B G♯sus G♯
e - vil like a cloud co - vers the peo - ple; but the
rise, you sleep - ers, Christ will shine on you:__ take the
kin - dles brigh - ter flames in our tremb - ling hearts: Liv - ing
lights in ev - ery street turn - ing night to day:__ and the
E F♯m7 B E F♯m7
Lord will rise u - pon____ you, and his glo - ry will ap -
Spir - it's flash - ing two - edged sword and with faith de - clare God's
Word, our lamp, come guide our feet – as we walk as one in
dark - ness shall not o - ver - come, till the full - ness of Christ's
B E C♯m7 F♯m Bsus B
- pear on you, na - tions will come__ to your light.______
migh - ty word; stand up, and in his strength be strong!______
light and peace, jus - tice and truth shine like the sun.______
king - dom comes, dawn - ing to God's e - ter - nal day.______

Words and music: © 1985 Kingsway's Thankyou Music,
PO Box 75, Eastbourne, East Sussex BN23 6NW

Chorus
F♯m/B B E G♯m C♯m G♯m C♯m A
A - rise, shine, your light has come, the glo-ry of the Lord has
F♯m A/B E G♯m A G♯m Amaj7
risen on you; a - rise, shine, your light has come –
A♯dim 3 E/B G♯m 1-3. A A/B
Je - sus the light of the world has
E G♯7 4. A A♯dim 3 E/B G♯m
come. world, Je - sus the light of the
A A♯dim 3 E/B G♯m A A/B E
world, Je - sus the light of the world has come.

28 Emmanuel

Capo 3(D)

Words and music: Michael W Smith
Isaiah 7.14

Words and music: © 1983 Meadowgreen Music

B♭ (G) Am7 (F♯m7) Dm (Bm) E♭ (C)
Prince of peace, migh-ty God, ho - ly One, Em -
E♭maj7 (Cmaj7) F (D) E♭ (C) F (D) Dm (Bm) B♭ (G)
1. Csus (Asus) C (A)
- man - u - el, Em - man - u -
F (D)
2. Csus (Asus) C (A) D♭9 (B♭9)
- el, Em - Em - man - u - el.
Csus (Asus) B♭m7 (Gm7)
to repeat
Csus C (Asus)(A) F (D)
D.𝄋
to end
Csus C (Asus)(A) F (D)
Em -

29 Eternal God and Father

Words: from The Alternative Service Book 1980
Music: Chris Rolinson

Worshipfully
Em A D Bm7
E - ter - nal God and Fa - ther, e - ter - nal
Em7 D/A A
1. D D/F♯
2. D D/F♯
God and Fa - ther, e - ter - nal Fa - ther, You cre -
G A A/G F♯m7 Bm7
- ate us by your power and re - deem us by your love: guide and
Em G/A D D/F♯
streng-then us by your Spi - rit, that we may

Words and music: © 1987 Kingsway's Thankyou Music,
PO Box 75, Eastbourne, East Sussex BN23 6NW

Words: © 1980 The Central Board of Finance
of the Church of England
Used by permission

G A A/G F♯sus F♯/A♯ Bm Bm/A 3
give our - selves in love and ser - vice to one a -
G Em7 1. Asus A
- no - ther and to you; E - ter - nal
2. Asus A F♯sus F♯/A♯ Bm A D
you; through Je - sus Christ our Lord. A -
G G/F♯ Em7 Asus A B♭ G D
- men, a - men.

30 Father God, I wonder

I will sing your praises

Words and music: Ian Smale
Romans 8.15, Galatians 4.5, Ephesians 1.5

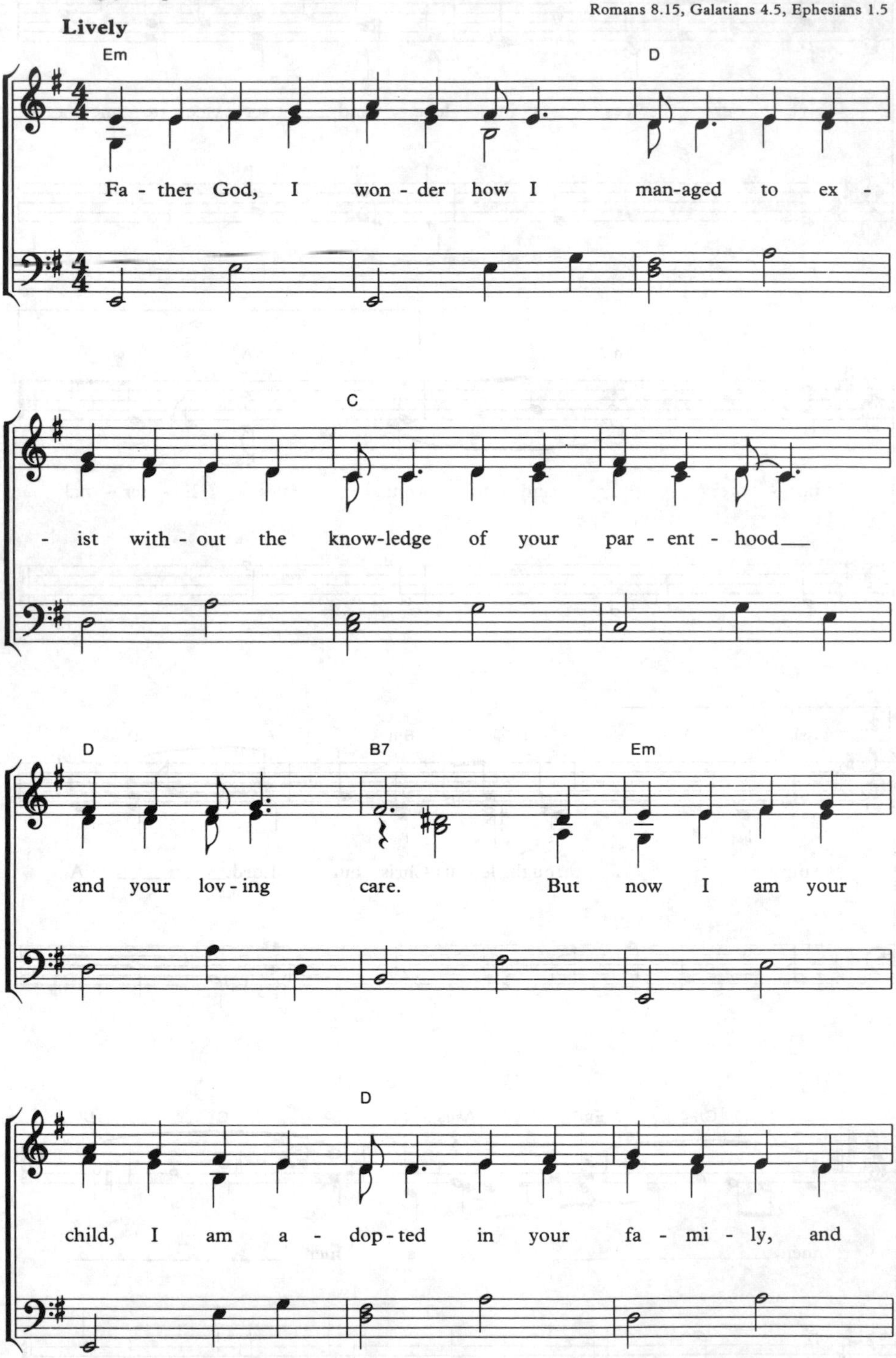
Lively
Em
D
Fa - ther God, I won - der how I man-aged to ex -
C
- ist with - out the know-ledge of your par - ent - hood
D
B7
Em
and your lov - ing care. But now I am your
D
child, I am a - dop - ted in your fa - mi - ly, and

Words and music: © 1984 Kingsway's Thankyou Music,
PO Box 75, Eastbourne, East Sussex BN23 6NW

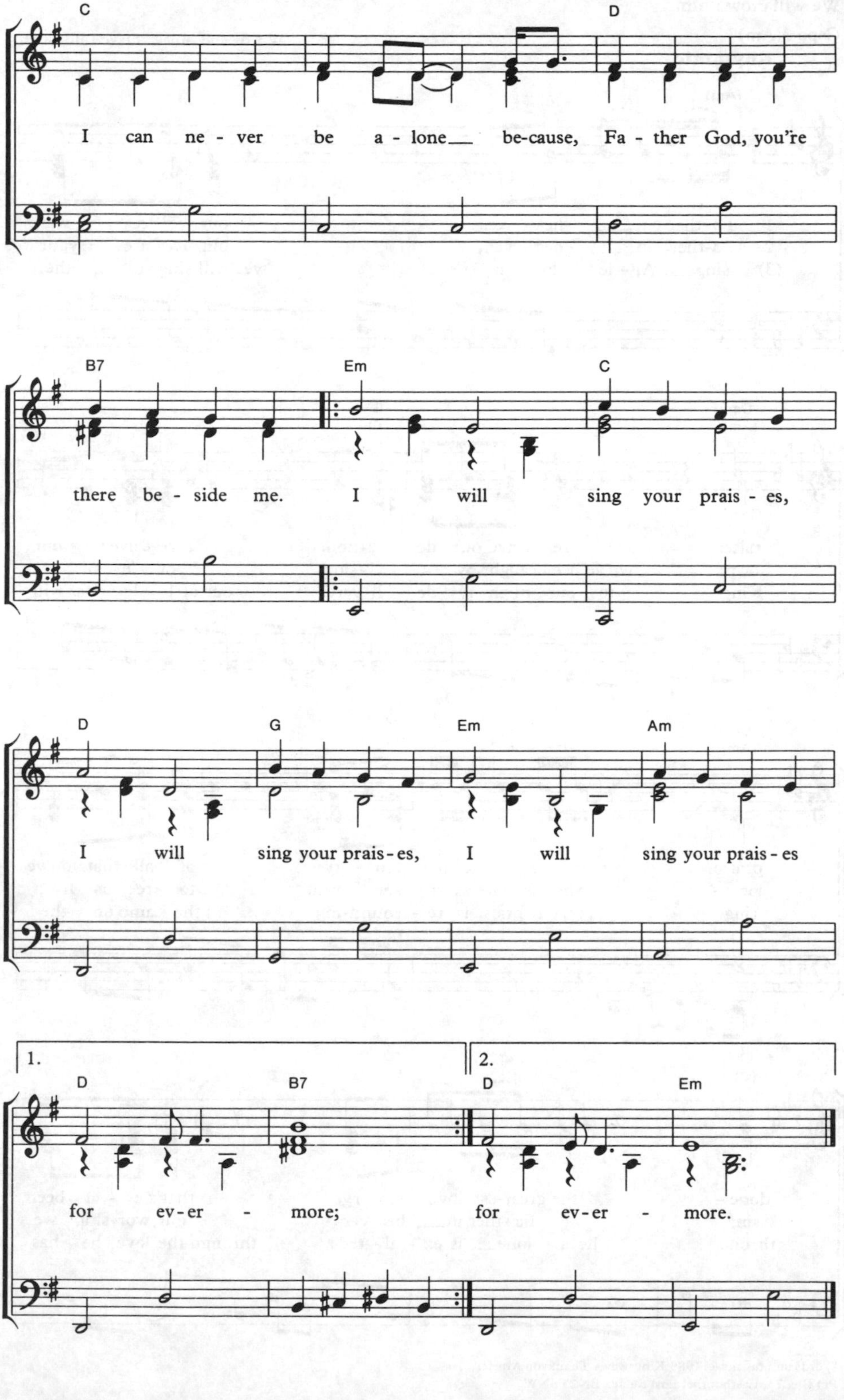
C D
I can ne - ver be a - lone__ be-cause, Fa - ther God, you're
B7 Em C
there be - side me. I will sing your prais - es,
D G Em Am
I will sing your prais - es, I will sing your prais - es
1. 2.
D B7 D Em
for ev - er - more; for ev - er - more.

31 Father in heaven

We will crown him

Capo 3(Am)

Words and music: Dave Bilbrough

Rhythmic
Cm
(Am)
G
(E)
1 Fa-ther in hea - ven, our voi - ces we
2 Fa-ther, in hea - ven, our lives are your
(3) sing Al - le - lu - ia, we will sing to the
raise: re - ceive our de - vo-tion, re-ceive now our
own; we've been caught by a vi - sion of Je - sus a -
King, to our migh - ty de - li-verer our al-le - lu - ias will
Ab
(F)
praise as we sing of the glo - ry of all that you've
- lone – who came as a ser - vant to free us from
ring. Yes, our praise is re - sound-ing to the Lamb on the
Eb
(C)
Bb
(G)
done – the great-est love - sto - ry that's ev - er been
sin: Fa - ther in hea-ven, our wor-ship we
throne: he a - lone is ex - al - ted through the love he has

Words and music: © 1985 Kingsway's Thankyou Music,
PO Box 75, Eastbourne, East Sussex BN23 6NW

Chorus
G (E)
Cm (Am)
B♭ (G)
Cm (Am)
sung.
bring.
shown.
And we will crown you Lord of all, yes, we will
B♭ (G)
Cm (Am)
A♭ (F)
B♭ (G)
crown you Lord of all, for you have won the
G (E)
Cm (Am)
B♭ (G)
1.
Cm (Am)
vic - to - ry: yes, we will crown you Lord of all.
2.
Cm (Am)
all.
3 We will
3.
Cm (Am)
all.

32 Father in heaven, how we love you

Blessed be the Lord God Almighty

Words and music: Bob Fitts
arranged Geoff Baker

Majestically
C Cmaj7 Dm
Fa - ther in hea-ven, how_ we love you:_____ we
G G7 C Fmaj7 G
lift your name in all the earth._______ May your
C Cmaj7 Dm
king - dom_ be es-tab - lished_ in our prais - es_______ as your
G9 C G7 C Em
peo-ple_ de-clare your migh-ty works. Bless - ed be the Lord God al -

Words and music: © 1984 Scripture in Song/CopyCare Ltd,
PO Box 77, Hailsham, East Sussex BN27 3EF

F G G9 C G7
- migh - ty who was and is and is to come: bless-ed be the
C Em7 F G G9 1. C
Lord God al - migh - ty who reigns for ev - er - more!
2. C A7 D F♯m7 G
more Bless-ed be the Lord God al - migh - ty who
A A9 D A7 D F♯m7
was and is and is to come: bless-ed be the Lord God al -
G A A9 D
- migh - ty who reigns for ev - er - more!

33 Father God in heaven

Kum ba yah 8 8 8 5

Words: From *The Lord's Prayer*
J E Seddon (1915–1983)
Matthew 6.9, Luke 11.2
Music: traditional melody
arranged David Peacock

D G D
1 Fa - ther God in heaven, Lord most high: hear your
2 May your king - dom come here on earth; may your
3 Give us dai - ly bread day by day, and for -
D/F♯ G A D G
child-ren's prayer, Lord most high: hal-lowed be your name, Lord most
will be done here on earth, as it is in heaven so on
- give our sins day by day, as we too for - give day by
D G/B D/A A7 D
high – O Lord, hear our prayer.
earth – O Lord, hear our prayer.
day – O Lord, hear our prayer.

4 Lead us in your way,
make us strong;
when temptations come
make us strong;
save us all from sin,
keep us strong –
O Lord, hear our prayer.

5 All things come from you,
all are yours –
kingdom, glory, power,
all are yours;
take our lives and gifts,
all are yours –
O Lord, hear our prayer.

Music arrangement: © David Peacock / Jubilate Hymns †
Words: © Mrs M Seddon / Jubilate Hymns †

34 Father, we adore you

Capo 1(E)

Words and music: Terry Coelho

Slowly, sustained

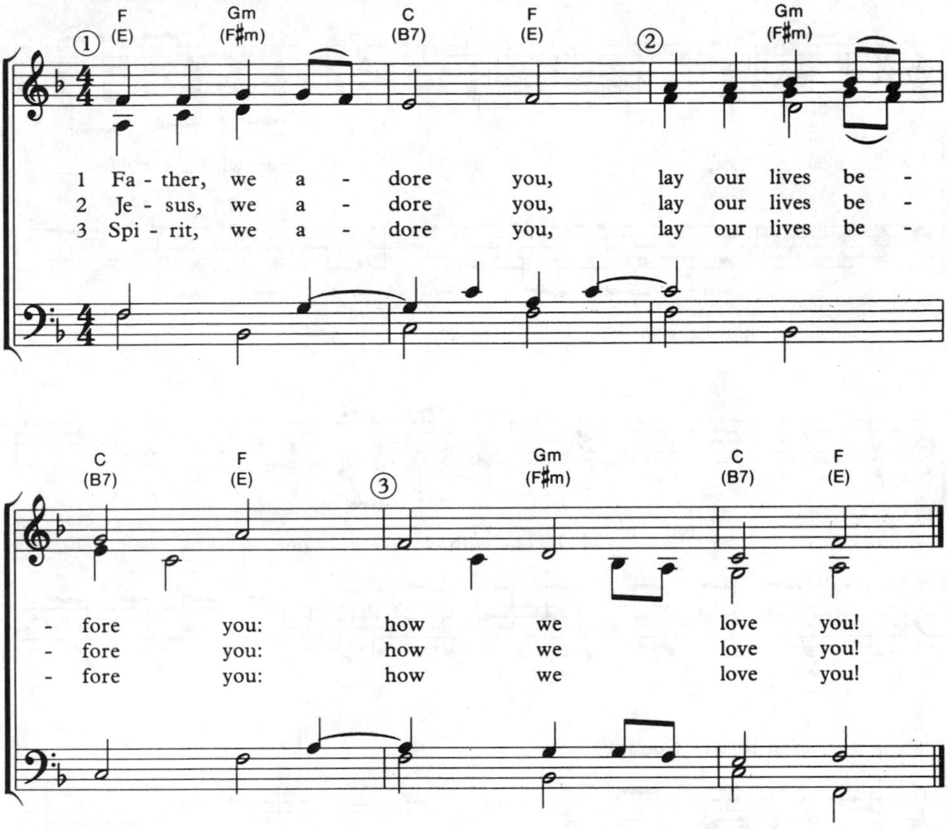
F (E)
Gm (F♯m)
C (B7)
F (E)
Gm (F♯m)
1 Fa - ther, we a - dore you, lay our lives be -
2 Je - sus, we a - dore you, lay our lives be -
3 Spi - rit, we a - dore you, lay our lives be -
C (B7)
F (E)
Gm (F♯m)
C (B7)
F (E)
- fore you: how we love you!
- fore you: how we love you!
- fore you: how we love you!

This may be sung as a 3-part round.

34A PRAISE SHOUT

LEADER It is good to praise you, Lord,
ALL **and make music to your name:**

LEADER To proclaim your constant love in the morning,
ALL **and tell your faithfulness in the evening**

LEADER For you, O Lord, are exalted for ever.
ALL **Amen.**

From Psalm 92

Words and music: © 1972 Maranatha! Music/CopyCare Ltd,
PO Box 77, Hailsham, East Sussex BN27 3EF

35 Fear not for I am with you

Words and music: Phil Pringle
Isaiah 43.1
Music arranged David Peacock

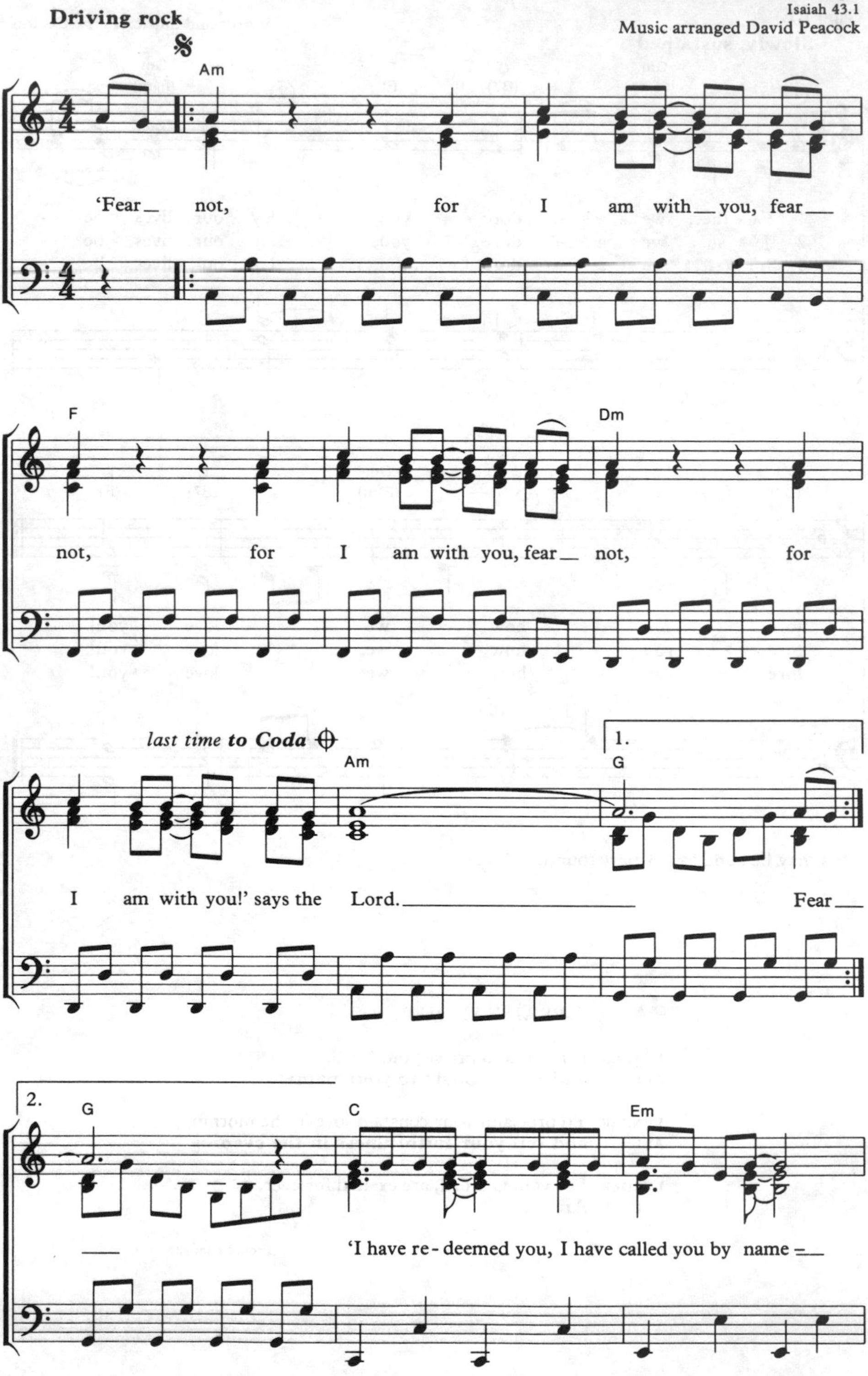
Driving rock
Am
'Fear — not, for I am with — you, fear —
F
not, for I am with you, fear — not,
Dm
for
last time to Coda
Am
I am with you!' says the Lord. —
1.
G
Fear —
2.
G
C
Em
'I have re-deemed you, I have called you by name —

Words and music: © 1984 Seam of Gold/Kingsway's Thankyou Music,
PO Box 75, Eastbourne, East Sussex BN23 6NW

F
C
child, you are mine:
when you walk through the wa-ters
Em
F
G
I'll be there;
and through the flame,
you'll
Am
Em
Am
not (no way!) be drowned,
you'll not (no way!) be
Em
F
G
Am
burned,
for I am with you.'
CODA
D.%
Am
Am
Fear
Lord.

36 Fling wide your doors

Capo 2(C)

From Psalm 24
Words and music: Graham Kendrick

With vigour ♩= 133

D (C)
Fling wide your doors, O you streets, o-pen up you hearts of men, that the
Bm7 (Am7) Em7 (Dm7) A7 (G7) D (C)
King of glo-ry may come in; fling wide your doors, O you streets, o-pen
3rd time to Coda
Bm7 (Am7) Em7 (Dm7) A7 (G)
up you hearts of men, that the King of glo - ry may come
D (C) D7 (C7) G (F) D (C) Bm7 (Am7)
WOMEN
MEN
in! Who is this King of glo - ry? The Lord, strong and

Words and music: © 1988 Make Way Music,
PO Box 263, Croydon, Surrey CR9 5AP.
International copyright secured. All rights reserved. Used by permission.

D/A (C) G (A) G (F) Bm (Am)
WOMEN MEN
might - ty. Who is this King, this King of glo - ry? The
E7 (D7) G/A (F) A (G) G/A (F) A (G)
ALL
Lord – his name is Je - sus! Fling wide your
CODA
D (C)
LEADER ALL LEADER
in Fling wide your doors, fling wide your doors, O you
Bm7 (Am7) Em7 (Dm7) A7 (G7)
ALL
streets, O you streets – o - pen up you hearts of
1. D (C) 2. D (C) D7 (C7)
LEADER
men! Fling wide your doors, men!

37 For I'm building a people of power

Words and music: Dave Richards
arranged David Peacock

Brightly

C F C
For I'm build - ing a peo - ple of pow - er and I'm
G7 C
mak - ing a peo - ple of praise, that will
F C
move through this land by my Spi - rit, and will
Dm7 G7 C C7
glo - ri - fy my ho - ly name. Build your

Words and music: © 1977 Kingsway's Thankyou Music,
PO Box 75, Eastbourne, East Sussex BN23 6NW

F Dm7 C Am7
Church, Lord; make us strong, Lord, join our
Dm7 G7 C C7
hearts, Lord, through your Son; make us
F Dm7 C A7
one, Lord, in your Bo - dy, in the
Dm7 G7 C
king - dom of your Son!

38 Forth in the peace of Christ

Duke Street 8 8 8 8 (LM)

Words: James Quinn S.J.
Music: J Hatton (died 1793)
arranged David Peacock

Triumphantly

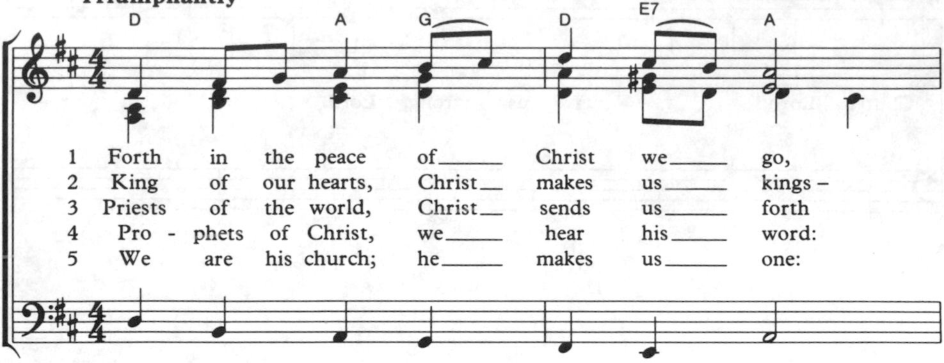

D A G D E7 A
1 Forth in the peace of___ Christ we___ go,
2 King of our hearts, Christ___ makes us___ kings –
3 Priests of the world, Christ___ sends us___ forth
4 Pro - phets of Christ, we___ hear his___ word:
5 We are his church; he___ makes us___ one:

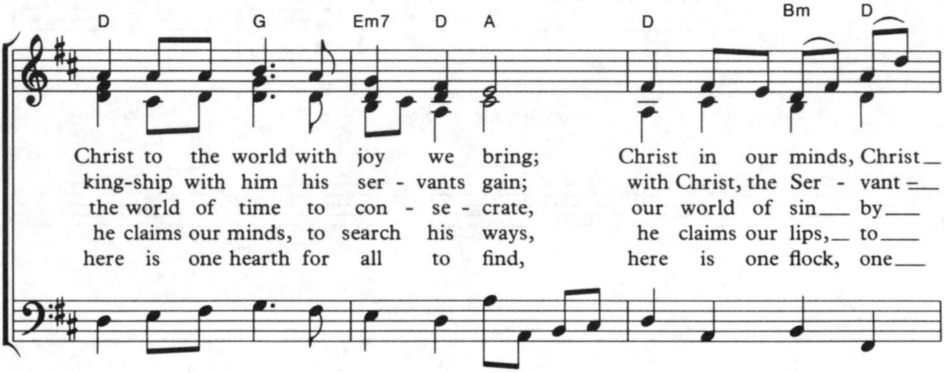

D G Em7 D A D Bm D
Christ to the world with joy we bring; Christ in our minds, Christ___
king-ship with him his ser - vants gain; with Christ, the Ser - vant –___
the world of time to con - se - crate, our world of sin___ by___
he claims our minds, to search his ways, he claims our lips,___ to___
here is one hearth for all to find, here is one flock, one___

Fine
G Em7 A D G D D/A A D
on___ our___ lips, Christ in our hearts, the world's true king.
Lord of___ all, Christ's world we serve to share Christ's reign.
grace to___ heal, Christ's world in Christ to re - cre - ate.
speak his___ truth, he claims our hearts, to sing his praise.
Shep - herd - King, here is one faith, one heart, one mind.

Link
D.C.
G D/F♯ Em7 Asus A

Words: © 1969, 1987 James Quinn S.J.
reprinted by permission of Geoffrey Chapman,
a division of Cassell Publishers Ltd,
Villiers House, 41-7 Strand, London WC2N 5JE

Music arrangement: © David Peacock / Jubilate Hymns †

39 For this purpose

Capo 2(C)

Words and music: Graham Kendrick
1 John 3.8

Flowing
D (C) A (G) Bm (Am) F♯m (Em) G (F)
Introduction
Asus (Gsus) A (G)
Verse
D (C) A (G)
1 For this
2 In the
Bm (Am) F♯m (Em) G (F) A (G) D (C)
pur - pose Christ was re - vealed,
name of Je - sus we stand;
Bm (Am) Bm/A (Am7) Asus/E (Gsus)
to de - stroy all the works of the ev - il
by the power of his blood we now claim this

Words and music: © 1985 Kingsway's Thankyou Music,
PO Box 75, Eastbourne, East Sussex BN23 6NW

A (G) D (C) A (G) Bm (Am) F♯m (Em)
one; Christ in us has
ground: Sa - tan has no au -
G (F) F♯ (E) Bm (Am) Bm/A (Am7)
ov - er - come, so with glad-ness we sing
- tho - ri - ty here, powers of dark-ness must flee,
Bm/G♯ (Am) Asus (Gsus)
and wel - come his king - dom in.
for Christ has the vic - to - ry.
Rhythmic
Chorus
A (G) D (C) G (F) D (C)
MEN
WOMEN
Ov - er sin he has con-quered: Al - le -

G (F) D (C) G (F) D (C) E (D) A (G) E (D)
MEN
WOMEN
- lu - ia! he has con-quered. Ov - er death vic - tor - ious: Al - le -
A (G) E (D) A (G) E (D) F♯ (E) Bm (Am) F♯ (E)
MEN
WOMEN
- lu - ia! vic - tor - ious. Ov - er sick - ness he has tri-umphed: Al - le -
Bm (Am) F♯ (E) Bm (Am) F♯ (E) G (F)
ALL
- lu - ia! he has tri-umphed. Je - sus
Asus (Gsus) A7 (G7) D (C) G (F) D (C) Asus (Gsus) D (C)
reigns ov - er all!

40 From heaven you came

The servant king

Capo 3(Am)

Words and music: Graham Kendrick

Mark 10.45 and 14.36, Matthew 20.28, John 20.27

Music arranged David Peacock

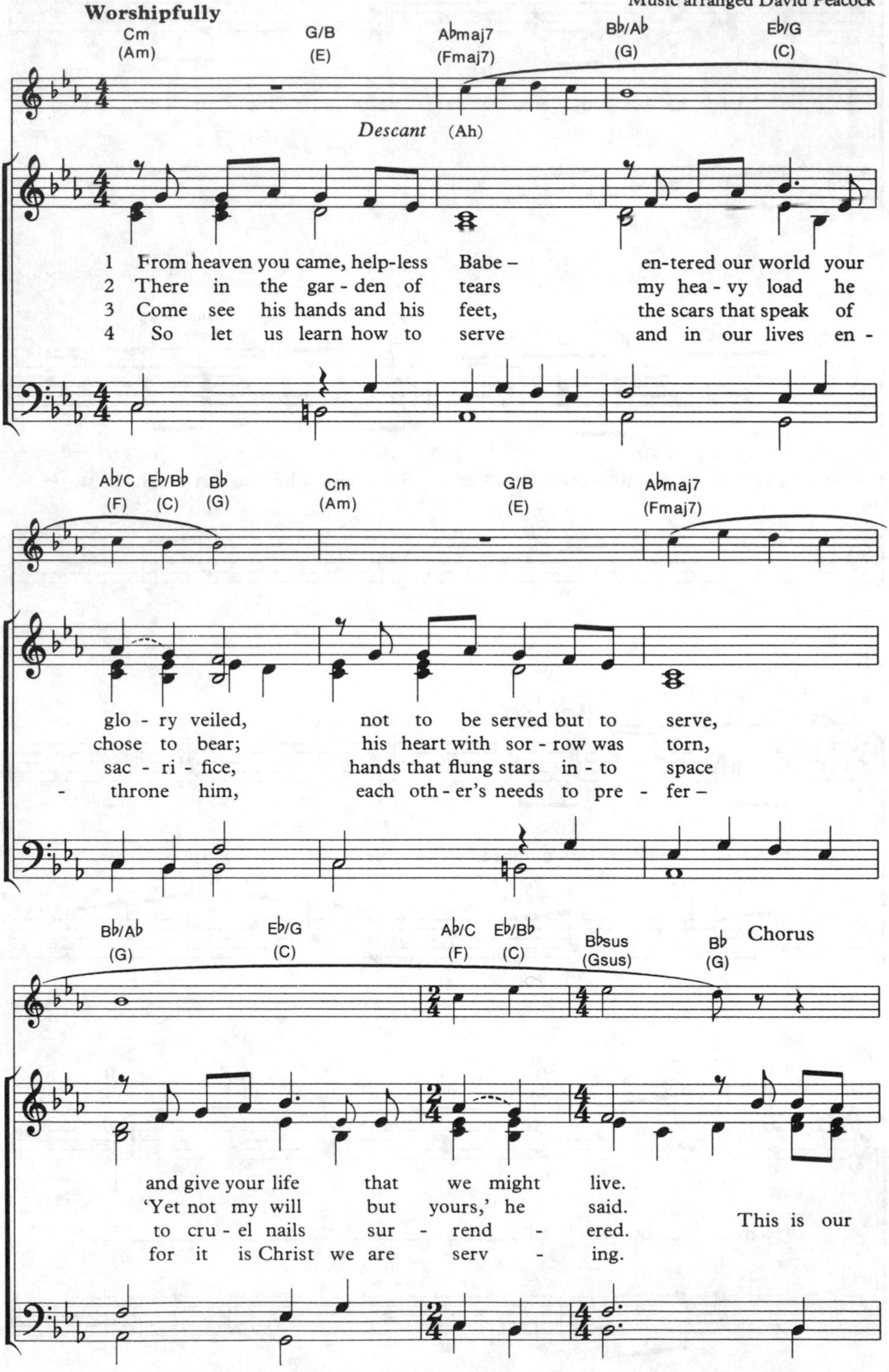
Worshipfully
Cm (Am) G/B (E) A♭maj7 (Fmaj7) B♭/A♭ (G) E♭/G (C)
Descant (Ah)
1 From heaven you came, help-less Babe – en-tered our world your
2 There in the gar - den of tears my hea - vy load he
3 Come see his hands and his feet, the scars that speak of
4 So let us learn how to serve and in our lives en -
A♭/C (F) E♭/B♭ (C) B♭ (G) Cm (Am) G/B (E) A♭maj7 (Fmaj7)
glo - ry veiled, not to be served but to serve,
chose to bear; his heart with sor - row was torn,
sac - ri - fice, hands that flung stars in - to space
- throne him, each oth - er's needs to pre - fer –
B♭/A♭ (G) E♭/G (C) A♭/C (F) E♭/B♭ (C) B♭sus (Gsus) B♭ (G) Chorus
and give your life that we might live.
'Yet not my will but yours,' he said.
to cru - el nails sur - rend - ered. This is our
for it is Christ we are serv - ing.

Words and music: © 1983 Kingsway's Thankyou Music,
PO Box 75, Eastbourne, East Sussex BN23 6NW

E♭ (C) B♭ (G) Cm (Am) Cm/B♭ (Am7) A♭ (F) B♭ (G)
Part II This is our God the ser-vant king he calls us now to
God – the ser-vant king, he calls us now to fol-low
E♭ (C) B♭ (G) E♭ (C) E♭/D♭ (C7) A♭/C (F) D (B)
fol-low him to bring our lives an off-er-ing
him, to bring our lives as a dai-ly of-fer-ing of wor-ship
1.2.3.
4.
E♭ (C) B♭ (G) E♭ (C) Dm7 (Bm7) G7 (E7) E♭ (C)
of wor-ship to the ser-vant king. king.
to the ser-vant king. king.

41 From the sun's rising

Capo 2(C)

Words and music: Graham Kendrick
Psalm 50.1, Isaiah 45.6, Matthew 28.19

Steadily
D (C) G (F) D (C) A (G) D (C) G (F)
1 From the sun's ris - ing un - to the sun's set - ting Je - sus our Lord shall be
2 To ev - ery tongue, tribe and na - tion he sends us, to make di - sci - ples, to
3 Come let us join with the church from all na-tions, cross ev - ery bor - der, throw
D (C) Asus (Gsus) A (G) D (C) G (F) D (C) A (G)
great in the earth; and all earth's kingdom shall be his do - minion –
teach and bap - tize; for all au - tho - ri - ty to him is gi - ven –
wide ev - ery door: wor-kers with him as he ga - thers his har - vest,
D (C) G (F) Bm (Am) G/A (F) A7 (G7) D (C) Dsus (Csus) D (C)
all of cre - a - tion shall sing of his worth.
now as his wit - nes - ses we shall a - rise.
till earth's far cor - ners our sav - iour a - dore.
Chorus
Bm (Am) F♯m (Em) G (F) D (C) Em (Dm)
Let ev - ery heart, ev - ery voice, ev - ery tongue join with spi - rits a -

Words and music: © 1988 Make Way Music,
PO Box 263, Croydon, Surrey CR9 5AP.
International copyright secured. All rights reserved. Used by permission.

Asus (Gsus) A (G) Bm (Am) F♯m (Em) G (F) D (C)
- blaze: one in his love we will cir - cle the world with the
Em (Dm) F♯sus (Esus) F♯ (E) Em7 (Dm7) A (G)
song of his praise. O let all his peo - ple re -
last time to Coda
Bm (Am) G (F) A (G) D (C) Dsus (Csus) D (C) Asus (Gsus) A (G)
- joice, and let all the earth hear his voice!
CODA
Bm (Am) Em (Dm) A (G) Bm (Am)
voice! Let all his peo - ple re - joice,
G (F) A (G) D (C) Dsus (Csus) D (C)
and let all the earth hear his voice!

42 Give thanks with a grateful heart

Capo 3(D)

Words and music: Henry Smith
2 Corinthians 8.9 and 12.9, Hebrews 1.34
Music arranged David Peacock

Unhurried

F (D) C/E (A) Dm (Bm)
Give thanks with a grate-ful heart, give thanks to the
Am (F♯m) B♭ (G) F/A (D)
Ho - ly One; give thanks because he's gi - ven Je - sus
E♭ (C) Gm7/C (Em7) C7 (A7) F (D) C/E (A)
Christ, his Son. Give thanks with a grate-ful heart, give
Dm (Bm) Am (F♯m) B♭ (G)
thanks to the Ho - ly One; give thanks because he's

Words and music: © 1978 Integrity's Hosanna! Music, administered in Europe
(excl. German speaking countries), by Kingsway's Thankyou Music, PO Box 75, Eastbourne, East Sussex BN23 6NW

F/A (D)
E♭ (C)
Gm7/C (Em7)
C7 (A7)
C/B♭
gi - ven Je - sus Christ, his Son. And
Am7 (F♯m7)
Dm7 (Bm7)
C/D (A)
Dm (Bm)
Gm7 (Em7)
now let the weak say 'I am strong', let the
C (A)
B♭/D (G)
C/E (A)
Fmaj7 (Dmaj7)
Am/E (F♯m7)
Dm7 (Bm7)
poor say 'I am rich', be-cause of what the Lord has
1.3.
2.
E♭ (C)
Gm7/C (Em7)
C (A)
C/B♭
D.𝄋
done for us; and done for us. Give
4.
Gm7/C (Em7)
C (A)
Csus (Asus)
F (D)
C/F (A)
B♭/F (G)
done for us.

43 Glory in the highest

Words: from *Gloria in excelsis*
Christopher Idle
Matthew 28.6, Luke 2.14 and 24.34, Hebrews 1.3
Music: E Elgar (1857–1934)
arranged Noël Tredinnick

Land of hope and glory

Capo 3(G)

B♭ (G) F7/C (D7) Gm/D (Em) B♭/D (G) E♭ (C) B♭/F (G)
1 Glo - ry in___ the high - est to the God__ of
2 Je - sus Christ is ris - en, God the Fa - ther's
3 Christ the world's true Sav - iour, high and ho - ly
C7/G (A7) F (D) B♭ (G) C7/B♭ (A7) F/A (D) Dm (Bm)
heaven! Peace to all___ your peo - ple
Son! With the Ho - ly Spi - rit,
one, seat - ed now___ and reign - ing
Gm (Em) C7 (A7) F (D) F7 (D7) B♭ (G) F7/C (D7)
through the earth_ be given! Migh - ty God__ and
you are Lord_ a - lone! Lamb once killed for
from your Fa - ther's throne: Lord and God,_ we

Music arrangement: © Noel Tredinnick / Jubilate Hymns †

Words: © Christopher Idle / Jubilate Hymns †

Gm/D (Em) Bb/D (G) Eb/G (C) Bb/F (G) C7/E (A7) F7 (D7) Bb (G) C7/Bb (A7)
Fa - ther, thanks and praise we bring, sing-ing Al - le -
sin - ners, all our guilt to bear, show us now your
praise you! High - est heaven a - dores: in the Fa - ther's
F/A (D) Dm (Bm) Eb/G (C) F7 (D7) Bb (G) Bb7 (G7)
- lu - ia to our heaven - ly king;
mer - cy, now re - ceive_ our prayer;
glo - ry, all the praise be yours;
Eb (C) F7/Eb (D7) Bb/D (G) Gm (Em) Cm7 (Am7) F7 (D7) Bb (G)
sing-ing Al - le-lu - ia to our heaven - ly king.
show us now_ your mer - cy, now re - ceive our prayer.
in the Fa - ther's glo - ry, all the praise be yours!

44 Glory and honour

Words: from Revelation 4 and 5
derived from the 'Daily Office'
of the Joint Liturgical Group
Music: Chris Rolinson
arranged David Peacock

Not too fast but with bounce
D A Bm7 G9 A7 D A Bm7
G9 A7 D A Bm Bm/A G A/G
Glo - ry and hon - our and power are yours by right, O
F♯m7 Bm7 G A/G F♯m7 Bm7
Lord our God; for you cre - a - ted all things, and
Em7 D/A A Dsus D G/A
by your will they have their be - ing. Glo - ry and
D A Bm Bm/A G A/G
hon - our and power are yours by right, O

Music: © 1987 Kingsway's Thankyou Music,
PO Box 75, Eastbourne, East Sussex BN23 6NW

Words: © Joint Liturgical Group

F♯m7 Bm7 G A/G F♯m7 Bm7
Lamb who was slain; for by your blood you ran-somed us for
Em7 G/A A A♯dim Bm
God: from ev-ery race and lan-guage, from
A/C♯ D G
ev-ery peo-ple and na-tion: to make us a
F♯m7 Bm Bm/A
king-dom of priests to
optional repeat from 𝄋
G F♯m7 Em Asus A
stand and serve be-fore our God.

D A Bm Bm/A G A/G
To him who sits on the throne and to the
F♯m7 Bm7 G A/G F♯m7 Bm7
Lamb, be praise and honour, glory and might, for
Em7 D/A A7 Dsus D
ever and ever and ever.
C G/A D
A - - - men,
C G/A D
a - - - men.

45 God, we praise you

Ode to Joy 8 7 8 7 D
Capo 5(C)

Words: from *Te Deum*, Christopher Idle
Isaiah 61.1, Matthew 11.5, Luke 7.22
Music: Ludwig van Beethoven (1770–1827)

F (C) Gm7/F (Dm7) F (C) Dm7 (Am7) F (C) C (G) F (C) C (G) F (C) F/C (C) C (G)
1 God, we praise you! God, we bless you! God, we name you sov-ereign Lord!
2 True a - pos - tles, faith-ful pro-phets, saints who set their world a - blaze,
3 Je - sus Christ, the king of glo - ry ev - er - last - ing Son of God,
4 Christ, at God's right hand vic - tor - ious, you will judge the world you made;
F (C) Gm7/F (Dm7) F (C) Dm7 (Am7) F (C) C (G) F (C) C (G) F (C) Csus (Gsus) C (G) F (C)
Migh-ty king whom an - gels wor-ship, Fa-ther, by your church a-dored:
mar-tyrs, once un - known, un - heed-ed, join one grow-ing song of praise,
hum-ble was your vir - gin mo-ther, hard the lone-ly path you trod:
Lord, in mer - cy help your ser-vants for whose free-dom you have paid:
C (G) F/C (C) Dm7/C (Am7) C7 (G7) F/C (C) Dm7/C (Am7) C (G) A7/C♯ (E7) Dm (Am) G (D) Csus (Gsus) C (G)
all cre - a - tion shows your glo - ry, heaven and earth draw near your throne
while your church on earth con-fess - es one ma - jes - tic Tri - ni - ty:
by your cross is sin de - feat-ed, hell con-front-ed face to face,
raise us up from dust to glo - ry, guard us from all sin to - day;
F (C) E♭ (B♭) B♭/D (F) F (C) Gm (Dm) B♭ (F) F/A (C) C7/G (G7) F (C) Csus (Gsus) C (G) F (C)
sing-ing 'Ho - ly, ho - ly, ho - ly,' Lord of hosts, and God a - lone!
Fa-ther, Son, and Ho - ly Spi - rit, God, our hope e - ter - nal - ly.
hea-ven open-ed to be - lie-vers, sin-ners jus - ti - fied by grace.
King en-throned a - bove all prai-ses, save your peo - ple, God, we pray.

Words: © Christopher Idle / Jubilate Hymns †

46(i) Go forth and tell

(FIRST TUNE)

Woodlands 10 10 10 10

Words: J E Seddon (1915–1983)
Mark 16.15
Music: W Greatorex (1877–1949)

A D G A D
1 Go forth and tell! O church of — God, a - wake!
2 Go forth and tell! God's love em - bra - ces all;
3 Go forth and tell! where still the — dark-ness lies;
4 Go forth and tell! The doors are o - pen wide:
5 Go forth and tell! O church of — God, a - rise!
A Bm D A7 D Em Em/G F♯
God's sav - ing news to all the na - tions take:
he will in grace res - pond to all who call:
in wealth or want, the sin - ner sure - ly dies:
share God's good gifts – let no one be de - nied;
go in the strength which Christ your Lord sup - plies;
B7 Em Em7/D A7
pro - claim Christ Je - sus, sav - iour, Lord, and king,
how shall they call if they have ne - ver heard
give us, O Lord, con - cern of heart and mind,
live out your life as Christ your Lord shall choose,
go till all na - tions his great name a - dore
D G D G A D Em7/G A Asus D
that all the world his wor - thy praise may sing.
the gra - cious in - vi - ta - tion of his word?
a love like yours which cares for hu - man - kind.
your ran - somed powers for his sole glo - ry use.
and serve him, Lord and king for ev - er - more.

Music: © Oxford University Press,
3 Park Road, London NW1 6XN

Words: © Mrs M Seddon / Jubilate Hymns †

46(ii) Go forth and tell

(SECOND TUNE)

Yanworth 10 10 10 10

Capo 3(D)

Words: J E Seddon (1915–1983)
Mark 16.15
Music: John Barnard

F (D) Bb (G) F (D) Gm (Em) F (D) Bb (G)
1 Go forth and tell! O church of God, a - wake! God's
2 Go forth and tell! God's love em - bra - ces all; he
3 Go forth and tell! where still the dark - ness lies; in
4 Go forth and tell! The doors are op - en wide: share
5 Go forth and tell! O church of God, a - rise! go
Gm7 (Em7) C7 (A7) F (D) Bb (G) C7 (A7) F (D) F/Eb
sav - ing news to all the na - tions take:
will in grace re - spond to all who call:
wealth or want, the sin - ner sure - ly dies:
God's good gifts – let no one be de - nied;
in the strength which Christ your Lord sup - plies;
Bb/D (G) Bb/C F7 (D7) Bb7 (G7) Eb (C)
pro - claim Christ Je - sus, sav - iour, Lord, and king,
how shall they call if they have ne - ver heard
give us, O Lord, con - cern of heart and mind,
live out your life as Christ your Lord shall choose,
go till all na - tions his great name a - dore
Cm (Am) D7 (B7) Gm (Em) Cm (Am) Bb (G) F (D) Bb (G)
that all the world his wor - thy praise may sing.
the gra - cious in - vi - ta - tion of his word?
a love like yours which cares for hu - man-kind.
your ran - somed powers for his sole glo - ry use.
and serve him, Lord and king for ev - er - more.

Music: © John Barnard / Jubilate Hymns †

Words: © Mrs M Seddon / Jubilate Hymns †

47 God is our strength and refuge

Dambusters March 7 7 7 5 7 7 11

Words: from Psalm 46
Richard Bewes
Music: Eric Coates (1886–1958)
arranged Noël Tredinnick

Stately

D/A
Introduction
Em/A
F♯m/A
mf
marcato
cresc.
Em7
F♯m/A Gmaj7/A
A7
Verses 1.2.
D
Em7
A7
1 God is our strength and re - fuge,
2 There is a flow - ing ri - ver,
D
F♯m
Gmaj7
Em6/G C♯dim/G
D/F♯
Bm
our pre - sent help in trou - ble; and we there - fore
with - in God's ho - ly ci - ty; God is in the
F♯m
B7
A/E
A/C♯
Bm7/D
E7
A
A7
will not fear, though the earth should change!
midst of her – she shall not be moved!

Music: © 1954 Chappell Music Ltd., London W1Y 3FA
Reproduced by permission of Chappell Music Ltd.
and International Music Publications

Words: © Richard Bewes / Jubilate Hymns †

D/F♯ Bm7 Em7 A7 Dmaj7 Gmaj7 Gmaj7/C♯ F♯7
Though moun-tains shake and trem-ble, though swirl-ing floods are__rag - ing,
God's help is swift-ly__giv - en, thrones van-ish at his__pres-ence –
Bm D♯dim7/A Em/G B7/F♯ Em G Gmaj7/A A7
1.
D A7/G D/F♯ A7/E
God the Lord of hosts is with us ev - er - more!
God the Lord of hosts is with us ev - er -
2.
D B♭ B♭7
more!
rit.
Verse 3 slower
E♭ Fm7 A♭/B♭ B♭7 E♭maj7 A♭maj7 B♭7/A♭
3 Come, see the works of our ma-ker, learn of his deeds all power-ful:

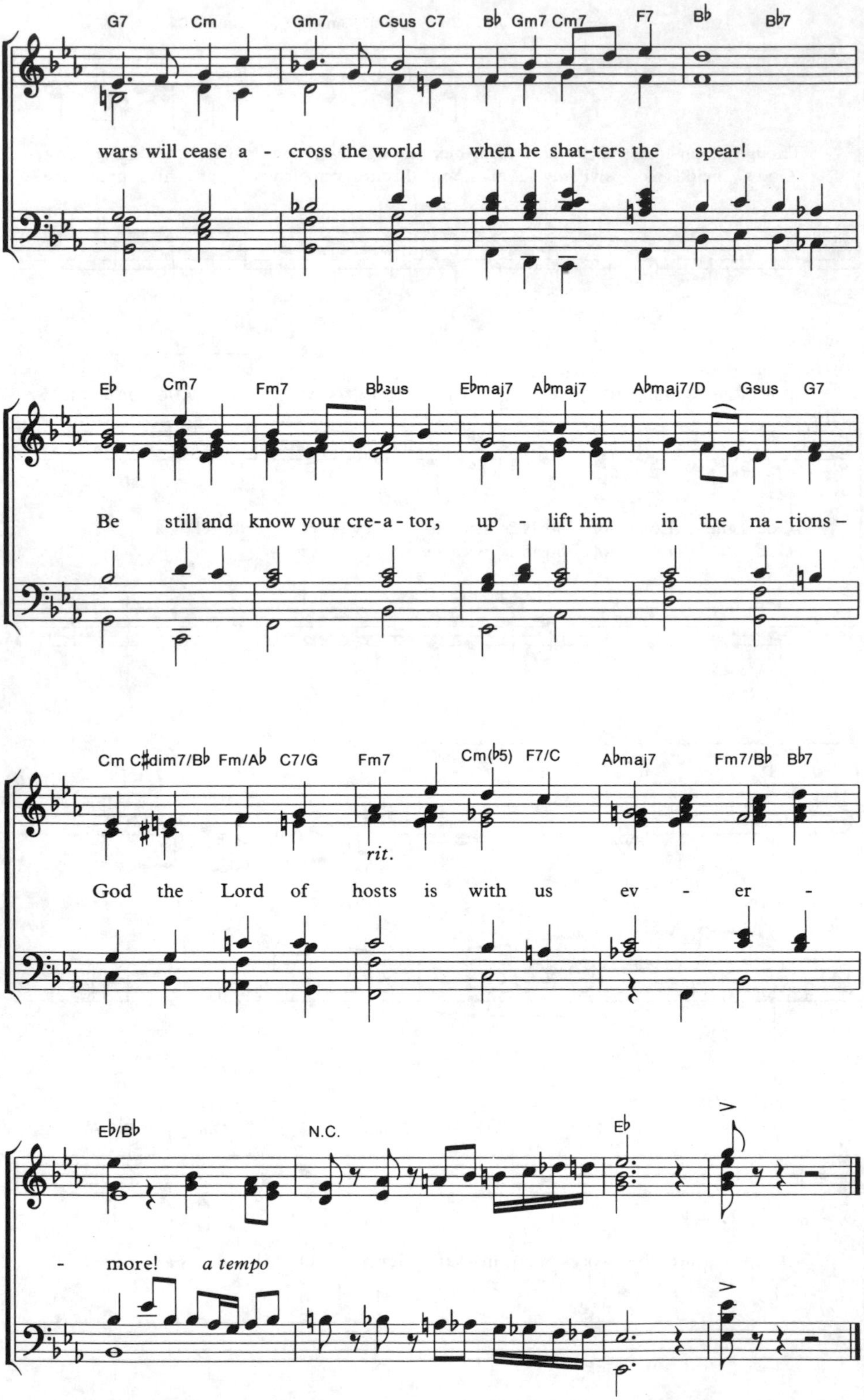
G7 Cm Gm7 Csus C7 B♭ Gm7 Cm7 F7 B♭ B♭7
wars will cease a - cross the world when he shat-ters the spear!
E♭ Cm7 Fm7 B♭sus E♭maj7 A♭maj7 A♭maj7/D Gsus G7
Be still and know your cre-a-tor, up - lift him in the na-tions –
Cm C♯dim7/B♭ Fm/A♭ C7/G Fm7 Cm(♭5) F7/C A♭maj7 Fm7/B♭ B♭7
rit.
God the Lord of hosts is with us ev - er -
E♭/B♭ N.C. E♭
- more! a tempo

48 God is the strength of my life

Show us your strength

Words and music: Graham Kendrick
Psalms 68.28, 80.1 and 118.14

Calypso
C
C♯dim7
Dm
G
gliss.
8va
C F C G
C
C♯dim
Dm
1 God is the strength of my life, my
2 Stir up your strength, O God, come
G7
C
C
C♯dim
joy, my song; I will sing prais - es to
near to save; let Sa - tan's strong-holds fall
Dm
G7
C
him and re - joice.
down in Je - sus' name.

Words and music: © 1985 Kingsway's Thankyou Music,
PO Box 75, Eastbourne, East Sussex BN23 6NW

Am F G
He has done great things for me out of his
Come set the pri - son - ers free, bring joy and
C Am F
mer - cy: O that the na-tions might see
glad - ness; now let your e - ne - mies see,
With strength
Chorus
G C Csus C Csus F A♭
that he is Lord!
that Christ is Lord.
Show us your strength, O
Csus Cm Csus Cm D♭ A♭ D♭ A♭ E♭
God,
sum-mon now your power, O

C
F
A♭
Lord; show us your strength, O
Csus Cm Csus Cm
D♭ A♭ D♭ A♭
E♭
God, may your king-dom come, O
1.
C
Fm/G
G
Lord!
2.
C
Lord!

49 God is good

Words and music: Graham Kendrick
Psalms 25.8 and 73.1, Luke 18.19
Music arranged Geoff Baker

Fast and rhythmic

Gm F Gm F Dm Gm F Gm
God is good – we sing and shout it, God is good –
E♭ D Gm F Gm F Dm
we ce-le-brate; God is good – no more we doubt it,
Gm F Gm F Gm
God is good – we know it's true!
Cm Gm D7
And when I think of his love for me, my heart fills with praise and I

Words and music: © 1985 Kingsway's Thankyou Music,
PO Box 75, Eastbourne, East Sussex BN23 6NW

Gm Dm7 Gm D7 Cm Gm
feel like danc-ing; for in his heart there is room for me, and I
A D D7
run with arms op-en wide.
Gm F Gm F Dm Gm F Gm
God is good – we sing and shout it, God is good –
E♭ D Gm F Gm F Dm
we ce-le-brate; God is good – no more we doubt it,
Gm F Gm F Gm
God is good – we know it's true!

50 God is love – his the care

Personent hodie 6 6 6 6 6 5 5 3 9

Words: P Dearmer (1867–1936)
1 John 4.16
Music: Piae Cantiones (1582)
arranged G Holst (1874–1934)

Brightly

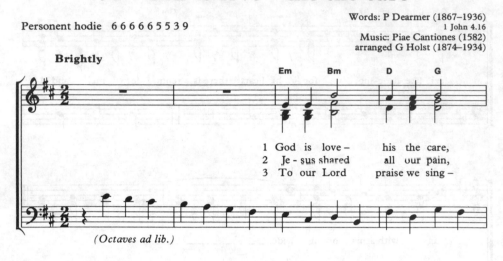

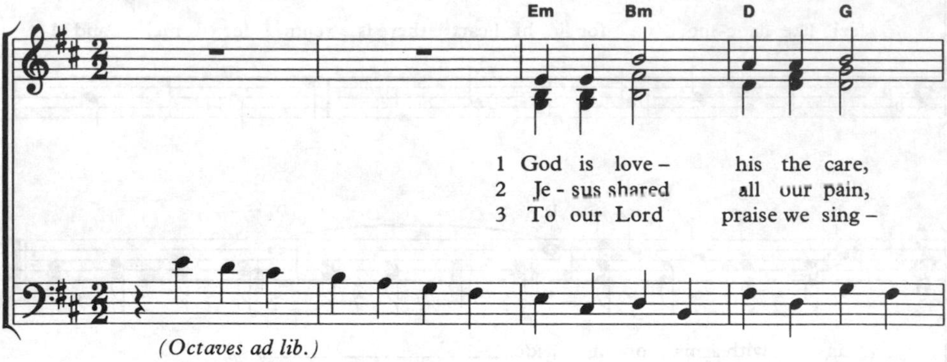
Em Bm D G
1 God is love – his the care,
2 Je - sus shared all our pain,
3 To our Lord praise we sing –
(Octaves ad lib.)

Em A F♯m D G D G D
tend - ing each, ev - ery - where; God is love –
lived and died, rose a - gain, rules our hearts,
light and life, friend and king, com - ing down

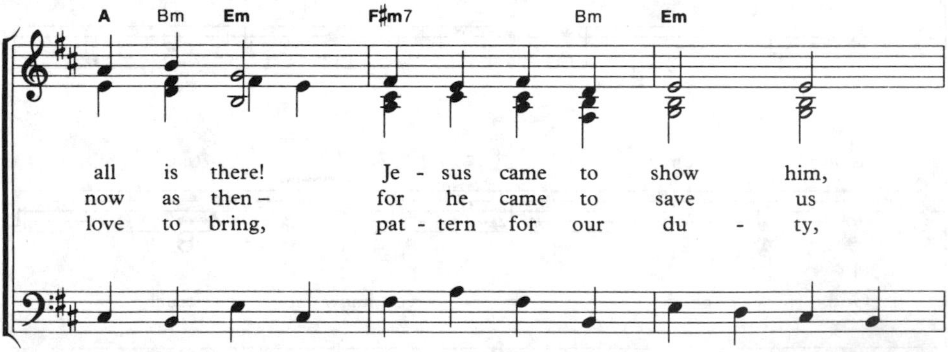
A Bm Em F♯m7 Bm Em
all is there! Je - sus came to show him,
now as then – for he came to save us
love to bring, pat - tern for our du - ty,

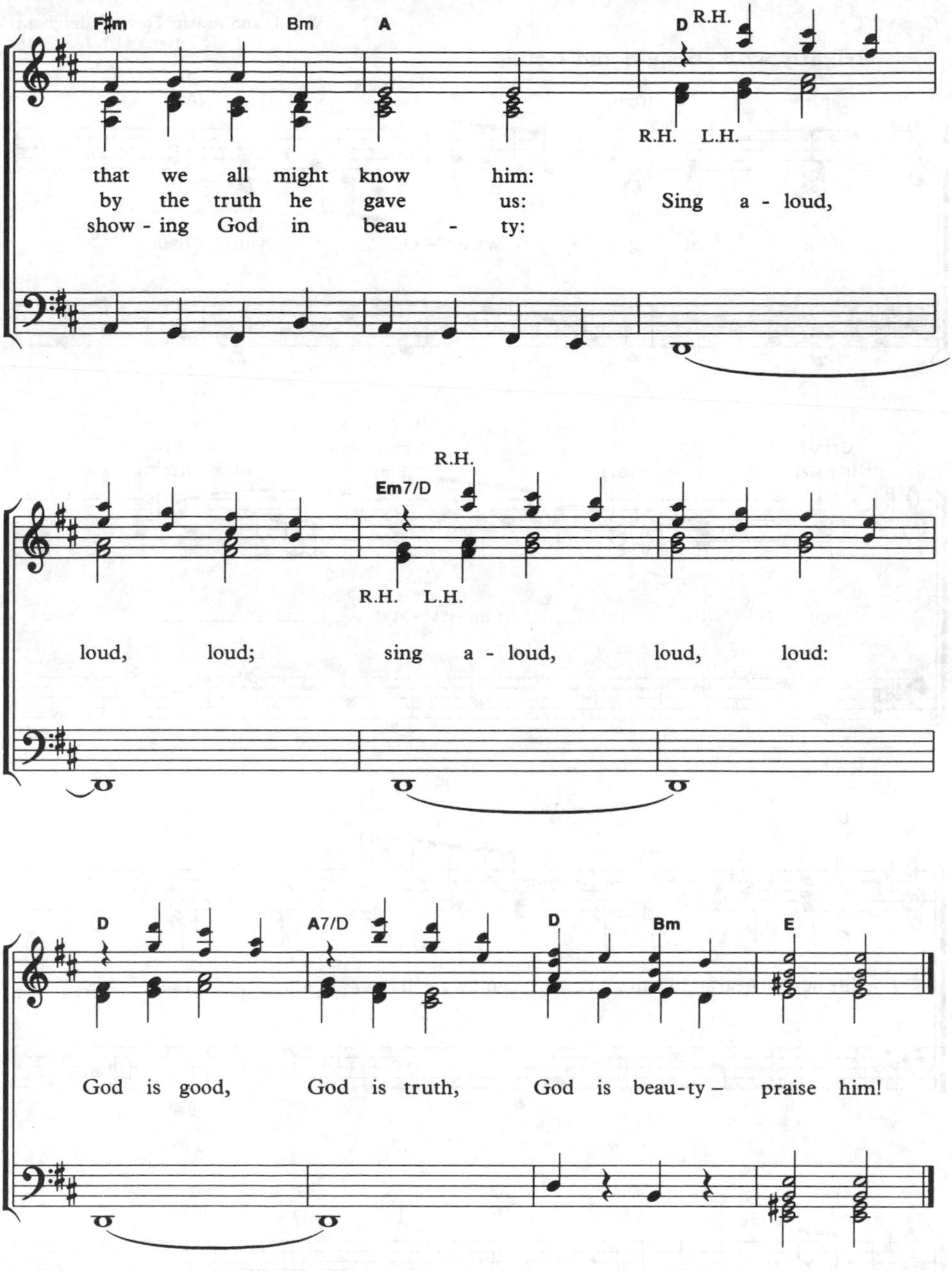
F♯m Bm A D
R.H.
R.H. L.H.
that we all might know him:
by the truth he gave us: Sing a - loud,
show - ing God in beau - ty:
R.H.
Em7/D
R.H. L.H.
loud, loud; sing a - loud, loud, loud:
D A7/D D Bm E
God is good, God is truth, God is beau - ty – praise him!

50A PRAISE SHOUT

LEADER Praise the Lord, all you nations;
ALL **extol him all you peoples!**

LEADER For his love protecting us is strong;
ALL **his faithfulness endures for ever!**

From Psalm 117

51 God of glory

Capo 2(C)

Words and music: Dave Fellingham

Isaiah 61.1, Luke 4.18

Brightly with strength and feeling

D (C) Em (Dm) F♯m (Em) Bm (Am)
God of glo - ry, we ex - alt your name,
Gmaj7 (Fmaj7) C♯7 (B7) F♯m (Em) A7/E (G7/D)
you who reign in ma-jes - ty; we
D (C) G (F) C7 (B♭7)
lift our hearts to you and we will wor - ship, praise and
D (C) Em (Dm) A7 (G7) D (C) G (F) D (C)
mag-ni-fy your ho - ly name. In power res -

Words and music: © 1982 Kingsway's Thankyou Music,
PO Box 75, Eastbourne, East Sussex BN23 6NW

Descant
Bm (Am)
F♯m (Em)
In power res - plen - dent you reign in glo - ry;
- plend - ent you reign in glo - ry; e - ter - nal
Em (Dm)
A (G)
e - ter - nal King, you reign for ev - er:
King, you reign for ev - er: your word is
Bm (Am)
F♯m (Em)
your word is migh - ty, re - leas - ing cap - tives,
migh - ty, re - leas - ing cap - tives, your love is
Em (Dm)
A7 (G7)
D (C)
G (F)
D (C)
your love is gra - cious – you are my God.
gra - cious – you are my God.

52 Grant to us your peace, Lord

Dona nobis pacem II

From Psalm 85
Words and music: Taizé – Jacques Berthier

Continuous Response

All ♩= 80

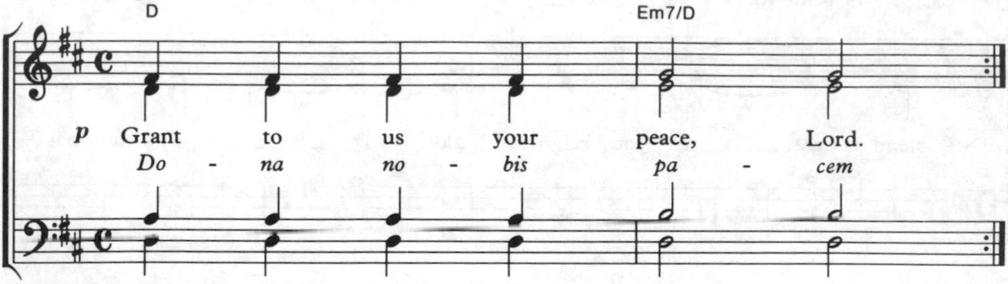
D
Em7/D
p Grant to us your peace, Lord.
Do - na no - bis pa - cem

Accompaniment

Keyboard

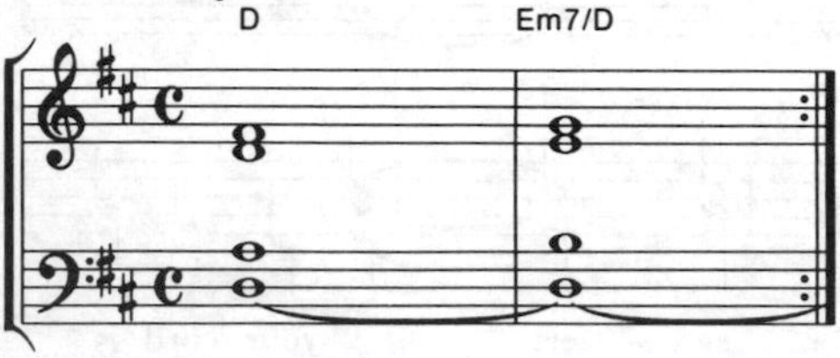
D
Em7/D

Solo verses (sung above continuous response)

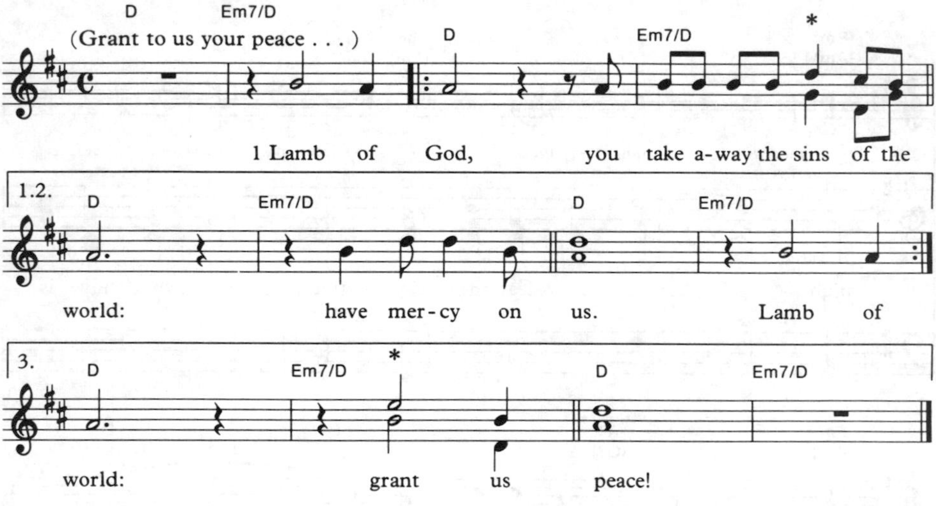
D Em7/D
(Grant to us your peace . . .)
D Em7/D *
1 Lamb of God, you take a-way the sins of the
1.2.
D Em7/D D Em7/D
world: have mer-cy on us. Lamb of
3.
D Em7/D * D Em7/D
world: grant us peace!

* Choose either part

Other verses

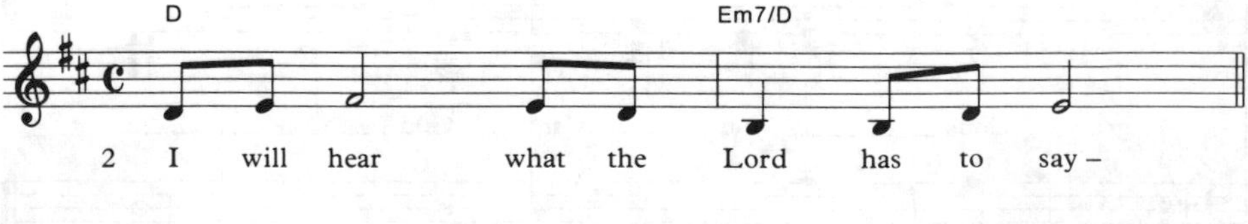
D
Em7/D
2 I will hear what the Lord has to say –

Words and music: © 1982, 1983 and 1984 Les Presses de Taizé (France).
Published by HarperCollins*Religious* and used with permission.

D Em7/D D
a voice that speaks of peace; peace for his peo-ple and
Em7/D D Em7/D
peace for his friends, and peace for those who turn to him _____ in their hearts.
D Em7/D
3 His help is near for those who a - dore him,
D Em7/D
his glo - ry will dwell _____ in our land.
D Em7/D
4 Mer - cy and faith - ful - ness have met,
D Em7/D D
jus-tice and peace have em - braced; faith-ful-ness shall spring from the
Em7/D D Em7/D
earth, and jus - tice look down from hea - ven.
D Em7/D
5 The Lord will grant us his joy, and our
D Em7/D D
earth shall yield its fruit; jus - tice shall walk be -
Em7/D D Em7/D
- fore him, and peace shall fol - low his steps.

Various accompaniments and solos

Guitar

Flute

Oboe

Bassoon or Cello

53 God has spoken

Words: Willard Jabusch
Music: Israeli folk melody
arranged Norman Warren
descant Angela Reith

Hebrew style
Chorus
Am
Descant
E
God has spo - ken to his peo - ple Al - le - lu - ia,
God has spo - ken to his peo - ple Al - le - lu - ia,
E7
Am
Fine
and his words are words of wis - dom. al - le - lu - ia!
and his words are words of wis - dom. al - le - lu - ia!
Verses
E
E7
Am
E
1 O - pen your ears, O Christ-ian peo - ple, o - pen your ears and hear good news;
2 They who have ears to hear his mes - sage, they who have ears, then let them hear;
3 Is - rael comes to greet the sav - iour, Ju - dah is glad to see his day;
E
E7
Am
Dm7
E7
D.C.
o - pen your hearts, O roy - al priest-hood, God has come to you,
they who would learn the way of wis - dom, let them hear God's word,
from east and west the peo - ples tra - vel, he will show the way,

Music arrangement: © Norman Warren / Jubilate Hymns †
Descant: © Angela Reith
Words: © 1966 Willard Jabusch

54 Great is your faithfulness

11 10 11 10 and refrain

Capo 3(C)

Words: T O Chisholm (1866–1960)
in this version Jubilate Hymns
Lamentations 3.23
Music: W M Runyan (1870–1957)

E♭ (C) Fm (Dm) B♭7 (G7) E♭ (C)
1 Great is your faith - ful-ness, O God my Fa - ther,
2 Sum - mer and win - ter, and spring-time and har - vest,
3 Par - don for sin, and a peace ev - er - last - ing,
A♭ (F) E♭ (C) F7 (D7) B♭ (G)
you have ful - filled all your pro - mise to me;
sun, moon and stars in their cours - es a - bove
your liv - ing pre - sence to cheer and to guide;
B♭7 (G7) E♭ (C) Fm (Dm)
you ne - ver fail and your love is un - chang - ing –
join with all na - ture in e - lo - quent wit - ness
strength for to - day, and bright hope for to - mor - row –
F♯dim (E♭dim) E♭/B♭ (C) B♭7 (G7) E♭ (C)
all you have been you for ev - er will be.
to your great faith - ful-ness, mer - cy and love.
these are the bless - ings your love will pro - vide.

Words and music: © 1923, Renewal 1951 by Hope Publishing Company,
Carol Stream, Illinois 60188, USA. This version © 1982 by Jubilate Hymns † / Hope Publishing Company.
All rights reserved. Used by permission.

B♭ (G) E♭ (C) C (A) Fm (Dm)
Great is your faith-ful-ness, great is your faith-ful-ness,
B♭ (G) E♭ (C) B♭/F (G) F7 (D7) B♭ (G)
morn - ing by morn - ing new mer - cies I see;
B♭7 (G7) E♭ (C) Fm (Dm)
all I have need - ed your hand has pro - vid - ed –
F♯dim (E♭dim) E♭/B♭ (C) B♭7 (G7) E♭ (C)
great is your faith - ful-ness, Fa - ther, to me.

55 Great and wonderful are your deeds

Words: from Revelation 15
derived from the 'Daily Office'
of the Joint Liturgical Group
Music: Chris Rolinson
arranged David Peacock

Bouncy

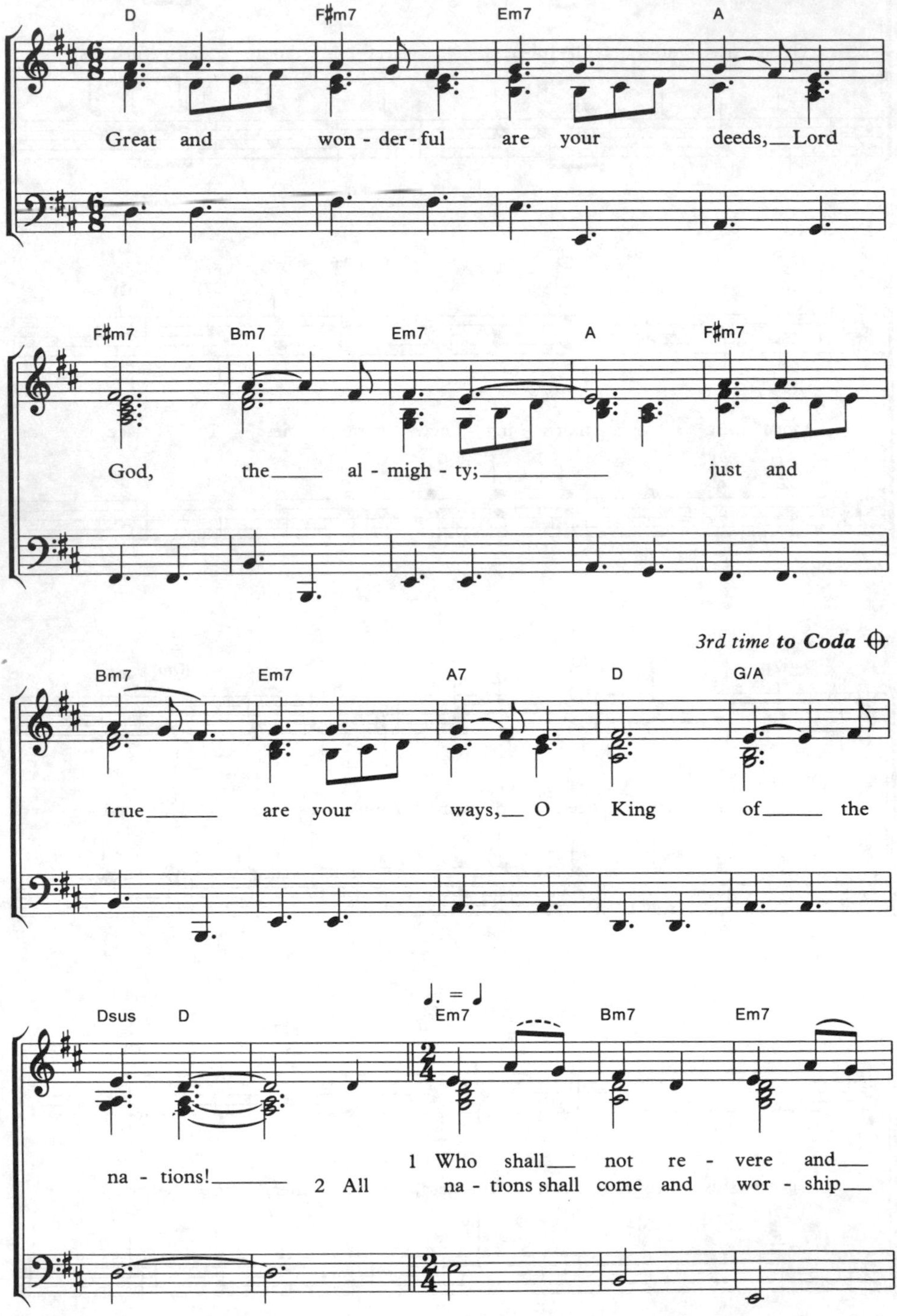
D
F♯m7
Em7
A
Great and won - der - ful are your deeds, Lord
F♯m7
Bm7
Em7
A
F♯m7
God, the al - migh - ty; just and
3rd time to Coda
Bm7
Em7
A7
D
G/A
true are your ways, O King of the
Dsus
D
Em7
Bm7
Em7
na - tions!
1 Who shall not re - vere and
2 All na - tions shall come and wor - ship

Music: © 1987 Kingsway's Thankyou Music,
PO Box 75, Eastbourne, East Sussex BN23 6NW

Words: © Joint Liturgical Group

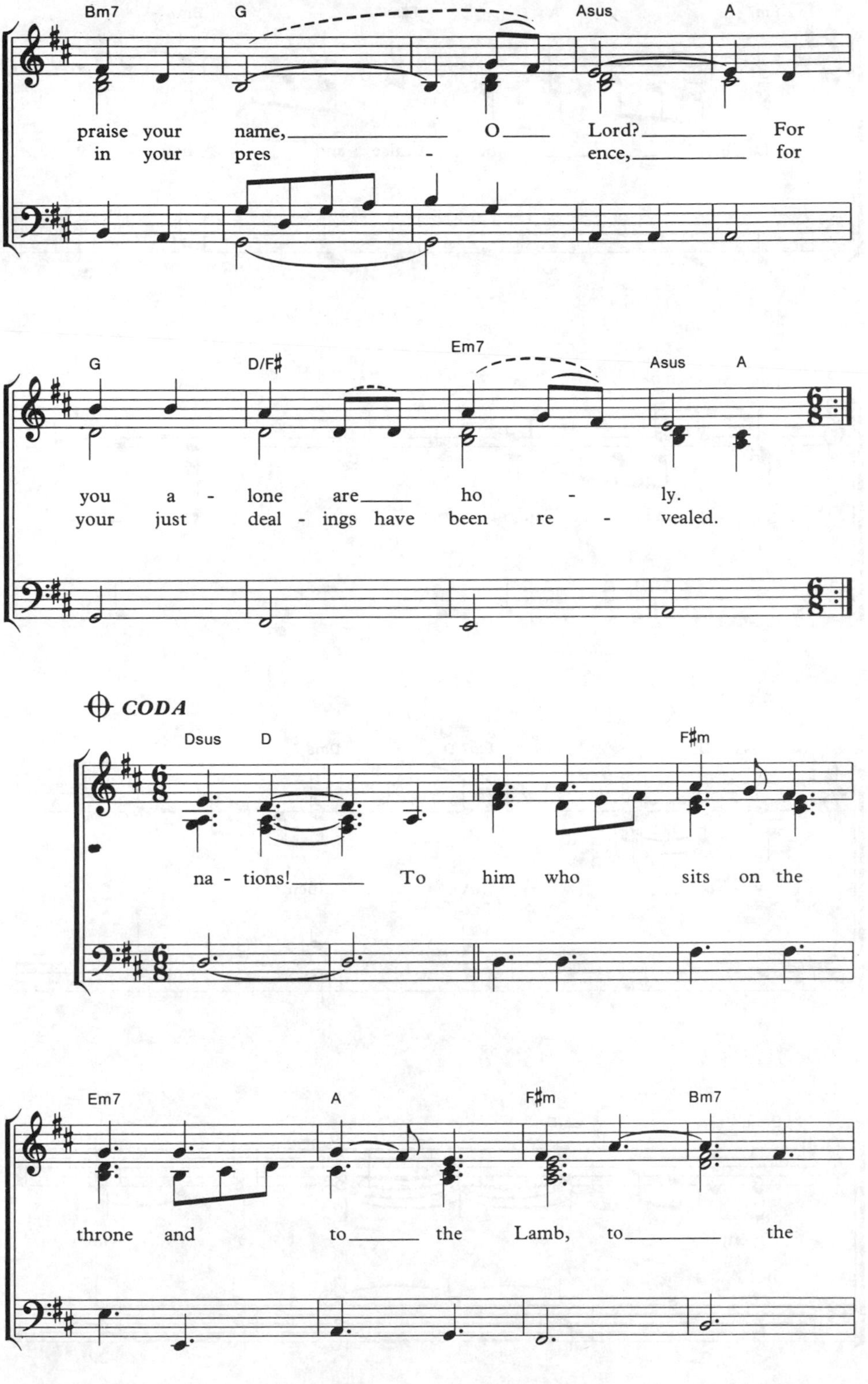
Bm7 G Asus A
praise your name, O Lord? For
in your pres - ence, for
G D/F♯ Em7 Asus A
you a - lone are ho - ly.
your just deal - ings have been re - vealed.
CODA
Dsus D F♯m
na - tions! To him who sits on the
Em7 A F♯m Bm7
throne and to the Lamb, to the

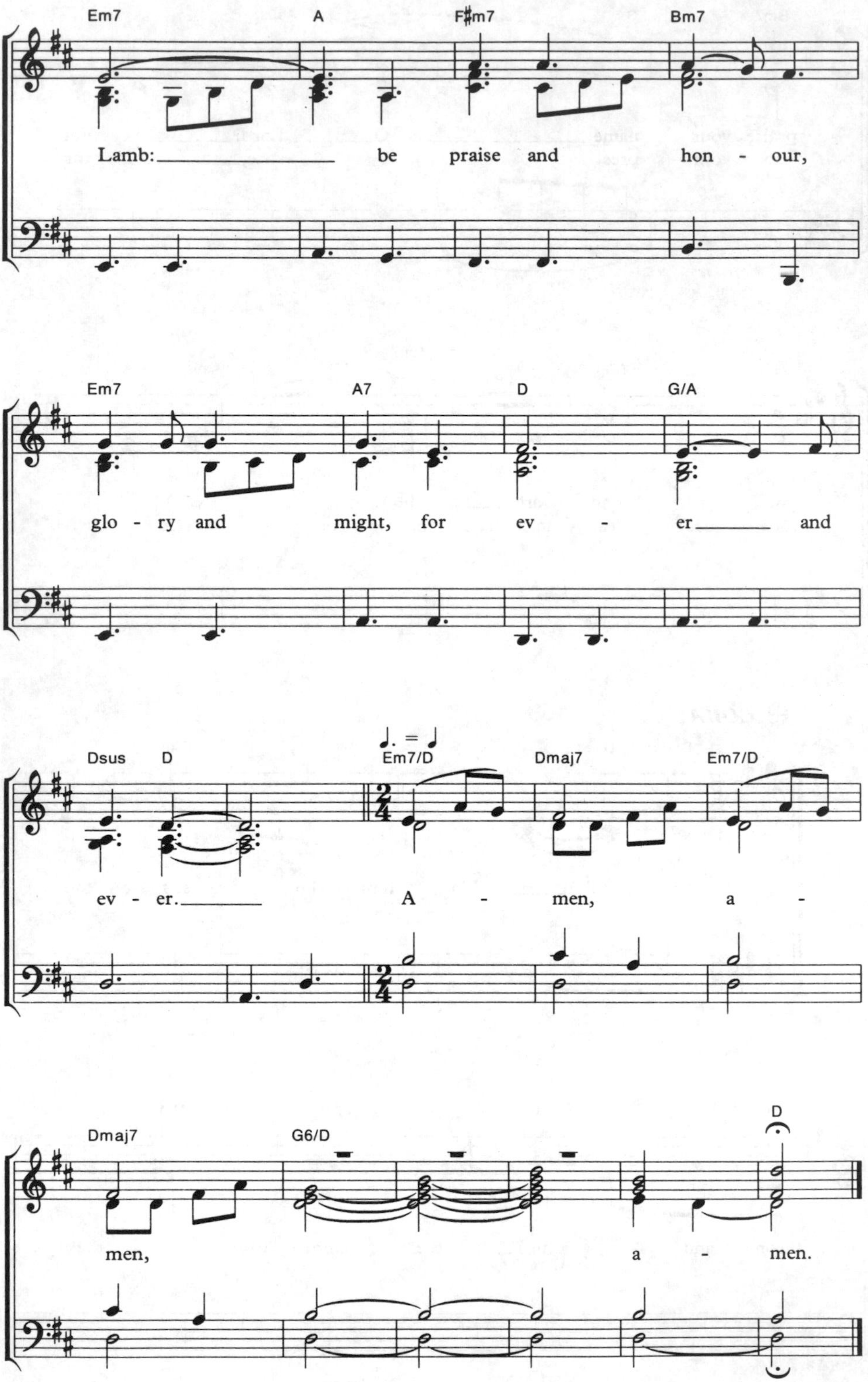
Em7 A F♯m7 Bm7
Lamb: be praise and hon - our,
Em7 A7 D G/A
glo - ry and might, for ev - er and
Dsus D Em7/D Dmaj7 Em7/D
ev - er. A - men, a -
Dmaj7 G6/D D
men, a - men.

56 He gave his life

Selfless love 8 6 8 6 D (DCM)

Words: Christopher Porteous
and in this version Jubilate Hymns
Music: Andrew Maries

D7 G Em A7 D Em A7 D
1 He gave his life in self-less love, for sin-ners once he came;
2 He did not come to call the good but sin-ners to re-pent;
3 They heard him call his Fa-ther's name – then 'Fin-ished!' was his cry;
4 His bo-dy bro-ken once for us is glor-ious now a-bove;
D/F♯ Em7 A D F♯m C7 F♯m
he had no stain of sin him-self but bore our guilt and shame:
it was the lame, the deaf, the blind for whom his life was spent:
like them we have for-sa-ken him and left him there to die:
the cup of bless-ing we re-ceive, a shar-ing of his love:
D7 G Em A7 D Em7 A7 D
he took the cup of pain and death, his blood was free-ly shed;
to heal the sick, to find the lost – it was for such he came,
the sins that cru-ci-fied him then are sins his blood has cured;
as in his pre-sence we par-take, his dy-ing we pro-claim
G F♯ Bm F♯m7 G Asus A7 D
we see his bo-dy on the cross, we share the liv-ing bread.
and round his ta-ble all may come to praise his ho-ly name.
the love that bound him to a cross our free-dom has en-sured.
un-til the hour of ma-jes-ty when Je-sus comes a-gain.

Music: © Andrew Maries

Words: © Christopher Porteous
and in this version Jubilate Hymns †

57 Happy is the one

Capo 4(C)

From Psalm 32.1–6
Words and music: Bill Batstone

Joyfully

Words and music: © 1984 Maranatha! Music/CopyCare Ltd,
PO Box 77, Hailsham, East Sussex BN27 3EF

Amaj7 (Fmaj7) G♯m7 (Em7) Amaj9 (Fmaj9)
__ no more when my guilt in me re - mained; __ I
__ be known and my con - fes - sion made, __
D2 (B♭) A/C♯ (F) D (B♭) Bsus (G)
D.C.
fell be-neath the burn - ing sun till for - give-ness brought the rain. __
then I saw your mer - cy flow to __ wash my guilt a - way. __
E (C) B/E (G) E (C) A/E (F) E (C) B/E (G) E (C)
Hap - py is __ the one __ whose sin __ free - ly is __ for -
A (F) B/D♯ (G) E (C) B/E (G) E (C) A/E (F) E (C)
- giv - en, whose in - no - cence has been __ de - clared __

C♯m7 (Am7) G♯m7 (Em7) F♯m7 (Dm7) Amaj7/B (Fmaj7) E (C) E2sus (C2sus) E (C)
by the Lord of hea - ven.
1. A/E (F) Esus (Csus)
2. Esus (Csus) A/B (F)
- ven.
F (C♯) C/F (G♯) F (C♯) B♭2 (F♯) F/G (C♯)
B♭/C (F♯) C7 (G♯7) Fmaj7 (C♯)
3 Peo-ple, let your voice be heard in prayer be-fore your God:
C/D (G♯) F/G (C♯) B♭/C (F♯) Fmaj7 (C♯)
he a-lone can res - cue you from

B♭maj9 (F♯)
A2/C♯ (F)
F♯m7 (Dm7)
A/B (F)
trou-ble like a flood.
B (G)
E (C) B/E (G) E (C) A/E (F) E (C)
Hap-py is the one whose sin
E (C) B/E (G) E (C) A/E (F) B/D♯ (G)
E (C) B/E (G) E (C) A/E (F)
free-ly is for - giv - en, whose in-no - cence has been
E (C) C♯m (Am) G♯m7 (Em7) F♯m7 (Dm7) Amaj7/B (Fmaj7) E (C)
de-clared by the Lord of hea - ven.

58 He has shown you

Words and music: Graham Kendrick
Micah 6.8

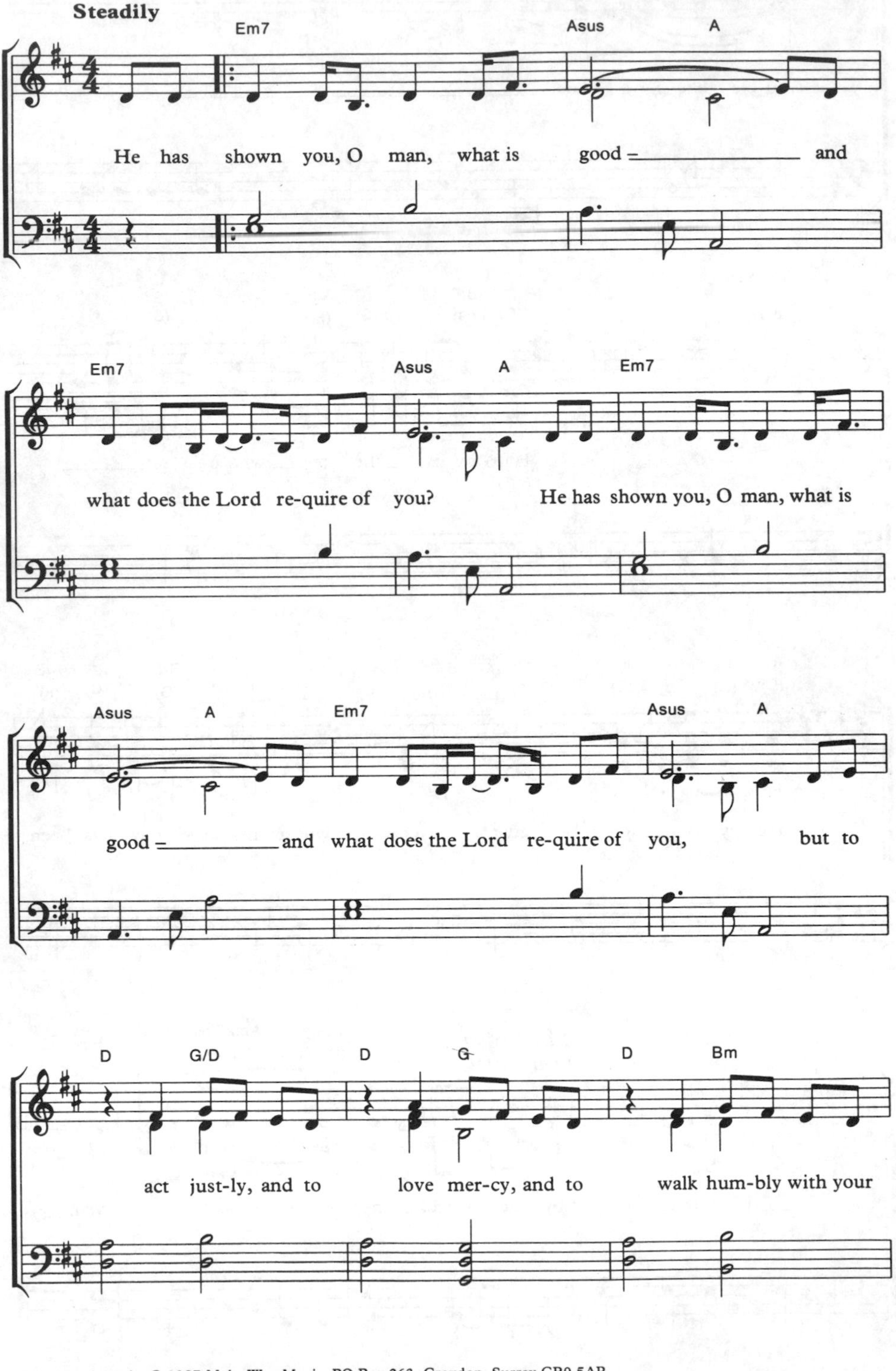
Steadily
Em7 Asus A
He has shown you, O man, what is good — and
Em7 Asus A Em7
what does the Lord re-quire of you? He has shown you, O man, what is
Asus A Em7 Asus A
good — and what does the Lord re-quire of you, but to
D G/D D G D Bm
act just-ly, and to love mer-cy, and to walk hum-bly with your

Words and music: © 1987 Make Way Music, PO Box 263, Croydon, Surrey CR9 5AP.
International copyright secured. All rights reserved. Used by permission.

58A PRAISE SHOUT

LEADER Praise the Lord, O my soul;
ALL **all my being, praise his name!**

LEADER Praise the Lord, O my soul;
ALL **and forget not all his blessings!**

LEADER Praise the Lord, O my soul.
ALL **Praise the Lord! Amen.**

From Psalm 103

59 He is Lord

Words: verse 1: Marvin Frey
verse 3: Michael Baughen
Philippians 2.10, Mark 13.26 and 13.35
Music: Marvin Frey
arranged Norman Warren
descant: Angela Reith

Capo 1(A)

Gently

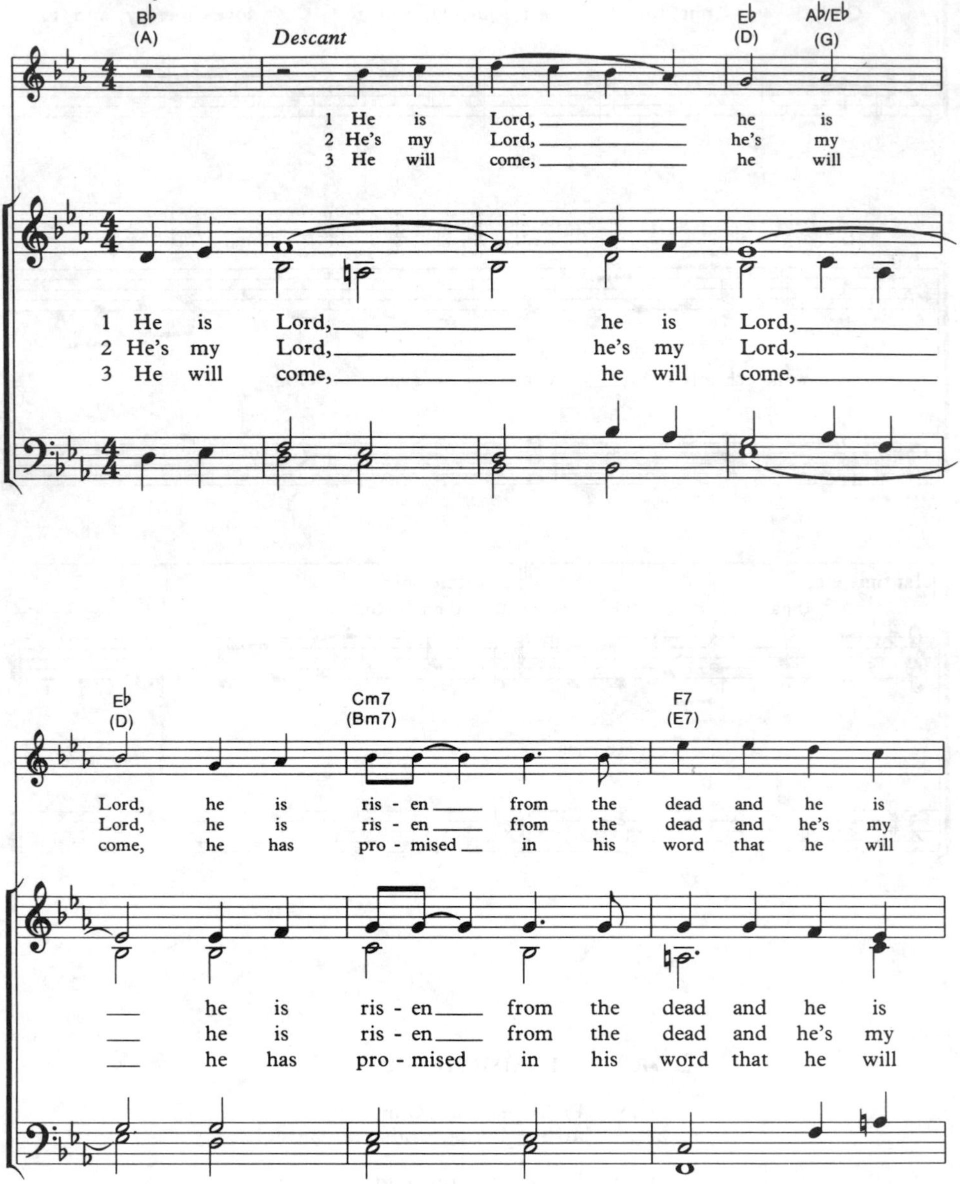

B♭ (A)
Descant
E♭ (D)
A♭/E♭ (G)
1 He is Lord, he is
2 He's my Lord, he's my
3 He will come, he will
1 He is Lord, he is Lord,
2 He's my Lord, he's my Lord,
3 He will come, he will come,
E♭ (D)
Cm7 (Bm7)
F7 (E7)
Lord, he is ris - en from the dead and he is
Lord, he is ris - en from the dead and he's my
come, he has pro - mised in his word that he will
he is ris - en from the dead and he is
he is ris - en from the dead and he's my
he has pro - mised in his word that he will

Music: © Marvin Frey
Descant: © Angela Reith
Music arrangement: © Norman Warren / Jubilate Hymns †
Words: verse 1: © Marvin Frey
Words: verse 3: © Michael Baughen / Jubilate Hymns †

B♭ (A)
B♭7 (A7)
E♭ (D)
Lord! Ev - ery knee, ev - ery
Lord! Ev - ery knee, ev - ery
come; some glad day, some glad
Lord! Ev - ery knee shall
Lord! Ev - ery knee shall
come; some glad day or
E♭7 (D7)
A♭ (G)
Fm (Em)
knee shall bow, tongue con - fess that
knee shall bow, tongue con - fess that
day or night, power and might, the
bow, ev - ery tongue con - fess that
bow, ev - ery tongue con - fess that
night, with great power and might, the
E♭/B♭ (D)
B♭7 (A7)
E♭ (D)
Fm7/E♭ (Em7)
E♭ (D)
Je - sus Christ is Lord.
Je - sus Christ is Lord.
ris - en Lord will come.
Je - sus Christ is Lord.
Je - sus Christ is Lord.
ris - en Lord will come.

60 He is risen

Words and music: Unknown
Matthew 28.6, Mark 16.6, Luke 24.34
Music arranged David Peacock

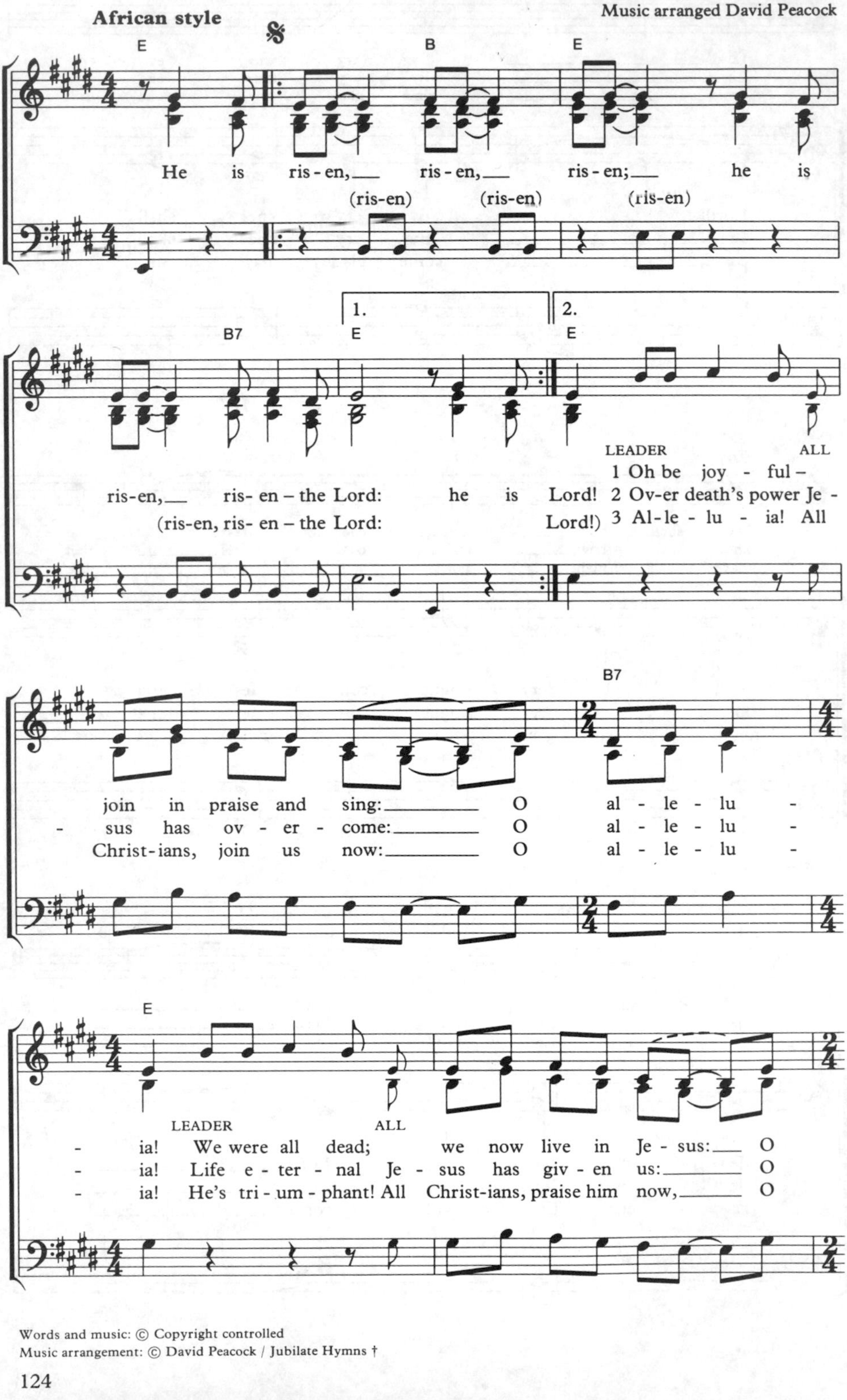
African style
E
B
E
He is ris-en,___ ris-en,___ ris-en;___ he is
(ris-en) (ris-en) (ris-en)
1.
2.
B7
E
E
ris-en,___ ris-en – the Lord: he is Lord!
(ris-en, ris-en – the Lord: Lord!)
LEADER
ALL
1 Oh be joy - ful –
2 Ov-er death's power Je -
3 Al-le - lu - ia! All
join in praise and sing:_____ O al - le - lu -
- sus has ov - er - come:_____ O al - le - lu -
Christ-ians, join us now:_____ O al - le - lu -
B7
E
LEADER
ALL
- ia! We were all dead; we now live in Je - sus:___ O
- ia! Life e - ter - nal Je - sus has giv - en us:___ O
- ia! He's tri - um - phant! All Christ-ians, praise him now,___ O

Words and music: © Copyright controlled
Music arrangement: © David Peacock / Jubilate Hymns †

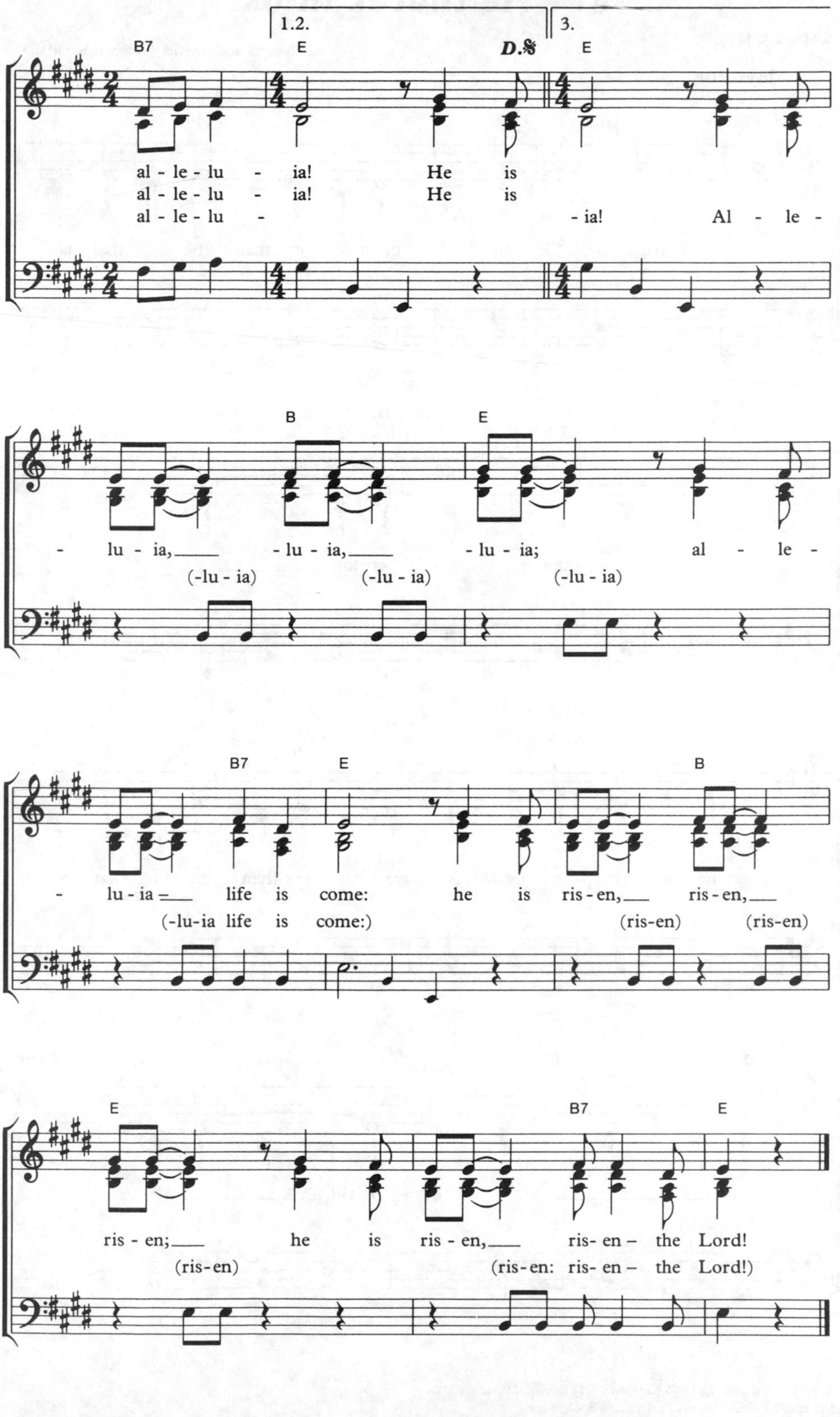
1.2.
3.
B7
E
D.𝄋
E
al - le - lu - ia! He is
al - le - lu - ia! He is
al - le - lu - ia! Al - le -
B
E
- lu - ia, - lu - ia, - lu - ia; al - le -
(-lu - ia) (-lu - ia) (-lu - ia)
B7
E
B
- lu - ia — life is come: he is ris - en, ris - en,
(-lu-ia life is come:) (ris-en) (ris-en)
E
B7
E
ris - en; he is ris - en, ris - en – the Lord!
(ris - en) (ris - en: ris - en – the Lord!)

61 He that is in us

Capo 2(C)

Words and music: Graham Kendrick
1 John 4.4

Joyfully
D (C) G (F) A (G) Bm (Am)
He that is in us is great - er than he that is
Em7 (Dm7) A7 (G7) D (C)
in the world;
G (F) A (G) Bm (Am)
he that is in us is great - er than he that is
Em (Dm) A7 (G7) D (C)
Fine
in the world.

Words and music: © 1986 Kingsway's Thankyou Music,
PO Box 75, Eastbourne, East Sussex BN23 6NW

G (F) A/G (G7) F♯m (Em) Bm (Am)
1 There-fore I will sing and I will re - joice for his
2 All the powers of death and hell and sin lie
Em (Dm) A7 (G7) D (C)
Spi - rit lives in me:
crushed be - neath his feet:
G (F) A/G (G7) F♯m (Em) F♯ (E) Bm (Am)
Christ the liv - ing One has ov - er - come, and we
Je - sus owns the name a - bove all names, crowned with
Em7 (Dm7) Asus (Gsus) A (G) D (C)
share in his vic - to - ry.
hon - our and ma - jes - ty.

62 He's got the whole world in his hands

Words and music: unknown
Music arranged D J Crawshaw

Bouyantly
E
F♯m7
B7
E
ALL 1&5 He's got the whole world in his hands, he's got the whole wide world
ALL 2 He's got ev-ery-bo-dy here in his hands, he's got ev-ery-bo-dy here
WOMEN 3 He's got you and me, sis-ter, in his hands, he's got you and me, sis-ter,
MEN 4 He's got you and me, bro-ther, in his hands, he's got you and me bro-ther
2nd part He's got the whole world, he's got the
B7

Words and music: © Marshall, Morgan & Scott/HarperCollins*Religious*/CopyCare Ltd,
PO Box 77, Hailsham, East Sussex BN27 3EF

E
in his hands, he's got the whole world
in his hands, he's got every-bo-dy here
in his hands, he's got you and me, sis-ter,
in his hands, he's got you and me bro-ther
whole world, he's got the
1-4. 5.
B7
E
E
in his hands, he's got the whole world in his hands! hands!
in his hands, he's got the whole world in his hands!
in his hands, he's got the whole world in his hands!
in his hands, he's got the whole world in his hands!
whole world, he's got the whole world in his hands! hands!

63 Here I am

Capo 3(D)

Words and music: Chris Bowater
Matthew 5.13, John 4.35

Worshipfully

Words and music: © 1981 Sovereign Lifestyle Music,
PO Box 356, Leighton Buzzard LU7 8WP. Used by permission.

F (D) C/E (A) Dm (Bm) Dm7/C (Bm7)
fields are white unto harvest but
time is right in the nation for
salt are we ready to savour, in
B♭ (G) C7 (A7) F (D) B♭/C (G)
oh, the labourers are so few; so
works of power and authority; God's
darkness are we ready to be light; God's
F (D) C/E (A) Dm (Bm)
Lord I give myself to help the reaping, to
looking for a people who are willing to be
seeking out a very special people to
B♭ (G) B♭m (Gm) C7 (A7) F (D) B♭/C (G) D.C.
gather precious souls unto you.
counted in his glorious victory.
manifest his truth and his might.

64 Holy holy, holy is the Lord

Words: from Revelation 4
Music: unknown
arranged with descant Norman Warren

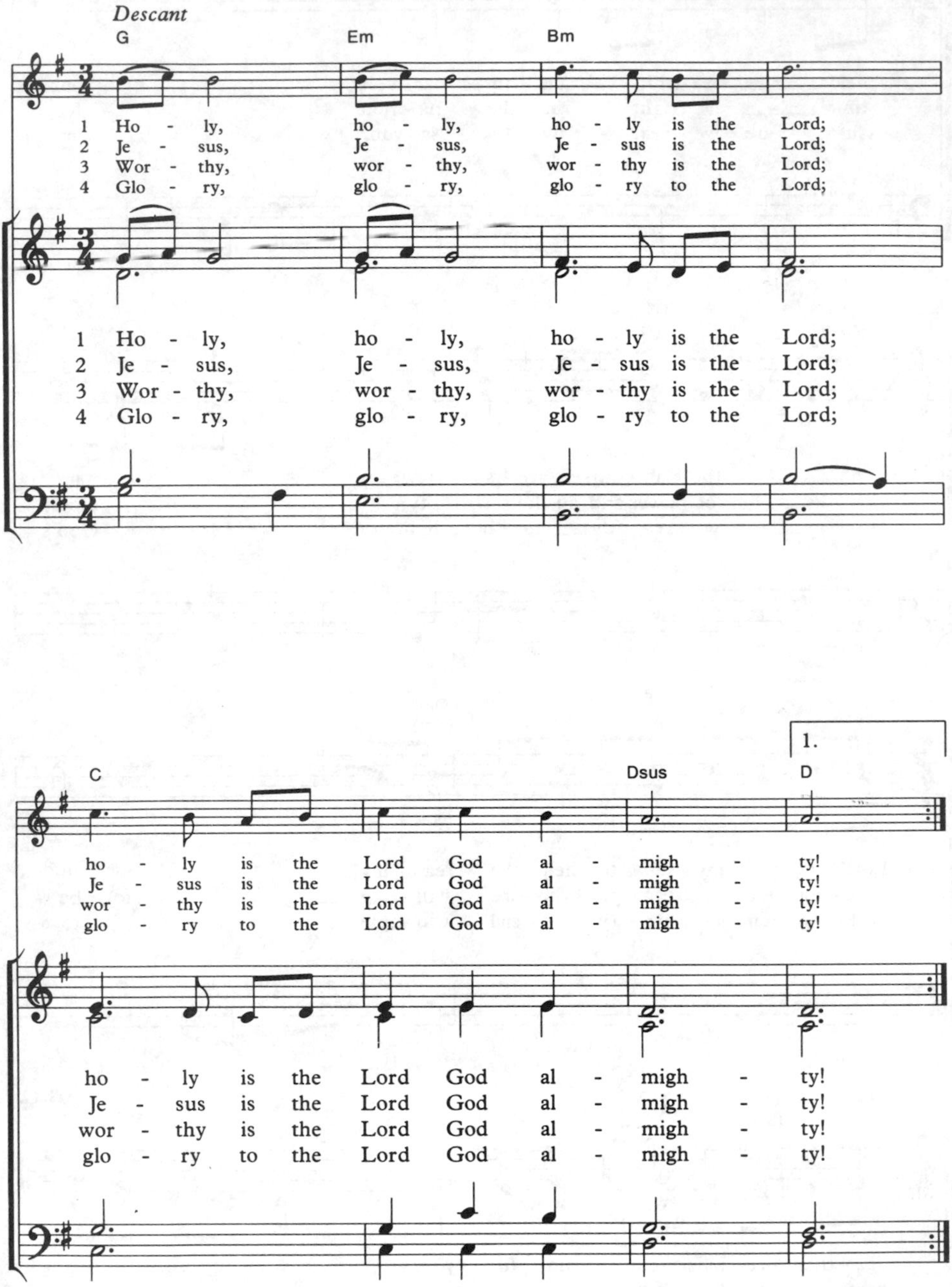
Descant
G
Em
Bm
1 Ho - ly, ho - ly, ho - ly is the Lord;
2 Je - sus, Je - sus, Je - sus is the Lord;
3 Wor - thy, wor - thy, wor - thy is the Lord;
4 Glo - ry, glo - ry, glo - ry to the Lord;
1 Ho - ly, ho - ly, ho - ly is the Lord;
2 Je - sus, Je - sus, Je - sus is the Lord;
3 Wor - thy, wor - thy, wor - thy is the Lord;
4 Glo - ry, glo - ry, glo - ry to the Lord;
1.
C
Dsus
D
ho - ly is the Lord God al - migh - ty!
Je - sus is the Lord God al - migh - ty!
wor - thy is the Lord God al - migh - ty!
glo - ry to the Lord God al - migh - ty!
ho - ly is the Lord God al - migh - ty!
Je - sus is the Lord God al - migh - ty!
wor - thy is the Lord God al - migh - ty!
glo - ry to the Lord God al - migh - ty!

Words and music: © Copyright controlled
Music arrangement and descant: © Norman Warren / Jubilate Hymns †

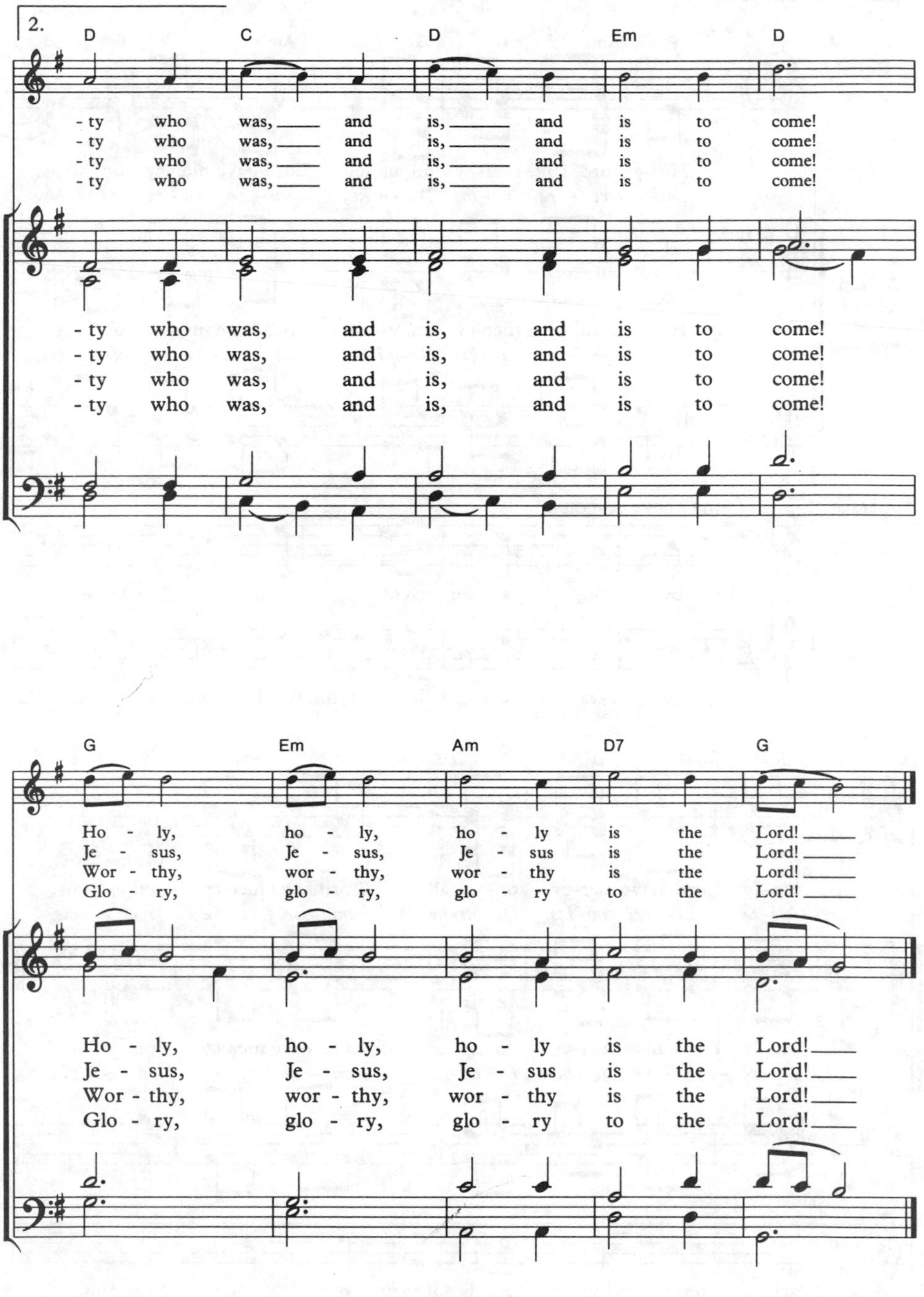

2.

Chords: D, C, D, Em, D

-ty who was,____ and is,____ and is to come!
-ty who was,____ and is,____ and is to come!
-ty who was,____ and is,____ and is to come!
-ty who was,____ and is,____ and is to come!

-ty who was, and is, and is to come!
-ty who was, and is, and is to come!
-ty who was, and is, and is to come!
-ty who was, and is, and is to come!

Chords: G, Em, Am, D7, G

Ho - ly, ho - ly, ho - ly is the Lord!____
Je - sus, Je - sus, Je - sus is the Lord!____
Wor - thy, wor - thy, wor - thy is the Lord!____
Glo - ry, glo - ry, glo - ry to the Lord!____

Ho - ly, ho - ly, ho - ly is the Lord!____
Je - sus, Je - sus, Je - sus is the Lord!____
Wor - thy, wor - thy, wor - thy is the Lord!____
Glo - ry, glo - ry, glo - ry to the Lord!____

65 Holy Lord, have mercy on us all

Miserere nobis

Continuous Response

From Psalm 123
Words and music: Taizé – Jacques Berthier
Psalm 123.2, Luke 18.13

♩ = 69
E Am7 D G C Am B7 Em B
Equal voices
Ho-ly Lord, have mer-cy on us all, Lord have mer-cy on us;
Mi-se-re-re no-bis Do-mi-ne, mi-se-re-re no-bis;
Mixed voices and keyboard
p
Ho-ly Lord, have mer-cy on us all, Lord have mer-cy on us;
Mi-se-re-re no-bis Do-mi-ne, mi-se-re-re no-bis;
Verses
(sung above response)
Solo
1 Be-hold, as the eyes of ser-vants
Solo
2 Our eyes are fixed on the Lord our God

E Am7 D G C Am Em B Em
Ho-ly Lord, have mer-cy on us all, Lord have mer-cy on us.
Mi-se-re-re no-bis Do-mi-ne, mi-se-re-re no-bis.
Ho-ly Lord, have mer-cy on us all, Lord have mer-cy on us.
Mi-se-re-re no-bis Do-mi-ne, mi-se-re-re no-bis.
are on the hands of their mas-ters:
un-til he shows us his mer-cy.

Words and music: © 1978, 1980 and 1981 Les Presses de Taizé (France).
Published by HarperCollins*Religious* and used with permission.

Flute

Oboe

B♭ Clarinet

66 Holy, holy, holy Lord

Sanctus Dominus II

Words and music: Taizé – Jacques Berthier
Psalm 34.1. Isaiah 6.3, Luke 18.13

Continuous Response

All

♩. = 56
D
Em7/D
mp
Ho - ly, ho - ly, ho - ly Lord,
San - ctus, san - ctus, Do - mi - nus,

Alternative response

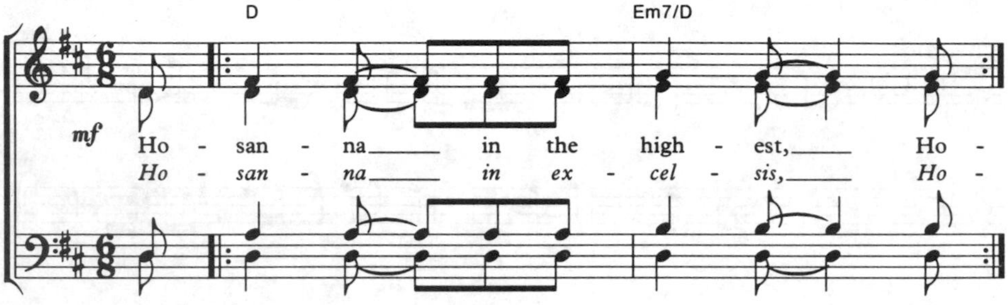
D
Em7/D
mf
Ho - san - na in the high - est, Ho -
Ho - san - na in ex - cel - sis, Ho -

Accompaniment

Keyboard

D
Em7/D

Verses (sung above continuous response)

Solo

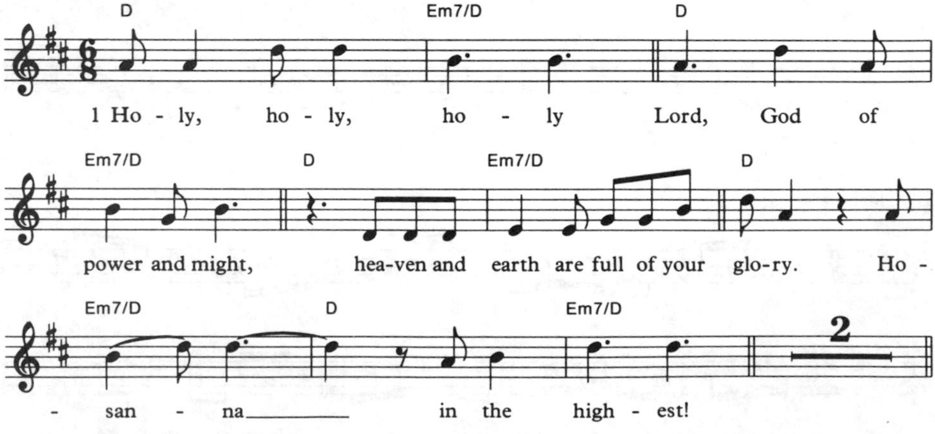
D
Em7/D
D
1 Ho - ly, ho - ly, ho - ly Lord, God of
Em7/D
D
Em7/D
D
power and might, hea-ven and earth are full of your glo-ry. Ho -
Em7/D
D
Em7/D
2
- san - na in the high - est!

Words and music: © 1982, 1983 and 1984 Les Presses de Taizé (France).
Published by HarperCollins*Religious* and used with permission.

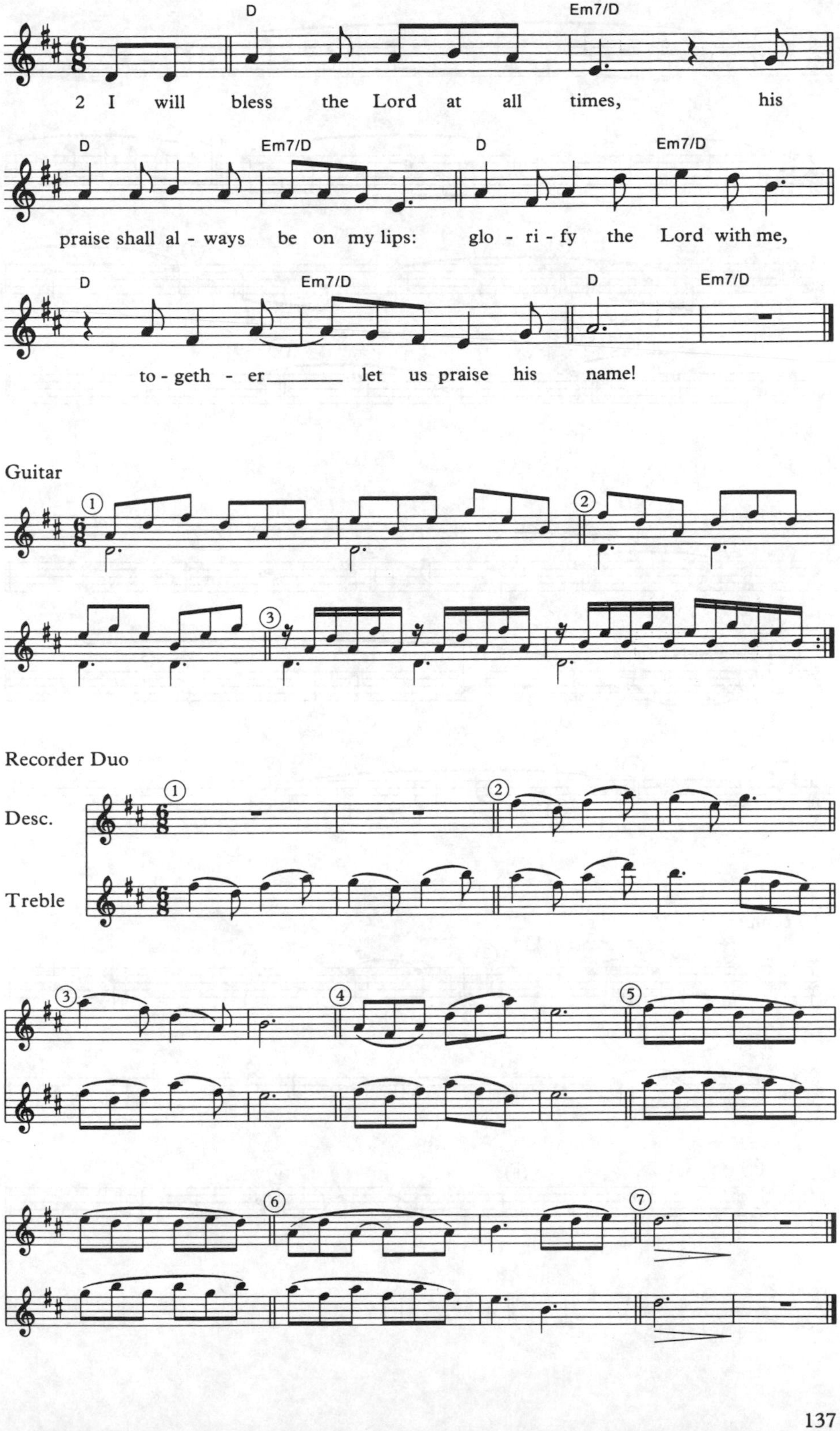
D
Em7/D
2 I will bless the Lord at all times, his
D
Em7/D
D
Em7/D
praise shall al - ways be on my lips: glo - ri - fy the Lord with me,
D
Em7/D
D
Em7/D
to - geth - er let us praise his name!
Guitar
Recorder Duo
Desc.
Treble

Oboe

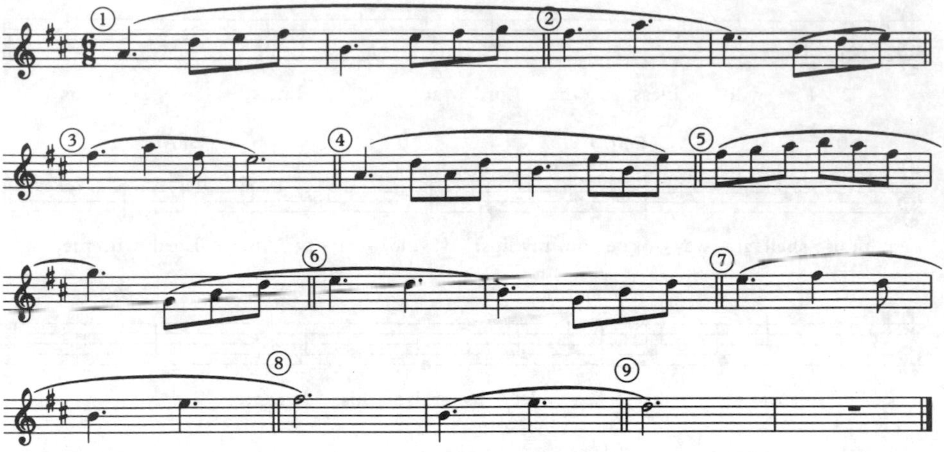

French horn

B♭ Trumpet

67 Holy Spirit, come to us

Veni Sancte Spiritus

Words and music: Taizé – Jacques Berthier

Continuous Response

All

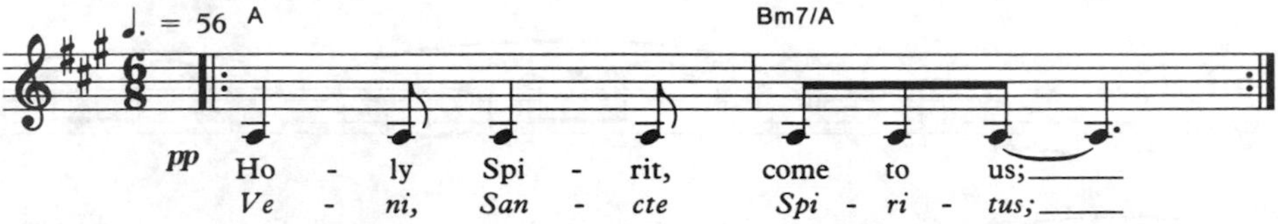
♩. = 56
A
Bm7/A
pp
Ho - ly Spi - rit, come to us;
Ve - ni, San - cte Spi - ri - tus;

Womens' voices

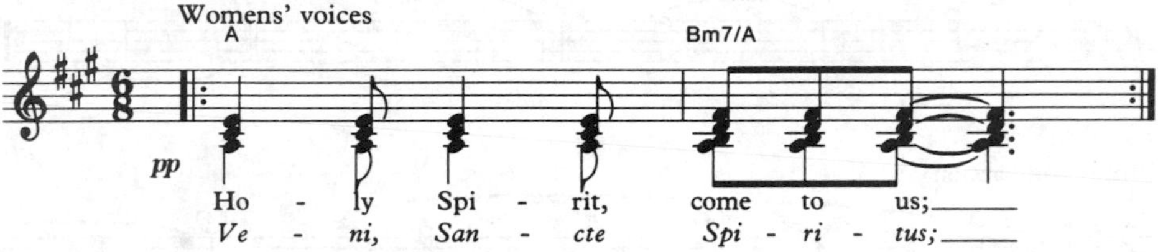
A
Bm7/A
pp
Ho - ly Spi - rit, come to us;
Ve - ni, San - cte Spi - ri - tus;

Mixed voices and accompaniment

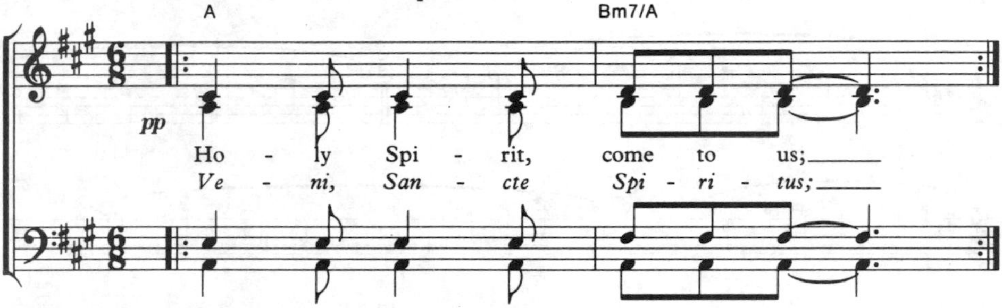
A
Bm7/A
pp
Ho - ly Spi - rit, come to us;
Ve - ni, San - cte Spi - ri - tus;

To begin this response, the four mixed voices should make their entrances in the order: Bass, Alto, Soprano, Tenor.

Verses

As the response continues, vocal and instrumental verses are sung or played as desired with some space always left between the verses (after the soloist's 'Holy Spirit come to us')

Solo

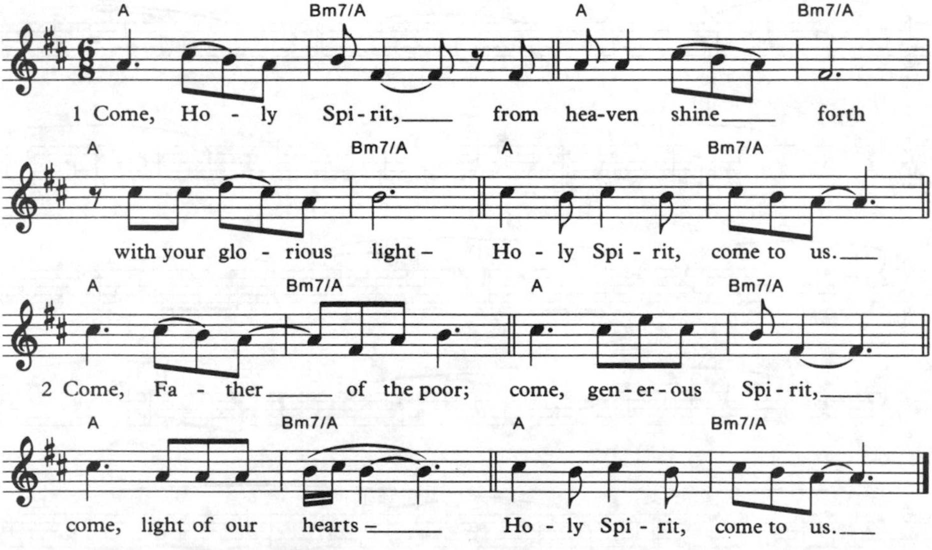
A Bm7/A A Bm7/A
1 Come, Ho - ly Spi - rit, from hea-ven shine forth
A Bm7/A A Bm7/A
with your glo - rious light – Ho - ly Spi - rit, come to us.
A Bm7/A A Bm7/A
2 Come, Fa - ther of the poor; come, gen - er - ous Spi - rit,
A Bm7/A A Bm7/A
come, light of our hearts – Ho - ly Spi - rit, come to us.

Words and music: © 1978, 1980 and 1981 Les Presses de Taizé (France).
Published by HarperCollins*Religious* and used with permission.

Flute (1st version)

Flute (2nd version)

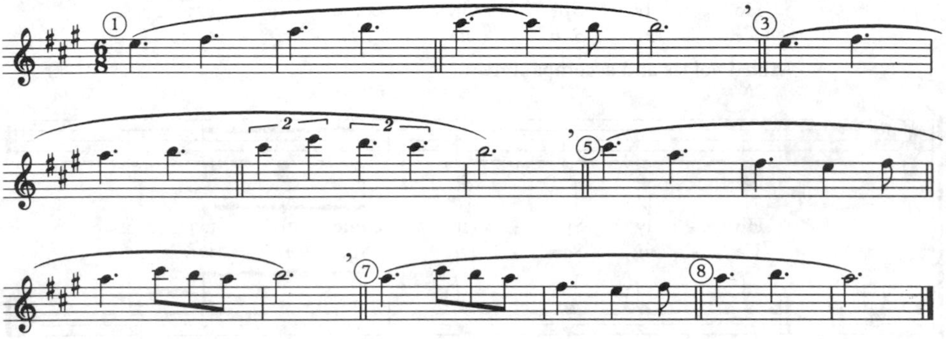

Oboe

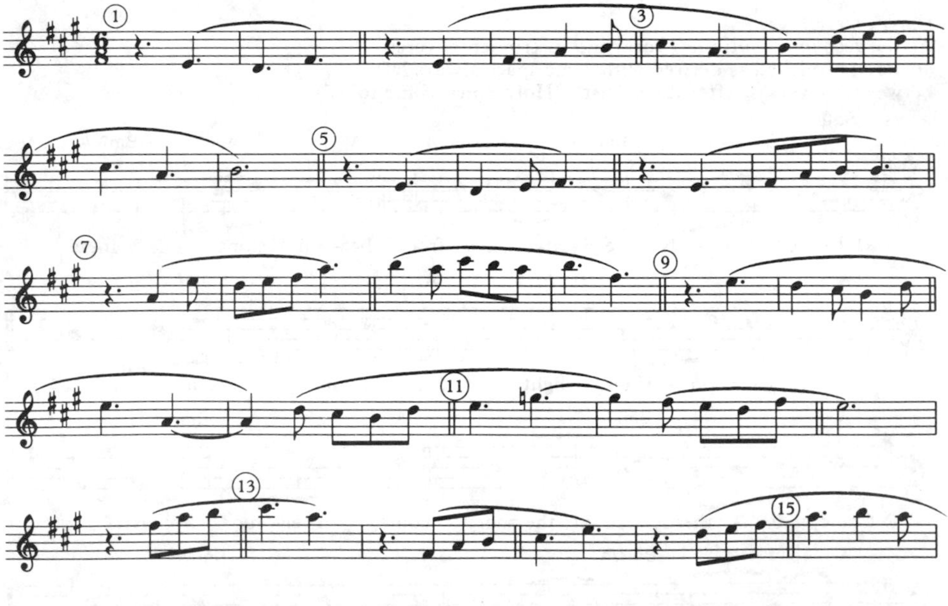

B♭ Clarinet

B♭ Trumpet

Trombone

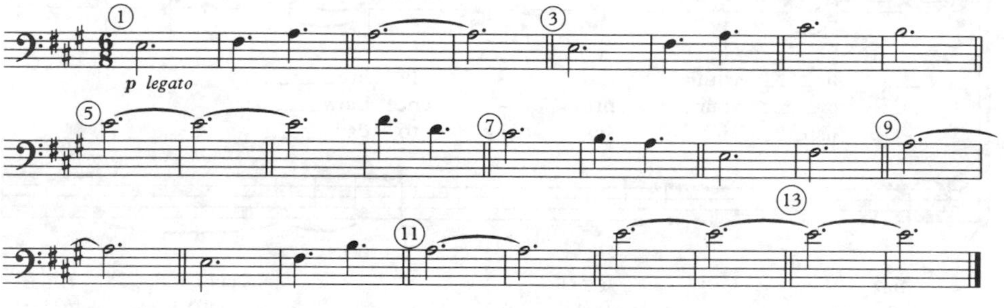

Cello

68 Holy Spirit, we welcome you

Capo 3(A)

Words and music: Chris Bowater

Prayerfully
C (A) Dm/C (Bm) Cmaj7 (Amaj7)
1 Ho - ly Spi - rit, we wel - come you,
2 Ho - ly Spi - rit, we wel - come you,
3 Ho - ly Spi - rit, we wel - come you,
1. Csus (Asus)
2. B♭/C (G) C7 (A7) Fmaj7 (Dmaj7)
Move a - mong
Let the breeze
Please ac - comp -
G/F (F) Em7 (C♯m7) Am7 (F♯m7)
us with ho - ly fire
of your pres - ence blow
- lish in us to - day
Dm7 (Bm7) G7 (E7) Cmaj7 (Amaj7) C7sus (A7sus)
as we lay a - side all earth - ly de - sire,
that your child - ren here might tru - ly know
some new work of lov - ing grace, we pray

Words and music: © 1986 Sovereign Lifestyle Music,
PO Box 356, Leighton Buzzard LU7 8WP. Used by permission.

C7 (A7)
Fmaj7 (Dmaj7)
G/F (E)
hands reach out and our
how to move in the
un - re - serv - ed - ly -
Em7 (C♯m7)
Am7 (F♯m7)
F (D)
hearts as - pire.
Spi - rit's flow. Ho - ly Spi - rit,
have your way.
C (A)
Dm7 (Bm7)
Ho-ly Spi - rit, Ho-ly Spi - rit,
1.2.
3.
F/G (D)
G7sus (E7sus)
C (A)
Dm/C (Bm)
C (A)
we wel-come you!

69 How I love you

You are the One

Words and music: Keith Green
John 14.6

Brightly
G D G G/B C G/B Am7 D7
How I love you: you are the One, you are the One;
4th time to Coda
G D G G/B C D7 G D7
how I love you: you are the One for me!
G D G G/B C G/B Am7 D7
1 I was so lost but you showed the way – for you are the Way;
2 I was lied to, but you told the truth – for you are the Truth;
3 I was dy - ing, but you gave me life – for you are the Life;
G D G G/B C D7 G D7
I was so lost, but you showed the way to me.
I was lied to, but you showed the truth to me.
I was dy - ing, but you gave your life for me.

Words and music: © 1982 Birdwing Music/Cherry Lane Music/EMI Music,
127 Charing Cross Road, London WC2H OEA

CODA
C G/B Am7 3 G/B C D7 G D7
you are the One, God's ri-sen Son, you are the One for ___ me!
G D G G/B C G/B
4 Al - le - lu - ia, you are the One, ___
How I love you: you are the One, ___
Am7 D7 G D G G/B
you are the One; ___ al - le - lu - ia,
you are the One; ___ how I love you:
1. 2.
C D7 G D7 G
you are the One for me!
you are the One for me!

70 How lovely is your dwelling-place

Moderately

From Psalm 84
Words and music: Tom Howard

Verse 1 and Chorus

C G/C F/C C Dm7 G7
1 How love-ly is__ your dwell-ing-place, al-migh-ty Lord!_
C G/B Am D7
__ There's a hun-ger__ deep in-side__ my
Gsus G C G/C F/C
soul:________ on-ly in__ your pres-
C B7sus E Am Am/G
-ence__ are my heart and flesh__ re-stored– how

Words and music: © 1982 Maranatha! Music/CopyCare Ltd,
PO Box 77, Hailsham, East Sussex BN27 3EF

1.
2.3.4.
Fmaj7 Gsus G7 F
love - ly. How love - ly is your
Gsus G C F/C G/C C
Fine
dwell - ing place. 3 A
Verse 2
F/C G/C C F/C G/C
2 In your courts there's shel - ter for the great-est and the small;
C Dm C2/E F F/G
the spar - row has a place to build her nest,

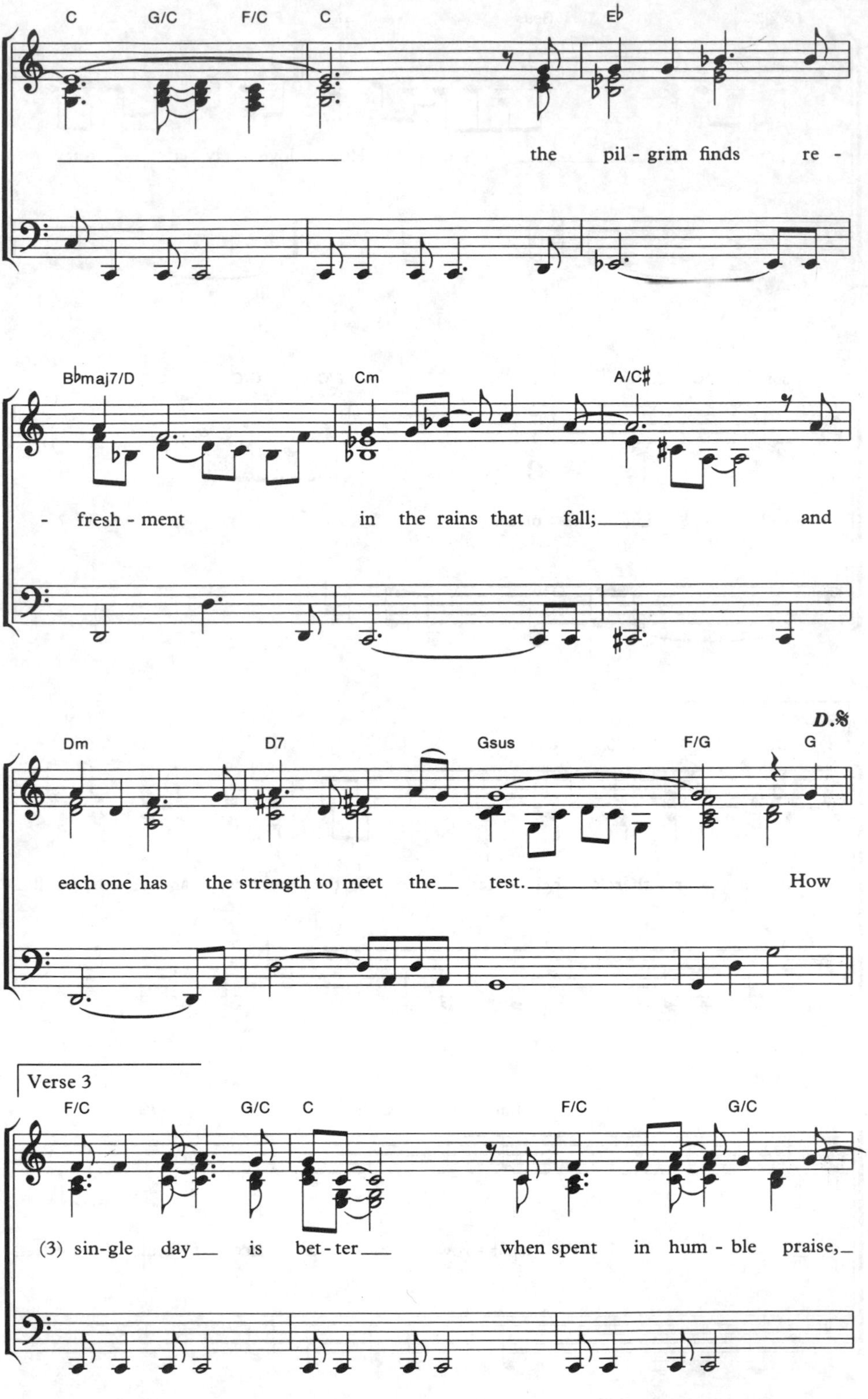
C G/C F/C C Eb
the pil - grim finds re -
Bbmaj7/D Cm A/C#
- fresh - ment in the rains that fall; and
Dm D7 Gsus F/G G
D.S.
each one has the strength to meet the test. How
Verse 3
F/C G/C C F/C G/C
(3) sin-gle day is bet - ter when spent in hum - ble praise,

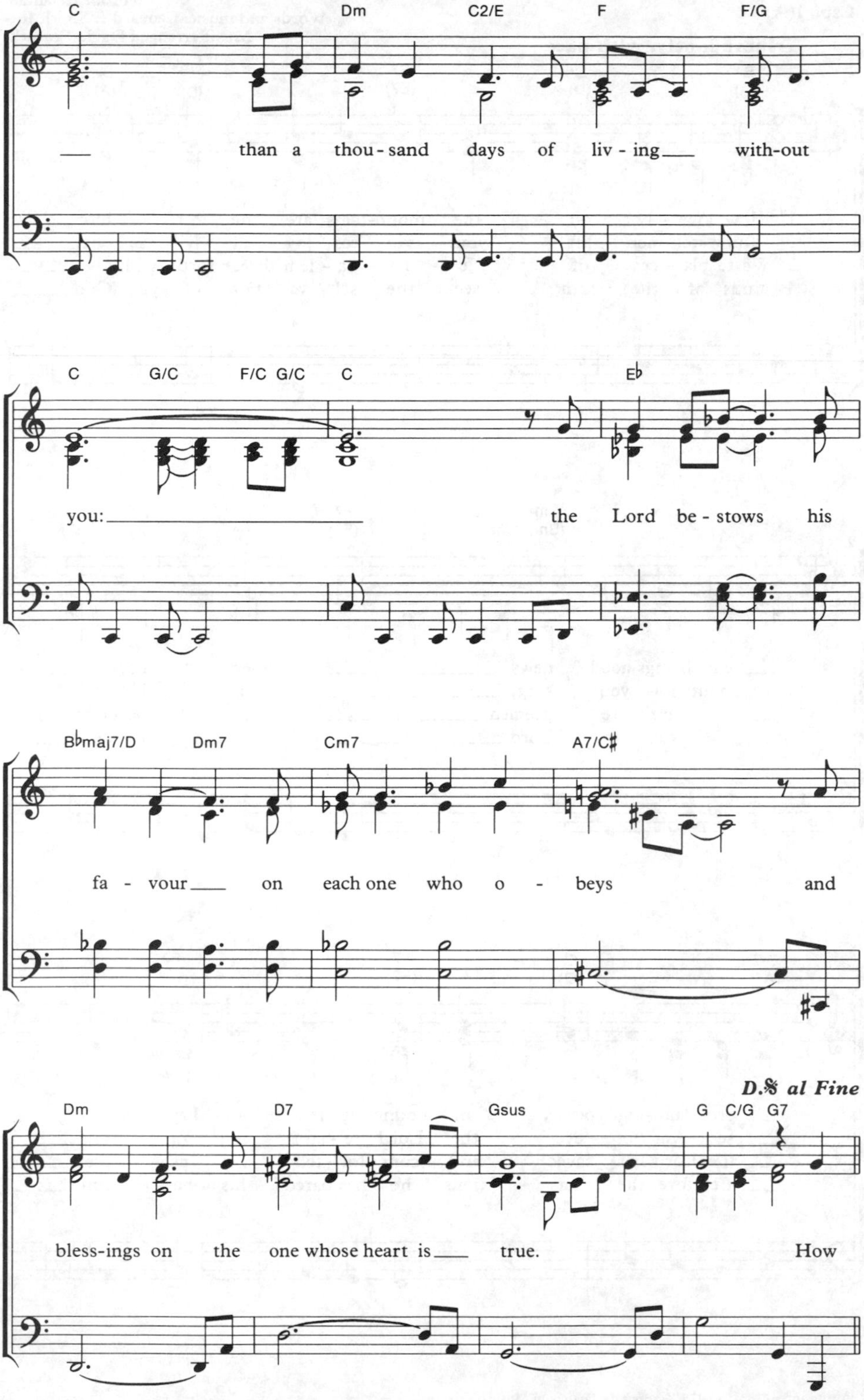
C Dm C2/E F F/G
than a thou-sand days of liv-ing with-out
C G/C F/C G/C C E♭
you: the Lord be-stows his
B♭maj7/D Dm7 Cm7 A7/C♯
fa - vour on each one who o - beys and
D.𝄋 al Fine
Dm D7 Gsus G C/G G7
bless-ings on the one whose heart is true. How

71 How lovely on the mountains

From Isaiah 52
Words and music: Leonard E Smith Jnr
Music arranged David Peacock

Capo 1(A)

Triumphantly, with pace

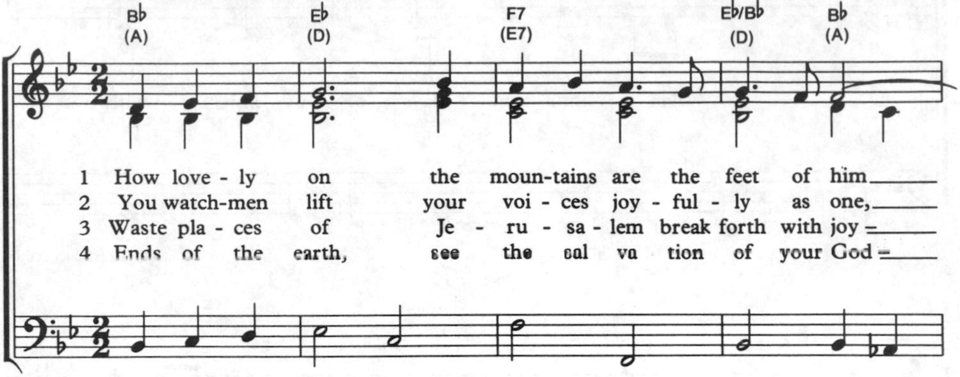

Bb (A) Eb (D) F7 (E7) Eb/Bb (D) Bb (A)
1 How love - ly on the moun-tains are the feet of him
2 You watch-men lift your voi - ces joy - ful - ly as one,
3 Waste pla - ces of Je - ru - sa - lem break forth with joy –
4 Ends of the earth, see the sal va tion of your God –

G (F♯) Cm (Bm) F7 (E7) Bb (A) F7 (E7)
who brings good news, good news,
shout for your king, your king;
we are re - deemed, re - deemed;
Je - sus is Lord, is Lord!

Bb7 (A7) Eb (D) F7 (E7) Eb/Bb (D) Bb (A)
pro-claim-ing peace, an - nounc-ing news of hap - pi-ness:
see eye to eye the Lord re - stor - ing Zi - on:
the Lord has saved and com - for - ted his peo - ple:
Be - fore the na - tions he has bared his ho - ly arm:

Words and music: © 1978 Kingsway's Thankyou Music,
PO Box 75, Eastbourne, East Sussex BN23 6NW

G (F♯) Cm (Bm) F7 (E7) B♭ (A) E♭/B♭ (D)
our God reigns, our God reigns!
(vv.2.3.4.)
your God reigns, your God reigns!
B♭7 (A7) E♭ (D) Cm (Bm) F7 (E7) B♭ (A)
Our God reigns, our God reigns,
Your God reigns, your God reigns,
Gm (F♯m) B♭7 (A7) E♭ (D) Cm7 (Bm7) F7 (E7) B♭ (A) E♭/B♭ (D) B♭ (A)
our God reigns, our God reigns!
your God reigns, your God reigns!

72 Hosanna, hosanna, hosanna

Words and music: Carl Tuttle
Psalm 118.26, Matthew 21.9, Mark 11.9,
Luke 19.38, John 12.13

Lively
G D Em C D
1 Ho - san - na, ho - san - na, ho - san-na in the high - est. Ho -
2 Glo - ry, glo - ry, glo-ry to the King of kings;
G D Em C D
- san - na, ho - san - na, ho - san-na in the high - est.
glo - ry, glo - ry, glo-ry to the King of kings:
C D G C D G
Lord, we lift up your name, with hearts full of praise.
C D G D/F♯ Em C D G
Be ex-alt-ed, O ___ Lord my God – ho - san-na in the high - est.
glo-ry to the King of kings.

Words and music: © 1985 Mercy Publishing/Kingsway's Thankyou Music,
PO Box 75, Eastbourne, East Sussex BN23 6NW

73 I see perfection

Children of the King

Words and music: Chris Eaton
Music arranged Christopher Hayward

Flowing
Em D/E Em D
1 I see per - fec - tion as I
2 Your Ho - ly Spi - rit will for
C G/B C Dsus D Em D/E
look in your eyes, Lord; there's no re -
ev - er con - trol me! I give my
Em D C G/B C Dsus D
- jec - tion as I look in your eyes, Lord.
pre - sent, fu - ture, past, to you com - plete - ly.
Animated
Em G
You are a ri - ver that is ne - ver dry,

Words and music: © 1983 Clouseau Music, SGO Music Management,
101 Wardour Street, London WC2H OEA

Em
Am7
D
C/D
D
you are — the star that lights the eve - ning sky, —
Em
G
you are — my God and I — will fol - low you,
Em
Am7
D
C/D
D
and now — I know just where I'm go - ing — to. —
Triumphantly
Chorus
G
D/G
C/G
G
We are child - ren, child-ren of — the King

G D/F♯ Am7 G/C D C/D D C B7
we will praise your name, glo-ri-fy you, mag-ni-fy __ you
Em Cm6 G/D C/D G/D
Je - sus, we __ can ne-ver de - ny __ your love for us __
C/D G/D C/D Am/D G D/G C/G G/D
on the cross now you've made us child-ren of the King.
1.
C Am7 Dsus D
2.
C/D Am/D G D/G G
now you've made us child-ren of the King.

74 I am a new creation

Capo 3(C)

Words and music: Dave Bilbrough

2 Corinthians 5.17

With drive
E♭ (C) B♭ (G) E♭ (C)
I am a new cre-a - tion, no more in con -
A♭ (F) E♭ (C) A♭ (F) B♭ (G)
- dem - na - tion, here in the grace of God I stand;
E♭ (C) A♭ (F) B♭ (G) E♭ (C) B♭ (G)
my heart is ov - er-flow - ing,
E♭ (C) A♭ (F) E♭ (C)
my love just keeps on grow-ing, here in the grace
A♭ (F) B♭ (G) E♭ (C) A♭ (F) E♭ (C)
of God I stand: and I will praise

Words and music: © 1983 Kingsway's Thankyou Music,
PO Box 75, Eastbourne, East Sussex BN23 6NW

Ab (F) Bb (G) Eb (C) Ab (F) Bb (G)
you, Lord, yes I will praise you, Lord,
Eb (C) Cm (Am) Ab (F) Bb (G)
and I will sing of all that you have done.
Eb (C) Bb (G) Eb (C)
A joy that knows no lim - it, A light-ness in
Ab (F) Eb (C) Ab (F) Bb (G)
my spi - rit - here in the grace of God I stand.
to repeat
last time only
Eb (C) Ab (F) Bb (G) Eb (C) Ab (F) Eb (C)

75 I call to you

My soul waits

From Psalm 130
Bill Batstone

With assurance ♩ = 80

B2/D♯ B/E B2/D♯ B/E A/C♯ E/B
Bm F♯m/B Em7 F♯m7 B2/D♯
1 I call to you __ from out of the deep, O Lord, ____ most
B/E Bm A/B Em7 F♯m7
high; a - ware of my sin and the __ dis - tance I keep from the
Chorus
Gmaj7 E/F♯ F♯/A♯ B F♯/B
Light, O __ Lord. But __ there is __ for-give-ness with

Words and music: © 1986 Maranatha! Music/CopyCare Ltd,
PO Box 77, Hailsham, East Sussex BN27 3EF

E2/B E/B F♯/B B F♯/B E2/B E/G♯ F♯/A♯
you! In___ won-der__ I fall on__my knees; my soul
B F♯/B C♯m G♯m7
waits for the Lord in the hope of his pro-mise – in the
E B/D♯ B C♯m E/G♯ F♯/A♯
hope of his pro - mise de - liv - erance will come. My soul
B F♯/B C♯m G♯m
waits for the Lord through the night to the morn-ing, like a

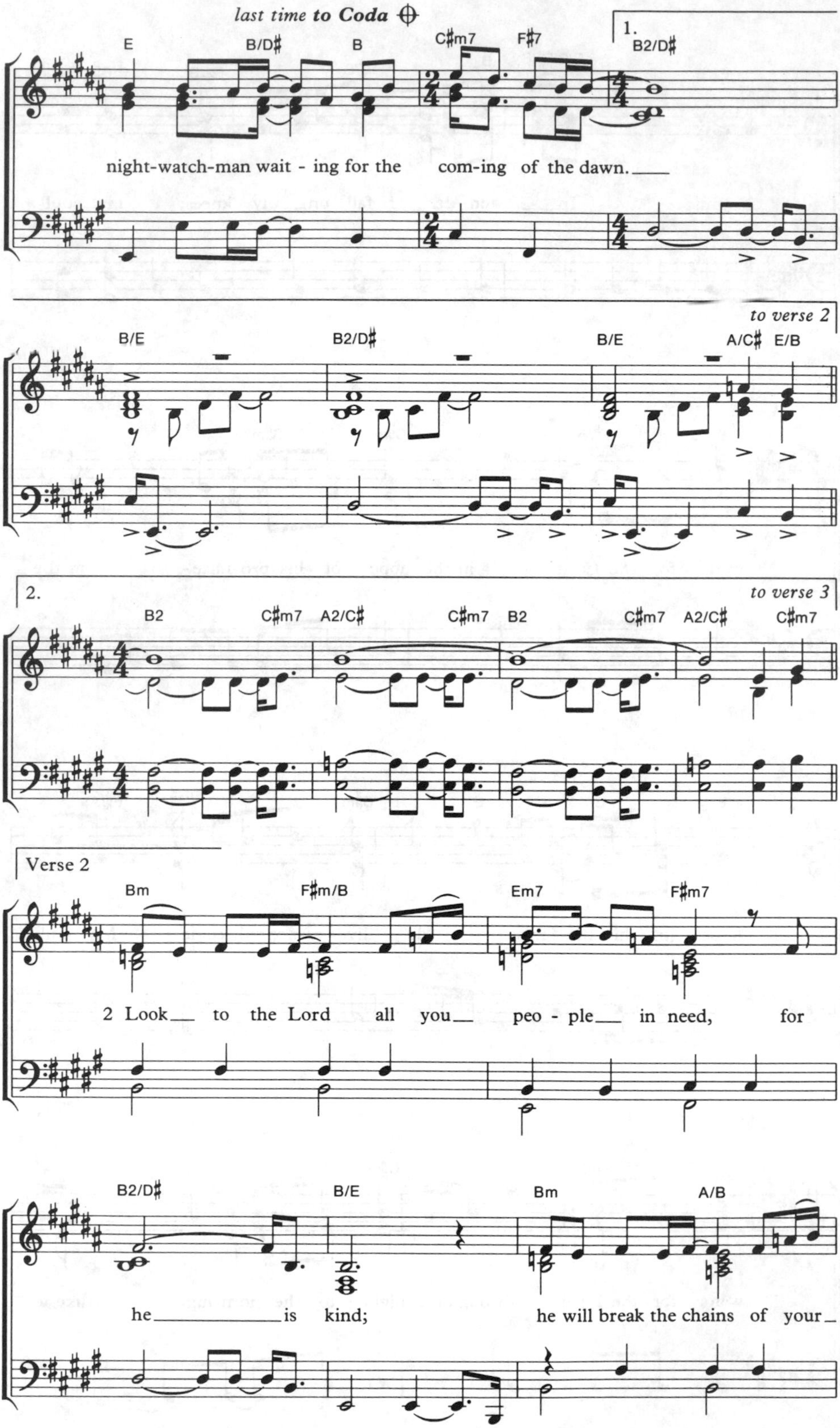
last time to Coda
1.
E B/D♯ B C♯m7 F♯7 B2/D♯
night-watch-man wait - ing for the com-ing of the dawn.
to verse 2
B/E B2/D♯ B/E A/C♯ E/B
2.
to verse 3
B2 C♯m7 A2/C♯ C♯m7 B2 C♯m7 A2/C♯ C♯m7
Verse 2
Bm F♯m/B Em7 F♯m7
2 Look to the Lord all you peo - ple in need, for
B2/D♯ B/E Bm A/B
he is kind; he will break the chains of your

Chorus D.𝄋
Em7 F♯m Gmaj7 E/F♯ F♯/A♯
soul's sla-ve-ry — for all time, O — Lord. But —
Verse 3
F♯m B F♯m B
3 Tell me who could stand in the Lord's right-eous reck-on-ing —
F♯m B F♯m B
if our lives faced his light?
G♯m C♯ G♯m C♯
Then, if all our deeds were re-vealed at God's beck-on-ing, —
D.𝄋 al Coda
G♯m F♯2 E2
who could hold their head high? But
CODA
C♯m7 F♯7 B
com-ing of the dawn. —

76 I have decided

Capo 3(D)

Words and music: Michael Card

With conviction

F (D) F (D) F/A Bb (G) F (D)
mf
I have de - cid-ed I'm go-ing to live like a be-liev-er, turn my back
mp mf
Bb (G) F (D) Bb/C (G) F (D) Bbmaj7 (Gmaj7)
on the de-ceiv - er, go-ing to live what I be-lieve: I have de -
F (D) F/A Bb (G) F (D)
cid - ed be - ing good is just a fa - ble – I just can't
1.2. to verses 3. Fine
Bb (G) F (D) Bb/C (G) F (D) Bb/C (G) F (D)
'cause I'm not a - ble, go-ing to leave it to the Lord. leave it to the Lord.

Words and music: © Whole Armor Publishing Co for the World excluding North, Central and South America.
Whole Armor Publishing c/o TKO Publishing Ltd, PO Box 130, Hove, East Sussex BN3 6QU

F (D) C (A) Bb (G) F (D)
mp
1 There's a wealth of things that I pro-fessed, I said that I be-lieved, but
2 So, for-get the game of be-ing good and all self-right-eous things, 'cause the
mp
Bb (G) F (D) C (A) C7 (A7)
deep in-side I ne-ver changed, I guess I'd been de-ceived, a
on-ly good in-side your heart is the good that Je-sus brings; when the
F (D) C (A) Bb (G) F (D)
voice in-side kept tell-ing me that I'd change by and by, but the
world be-gins to see you change, don't ex-pect them to ap-plaud, keep your
Bb (G) F (D) Bb/C (G) F (D) Bb/C (G)
D.S.
Spi-rit made it clear to me that kind of life's a lie.
eyes on him and tell your-self I've be-gun the work of God. I have de-
mf

77 I love you, I love you, Jesus

Words and music: Gary Houston
Music arranged David Peacock

Driving rock
G
I love, I love you, Je - sus,
I love, I love you, Je - sus;
Em
you are the
light with - in me:
C
I love you,
D
I love you, Je - sus!
last time to Coda
C
D
Cmaj7
I will sing a new song to you,

Words and music: © copyright controlled

G
C/G
G
Cmaj7
Lord, I will lift my hands
to you; I'll sing and tell the world that
Am9
D
Cmaj7
G
you're my king and you're the one who saved me:
C/G
Cmaj7
you're my strength and my rock O
Am9
D
D.C.
CODA
G
Lord, you're beau - ti - ful!

78 I love you, O Lord, you alone

Jane 8888D

Words: from Psalm 18
Christopher Idle
Music: David Peacock

With assurance

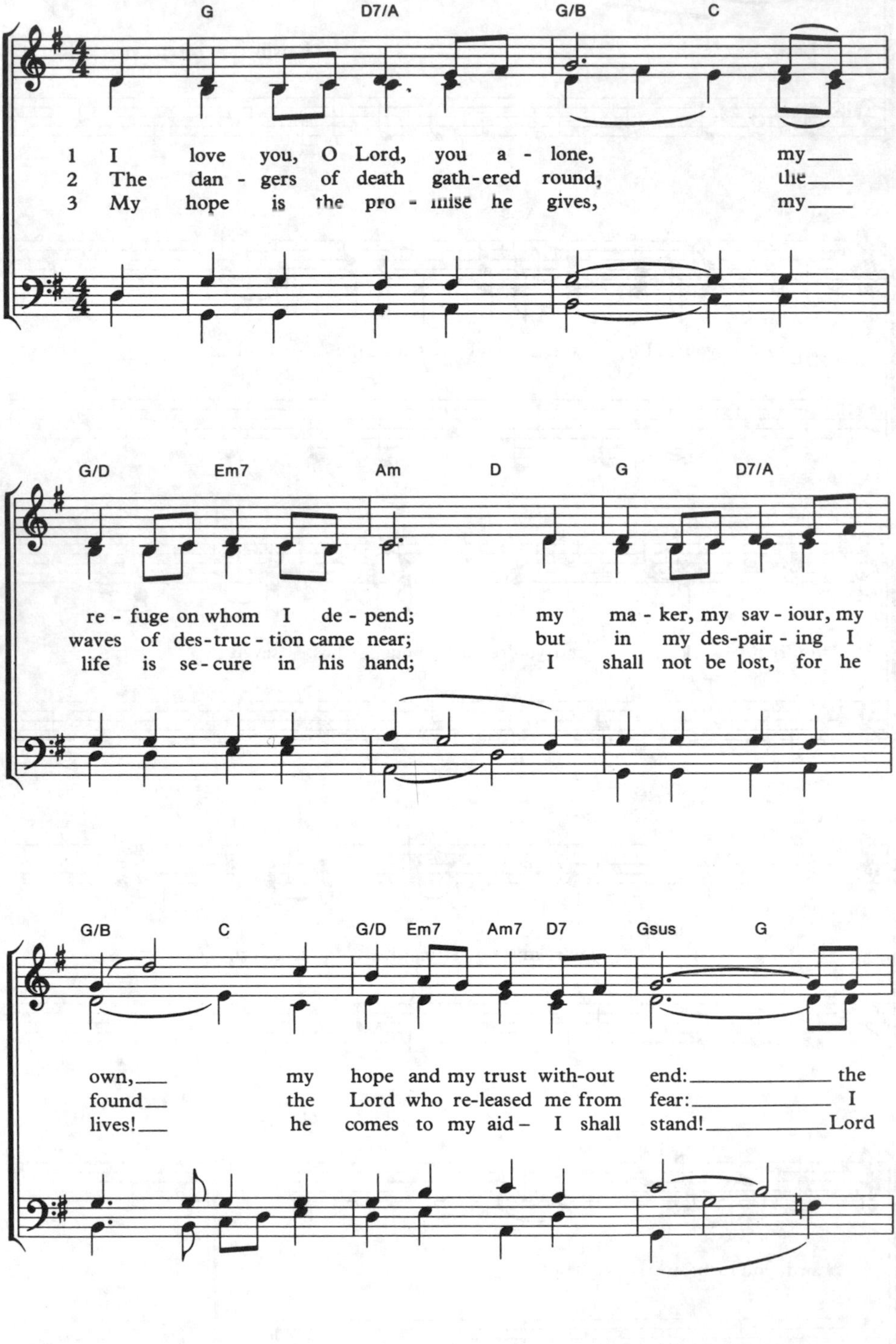
G D7/A G/B C
1 I love you, O Lord, you a - lone, my
2 The dan - gers of death gath - ered round, the
3 My hope is the pro - mise he gives, my
G/D Em7 Am D G D7/A
re - fuge on whom I de - pend; my ma - ker, my sav - iour, my
waves of des - truc - tion came near; but in my des - pair - ing I
life is se - cure in his hand; I shall not be lost, for he
G/B C G/D Em7 Am7 D7 Gsus G
own, my hope and my trust with-out end: the
found the Lord who re-leased me from fear: I
lives! he comes to my aid – I shall stand! Lord

Music: © David Peacock / Jubilate Hymns †

Words: © Christopher Idle / Jubilate Hymns †

E♭ A♭ Gm7 C7
Lord is my strength and my song, de -
called for his help in my pain, to
God, you are power - ful to save, your
Fm Cm Dsus D G D7/A
- fen - der and guide of my ways; my mas - ter to whom I be -
God my sal - va - tion I cried; he brought me his com - fort a -
Spi - rit will spur me to pray; your Son has de - feat - ed the
G/B C G/D Em7 Am7 D7 Gsus G
- long, my God who shall have all my praise.
- gain, I live by the strength he sup - plied.
grave: I trust and I praise you to - day!

79 I rest in God alone

From Psalm 62
Words and music: John Daniels
Music arranged Christopher Norton

Capo 3(D)

Steadily

F (D) C/B♭ (A) Cm/E♭ (A♭) D7 (B7)
Gm (Em) C (A) F (D) B♭/F (G)
F (D) Am (F♯m) Dm (Bm) Am (F♯m) B♭ (G)
I rest in God a - lone, from him comes
Gm7 (Em7) F/C (D) B♭/C (G) C7 (A7) F (D)
my sal - va - tion; my soul finds
Am (F♯m) Dm (Bm) Am (F♯m) B♭ (G)
rest in him, my for - tress –

Words and music: © 1985 HarperCollins*Religious*/CopyCare Ltd,
PO Box 77, Hailsham, East Sussex BN27 3EF

Gm7 (Em7) F/C (D) C (A) B♭/C (G) C (A) F/A (D)
I'll not be sha - ken.
1 My hope is in
2 O trust in him,
B♭ (G) C (A) A/C♯ (F♯) Dm (Bm)
the Lord my hon-our and strength; my re-fuge is in
you peo - ple, pour out your hearts, for God is our re -
G (E) B♭/C (G) C7 (A7) B♭/C (G) C (A) F/A (D)
him for ev - er,
- fuge for ev - er,
my trust and
C/B♭ (A) Cm/E♭ (Am) D7 (B7) Gm7 (Em7)
all of my heart in him a - lone
after verse 2 D.𝄋
1.
to end
B♭/C (G) F (D) B♭/F (G) F (D) B♭/F (G) F (D)
my soul finds rest.

80 I tell you . . .
(Jesus is all that you need)

Leben

Original words and music: Christoph Haus, Burkhard Bahr and Joachim Gnep
Words: Michael Perry
Luke 15.13, John 14.6, Acts 4.12, Philippians 1.21 and 3.7
Music arranged David Peacock

Medium paced with a swing

A E B E
I tell you . . . Je - sus is all that you need,
A E D B A E
Je - sus – hear what I say! Je - sus – I tell you,
B C#m A A7/B 1. E
he is the Life: he is the Truth and the Way. I tell you . . .
2. E Fine G# C#m
1 Once I was dis - sat - is - fied and
2 Once I walked the road a - lone, and

Original words and music: © 1987 Oncken Verlag, Wuppertal
Music arrangement: © David Peacock / Jubilate Hymns †
English words: © Michael Perry / Jubilate Hymns †

A B E F♯m7 G♯7
tired of stand-ing still; tast-ing plea-sure
tried hard to be brave— for, you see, I'd
C♯m A F♯m7 B7
far and wide, I'd just had my fill.
ne-ver known that Je-sus can save.
G♯ C♯m A B
Then I met the One who died— now ri-sen from the dead—
Now with him up-on the throne I all my days will spend—
E F♯m7 G♯m7 C♯m A
Je-sus Christ, the Cru-ci-fied: he
glad-ly tell-ing ev-ery-one that
D.𝄋
F E G B7
gave me life in-stead!
Je-sus is their Friend! I tell you . . .

81 I look up to the mountains

From Psalm 121
Words and music: Bill Batstone

Capo 2(D)
Relaxed with a soul feel
E (D) A2 (G2) E (D)
1 I look up to the mountains, to the hills I turn my eyes:
(2) One who watch-es Is-ra-el will his vi-gil keep,
B (A)
who will come to help me, can I find a place to hide? The
through the burn-ing sun-light and in the dark-ness deep;
E (D) E/G♯ (D) A2 (G2) F♯m (Em)
One who made the hea-vens and the earth will hear my call, the
con-stant-ly beside you – you need not fear at all, the
E/B (D) B2 (A2) A2 (G2) E (D)
Lord will come to help me and he will not let me fall.
Lord is there to help you, and he will not let you fall. He

Words and music: © 1984 Maranatha! Music/CopyCare Ltd,
PO Box 77, Hailsham, East Sussex BN27 3EF

E (D)
A (G)
E (D)
will not let_you fall,___ he will not let_you fall;_
B (A)
A (G)
E (D)
D.𝄋
he is ne-ver wea-ry, and he will not let_you fall._ He
2 The
3 So
E (D)
A2 (G2)
E (D)
when you are_in dan-ger, when by trou-ble you are found, and your
B (A)
ve-ry soul is threat-ened by_ the___e-vil__all a-round;

E (D)
E/G♯ (D)
A2 (G2)
F♯m (Em)
in all of your ways and in your trou-bles great and small,
E/B (D)
B2 (A2)
A2 (G2)
E (D)
now and ev-er af - ter he will not let you fall. He
E (D)
A (G)
E (D)
will not let you fall, he will not let you fall;
Fine
B (A)
A (G)
E (D)
he is ne-ver wea - ry, and he will not let you fall. He

82 I want to serve you, Lord

I want to give my all

Words and music: Chris Rolinson

Slowly and steadily with strength

D E F♯m F♯m/E A/C♯ E7sus E7
1 I want to serve you, Lord, in to - tal a - ban - don -
2 I want to give my all in to - tal a - ban - don -
3 I want to come to you in to - tal a - ban - don -
A D Amaj7/C♯ Bm7 B7 E
- ment, I want to yield my heart to you;
- ment, re - leas - ing all with - in my grasp;
- ment – Lord, will you set my heart a - blaze?
C♯sus C♯7 F♯m E A C♯sus/G♯ C♯7sus C♯7
I want to give my life in all sur - ren -
I want to live my life in all its ful -
I want to love you with all my soul and
D+9 D Bm7 E7sus E7 A D/A A
- der, I want to live for you a - lone.
- ness, I want to wor - ship Christ a - lone.
strength, I want to give you all my days.

Words and music: © 1988 Kingsway's Thankyou Music,
PO Box 75, Eastbourne, East Sussex BN23 6NW

83 I want to sing

Words and music: Tim Mayfield

Lively
D G D
I want to sing a praise song to you, I want to lift the name of
A D D7 G
Je - sus high - er; I want to sing, I want to move my feet
D A7 D D7 G
Lord, I'm going to wor - ship you! I want to praise,
A7 D D7
praise you Lord, I want to

Words and music: © 1987 Kingsway's Thankyou Music,
PO Box 75, Eastbourne, East Sussex BN23 6NW

G A7 D
praise, praise you Lord,
D7 G A
I want to praise you Lord:
F♯m Bm7 G
you're wor-thy to be praised – praise the Lord
to repeat
to end
A D A
with me!

84 I will build my church

Words and music: Graham Kendrick
Matthew 16.18, Philippians 2.10

Brightly ♩ = 130

MEN 'I will build my church, and the
WOMEN I will build my church,
gates of hell, shall not pre - vail, a -
and the gates of hell, shall not pre-vail, a -
1.
2.
ALL
MEN
ALL
- gainst it.' I will - gainst it.' So you
Chorus
powers in the hea - vens a - bove, bow down! And you

Words and music: © 1984 Make Way Music,
PO Box 263, Croydon, Surrey CR9 5AP.
International copyright secured. All rights reserved. Used by permission.

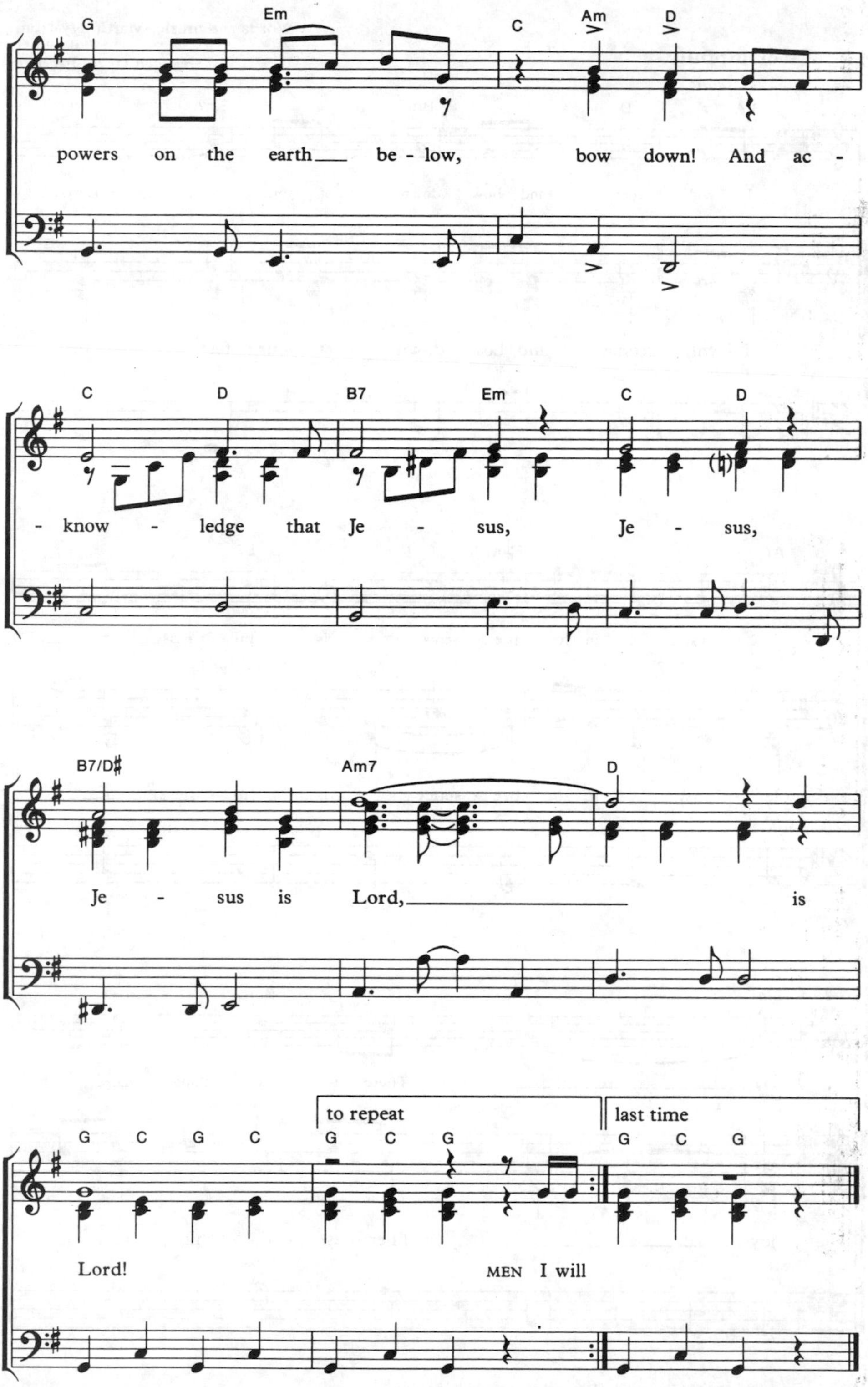
G Em C Am D
powers on the earth ___ be - low, bow down! And ac -
C D B7 Em C D
- know - ledge that Je - sus, Je - sus,
B7/D♯ Am7 D
Je - sus is Lord, ___ is
to repeat
last time
G C G C G C G G C G
Lord! MEN I will

85 I will come and bow down

Words and music: Martin Nystrom
Psalm 16.11
arranged David Peacock

Worshipfully

Descant
G/A
D
Bm
Em7
I will come and bow down at your feet, Lord
I will come and bow down at your feet, Lord
A7
F♯m
B7
Je - sus; in you pre - sence is ful - ness of
Je - sus; in you pre - sence is ful - ness of
Em
A7
Bm
joy. There is no - thing, there is
joy. There is no - thing, there is

Words and music: © 1984 Integrity's Hosanna! Music, administered in Europe (excl. German speaking countries), by Kingsway's Thankyou Music, PO Box 75, Eastbourne, East Sussex BN23 6NW

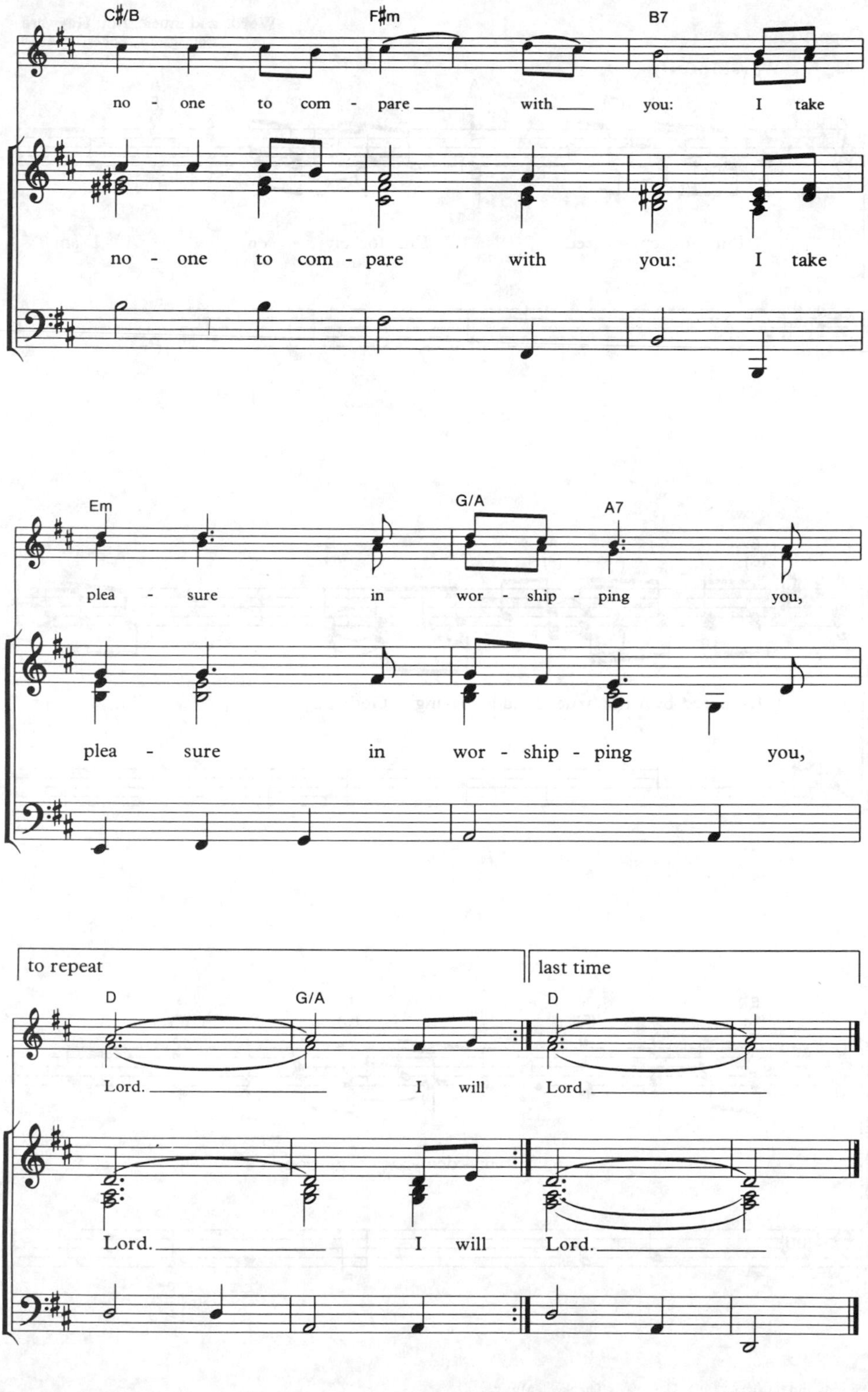

no - one to com - pare _____ with _____ you: I take

no - one to com - pare with you: I take

plea - sure in wor - ship - ping you,

plea - sure in wor - ship - ping you,

to repeat

last time

Lord. _____ I will Lord.

Lord. _____ I will Lord. _____

86 I'm accepted

Capo 4(C)

Words and music: Rob Hayward
Romans 8.1, Ephesians 4.1–8

Worshipfully

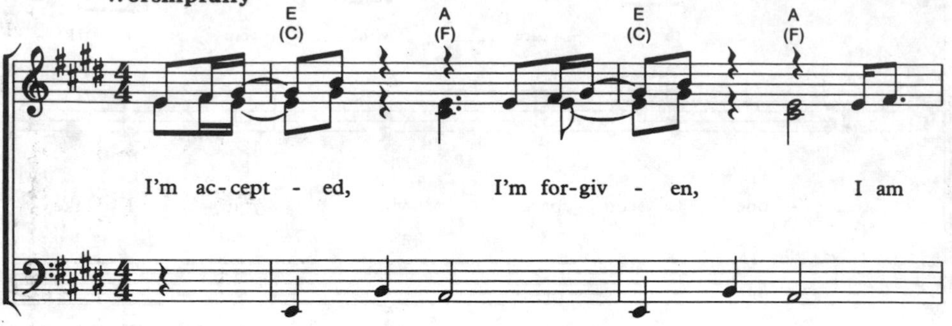
E (C)
A (F)
E (C)
A (F)
I'm ac-cept - ed, I'm for-giv - en, I am

E (C)
A (F)
B (G)
fa-thered by the true_ and liv-ing God:_ I'm ac-cept -

E (C)
A (F)
E (C)
A (F)
- ed – no con-dem-na - tion, I am

Words and music: © 1985 Kingsway's Thankyou Music,
P.O Box 75, Eastbourne, East Sussex BN23 6NW

E (C) A (F) B (G) E (C) E7 (C7)
loved by the true and liv-ing God. There's no
A (F) B (G) G♯m (Em) C♯m (Am)
guilt or fear as I draw near to the
A (F) B (G) E (C) A (F) B (G)
sav-iour and cre-a-tor of the world; there is joy and peace as
G♯m (Em) C♯m (Am) A (F) B (G) E (C)
I re - lease my wor - ship to you, O Lord.

87 If my people

Capo 4(Am)

Words and music: Graham Kendrick
2 Chronicles 7.14

Gently

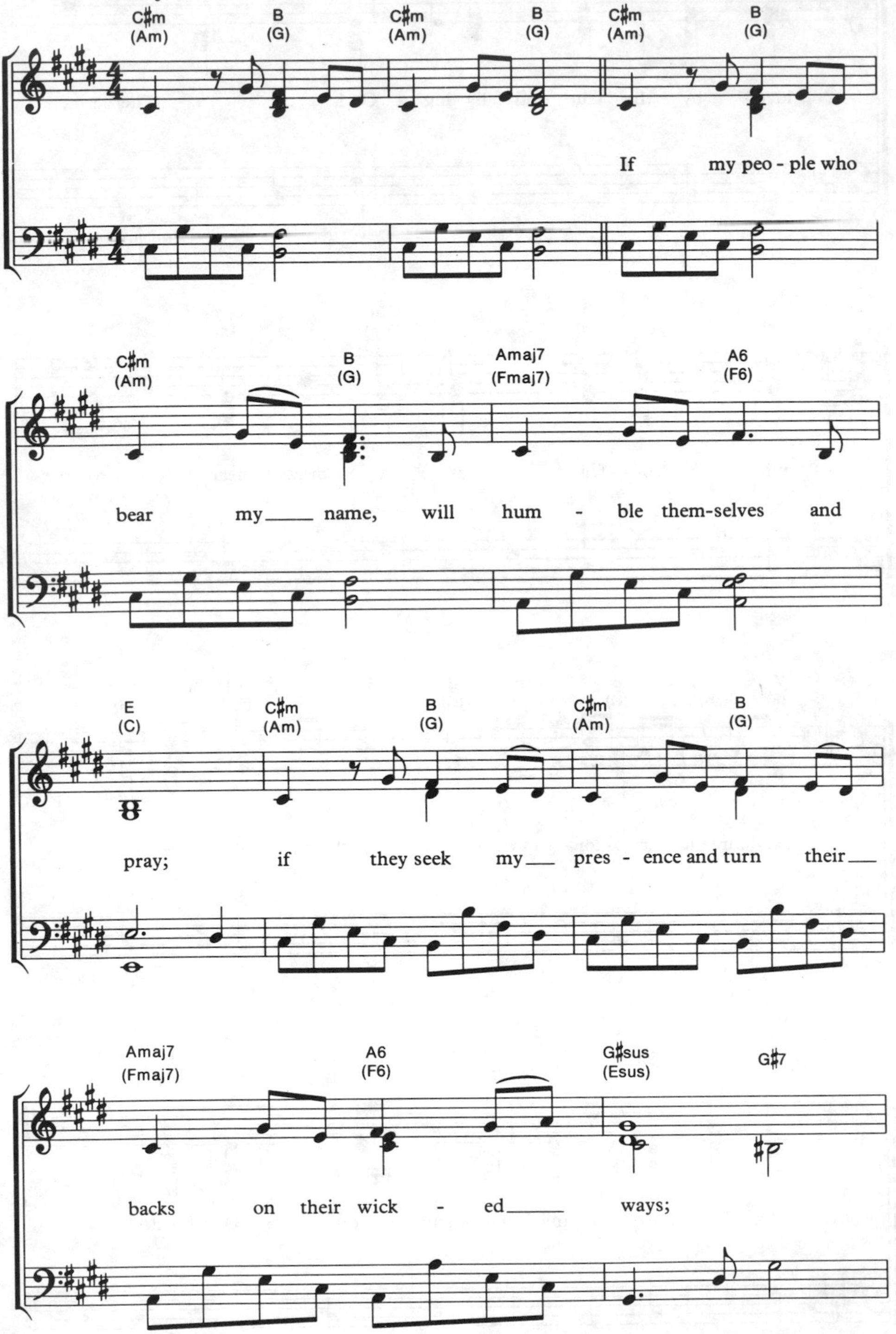
C♯m (Am) B (G) C♯m (Am) B (G) C♯m (Am) B (G)
If my peo - ple who
C♯m (Am) B (G) Amaj7 (Fmaj7) A6 (F6)
bear my name, will hum - ble them-selves and
E (C) C♯m (Am) B (G) C♯m (Am) B (G)
pray; if they seek my pres - ence and turn their
Amaj7 (Fmaj7) A6 (F6) G♯sus (Esus) G♯7
backs on their wick - ed ways;

Words and music: © 1987 Make Way Music,
PO Box 263, Croydon, Surrey CR9 5AP.
International copyright secured. All rights reserved. Used by permission.

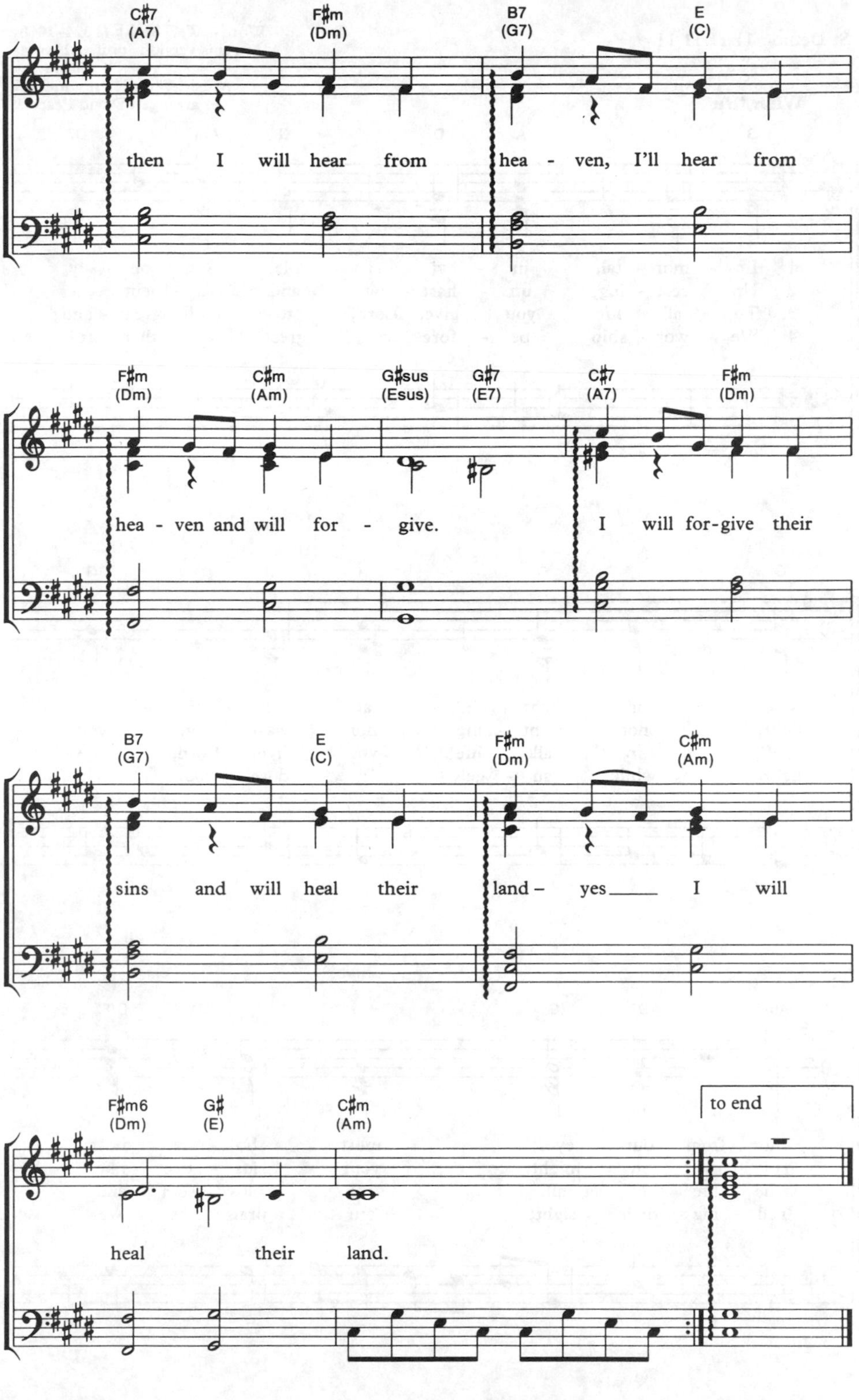
C♯7 (A7) F♯m (Dm) B7 (G7) E (C)
then I will hear from hea - ven, I'll hear from
F♯m (Dm) C♯m (Am) G♯sus (Esus) G♯7 (E7) C♯7 (A7) F♯m (Dm)
hea - ven and will for - give. I will for-give their
B7 (G7) E (C) F♯m (Dm) C♯m (Am)
sins and will heal their land – yes I will
F♯m6 (Dm) G♯ (E) C♯m (Am)
heal their land.
to end

88 Immortal, invisible

St Denio 11 11 11 11

Words: W C Smith (1824–1908)
in this version Jubilate Hymns
1 Timothy 1.7
Music: Welsh hymn melody
arranged David Peacock

With life

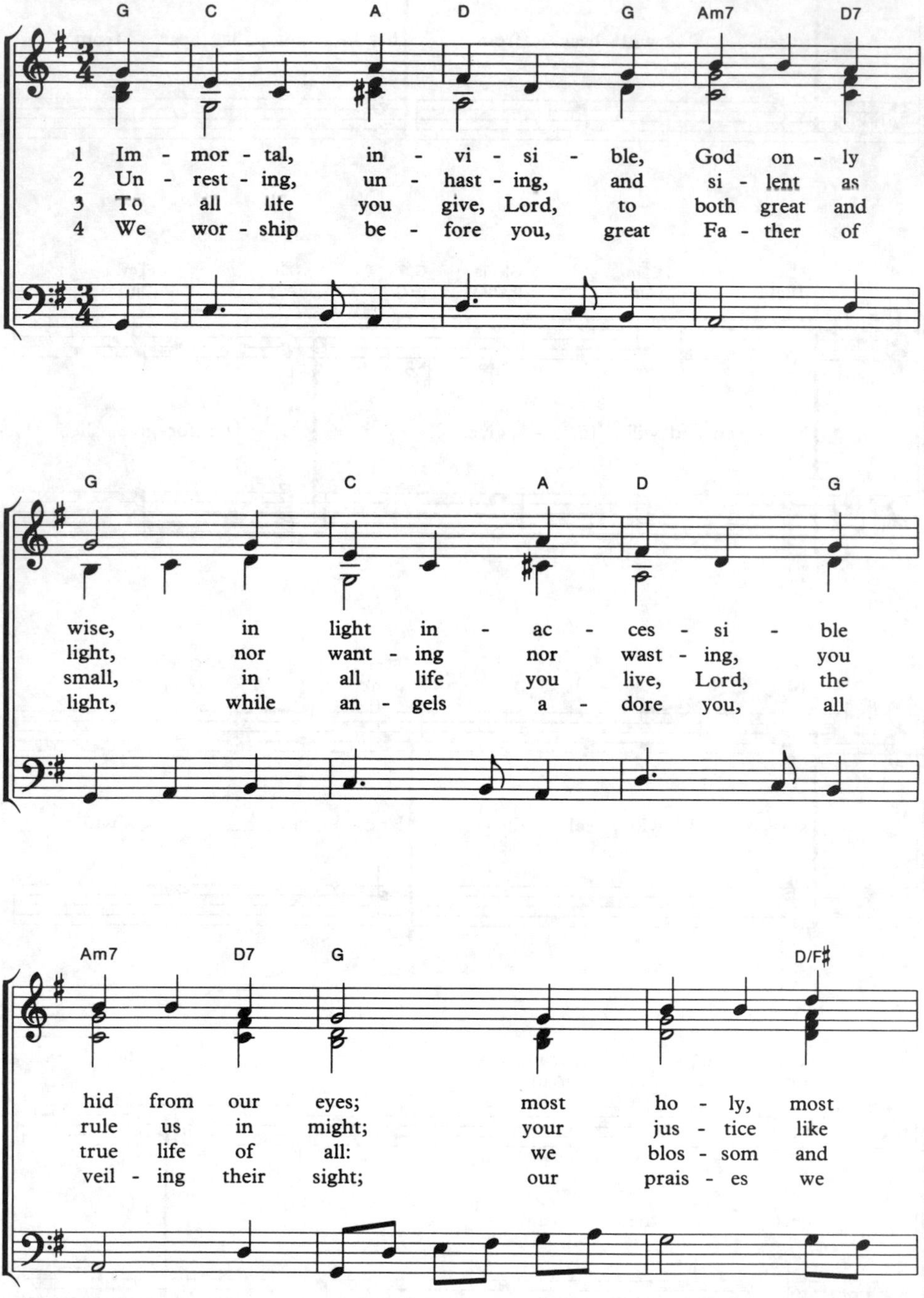
G C A D G Am7 D7
1 Im - mor - tal, in - vi - si - ble, God on - ly
2 Un - rest - ing, un - hast - ing, and si - lent as
3 To all life you give, Lord, to both great and
4 We wor - ship be - fore you, great Fa - ther of
G C A D G
wise, in light in - ac - ces - si - ble
light, nor want - ing nor wast - ing, you
small, in all life you live, Lord, the
light, while an - gels a - dore you, all
Am7 D7 G D/F♯
hid from our eyes; most ho - ly, most
rule us in might; your jus - tice like
true life of all: we blos - som and
veil - ing their sight; our prais - es we

Music arrangement: © David Peacock / Jubilate Hymns †

Words: © in this version Jubilate Hymns †

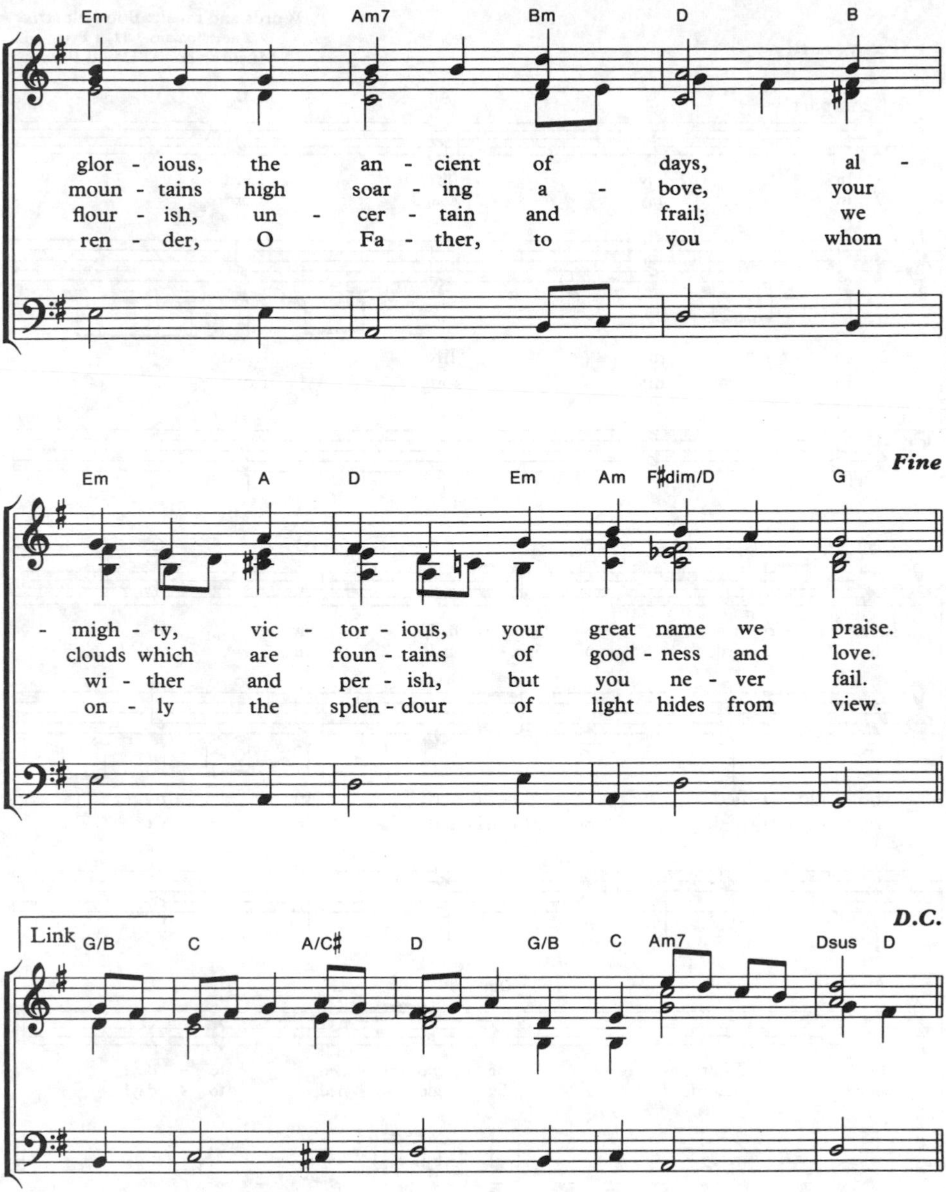
Em Am7 Bm D B
glor - ious, the an - cient of days, al -
moun - tains high soar - ing a - bove, your
flour - ish, un - cer - tain and frail; we
ren - der, O Fa - ther, to you whom
Fine
Em A D Em Am F♯dim/D G
- migh - ty, vic - tor - ious, your great name we praise.
clouds which are foun - tains of good - ness and love.
wi - ther and per - ish, but you ne - ver fail.
on - ly the splen - dour of light hides from view.
D.C.
Link G/B C A/C♯ D G/B C Am7 Dsus D

88A PRAISE SHOUT

LEADER O Lord, our Lord,
ALL **how glorious is your name**
in all the earth!

LEADER High above the heavens
ALL **your majesty is praised.**
Alleluia!

From Psalm 8

89 In my life, Lord

Words and music: Bob Kilpatrick
2 Thessalonians 1.11, 1 Peter 4.11
Music arranged David Peacock

Prayerfully

2nd part
C G Am C
1 In my life, Lord,
2 In my song, Lord,
Dm B♭ G7 C G
be glo - ri - fied, be glo - ri - fied; in my
Am C Dm G7 C
life, Lord, be glo - ri - fied to - day!
song, Lord, be glo - ri - fied to - day!

3 In your church, Lord,
be glorified, be glorified;
in your church, Lord,
be glorified today!

4 In my speech, Lord,
be glorified, be glorified;
in my speech, Lord,
be glorified today!

Words and music: © 1978 Bob Kilpatrick Music/CopyCare Ltd,
PO Box 77, Hailsham, East Sussex BN27 3EF

90 In heavenly armour

Words and music: Jamie Owens-Collins

The battle belongs to the Lord

1 Samuel 17.47, 2 Chronicles 20.15,
Isaiah 54.17, Ephesians 6.11

Music arranged Geoff Baker

With excitement

Em D/E Em D/E Em D/E
Em D/E Em D/E Em
1 In hea-ven-ly ar - mour we'll en - ter the land – the
2 When the pow-er of dark-ness comes in like a flood, the
3 When your en - e - my pres - ses in hard, do not fear – the
Em D/E Em Em
bat-tle be-longs to the Lord; no wea-pon that's fash - ioned a - gainst
bat-tle be-longs to the Lord; he's raised up a stan - dard, the power
bat-tle be-longs to the Lord; take cour-age, my friend, your re-demp -

Words and music: © 1984 Fairhill Music/Word Music (UK)/CopyCare Ltd,
PO Box 77, Hailsham, East Sussex BN27 3EF

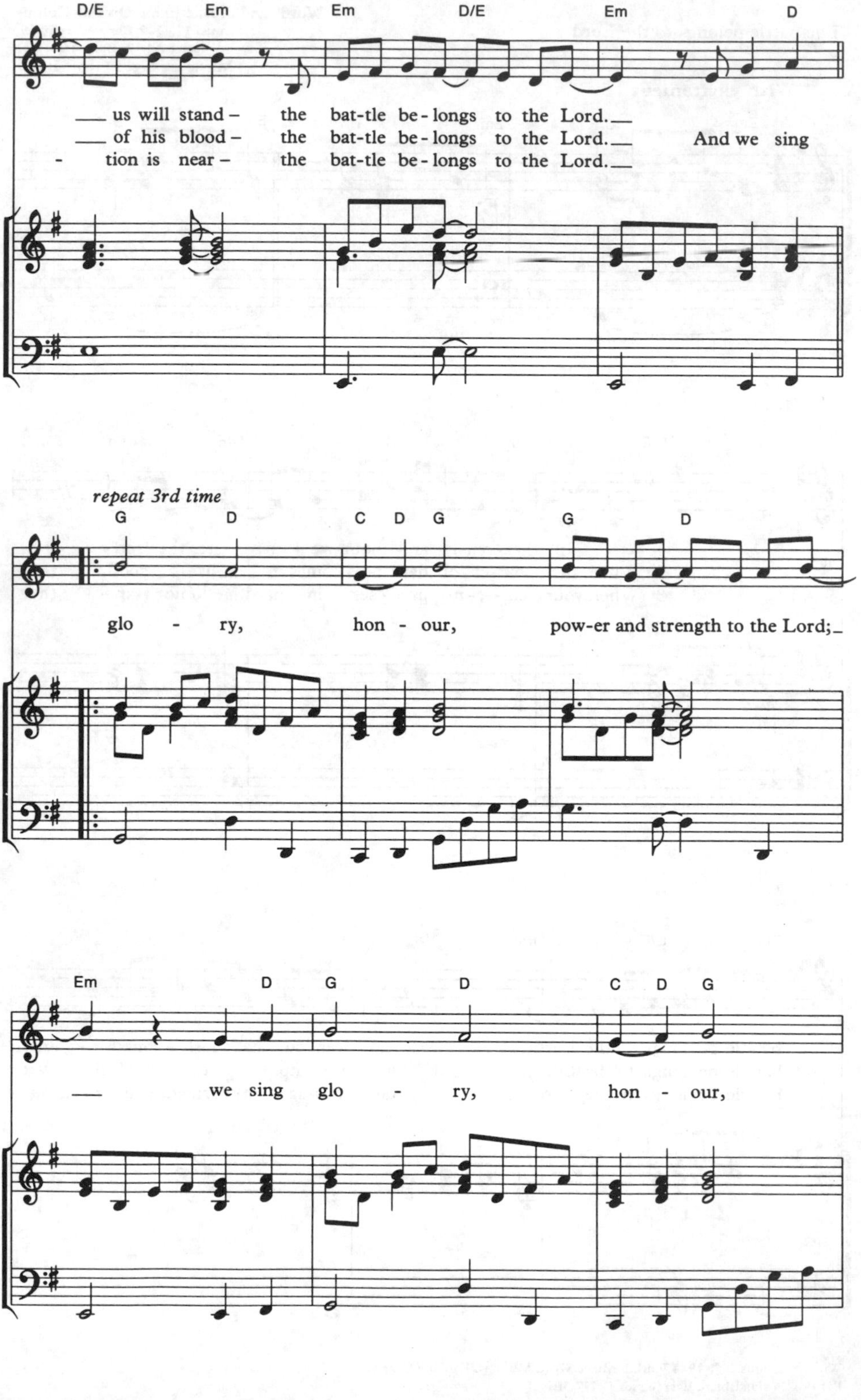
D/E Em Em D/E Em D
___ us will stand – the bat-tle be-longs to the Lord.__
___ of his blood – the bat-tle be-longs to the Lord.__ And we sing
- tion is near – the bat-tle be-longs to the Lord.__
repeat 3rd time
G D C D G G D
glo - ry, hon - our, pow-er and strength to the Lord;_
Em D G D C D G
__ we sing glo - ry, hon - our,

1.2.
D.𝄋
G D Em D/E Em D/E
pow-er and strength to the Lord!
3.
repeat chorus
4.
Em D Em D/E Em D/E
And we sing
Pow-er and strength to the
Em D/E Em D/E Em
Lord,
pow-er and strength to the Lord!
rall.

91 It was raining

(Light a candle)

Capo 2(G)

Words and music: Garth Hewitt
Matthew 27.45, Mark 15.33, Luke 23.44
Music arranged David Peacock

Flowing

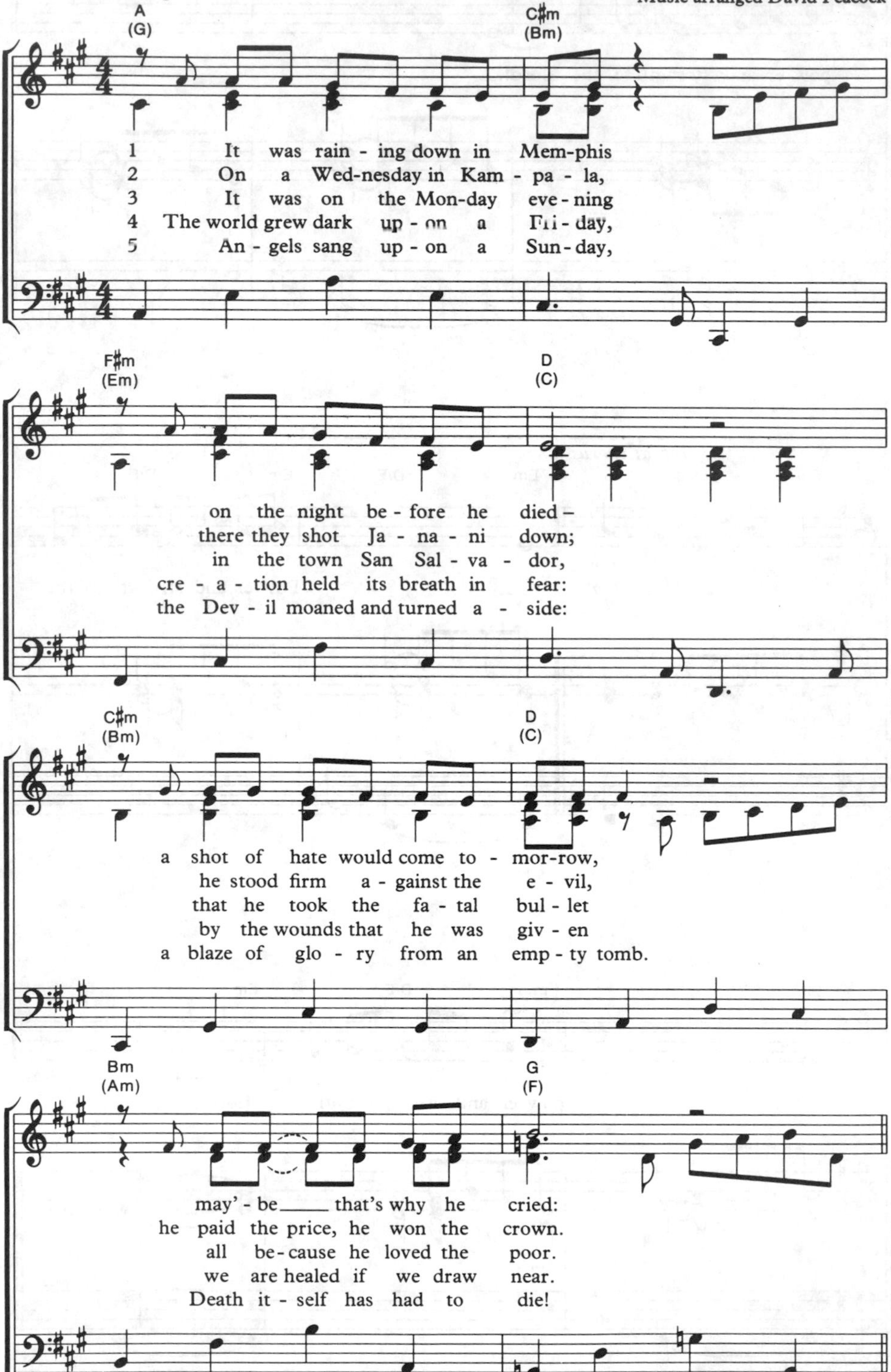
A (G)
C♯m (Bm)
1 It was rain - ing down in Mem-phis
2 On a Wed-nesday in Kam - pa - la,
3 It was on the Mon-day eve - ning
4 The world grew dark up - on a Fri - day,
5 An - gels sang up - on a Sun - day,
F♯m (Em)
D (C)
on the night be - fore he died –
there they shot Ja - na - ni down;
in the town San Sal - va - dor,
cre - a - tion held its breath in fear:
the Dev - il moaned and turned a - side:
C♯m (Bm)
D (C)
a shot of hate would come to - mor-row,
he stood firm a - gainst the e - vil,
that he took the fa - tal bul - let
by the wounds that he was giv - en
a blaze of glo - ry from an emp - ty tomb.
Bm (Am)
G (F)
may' - be ___ that's why he cried:
he paid the price, he won the crown.
all be-cause he loved the poor.
we are healed if we draw near.
Death it - self has had to die!

Words and music: © 1985 Word Music (UK)/CopyCare Ltd, PO Box 77, Hailsham, East Sussex BN27 3EF

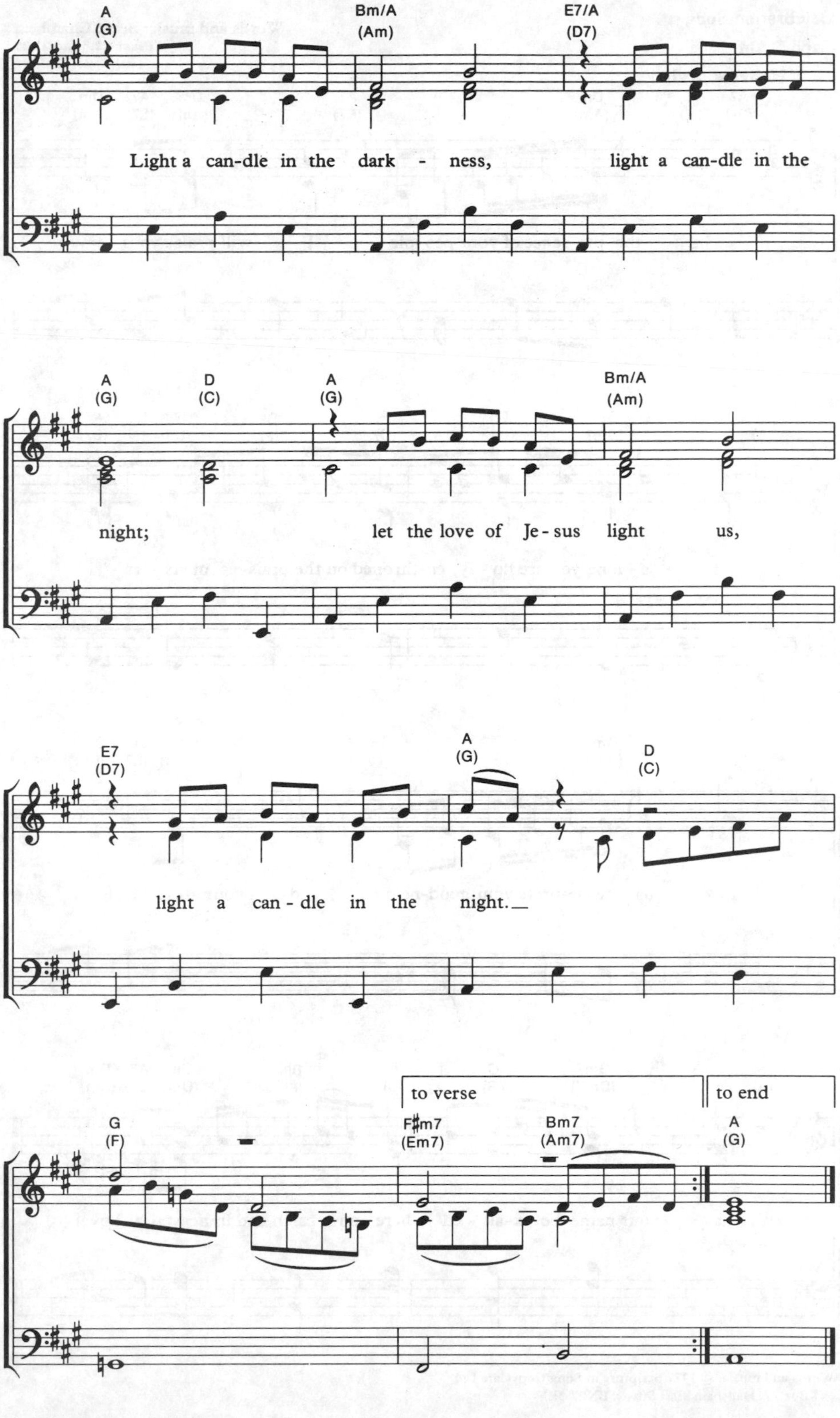
A
(G)
Bm/A
(Am)
E7/A
(D7)
Light a can-dle in the dark - ness, light a can-dle in the
A
(G)
D
(C)
A
(G)
Bm/A
(Am)
night; let the love of Je-sus light us,
E7
(D7)
A
(G)
D
(C)
light a can-dle in the night.
to verse
to end
G
(F)
F♯m7
(Em7)
Bm7
(Am7)
A
(G)

92 In the presence of your people

Celebration Song

Capo 5(Am)

Words and music: Brent Chambers

Psalm 22.3 and 22.25

Hebrew style

A7 (E7) Dm (Am) A7 (E7) Dm (Am) A7 (E7) Dm (Am)
In the pre-sence of your peo-ple I will praise your name,
D (A) Gm (Dm) C (G) F (C) B♭ (F) Gm (Dm) A7 (E7)
for a-lone you are ho-ly, en-throned on the prais-es of Is-ra-el.
Dm (Am) A7 (E7) Dm (Am) A7 (E7) Dm (Am)
Let us ce-le-brate your good-ness and your stead-fast love;
D (A) Gm7 (Dm7) C (G) F (C) B♭ (F) Gm (Dm) A7 (E7) Dm (Am)
may your name be ex-alt-ed here on earth and in heaven a-bove!

Words and music: © 1977 Scripture in Song/CopyCare Ltd,
PO Box 77, Hailsham, East Sussex BN27 3EF

93 Jesus is king

Capo 5(C)

Words and music: Wendy Churchill
Hebrews 4.14
Music arranged David Peacock

Joyfully
F (C) Am (Em) Dm (Am) B♭ (F) C (G) F (C)
1 Je - sus is king, and we will ex-tol him,
2 We have a hope that is stead - fast and cer - tain,
3 We come to him our Priest and A-pos - tle,
4 'O Ho-ly One, our hearts do a-dore you;
B♭ (F) C (G) F (C) Dm (Am) G (D) C (G)
give him the glo - ry, and hon - our his name;
gone through the cur - tain and touch - ing the throne;
clothed in his glo - ry and bear - ing his name,
thrilled with your good - ness we give you our praise!'
F (C) Am (Em) Dm (Am) B♭ (F) C (G) F (C)
he reigns on high, en-throned in the hea - vens
we have a Priest who is there in-ter-ced - ing,
lay - ing our lives with glad - ness be-fore him
An - gels in light with wor - ship sur-round him,
Gm (Dm) C (G) A (E) Dm (Am) Gm (Dm) C7 (G7) F (C)
Word of the Fa - ther, ex - alt - ed for us.
pour - ing his grace on our lives day by day.
filled with his Spi - rit we wor - ship the King:
Je - sus, our Sav - iour, for ev - er the same.

Words and music: © 1982 Springtide/Word Music (UK)/CopyCare Ltd,
PO Box 77, Hailsham, East Sussex BN27 3EF

94 Jehovah Jireh

Words and music: Ian Smale
Genesis 12.8, Exodus 17.15, Judges 6.24
Jeremiah 23.6, Ezekiel 48.35 etc.

Accelerating
Em
1 Je - ho - vah Ji - reh – God will pro-vide,
C
D
Je - ho - vah Ro - phe – God
B7
Em
heals; Je - ho-vah M'- ked - desh – God who
C
B
sanc - ti - fies, Je - ho - vah Nis - si – God is my

Words and music: © 1987 Kingsway's Thankyou Music,
PO Box 75, Eastbourne, East Sussex BN23 6NW

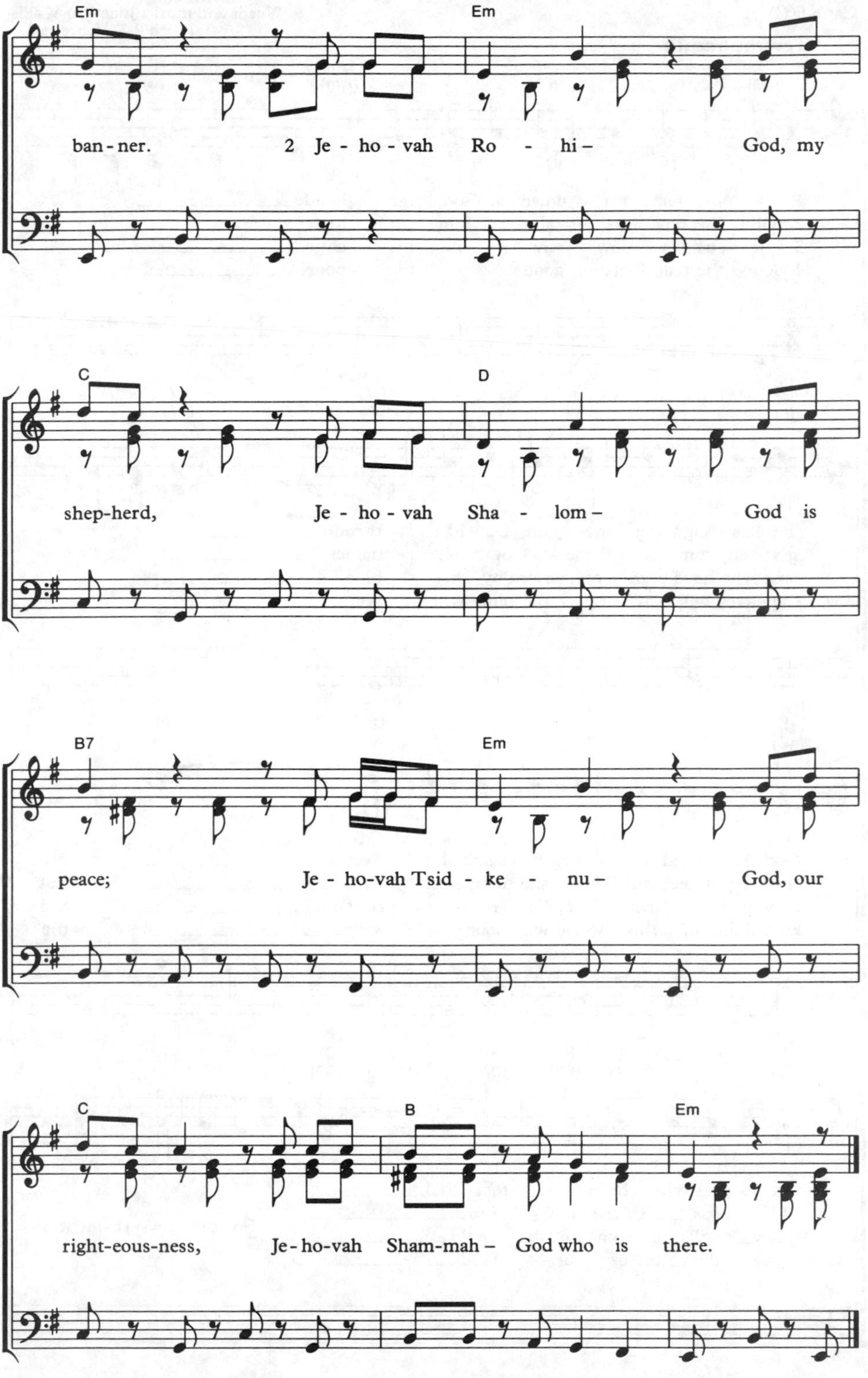
Em
Em
ban-ner.
2 Je-ho-vah Ro-hi–
God, my
C
D
shep-herd,
Je-ho-vah Sha-lom–
God is
B7
Em
peace;
Je-ho-vah Tsid-ke-nu–
God, our
C
B
Em
right-eous-ness,
Je-ho-vah Sham-mah–
God who is there.

95 Jesus has sat down

Capo 5(C)

Words and music: Jonathan Wallis
Isaiah 9.7, Hebrews 1.3

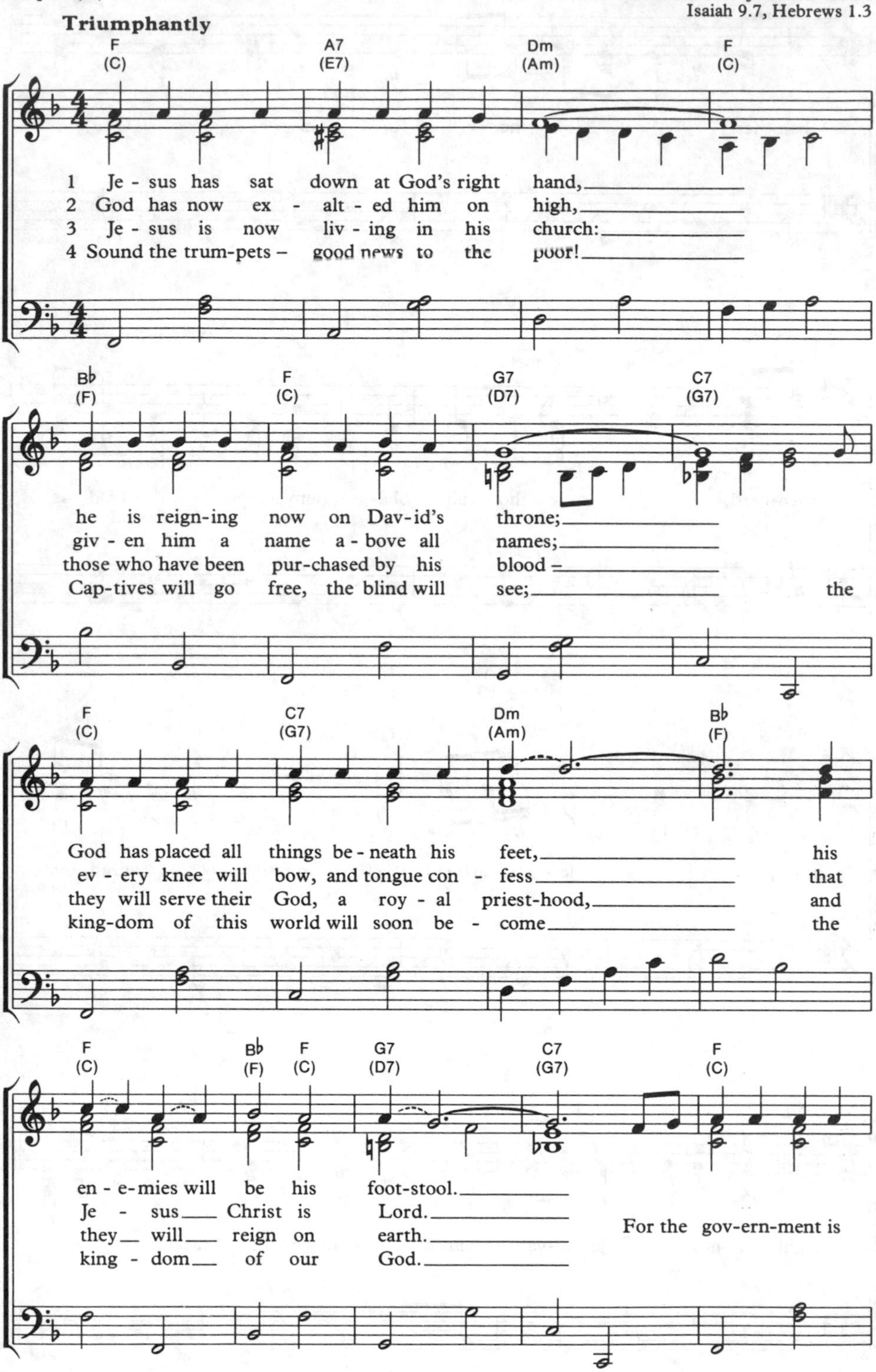
Triumphantly
F (C) A7 (E7) Dm (Am) F (C)
1 Je - sus has sat down at God's right hand,
2 God has now ex - alt - ed him on high,
3 Je - sus is now liv - ing in his church:
4 Sound the trum-pets – good news to the poor!
B♭ (F) F (C) G7 (D7) C7 (G7)
he is reign-ing now on Dav-id's throne;
giv - en him a name a - bove all names;
those who have been pur-chased by his blood –
Cap-tives will go free, the blind will see; the
F (C) C7 (G7) Dm (Am) B♭ (F)
God has placed all things be - neath his feet, his
ev - ery knee will bow, and tongue con - fess that
they will serve their God, a roy - al priest-hood, and
king-dom of this world will soon be - come the
F (C) B♭ (F) F (C) G7 (D7) C7 (G7) F (C)
en - e-mies will be his foot-stool.
Je - sus Christ is Lord.
they will reign on earth.
king - dom of our God.
For the gov-ern-ment is

Words and music: © 1983 Kingsway's Thankyou Music,
PO Box 75, Eastbourne, East Sussex BN23 6NW

C7 (G7) Dm (Am) Am (Em) F (C)
now up - on his shoul-der, for the gov - ern-ment is
C7 (G7) Dm (Am) Am (Em) F (C)
now up - on his shoul-der; and of the in-crease of his
A7 (E7) Dm (Am) B♭ (F) F (C)
gov - ern - ment and peace there will be no end, there will
Dm (Am) Am (Em) F/C (C) C7 (G7) F (C)
be no end, there will be no end.

96 Jesus, Jesus* fill us with your love

Chereponi

Words: Tom Colvin
Luke 10.29, John 13.5
Music: Ghana Folk Song
arranged Betty Pulkingham

With a gentle lilt

E
F♯m/E
Je - sus, Je - sus, fill us with your love; show
E
B7
E
Fine
us how to serve the neigh-bours we have from you.
E
F♯m7
B7
1 Kneels at the feet of his friends, si - lent - ly wash - es their
2 Neigh-bours are rich folk and poor; neigh-bours are black, brown and
3 These are the ones we should serve, these are the ones we should
4 Lov - ing puts us on our knees, serv - ing as though we were
G♯m
C♯m
F♯m/A B7
E
D.C.
feet – Mas - ter who acts as a slave to them:
white; neigh-bours are near - by and far a - way:
love; all these are neigh-bours to us and you:
slaves – this is the way we should live with you:

This folk song may be sung in four-part harmony, using chords in the right-hand piano part (basses sing melody). Sing the verses in unison. A very effective arrangement is achieved when voices sing alone, and a hand-drum is used to create poly-rhythms.

* In its original American version, this song has 'Jesu' throughout.

Words: © 1969 and Music arrangement: © 1980
Hope Publishing Company, Carol Stream, Illinois 60188, USA
International copyright secured. All rights reserved.
Used by permission.

97 Jesus shall reign

Duke Street 8 8 8 8 (LM)

Words: I Watts (1674–1748)
in this version Jubilate Hymns
Psalm 72.5, 72.8 etc
Music: J Hatton (died 1793)
arranged David Peacock

Triumphantly

D A G D E7 A
1 Je - sus shall reign where'er the sun
2 Peo - ple and realms of ev - ery tongue
3 Bless - ings a - bound where Je - sus reigns –
4 To him shall end - less prayer be made,
5 Let all cre - a - tion rise and bring
D G Em7 D A D Bm D
does his suc - ces - sive jour - neys run; his king - dom stretch from
de - clare his love in sweet - est song, and child - ren's voi - ces
the pri - soner leaps to lose his chains, the wea - ry find e -
and prin - ces throng to crown his head; his name like in - cense
the high - est hon - ours to our king; an - gels de - scend with
G Em7 A D G D D/A A D
Fine
shore to shore till moons shall rise and set no more.
shall pro - claim their ear - ly bless - ings on his name.
- ter - nal rest, the hun - gry and the poor are blessed.
shall a - rise with ev - ery morn - ing sac - ri - fice.
songs a - gain and earth re - peat the loud 'A - men!'
Link
G D/F♯ Em7 Asus A
D.C.

Music arrangement: David Peacock / Jubilate Hymns †

Words: © in this version Jubilate Hymns †

98 Jesus, we enthrone you

Words and music: Paul Kyle
Psalm 22.3, Revelation 22.20
Music arranged Geoff Baker

With reverence

G
G/F♯
Em
Em/D
Je - sus, we en - throne you,
C
Am7
G
D/F♯
we pro - claim you our king –
Em
Bm7
stand-ing here in the midst of us!
C
D
We raise you up with our praise.

Words and music: © 1980 Kingsway's Thankyou Music,
PO Box 75, Eastbourne, East Sussex BN23 6NW

G D/F♯ Em Em/D
And as we wor - ship, build a throne,
C D G D/F♯ Em
and as we wor - ship, build a throne,
C D G D/F♯ Em Em/D
and as we wor - ship, build a throne – come, Lord
C Am7 D9 G C/G G
Je - sus and take your place!

99 Jesus, you are the radiance

Capo 5(C)

Words and music: Dave Fellingham
Psalm 8.5, Hebrews 1.3 and 2.9

Light jazz waltz style
F (C) C/F (G) Bb/F (F) Esus (Bm) Em7 (Bm7) A (E) A7 (E7)
Je - sus, you are the rad - iance of the
Aaug (E) A (E) C/D (Am7) Dm (Am) Bb (F) Gm/Bb (Dm) F/A (C)
Fa - ther's glo - ry, you are the Son, the ap -
Bb (F) Gm/Bb (Dm) F/A (C) Gm7 (Dm7) F/A (C) Gm7/Bb (Dm7) C (G)
- point - ed heir, through whom all things are made;
C7 (G7) F (C) C/F (G) Bb/F (F) F (C)
you are the one who sus - tains all

Words and music: © 1985 Kingsway's Thankyou Music,
PO Box 75, Eastbourne, East Sussex BN23 6NW

things by your pow - er - ful word, you have
pu - ri - fied us from sin, you are ex - alt - ed, O Lord, ex -
- alt - ed, O Lord to the right hand of God:
last time
Crowned with glo - ry, crowned with hon - our
we wor - ship you;
repeat as required

100 Jesus, you have lifted me

Words and music: Dave Fellingham
Colossians 3.3

Slow, but with a 'soul' feel

Gm
C7
Fmaj7
Je - sus, you have lift - ed me,
Gm
C7
Fmaj7
Gm
C7
giv - en me your life;
you have heard my
Am
Dm
Gm
C7
F9
cry to you,
you have raised me up.
B♭
C
Am
Dm
My heart trusts in you and I am helped;

Words and music: © 1987 Kingsway's Thankyou Music,
PO Box 75, Eastbourne, East Sussex BN23 6NW

Bb C Fmaj7 Em7
you're my strength and shield. My heart
Bm7 Am Eb9
will re - joice, and with my song I thank you, Lord.
Gm C7 Fmaj7
You're my fort - ress and my rock –
Gm C7 Am D7 Bb C
I shall not be moved; my life's hid-den
Am Dm Gm9 C9 F
now with Christ in God I am now se - cure.

101 Just as I am

Woodworth 8 6 8 6 extended

Words: C Elliott (1789–1871)
in this version Jubilate Hymns
Luke 18.13, Ephesians 3.18
Music: W B Bradbury (1816–1868)
arranged David Peacock

With sensitivity

D Dmaj7
1 Just as I am, with -
(2) as I am, with -
(3) as I am, though
C/D D A Em7 A7
- out one plea but that you died to
- out de - lay your call of mer - cy
tossed a - bout with ma - ny a con - flict,
G/D D D/F♯
set me free, and at your bid - ding
I o - bey – your blood can wash my
ma - ny a doubt, fight - ings with - in and
G G♯dim D/A Bm7
'Come to me!' O Lamb of God, I
sins a - way: O Lamb of God, I
fears with - out, O Lamb of God, I

Music arrangement: © David Peacock / Jubilate Hymns †

Words: © in this version Jubilate Hymns †

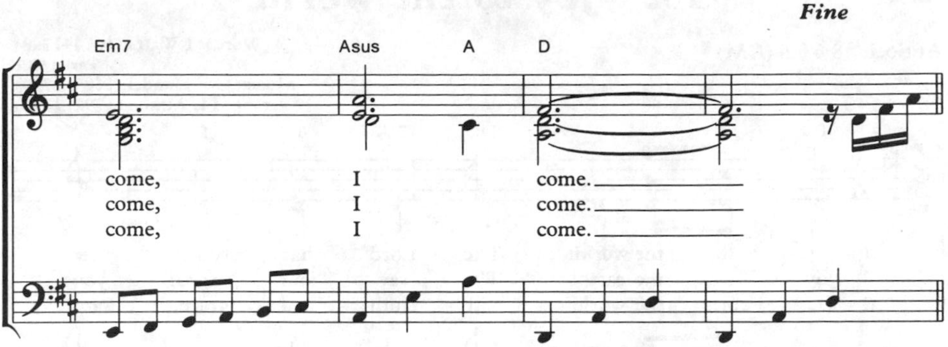

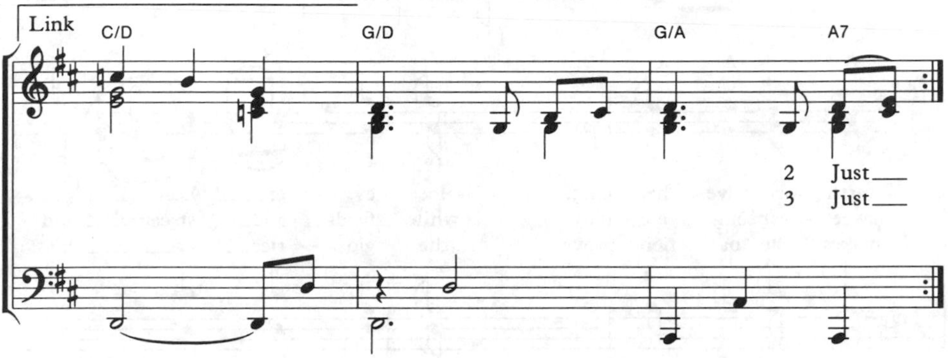

4 Just as I am, poor, wretched, blind!
Sight, riches, healing of the mind –
all that I need, in you to find:
O Lamb of God, I come, I come.

5 Just as I am! You will receive,
will welcome, pardon, cleanse, relieve:
because your promise I believe,
O Lamb of God, I come, I come.

6 Just as I am! Your love unknown
has broken every barrier down:
now to be yours, yes, yours alone,
O Lamb of God, I come, I come.

7 Just as I am! Of that free love
the breadth, length, depth and height to prove,
here for a time and then above,
O Lamb of God, I come, I come.

101A PRAISE SHOUT

LEADER Give thanks to the Lord, for he is good;
ALL **his love endures for ever.**

LEADER Tell of all his mighty acts;
ALL **and make his praises heard.**

LEADER Praise be to the Lord, the God of Israel:
ALL **from everlasting to everlasting.**

LEADER Let all the people say, 'Amen':
ALL **Amen, praise the Lord!**

From Psalm 106

102 Joy to the world

Antioch 8 6 8 6 (CM)

Words: I Watts (1674–1748)
Psalm 98.1
Music: G F Handel (1685–1759)
arranged L Mason (1792–1872)

D Em D/A A7 D
1 Joy to the world! The Lord has come: let
2 Joy to the earth! The sav - iour reigns: your
3 He rules the world with truth and grace, and
G A D G/D D
earth re-ceive her king, let ev - ery heart pre -
sweet - est songs em - ploy, while fields and streams and
makes the na - tions prove the glo - ries of his
G/D D
- pare him room and heaven and na - ture sing, and
hills and plains re - peat the sound-ing joy, re -
right - eous ness, the won - ders of his love, the
and heaven and na - ture
re - peat the sound-ing
the won - ders of his
A A7 D G/D D Em D/A A7 D
heaven and na - ture sing, and heaven, and heaven and na - ture sing!
- peat the sound-ing joy, re - peat, re - peat the sound-ing joy.
won - ders of his love, the won - ders, won - ders of his love.
sing, and heaven and na - ture sing, and heaven and na - ture sing!
joy, re - peat the sound-ing joy, re - peat the sound-ing joy.
love, the won - ders of his love, the won - ders of his love.

103 King of kings

Words: Sophie Conty and Naomi Batya
Isaiah 9.6, Revelation 17.14 and 19.16
Music: Ancient Hebrew folk song

Lively

Em
B7
Em
King of kings and Lord of___ lords,_ Glo - ry, al - le - lu - ia;
B7
Em
King of kings and Lord of___ lords,_ glo - ry, al - le - lu - ia!
*
B7
Em
Je - sus, Prince of peace,_ Glo - ry, al - le - lu - ia;
B7
Em
Je - sus, Prince of peace,_ glo - ry, al - le - lu - ia!

* To sing as a round in two parts,
group 2 should begin singing when group 1 arrives at this point.

Words and music arrangement: © 1980 Maranatha! Music/CopyCare Ltd,
PO Box 77, Hailsham, East Sussex BN27 3EF

104 King of kings, Lord of lords

The King of glory comes

Words and music: Graham Kendrick
Isaiah 9.7, John 1.1, Revelation 5.5, 17.14, 19.16

Capo 2(G)

Strongly ♩ = 86

F♯m (Em)
Dma7 (Cmaj7)
Esus (Dsus)
E (D)
F♯m (Em)
King of kings, Lord of lords,
Dmaj7 (Cmaj7)
Esus (Dsus)
E (D)
F♯m (Em)
Lion of Ju-dah, Word of God; King of kings,
Dmaj7 (Cmaj7)
Lord of lords, Lion of Ju-dah, Word of

Words and music: © 1988 Make Way Music,
PO Box 263, Croydon, Surrey CR9 5AP.
International copyright secured. All rights reserved. Used by permission.

Chorus
Esus (Dsus) E (D) A (G) F♯m (Em)
God! And here he comes, the
D (C) E (D) F♯m (Em) D (C) Bm (Am)
King of glo-ry comes, in right-eous-ness he comes to judge the
G (F) Esus (Dsus) E (D) A (G) F♯m (Em)
earth; and here he comes, the
D (C) E (D) F♯sus (Esus) F♯ (E) Bm (Am) Esus (Dsus) E (D) A (G)
King of glo-ry comes – with just-ice he'll rule the earth!

105 Led like a lamb

You're alive

Words and music: Graham Kendrick
Isaiah 53.7, John 20.1, Hebrews 1.3

Thoughtfully

Dm C Dm
G F C G Am
1 Led like a lamb to the slaugh - ter in
2 At break of dawn – poor Ma - ry, still
3 At the right hand of the Fa - ther, now
Fmaj7 Gsus G F C G Am
si - lence and shame, there on your back you car - ried a world of
weep - ing, she came: when through her grief she heard your voice now
seat - ed on high, you have be - gun your e - ter - nal reign of
Fmaj7 Gsus G Dm C
vio - lence and pain, bleed - ing, dy - ing,
speak - ing her name, MEN 'Ma - ry!' WOMEN 'Mas - ter!'
jus - tice and joy: Glo - ry, glo - ry,

Words and music: © 1983 Kingsway's Thankyou Music,
PO Box 75, Eastbourne, East Sussex BN23 6NW

Triumphantly
Chorus
Dm
Gsus
G
bleed - ing,
MEN 'Ma - ry!'
glo - ry,
dy - ing.
WOMEN 'Mas - ter!'
glo - ry!
ALL You're a -
Antiphonal Alleluias
C
Bb/C
F
Dm F/G
Al - le - lu - ia al - le - lu - ia
- live – you're a - live, you have ri - sen –
Al - le - lu - ia
and the
al - le - lu - ia al - le - lu - ia
power and the glo - ry is giv - en –
al - le - lu - ia
Je - sus to
1.2.
last time
you.
you.

106 Let our praise to you

Words and music: Brent Chambers
Psalm 141.2, Isaiah 6.3, Revelation 4.8

Worshipfully
D
C/D
Let our praise to you be as in - cense, let our
G/D
D
praise to you be as pil - lars of your throne;
C/D
let our praise to you be as in - cense, as we
G/D
D
come be - fore you and wor - ship you a - lone –

Words and music: © 1979 Scripture in Song/CopyCare Ltd,
PO Box 77, Hailsham, East Sussex BN27 3EF

G D
as we see you in your splen-dour, as we
G C G D G
gaze up-on your ma-jes-ty, as we join the hosts of
D C
an - gels and pro - claim to-ge - ther your
A D
ho-li-ness: Ho - ly, ho-ly,
to repeat to end
C/D G/D D D
ho - ly; ho - ly is the Lord! Lord!

107 Let the heavens shout for joy

Let the world sing (Jesus reigns)

Words and music: Phil Pringle
Isaiah 98.7, Matthew 24.30,
Mark 13.26, Revelation 1.7
Music arranged David Peacock

Slow, unhurried rock

G D Am7
Let the hea-vens shout for joy,
let the na-tions bow their knees,
G D C
let the earth bring forth its praise,
fall in awe up-on their face,
1. Em/C♯ C
let the seas roar,
for my Sav-iour comes;
D
2. Em/C♯
see him come in

Words and music: © 1987 Seam of Gold/Kingsway's Thankyou Music,
PO Box 75, Eastbourne, East Sussex BN23 6NW

C
D
clouds of right-eous-ness. Al-le -
G
C
- lu - ia, al-le-lu -
Am7
D
- ia, al-le -
Bm
Cmaj7
- lu - ia let the world
to repeat
to end
Em/C♯
Am7
D
Am7
D
G
sing: Je-sus reigns; Al-le -

108 Let there be love

Capo 1(E)

Words and music: Dave Bilbrough

1 John 3.14

Triumphantly

F (E) B♭ (A) Gm (F♯m) C (B7) F (E) F/E (E/D♯)
Let there be love shared a - mong us, let there be love in our
Dm (C♯m) Dm7 (C♯m7) B♭ (A) Gm (F♯m) C (B7) F (E)
eyes; may now your love sweep this na-tion, cause us, O Lord, to a -
F7 (E7) B♭ (A) Gm (F♯m) C (B7) F (E) A7 (G♯7)
- rise: give us a fresh un - der - stand-ing of bro-ther-ly love that is
Dm (C♯m) Dm7 (C♯m7) B♭ (A) Gm (F♯m) C (B7) B♭ (A) F (E)
real; let there be love shared a - mong us, let there be love!

Words and music: © 1979 Kingsway's Thankyou Music,
PO Box 75, Eastbourne, East Sussex BN23 6NW

109 Lift up your heads

Capo 2(G)

Words and music: Steven Fry
Matthew 2.11, Luke 21.28

Broadly

A (G) E7/B (D7) A/C# (G) D (C) E (D) E7/G# Asus (G) A A/G#
Lift up your heads to the com-ing King;
F#m (Em) D (C) E/D (D) A/C# (G) Bm7sus (Am) A/E (G) Esus (D) E
bow be-fore him and a-dore him, sing
A (G) E7/B (D7) A/C# (G) D (C) E (D) E7/G# Asus (G) A A/G#
to his ma-jes-ty: let your prais-es be
F#m (Em) D (C) E/D (D) A/C# (G) Bm (Am7) A/C# (G) Esus (Dsus) E (D) A (G)
pure and ho-ly, giv-ing glo-ry to the King of kings.

Words and music: © 1974 Birdwing Music/Cherry Lane Music/EMI Music,
127 Charing Cross Road, London WC2H OEA

110 Lift your voice and sing

Give him the glory

Words: Stephen Chapman
Philippians 2.10, Revelation 1.7
Music: Stephen Chapman and Brent Henderson

Light, with a lilt ♩ = 124

G F/G G Cmaj7/G
G F/G G Cmaj7/G
G D/F♯ C/E C G D/F♯ Em D
1 Lift your voice and sing – we serve the liv - ing
2 Lift your eyes and see his power and ma - jes -
mp
C Am7 D B7 Em
King; our lives are the throne where his glo - ry shown will
- ty! Our lives are the throne where his glo - ry shown will

Words and music: © 1984 Paragon Music Corp/Fine Balance Music/CopyCare Ltd, PO Box 77, Hailsham, East Sussex BN27 3EF

C D E♭ F B♭ Gm Cm7 F7 B♭ Gm7
draw peo-ple to Jesus. Give him the glory and honour and praise: he is the
draw peo-ple to Jesus. Give him the glory and honour and praise: he is the
cresc.
mf
Cm7 E♭/F Gm7 Gm7/F Edim7 Cm7 E♭/F
Lord of cre-a-tion al - ways – almighty God, worthy a-lone to be
King of cre-a-tion al - ways – almighty God, worthy a-lone to be
1.
2.
Dsus D E♭ Cm7 A♭maj7 Fm7 A♭/B♭
praised!
praised!
decresc.
E♭ B♭/D Cm7 B♭ E♭ B♭/D
3 Ev - ery eye will be-hold him, ev - ery
p

Cm7 B♭ G/F C/E Dm7 C
knee bow in prayer, ev - ery tongue will con-fess him,
mp
cresc.
G7 C/E Dm7 G7 C Am7
and all the earth will proclaim he is Lord. Give him the
Dm7 G7 C Am7 Dm7 G7
glo - ry and honour and praise: he is the King of cre - a - tion al -
Am7 F♯dim7 Dm G7
- ways – al-migh - ty God, worthy a - lone to be

C Am7 Dm7 G7 C Am7
praised! Give him the glo-ry and honour and praise: he is the
Dm7 G7 Am7 F♯dim7
Lord of cre-a-tion al-ways– al-migh-ty God,
Dm G7 C Am7 Dm7 G7
wor-thy a-lone to be praised, wor-thy a-lone to be
C Am7 Dm7 G7 Dm7 G C
praised, worthy alone to be praised!
8va

111 Light has dawned

Capo 2(G)

Words and music: Graham Kendrick
2 Corinthians 4.6

Strongly ♩ = 130

1 Light has dawned that ev - er shall blaze, dark-ness flees a - way; Christ the light has shone in our hearts, turn - ing night to day.
WOMEN 2 Sav - iour of the world is he, hea - ven's king come down; judge-ment, love and mer - cy meet at his thor - ny crown.
MEN 3 Life has sprung from hearts of stone, by the Spi - rit's breath; hell shall let her cap - tives go, life has con-quered death.
4 Blood has flowed that cleans - es from sin, God his love has proved; man may mock and dem - ons may rage – we shall not be moved!

Words and music: © 1988 Make Way Music,
PO Box 263, Croydon, Surrey CR9 5AP.
International copyright secured. All rights reserved. Used by permission.

F♯m (Em) E (D) Bm (Am) F♯m (Em) E (D) A (G) F♯m (Em) E (D) Bm (Am)
ALL
We pro - claim him King of ___ kings, we lift high his ___
Esus (Dsus) E (D) F♯m (Em) E (D) Bm (Am) F♯m (Em) E (D) F♯sus (Esus) F♯ (E)
name; heaven and earth shall bow at his feet,
1-3.
Bm (Am) Esus (Dsus) E (D) Asus (Gsus) A (G) E/A (D) A (G)
when he ___ comes to reign.
4.
Asus (Gsus) A (G)
D.𝄋
reign.
5.
A (G) D/A (C) E/A (D) D/A (C) A (G)
reign.

112 Lighten our darkness

Words: from The Alternative Service Book 1980
Isaiah 60.2, Luke 2.32, John 1.5
Music: Chris Rolinson

Prayerfully

G/A
G/D
D
3
SOLO
Light - en our dark - ness, Lord, we
Bm
G/A
G/D
D
pray,
ALL
light - en our dark - ness,
Lord, we pray;
Bm
Bm/A
SOLO
and
G
A/G
F♯m7
Bm
G
G/A
in your mer - cy de - fend us,
ALL
and in your mer - cy de -

Music: © 1987 Kingsway's Thankyou Music,
PO Box 75, Eastbourne, East Sussex BN23 6NW

Words: © 1980 The Central Board of Finance
of the Church of England
Used by permission

F♯m7 Bm Em7 G G/A A7 D
SOLO
ALL
- fend us from all pe - rils and dan - gers of this night, from all
Bm G G/A A7 D Bm
pe - rils and dan - gers of this night; for the love of your on - ly
A♯aug5 D/A G Dmaj7/F♯ Em9
SOLO
Son, our Sav - iour Je - sus Christ. A -
G/A D Bm G D Bm7
ALL
SOLO
- men, a - men, a -
G D Bm G D
ALL
- men, a - men!

113 Look around you

Kyrie eleison

Capo 2(D)

Words and music: Jodi Page Clark

With strength and intensity

E (D)
A (G)
B (A)
v.2
1 Look a-round you – can you see;
2 Walk a-mong them I'll go with you,
3 For-give us Fa - ther, hear our prayer:
E (D)
v.3
A (G)
B (A)
times are trou-bled, peo-ple grieve?
reach out to them with my hands:
we will walk with you a - ny-where –
E (D)
Am (Gm)
See the vio-lence, feel the hard-ness –
suf - fer with me, and to - ge - ther
through your suf-fering, with for-give-ness,

Words and music: © 1976 Celebration/Kingsway's Thankyou Music,
PO Box 75, Eastbourne, East Sussex BN23 6NW

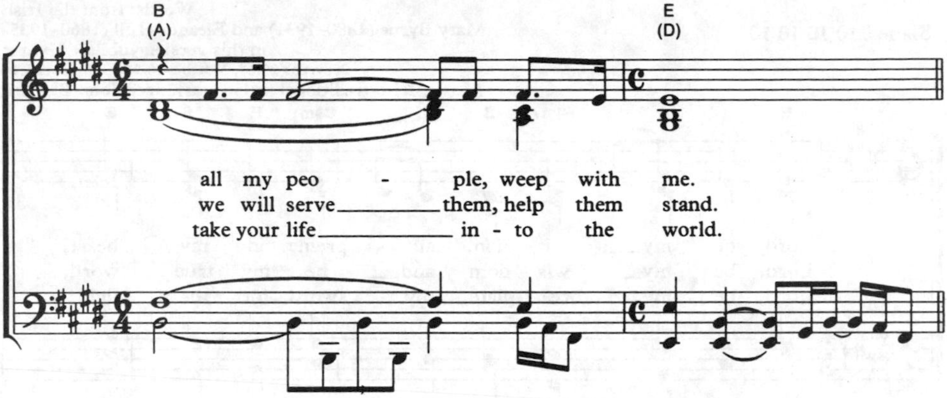
B
(A)
E
(D)
all my peo - ple, weep with me.
we will serve ________ them, help them stand.
take your life ________ in - to the world.

Chorus
E
(D)
A B
(G) (A)
E
(D)
A B
(G) (A)
Ky-ri - e e - lei-son, Chris-te e - lei-son,
Fa-ther, God, have mer-cy, Je-sus, have mer-cy,

E
(D)
A
(G)
B
(A)
E
(D)
Ky-ri - e e - le - - - i - son.
Spi-rit, Lord, have mer - - - cy!

113A PRAISE SHOUT

LEADER Let the people praise you, O God;
ALL **let all the people praise you!**

LEADER Let your ways be known on earth;
ALL **your saving power in all the world!**

From Psalm 67

114 Lord, be my vision

Slane 10 10 10 10

Words: from the Irish
Mary Byrne (1880–1931) and Eleanor Hull (1860–1935)
in this version Jubilate Hymns
Proverbs 29.18, Matthew 6.24, Ephesians 6.14
Music: Irish traditional melody, arranged John Barnard

E A F♯m7 B C♯m E A6 E
1 Lord, be my vision, supreme in my heart,
2 Lord, be my wisdom and be my true word,
3 Lord, be my breast-plate, my sword for the fight:
F♯m7 B A6 G♯m7 C♯m7 F♯m7 G♯m7 A B
bid every rival give way and depart:
I ever with you and you with me, Lord:
be my strong armour, for you are my might;
C♯m C♯m7/B F♯m E G♯m C♯m A G♯m/B A B
you my best thought in the day or the night,
you my great father and I your true child,
you are my shelter and you my high tower –
C♯m G♯m E A C♯m Emaj7/B A6 A A6 E
waking or sleeping your presence my light.
once far away, but by love reconciled.
raise me to heaven, O Power of my power.

4 I need no riches, nor earth's empty praise:
you my inheritance through all my days;
all of your treasure to me you impart,
high King of heaven, the first in my heart.

5 High King of heaven, when battle is done,
grant heaven's joy to me, bright heaven's sun;
Christ of my own heart, whatever befall,
still be my vision, O Ruler of all.

Music arrangement: © John Barnard / Jubilate Hymns †

Words: © in this version Jubilate Hymns †

115 Lord, come and heal your church

Worshipfully

Words and music: Chris Rolinson

D A/C♯ Bm F♯m/A
1 Lord, come and heal your church, take our lives and
2 Spi - rit of God, come in and re - lease our
3 Show us your power, we pray, that___ we may
G Em D/A Asus A D A/C♯
cleanse with your fi - re; let your de-liver - ance
hearts to___ praise you; make us___whole, for
share in your glo - ry: we shall a - rise, and
Bm F♯m/A G Em D/A Asus A/G
flow as we lift your name up___ high - er.
ho - ly___ we'll be - come and___ serve you,
go to pro-claim your works most__ ho - ly.
Chorus
F♯sus F♯ Bm Bm/A G D/F♯ Em7
We will draw near and sur - ren - der our__ fear:
A A/G D/F♯ Fdim Em7 D/F♯ G G/A A D
lift our hands to pro-claim, 'Ho-ly Fa - ther, you are___ here!'

Words and music: © 1987 Kingsway's Thankyou Music,
PO Box 75, Eastbourne, East Sussex BN23 6NW

116 Lord, for the years

Lord of the years 11 10 11 10

Words: Timothy Dudley-Smith
Music: Michael Baughen
arranged David Iliff
Descant and arrangement verse 5 John Barnard

C Dm7 C/E F Em Am
1 Lord, for the years your love has kept and
2 Lord, for that word, the word of life which
3 Lord, for our land, in this our ge - ne -
4 Lord, for our world; when we dis - own and
Organ
G7 C Am6 B Em Cm/E♭
gui - ded, urged and in - spired us,
fi - res us, speaks to our hearts and
- ra - tion, spi - rits op - pressed by
doubt him, love - less in strength, and
G/D Am D7 G C C/E
cheered us on our way, sought us and
sets our souls a - blaze; teach - es and
plea - sure, wealth and care; for young and
com - fort - less in pain; hun - gry and
F A7/E D G
saved us, par - doned and pro - vi - ded,
trains, re - bukes us and in - spires us;
old, for com - mon - wealth and na - tion,
help - less, lost in - deed with - out him;

Music: © Michael Baughen / Jubilate Hymns †
Music arrangement: © David Iliff / Jubilate Hymns †
Descant and arrangement verse 5 © John Barnard / Jubilate Hymns †
Words: © Timothy Dudley-Smith

Am Em F Dm G7 C
Lord of the years, we bring our thanks to - day.
Lord of the word, re - ceive your peo - ple's praise.
Lord of our land, be pleased to hear our prayer.
Lord of the world, we pray that Christ may reign.
Descant
C Dm7 C/E F Em Am
5 Lord, in liv - ing power re -
5 Lord, for our - selves; in liv - ing power re -
Dm7 G C B Em Cm6/E♭
- make us - self on the cross and
- make us - self on the cross and

G/D D7 G G7 C C/E F Em A7/E
Christ up - on the throne, for the
Christ up - on the throne, past put be - hind us,
Dm D G C/E
fu - ture take us, Lord of our
for the fu - ture take us, Lord of our
F Dm G7 C
lives, to live for Christ a - lone.
lives, to live for Christ a - lone.

117 Lord, your church on earth

Ode to Joy 8 7 8 7 D
Capo 5(C)

Words: Hugh Sherlock and Michael Saward
Matthew 28.19
Music: Ludwig van Beethoven (1770–1827)

F (C) Gm7/F (Dm7) F (C) Dm7 (Am7) F (C) C (G) F (C) C (G) F (C) F/C (C) C (G)
1 Lord, your church on earth is seek-ing power and wis-dom from a-bove:
2 You re-lease us from our bond-age, lift the bur-dens caused by sin;
3 In the streets of ev-ery ci-ty where the bruised and lone-ly live,
F (C) Gm7/F (Dm7) F (C) Dm7 (Am7) F (C) C (G) F (C) C (G) F (C) Csus (Gsus) C (G) F (C)
teach us all the art of speak-ing with the ac-cents of your love.
give new hope, new strength and cour-age, grant re-lease from fears with-in.
we will show the Sav-iour's pi-ty and his long-ing to for-give.
C (G) F/C (C) Dm7/C (Am7) C7 (G7) F/C (C) Dm7/C (Am7) C (G) A7/C♯ (E7) Dm (Am) G (D) Csus (Gsus) C (G)
We will heed your great com-mis-sion send-ing us to ev-ery place –
Light for dark-ness, joy for sor-row, love for ha-tred, peace for strife –
In all lands and with all ra-ces we will serve, and seek to bring
F (C) E♭ (B♭) B♭/D (F) F (C) Gm (Dm) B♭ (F) F/A (C) C7/G (G7) F (C) Csus (Gsus) C (G) F (C)
'Go, bap-tize, ful-fil my mis-sion; serve with love and share my grace!'
these and count-less bless-ings fol-low as the Spi-rit gives new life.
all the world to ren-der prais-es Christ, to you, re-deem-er King.

Words: © Methodist Publishing House, 20 Ivatt Way, Peterborough PE3 7PG

118 Lord, have mercy on us

Words and music: Graham Kendrick

Steadliy
E
G♯m
A
Lord, have mer - cy on us,
B
E
G♯m
come and heal our
A
B
C♯m
B
land
OR *world.*
Cleanse with your fire,
B♯dim
C♯m
Amaj7
heal with your touch:
hum - bly we

Words and music: © 1986 Kingsway's Thankyou Music,
PO Box 75, Eastbourne, East Sussex BN23 6NW

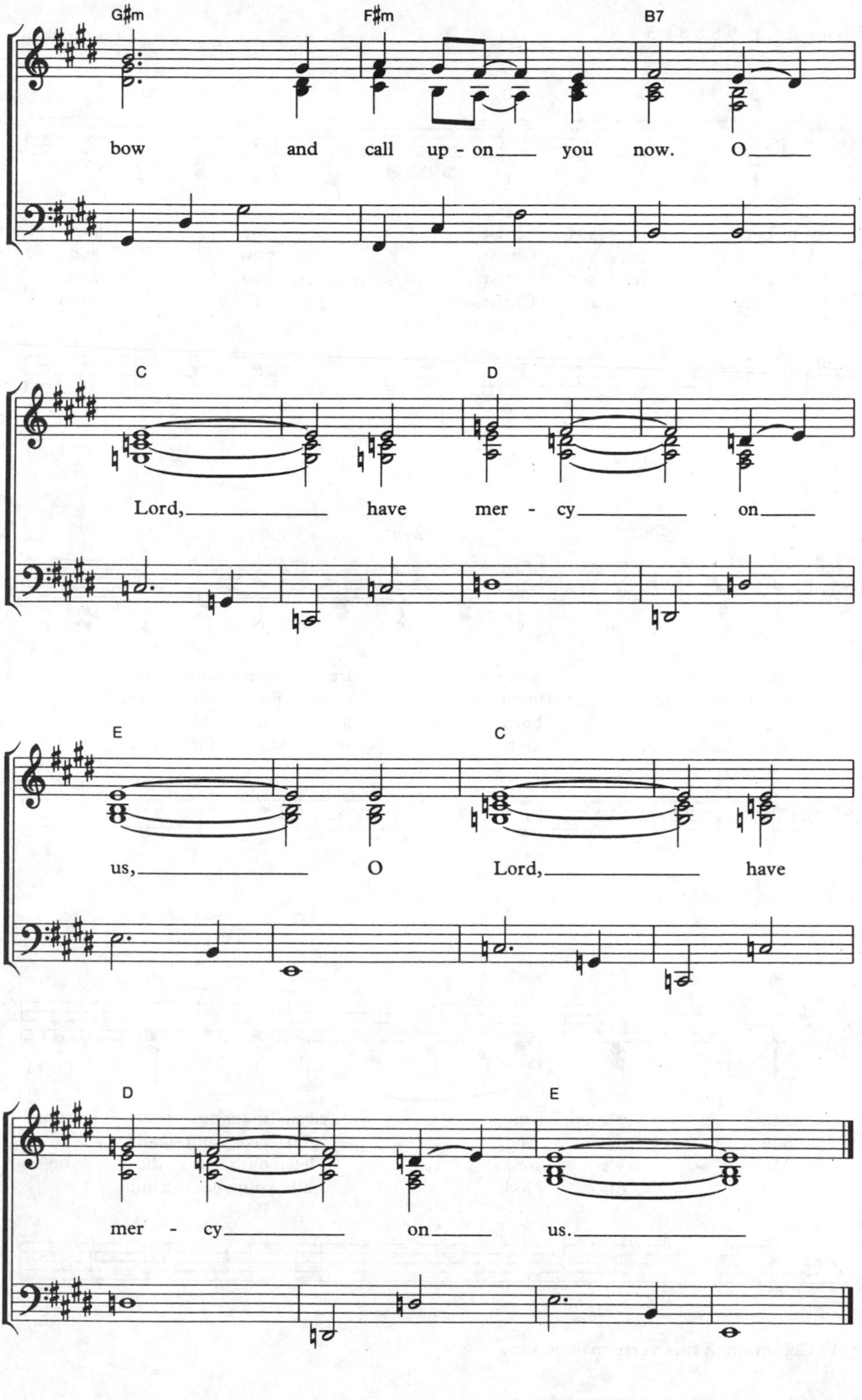
G♯m
F♯m
B7
bow and call up - on you now. O
C
D
Lord, have mer - cy on
E
C
us, O Lord, have
D
E
mer - cy on us.

119 Lord Jesus Christ

Living Lord 9 8 8 8 8 3

Words and music: Patrick Appleford

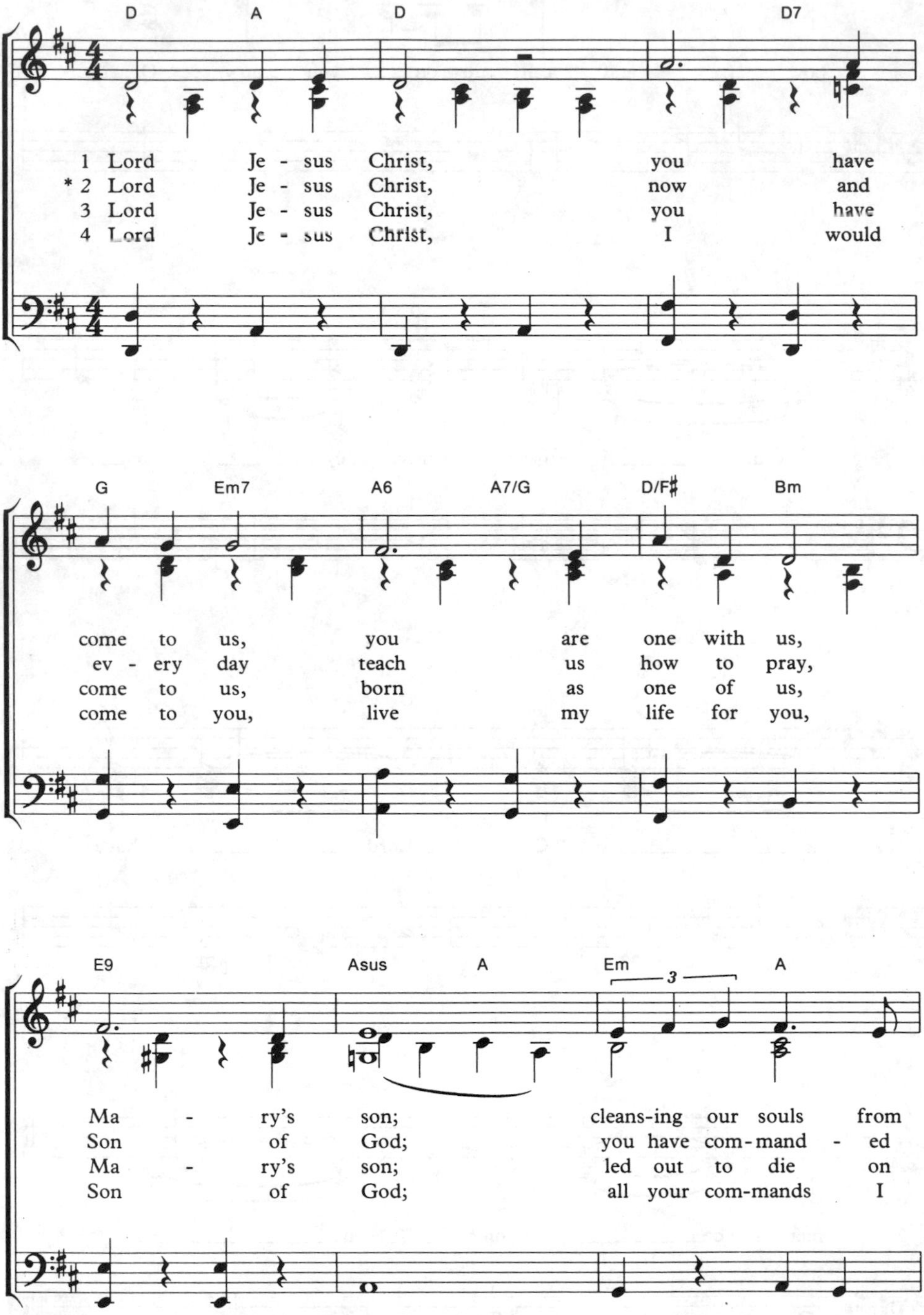
D A D D7
1 Lord Je - sus Christ, you have
*2 Lord Je - sus Christ, now and
3 Lord Je - sus Christ, you have
4 Lord Je - sus Christ, I would
G Em7 A6 A7/G D/F♯ Bm
come to us, you are one with us,
ev - ery day teach us how to pray,
come to us, born as one of us,
come to you, live my life for you,
E9 Asus A Em A
3
Ma - ry's son; cleans-ing our souls from
Son of God; you have com-mand - ed
Ma - ry's son; led out to die on
Son of God; all your com-mands I

* At Communion this verse may be sung

Words and music: © 1960 Josef Weinberger Ltd,
12–14 Mortimer Street, London W1N 7RD

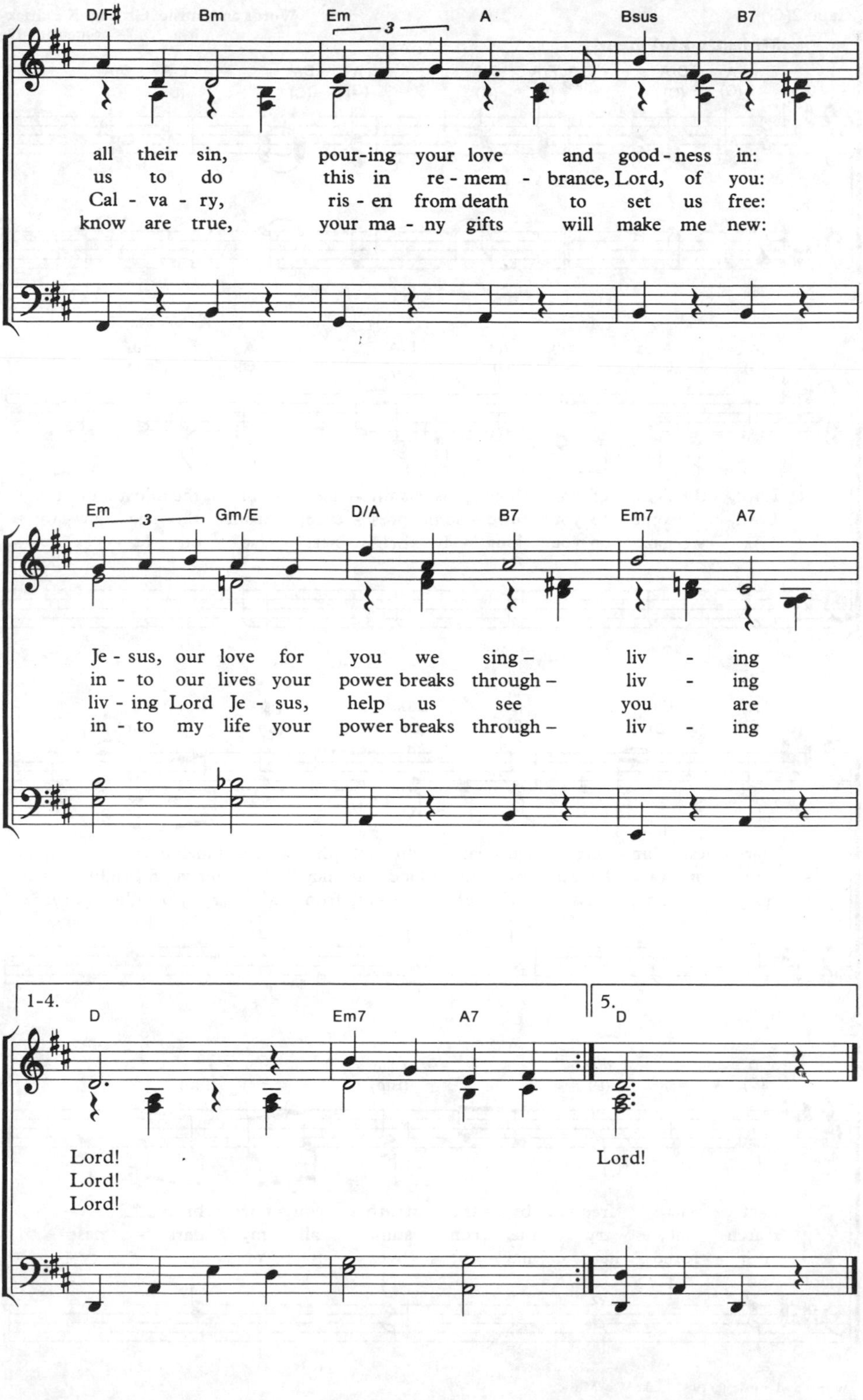
D/F♯ Bm Em 3 A Bsus B7
all their sin, pour-ing your love and good - ness in:
us to do this in re - mem - brance, Lord, of you:
Cal - va - ry, ris - en from death to set us free:
know are true, your ma - ny gifts will make me new:
Em 3 Gm/E D/A B7 Em7 A7
Je - sus, our love for you we sing – liv - ing
in - to our lives your power breaks through – liv - ing
liv - ing Lord Je - sus, help us see you are
in - to my life your power breaks through – liv - ing
1-4. D Em7 A7
5. D
Lord!
Lord!
Lord!
Lord!

120 Lord, the light of your love

Capo 2(G)

Words and music: Graham Kendrick
John 1.5, 2 Corinthians 3.18

Majestic and steady

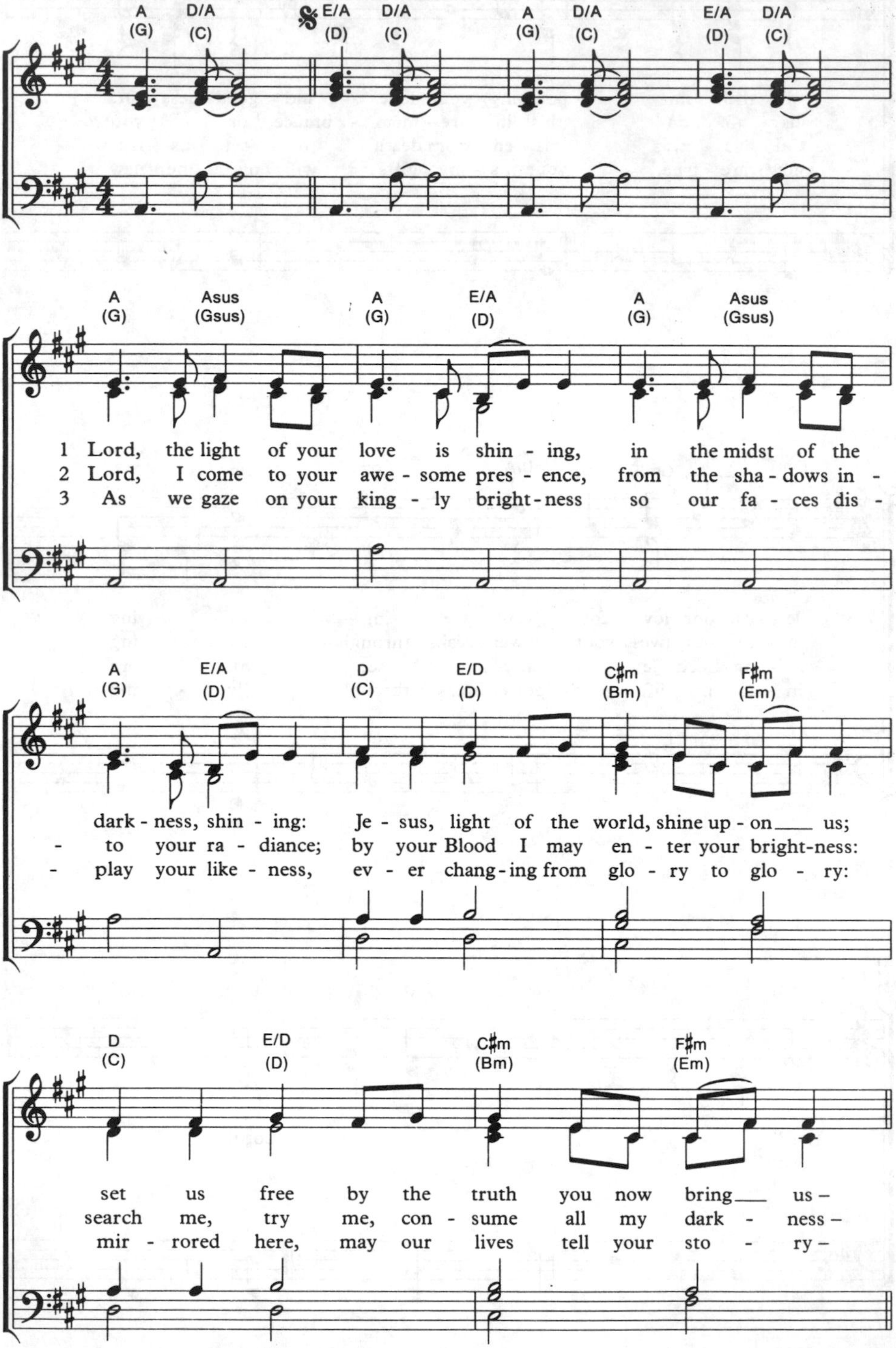
A (G) D/A (C) E/A (D) D/A (C) A (G) D/A (C) E/A (D) D/A (C)
A (G) Asus (Gsus) A (G) E/A (D) A (G) Asus (Gsus)
1 Lord, the light of your love is shin - ing, in the midst of the
2 Lord, I come to your awe - some pres - ence, from the sha - dows in -
3 As we gaze on your king - ly bright - ness so our fa - ces dis -
A (G) E/A (D) D (C) E/D (D) C♯m (Bm) F♯m (Em)
dark - ness, shin - ing: Je - sus, light of the world, shine up - on us;
- to your ra - diance; by your Blood I may en - ter your bright-ness:
- play your like - ness, ev - er chang - ing from glo - ry to glo - ry:
D (C) E/D (D) C♯m (Bm) F♯m (Em)
set us free by the truth you now bring us –
search me, try me, con - sume all my dark - ness –
mir - rored here, may our lives tell your sto - ry –

Words and music: © 1987 Make Way Music,
PO Box 263, Croydon, Surrey CR9 5AP.
International copyright secured. All rights reserved. Used by permission.

Chorus
G (F) Esus (Dsus) E (D) A (G) E/A (D) A (G) D (C) A (G)
shine on me, Shine, Je - sus, shine, fill this
Flow, ri - ver, flow, flood the
Bm (Am) Bm/A (Am7) Esus (Dsus) E (D) A (G) E/A (D) A (G) D (C)
land with the Fa - ther's glo - ry; blaze, Spi - rit, blaze,
na - tions with grace and mer - cy; send forth your word,
1.
A (G) Bm (Am) Bm/A (Am7) G (F) Esus (Dsus) E (D)
set our hearts on fire.
Lord, and
2.
Bm (Am) E7 (D7) A (G) D/A (C)
D.𝄋
last time
A (G)
let there be light!

121 Lord, your word shall guide us

Words: H W Baker (1821–1877)
in this version Jubilate Hymns
Psalm 119.105, 2 Timothy 3.16, Hebrews 4.12
Music: G Beaumont (1903–1970)

Chesterton 6 6 6 6 D

Capo 3(C)

E♭ (C) Fm7 (Dm7) G♯dim (Fdim) Gm (Em) G (E)
1 Lord your word shall guide us and with
2 When the storms di - stress us and dark
3 Word of mer - cy, giv - ing cour - age
Fm (Dm) B♭ (G) E♭ (C) Cm (Am) B♭ (G)
truth pro - vide us: teach us to re - ceive it -
clouds op - press us, then your word pro - tects us
to the liv - ing; word of life, sup - ply - ing
E♭ (C) Fm (Dm) B♭ (G) E♭ (C) Fm7 (Dm7) G♯dim (Fdim)
and with joy be - lieve it. When our foes are near us,
and its light di - rects us. Who can tell the plea-sure,
com-fort to the dy - ing: O that we dis-cern - ing

Music: © Paxton Music c/o Novello & Co, 8/9 Frith Street, London W1V 5TZ

Words: © in this version Jubilate Hymns †

Gm (Em) G (E) Fm (Dm) B♭ (G) Cm (Am) B♭7 (G7)
then your word shall cheer us – word of con - so -
who re - count the trea - sure by your word im -
its most ho - ly learn - ing, Lord, may love and
1.2.
Fm (Dm) C (A) Fm (Dm) B♭ (G) E♭ (C)
- la - tion, mes - sage of sal - va - tion.
- part - ed to the sim - ple - heart - ed?
fear you – ev - er - more be
3.
F♯dim (E♭dim) Fm (Dm) B♭7 (G7) B♭ (G) E♭ (C)
near ___ you!

122 Low in the grave he lay

Christ arose 6 5 6 4 and refrain

Words and music: R Lowry (1826–1899)
Matthew 27.62, Colossians 2.15

Capo 3(G)

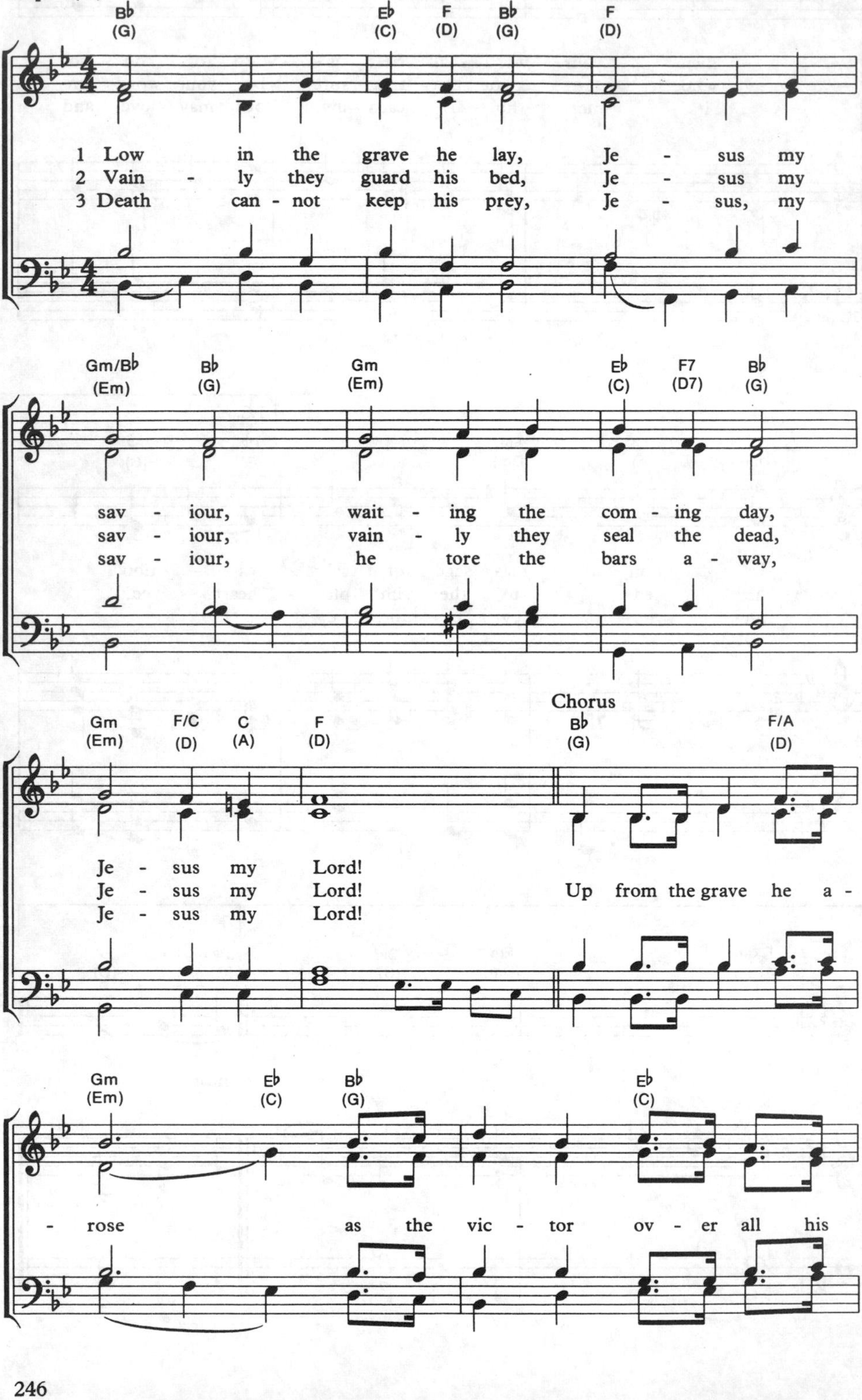
Bb (G) Eb (C) F (D) Bb (G) F (D)
1 Low in the grave he lay, Je - sus my
2 Vain - ly they guard his bed, Je - sus my
3 Death can - not keep his prey, Je - sus, my
Gm/Bb (Em) Bb (G) Gm (Em) Eb (C) F7 (D7) Bb (G)
sav - iour, wait - ing the com - ing day,
sav - iour, vain - ly they seal the dead,
sav - iour, he tore the bars a - way,
Gm (Em) F/C (D) C (A) F (D)
Je - sus my Lord!
Je - sus my Lord!
Je - sus my Lord!
Chorus
Bb (G) F/A (D)
Up from the grave he a -
Gm (Em) Eb (C) Bb (G) Eb (C)
- rose as the vic - tor ov - er all his

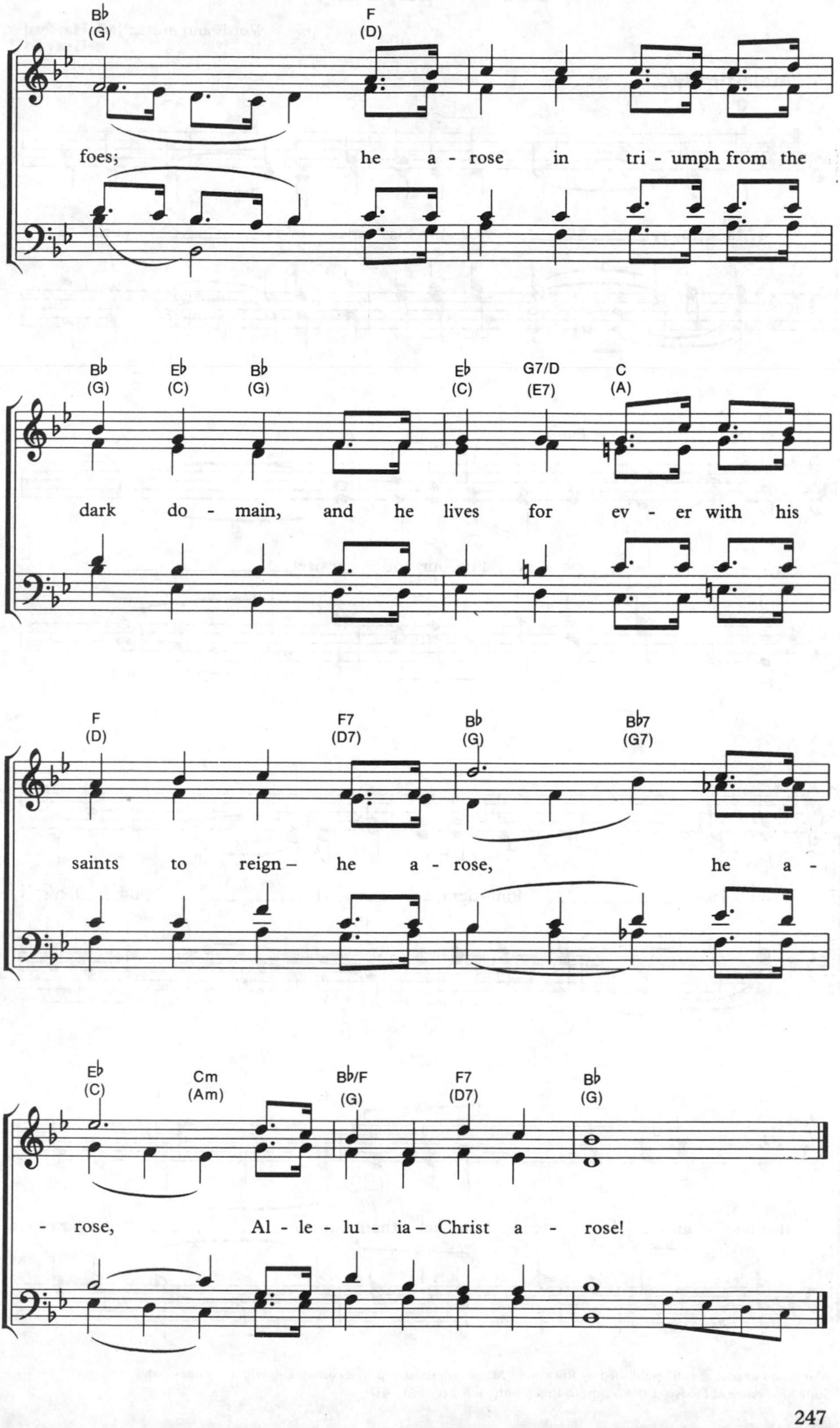
B♭ (G) F (D)
foes; he a - rose in tri - umph from the
B♭ (G) E♭ (C) B♭ (G) E♭ (C) G7/D (E7) C (A)
dark do - main, and he lives for ev - er with his
F (D) F7 (D7) B♭ (G) B♭7 (G7)
saints to reign – he a - rose, he a -
E♭ (C) Cm (Am) B♭/F (G) F7 (D7) B♭ (G)
- rose, Al - le - lu - ia – Christ a - rose!

123 Majesty

Words and music: Jack Hayford
Hebrews 1.3

Majestically

G C Am
Ma - jes- ty — worship his ma - jes-ty; — un - to
G Em Am D
Je - sus be glo - ry, hon-our and praise! —
G C Am
Ma - jes-ty, — king-dom, au - tho - ri - ty, — flow from his
G Em Am D G C G
throne un - to his own: his an - them raise! — So ex -

Words and music: © 1981 published by Rocksmith Music, administered by Leosong Copyright Services Ltd, Suite 8, Westmead House, 123 Westmead Road, Sutton, Surrey SM1 4JH

D Am D G
- alt, lift up-on high the name of Je - sus; mag-ni -
D Am D B7 D
- fy, come, glo-ri - fy Christ Je-sus the king.
G C Am
Ma - jes- ty worship his ma - jes-ty, Je-sus who
G Em Am D G C G
died, now glo - ri - fied, King of all Kings!

124 Make me a channel of your peace

From the traditional prayer
Words and music: Sebastian Temple
Matthew 5.9
Music arranged Norman Warren

Prayerfully

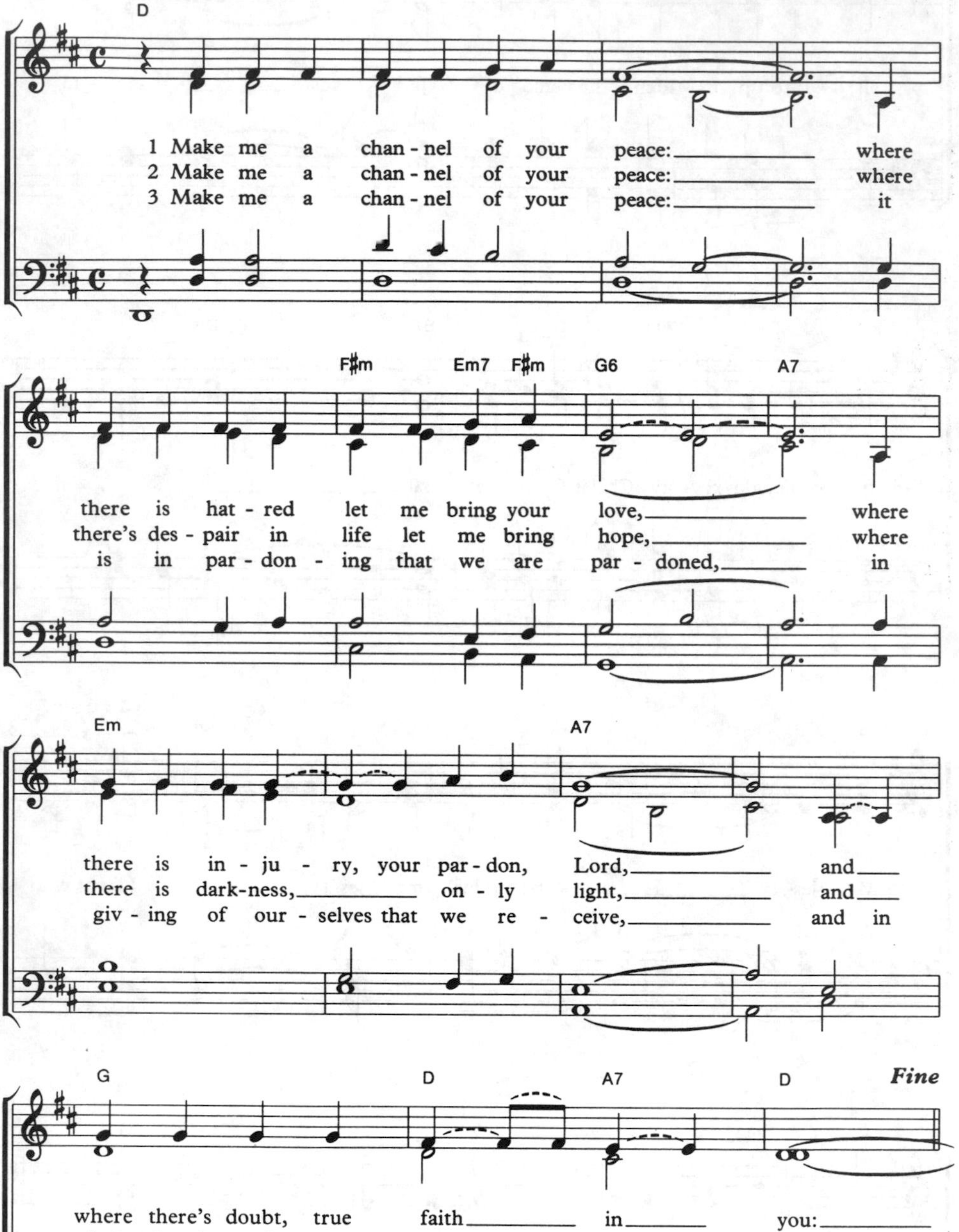
D
1 Make me a chan - nel of your peace: where
2 Make me a chan - nel of your peace: where
3 Make me a chan - nel of your peace: it
F♯m Em7 F♯m G6 A7
there is hat - red let me bring your love, where
there's des - pair in life let me bring hope, where
is in par - don - ing that we are par - doned, in
Em A7
there is in - ju - ry, your par - don, Lord, and
there is dark-ness, on - ly light, and
giv - ing of our - selves that we re - ceive, and in
G D A7 D Fine
where there's doubt, true faith in you:
where there's sad - ness, ev - er joy:
dy - ing that we're born to e - ter - nal life.

Words and music: © 1967 Franciscan Community Center
1229 South Santee Street, Los Angeles, California 90015, USA

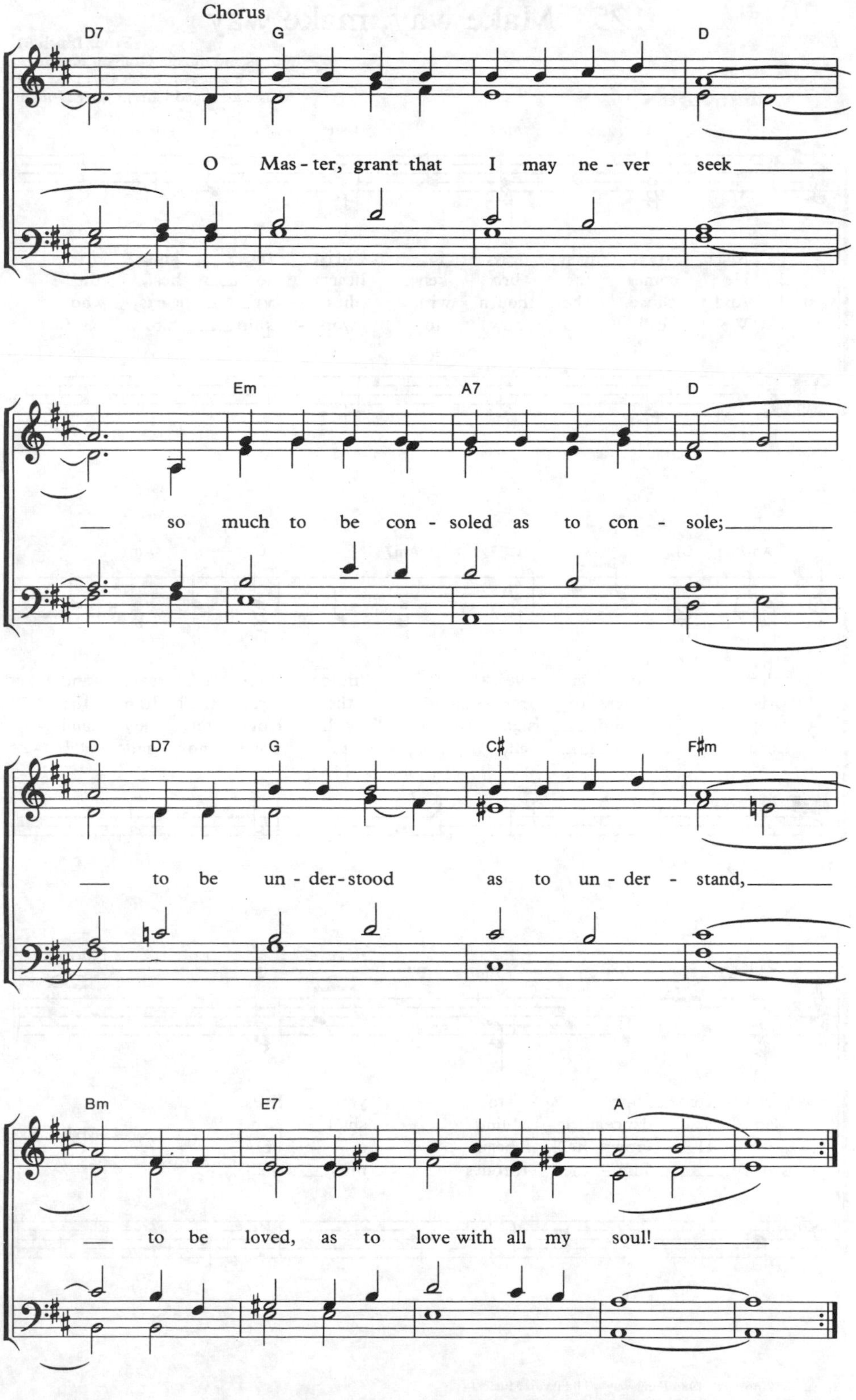
Chorus
D7 G D
O Mas-ter, grant that I may ne-ver seek
Em A7 D
so much to be con-soled as to con-sole;
D D7 G C♯ F♯m
to be un-der-stood as to un-der-stand,
Bm E7 A
to be loved, as to love with all my soul!

Make Way 1: procession song

125 Make way, make way

From Isaiah 61
Words and music: Graham Kendrick
Psalm 24.7, Isaiah 61.1, Luke 4.18
Music arranged Christopher Norton

With strength

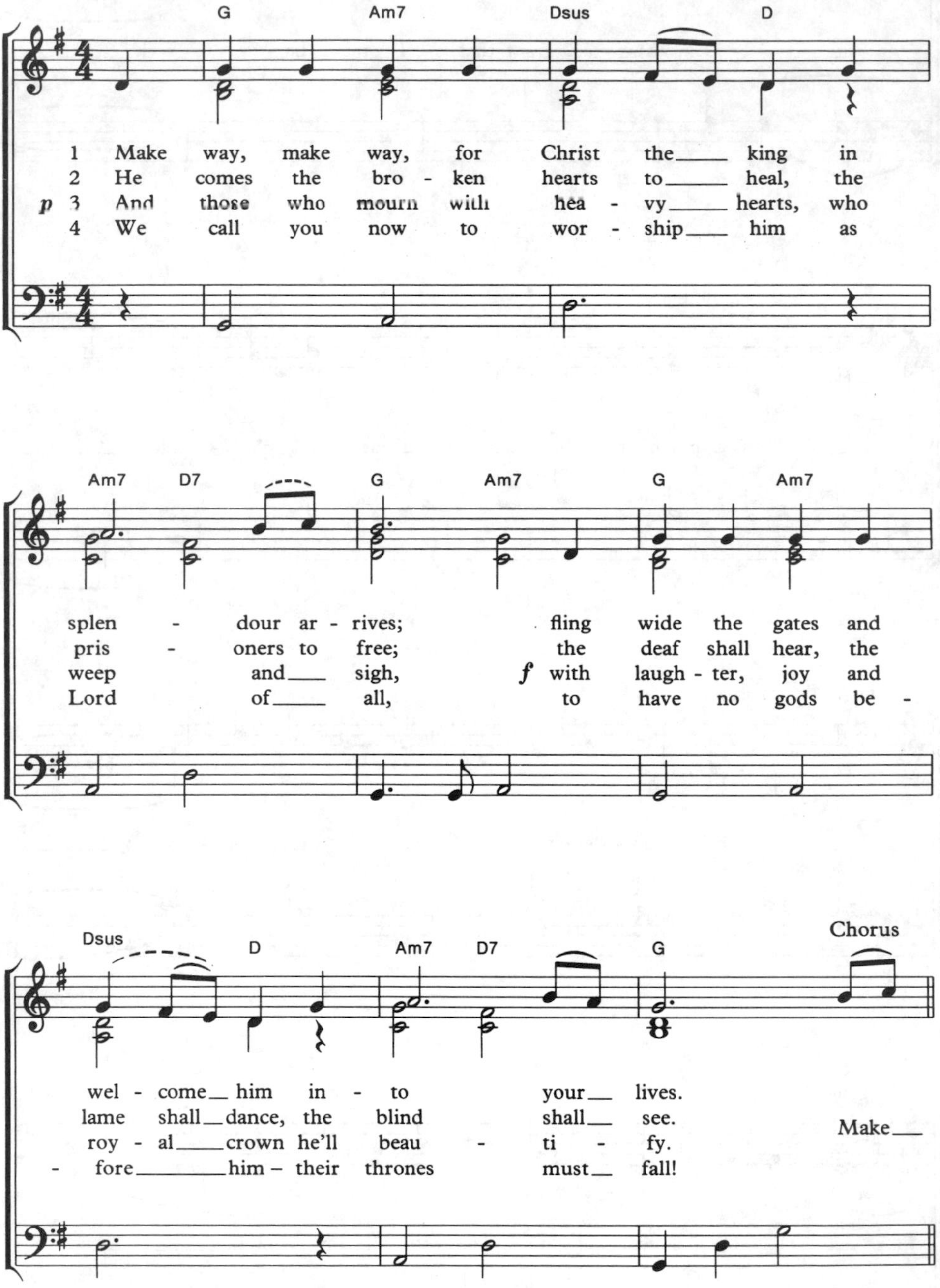
G Am7 Dsus D
1 Make way, make way, for Christ the king in
2 He comes the bro - ken hearts to heal, the
p 3 And those who mourn with hea - vy hearts, who
4 We call you now to wor - ship him as
Am7 D7 G Am7 G Am7
splen - dour ar - rives; fling wide the gates and
pris - oners to free; the deaf shall hear, the
weep and sigh, f with laugh - ter, joy and
Lord of all, to have no gods be -
Dsus D Am7 D7 G
Chorus
wel - come him in - to your lives.
lame shall dance, the blind shall see.
roy - al crown he'll beau - ti - fy.
- fore him – their thrones must fall!
Make

Words and music: © 1986 Kingsway's Thankyou Music,
PO Box 75, Eastbourne, East Sussex BN23 6NW

G Am7 Dsus D Em D
Part II make way, make way, for the
way, make way, for the King of kings;
Em D G Am7 Dsus D
King of kings; make way, make way,
make way, make way, and
Em D7sus D7 G C/G G
let his king - dom in!

B♭ melody version

1.
2.

Make Way 1: procession song

126 We declare

Words and music: Graham Kendrick
Luke 4.19 and 10.9

With strength

D F Em D
Chorus
D F Em D F Em
WOMEN we de-clare that the king-dom of God is
MEN We de-clare that the king-dom of God is here,
to continue
D F Em D F Em
here,
we de-clare that the king-dom of God is
we de-clare that the king-dom of God is here, a -
to end
D
Fine
D F Em D F Em
here a - mong you,
- here. -mong you, a -

Words and music: © 1986 Kingsway's Thankyou Music,
PO Box 75, Eastbourne, East Sussex BN23 6NW

D F Em D
a - mong you. The
- mong you,
Verse
C/D D
ALL blind see, the deaf hear, the lame men are walk - ing,
C/D D C/D
sick-ness - es flee at his voice; the dead live a - gain and the
D.𝄋 al Fine
D C/D Asus A
poor hear the good news: Je-sus is king – so re - joice!

Sequence: Chorus twice, Verse, Chorus, Verse, Chorus twice.

Make Way 1: procession song

127 Let God arise

Triumphantly

From Psalm 68
Words and music: Graham Kendrick

Chorus

D A6 D D7/F♯ G Bm A7 D
Let God a - rise, and let his en - e - mies be scat - tered, and
Em A7 Em A7 A7/C♯
let those who hate him flee be - fore___ him;___
D G D D7/F♯ G Bm A7 D
let God a - rise, and let his en - e - mies be scat - tered, and
Em A7 A D G/D D
Fine
let those who hate him flee a - way.

Words and music: © 1984 Kingsway's Thankyou Music,
PO Box 75, Eastbourne, East Sussex BN23 6NW

Verse
A A7 A D
WOMEN
the right - eous be
MEN
But let the right - eous be glad;
E E7 A F♯
glad, let them ex - ult be - fore God;
let them ex - ult be-fore God, let them re -
F♯ Bm Bm/A E7 E7/G♯ A
O let them re - joice for the king
- joice with glad - ness, build-ing up a high - way for the king.
D.C. al Fine
Asus A Asus A Asus G7 A
in the name of the Lord!
rit.
We go in the name of the Lord: let the shout go up in the name of the Lord!

Make Way 1: procession song

128 The earth is the Lord's

Words and music: Graham Kendrick
Psalm 24

With strength

Chorus
D G D
MEN The earth is the Lord's MEN The
WOMEN and ev - ery-thing in it.
Em A
earth is the Lord's, MEN The earth is the
WOMEN the work of his hands.
G D G
Lord's ALL and all things were
WOMEN and ev - ery - thing in it:
3rd time to Coda
D A7 D Dsus D
made for his glo - ry!

Words and music: © 1986 Kingsway's Thankyou Music,
PO Box 75, Eastbourne, East Sussex BN23 6NW

Verse
A7 D Bm Em
The moun-tains are his, the seas and the
A7 D Bm Em A
is-lands, the ci-ties and towns, the hou-ses and streets: let
D Bm Em A7 G
re-bels bow down and wor-ship be-fore him, for all things were
repeat twice
D A7 D Dsus D A7
made for his glo - ry! The

CODA
A7 D G D
MEN The earth is the Lord's WOMEN The
WOMEN and ev-ery-thing in it.
Em A
earth is the Lord's, MEN The earth is the
WOMEN the work of his hands.
G D G
Lord's ALL and all things were
WOMEN and ev - ery - thing in it:
D G D G
made, yes, all things were made, and all things were
D A7 D
made for his glo - ry!

Make Way 1: procession song

129 We believe in God the Father

Capo 2(Em)

Words and music: Graham Kendrick

With strength
1 We be - lieve in God the Fa - ther,
2 We be - lieve he sends his Spi - rit
mak - er of the u - ni - verse, and in Christ his
on his church with gifts of power; God, his word of
Son our sav - iour, come to us by vir - gin birth.
truth af - firm - ing, sends us to the na - tions now.
We be - lieve he died to save us, bore our sins, was
He will come a - gain in glo - ry, judge the liv - ing

Words and music: © 1986 Kingsway's Thankyou Music,
PO Box 75, Eastbourne, East Sussex BN23 6NW

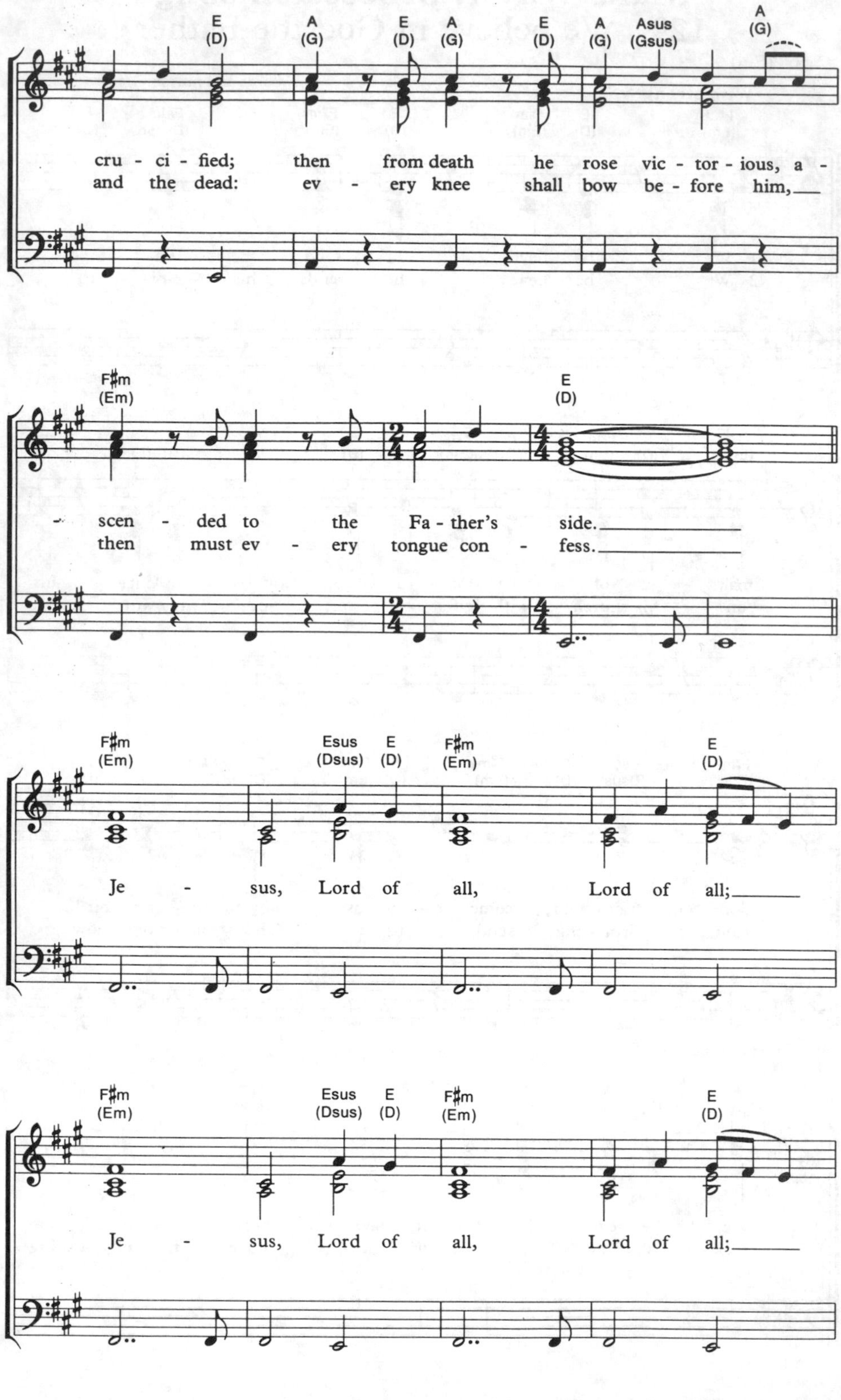
E (D) A (G) E (D) A (G) E (D) A (G) Asus (Gsus) A (G)
cru - ci - fied; then from death he rose vic - tor - ious, a -
and the dead: ev - ery knee shall bow be - fore him,
F♯m (Em) E (D)
- scen - ded to the Fa - ther's side.
then must ev - ery tongue con - fess.
F♯m (Em) Esus (Dsus) E (D) F♯m (Em) E (D)
Je - sus, Lord of all, Lord of all;
F♯m (Em) Esus (Dsus) E (D) F♯m (Em) E (D)
Je - sus, Lord of all, Lord of all;

A (G) Asus (Gsus) A (G) F♯m (Em) E (D)
Je - sus, Lord of all, Lord of all;
A (G) Asus (Gsus) A (G) F♯m (Em)
Je - sus, Lord of all, Lord of
E (D) F♯ (E) E (D)
all; name a - bove all names, name a - bove
F♯ (E) E (D) F♯ (E)
last time
rit.
all names! Name a - bove all names!

Make Way 1: procession song

130 Jesus put this song into our hearts

Capo 5(Am)

Words and music: Graham Kendrick
Psalms 40.3 and 126.5, Ephesians 4.13
arranged for piano Christopher Norton
Obligato: David Peacock

Hebrew style, getting faster

Dm
(Am)
A7
(E7)
1 Je - sus put this song in - to our hearts,
2 Je - sus taught us how to live in har - mo - ny,
3 Je - sus taught us how to be a fa - mi - ly,
4 Je - sus turned our sor - row in - to danc - ing,
5 *Instrumental*
Dm
(Am)
Je - sus put this song in - to our hearts;
Je - sus taught us how to live in har - mo - ny;
Je - sus taught us how to be a fa - mi - ly;
Je - sus turned our sor - row in - to danc - ing,
D7
(A7)
Gm
(Em)
it's a song of joy no - one can take a - way.
dif - ferent fa - ces, dif - ferent ra - ces, he made us one –
lov - ing one a - no - ther with the love that he gives –
changed our tears of sad - ness in - to ri - vers of joy –

Words and music: © 1986 Kingsway's Thankyou Music,
PO Box 75, Eastbourne, East Sussex BN23 6NW

A7
(E7)
Je - sus put this song ___ in - to our
Je - sus taught us how to live ___ in har - mo -
Je - sus taught us how to be ___ a fa - mi -
Je - sus turned our sor - rows ___ in - to a

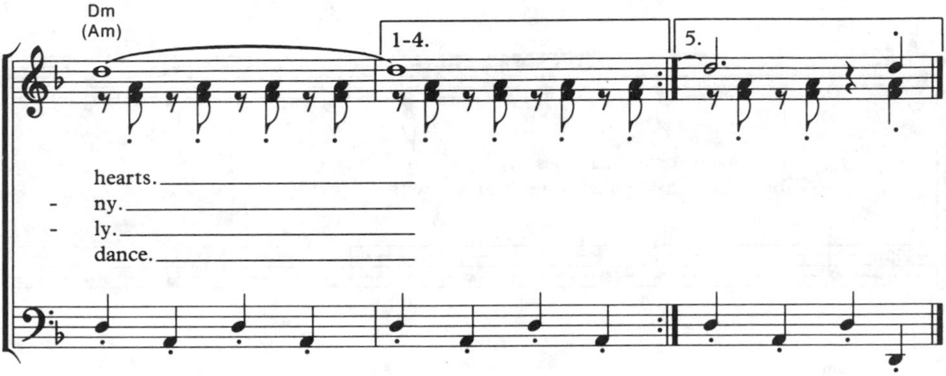
Dm
(Am)
1-4.
5.
hearts. ___
- ny. ___
- ly. ___
dance. ___

Obligato part (violins/flutes/oboes etc)

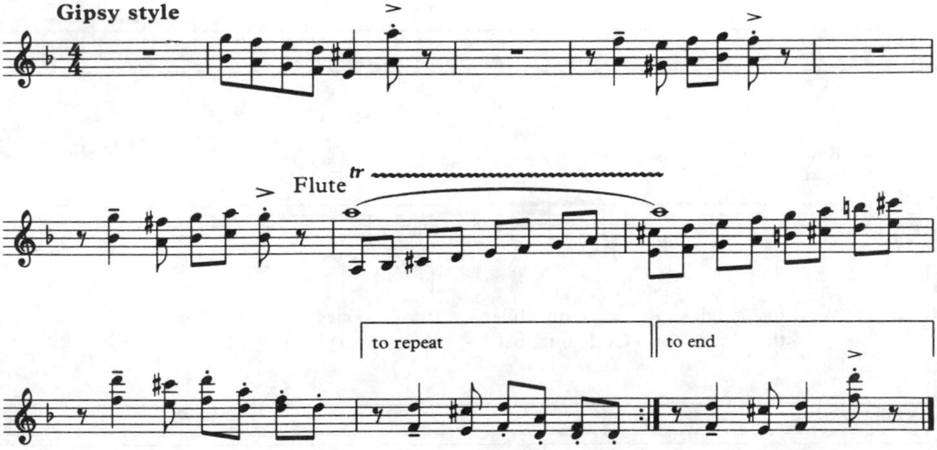
Gipsy style
Flute
tr
to repeat
to end

Make Way 1: procession song

131 The Lord is marching out

Capo 2(Am)

Words and music: Graham Kendrick

March

Bm
(Am)
A
(G)
1 The Lord is march-ing out in splen - dour,
2 His ar - my march - es out with danc - ing,
Bm
(Am)
A
(G)
in awe - some ma - jes - ty he rides
for he has filled our hearts with joy:
Bm
(Am)
A
(G)
for truth, hu - mil - i - ty and jus - tice;
be glad the King-dom is ad - vanc - ing,
Bm
(Am)
F♯
(E)
Chorus
his migh - ty ar - my fills the skies.
the love of God our bat - tle - cry.
O give

Words and music: © 1986 Kingsway's Thankyou Music,
PO Box 75, Eastbourne, East Sussex BN23 6NW

Bm (Am) A (G) F♯m (Em)
thanks to the Lord for his love en - dures; O give
Bm (Am) A (G) F♯m (Em)
thanks to the Lord for his love en - dures; O give
Bm (Am) A (G) F♯m (Em)
thanks to the Lord for his love en - dures for
Bm (Am) A (G) Bm (Am)
ev - er, for ev - er!
to repeat
to end
A (G) A (G) Bm (Am)
for ev - er!

Make Way 1: procession song

132 In the tomb so cold

Christ is risen

Words and music: Graham Kendrick
Matthew 27.60 and 28.6, Mark 15.46 and 16.9
Luke 23.53 and 24.34, John 19.41, 1 Corinthians 15.20
arranged for piano Christopher Norton

Triumphantly

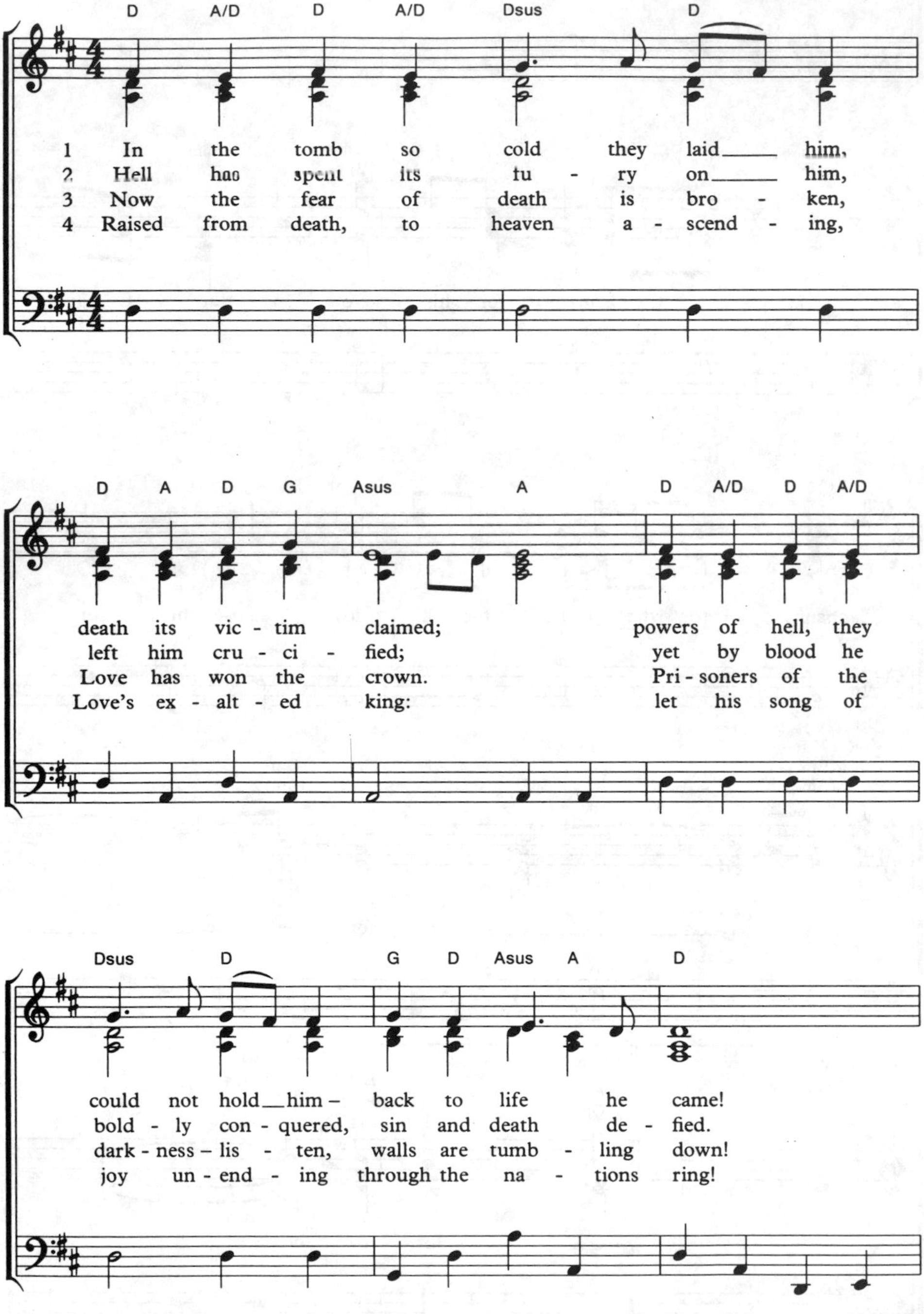
D A/D D A/D Dsus D
1 In the tomb so cold they laid him,
2 Hell has spent its fu - ry on him,
3 Now the fear of death is bro - ken,
4 Raised from death, to heaven a - scend - ing,
D A D G Asus A D A/D D A/D
death its vic - tim claimed; powers of hell, they
left him cru - ci - fied; yet by blood he
Love has won the crown. Pri - soners of the
Love's ex - alt - ed king: let his song of
Dsus D G D Asus A D
could not hold him – back to life he came!
bold - ly con - quered, sin and death de - fied.
dark - ness – lis - ten, walls are tumb - ling down!
joy un - end - ing through the na - tions ring!

Words and music: © 1986 Kingsway's Thankyou Music,
PO Box 75, Eastbourne, East Sussex BN23 6NW

D A D A D G D
WOMEN Christ is ris - en!
MEN Christ is ris - en, Death has been con-quered,
G D D A D
death has been con - quered!
Christ is ris - en,
A D G Bm Asus A
Christ is ris - en: ALL he shall reign for ev -
ALL he shall reign for ev -
last time
D Em A D
- er!

133 Love is his word

Words: Luke Connaughton (1917–1979)
Matthew 12.50 and 26.26, Mark3.35 and 14.22
Luke 8.21 and 22.14, John 13.34, 1 Corinthians 11.23
Music: Anthony Milner

Cresswell 8 8 9 7 10 7

With strength

C F Am G/D C/E F G Dm G
1 Love is his word, love is his way, feast-ing with all, fast-ing a-lone,
2 Love is his way, love is his mark, shar-ing his last Pass-ov-er feast,
3 Love is his mark, love is his sign, bread for our strength, wine for our joy,
C D7/A G/B Am D7 G
liv - ing and dy - ing, ris - ing a - gain, love, on - ly love, is his way:
Christ at his ta - ble, host to the twelve, love, on - ly love, is his mark:
'This is my bo - dy, this is my blood' – love, on - ly love, is his sign:
C C/E F G C F Dm G7 C
Rich - er than gold is the love of my Lord, bet - ter than splen-dour and wealth.

4 Love is his sign, love is his news,
'Do this,' he said,'lest you forget
all my deep sorrow, all my dear blood' –
love, only love, is his news:
Richer than gold . . .

5 Love is his news, love is his name,
we are his own, chosen and called,
family, brethren, cousins and kin,
love, only love, is his name:
Richer than gold . . .

6 Love is his name, love is his law,
hear his command, all who are his:
'Love one another, I have loved you' –
love, only love, is his law.
Richer than gold . . .

7 Love is his law, love is his word:
love of the Lord, Father and Word,
love of the Spirit, God ever one,
love, only love, is his word:
Richer than gold . . .

Words and music: © Mc Crimmon Publishing Co Ltd,
10–12 High Street, Great Wakering, Essex SS3 0EQ

134 May our worship be acceptable

Words and music: Graham Kendrick
Psalm 19.1

Prayerfully
E Emaj7 E6 Emaj7 Amaj7 A/B E A/B B
May our wor-ship be ac-cept-a-ble in your sight, O Lord;
E Emaj7 E6 Emaj7 Amaj7 A/B B6 E D/E E7
may our wor-ship be ac-cept-a-ble in your sight, O Lord;
Amaj7 B/A G♯m7 C♯m7 F♯9 Amaj7 Dmaj7 A/B
may the words of my mouth be pure, and the me-di-ta-tion of my heart;
B E Emaj7 E6 Emaj7 Amaj7 A/B B6 E
may our wor-ship be ac-cept-a-ble in your sight, O Lord.

Words and music: © 1988 Make Way Music,
PO Box 263, Croydon, Surrey CR9 5AP.
International copyright secured. All rights reserved. Used by permission.

135 May the fragrance of Jesus

Words and music: Graham Kendrick
Ephesians 5.2
Music arranged for piano Christopher Norton

Worshipfully
D Dmaj7 Gmaj7 G/A A7 D Dmaj7
WOMEN 1 May the fra-grance of
2 May the glo - ry of
3 May the beau - ty of
MEN
1 May the fra-grance of Je - sus fill this place,
2 May the glo - ry of Je - sus fill his church,
3 May the beau - ty of Je - sus fill my life,
Gmaj7 G/A A7 D Dmaj7 Gmaj7 G/A A7
Je - sus fill this place,
Je - sus fill his church,
Je - sus fill my life,
may the fra-grance of Je - sus fill this
may the glo - ry of Je - sus fill his
may the beau - ty of Je - sus fill my
D Dmaj7 Gmaj7 Asus A7 G Bm
love - ly fra - grance of Je - sus, ris - ing
ra - diant glo - ry of Je - sus, shin - ing
per - fect beau - ty of Je - sus, fill my
place; ris - ing
church; shin - ing
life: fill my

Words and music: © 1986 Kingsway's Thankyou Music, PO Box 75, Eastbourne, East Sussex BN23 6NW

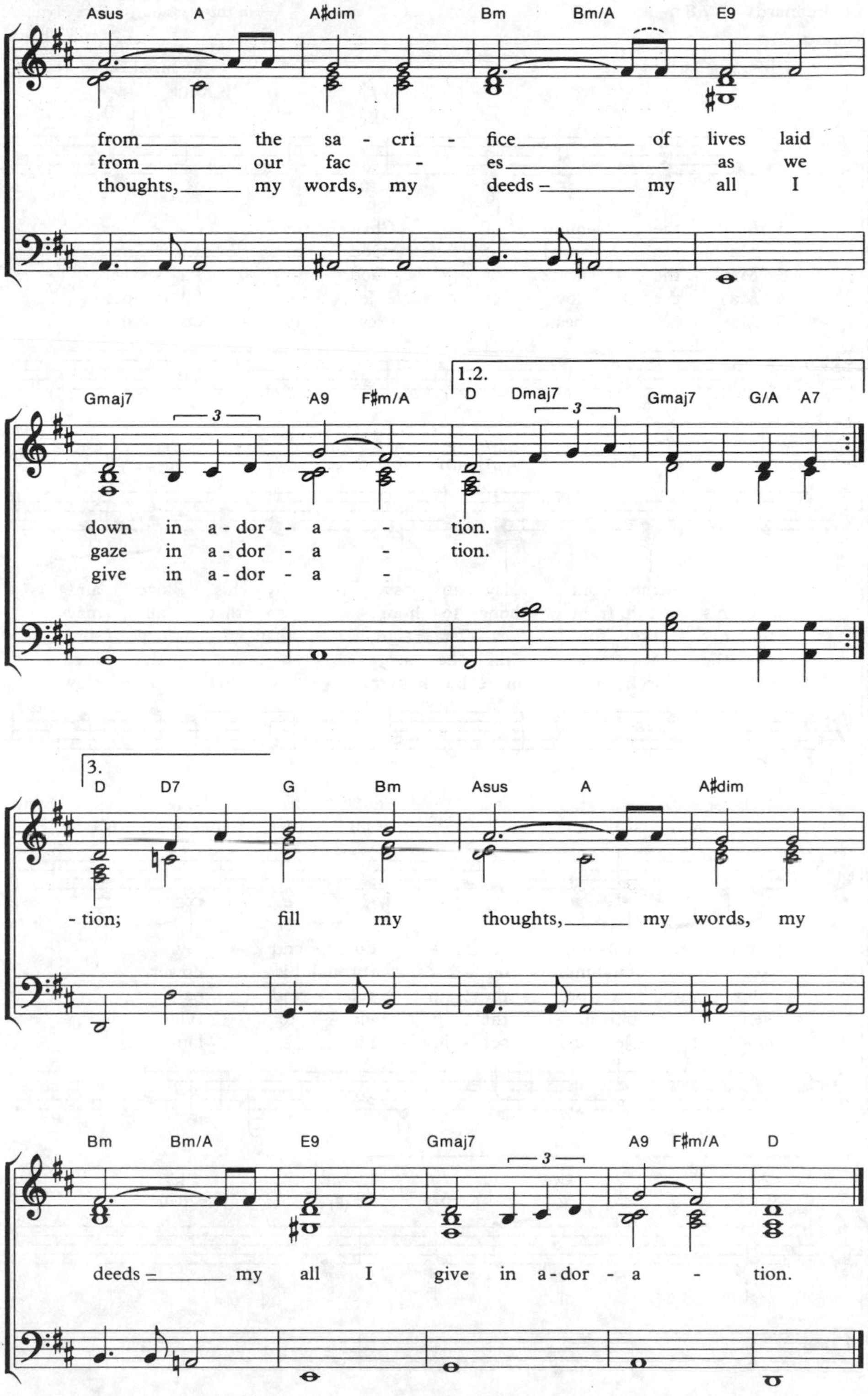
Asus A A♯dim Bm Bm/A E9
from the sa - cri - fice of lives laid
from our fac - es as we
thoughts, my words, my deeds – my all I
Gmaj7 A9 F♯m/A
1.2.
D Dmaj7 Gmaj7 G/A A7
3
down in a - dor - a - tion.
gaze in a - dor - a - tion.
give in a - dor - a -
3.
D D7 G Bm Asus A A♯dim
- tion; fill my thoughts, my words, my
Bm Bm/A E9 Gmaj7 A9 F♯m/A D
deeds – my all I give in a - dor - a - tion.

136 May the mind of Christ my saviour

St. Leonards 8 7 8 5
Capo 3(C)

Words: K B Wilkinson (1859–1928)
in this version Jubilate Hymns
Philippians 2.5
Music: A C Barham Gould
arranged David Peacock

Flowing
E♭ (C) A♭ (F) A♭/B♭ B♭7 (G7)
1 May the mind of Christ my sav - iour
2 May the word of God en - rich me
3 May the peace of God my Fa - ther
4 May the love of Je - sus fill me
5 May his beau - ty rest up - on me
E♭ (C) Cm7 (Am7) F (D) B♭ (G) E♭/G (C) Fm/A♭ (Dm) E♭/G (C)
live in me from day to day, by his love and
with his truth, from hour to hour; so that all may
in my life for ev - er reign, that I may be
as the wa - ters fill the sea, him ex - alt - ing,
as I seek to make him known; so that all may
B♭7/F (G7) Cm/E♭ (Am) A♭6 (F6) E♭/G (C) F7 (D7) Fm/B♭ (Dm) B♭7 (G7) E♭sus (Csus) E♭ (C) Fine
power con - trol - ling all I do and say.
see I tri - umph on - ly through his power.
calm to com - fort those in grief and pain.
self a - bas - ing – this is vic - to - ry!
look to Je - sus, see - ing him a - lone.
Link
Fm7 (Dm7) E♭/G (C) F7/A (D7) A♭/B♭ (F) B♭ (G) D.C.

Music: © Executors of the late A C Barham Gould
Words: © in this version Jubilate Hymns †

137 Morning has broken

Bunessan 10 9 10 9

Words: E Farjeon (1881–1965)
Music: Gaelic melody
arranged Noël Tredinnick

Gently

C C/E Dm/F G Dm7 G7
1 Morn - ing has bro - ken like the first morn - ing;
2 Sweet the rain's new fall, sun - lit from hea - ven,
3 Mine is the sun - light, mine is the morn - ing
C G/B Am C/E D7/F♯ Gsus G7
black - bird has spo - ken like the first bird:
like the first dew fall on the first grass:
born of the one light E - den saw play:
Em Am Dm7 C/E F Dm7 G7/D
praise for the sing - ing, praise for the morn - ing,
praise for the sweet - ness of the wet gar - den,
praise with e - la - tion, praise ev - ery morn - ing,
C C/G Dm7/F Gsus G7 C
praise from them spring - ing fresh from the word!
sprung in com - plete - ness where his feet pass.
God's re - cre - a - tion of the new day!

Music arrangement: © Noël Tredinnick/Jubilate Hymns †

Words: © David Higham Associates Ltd,
5–8 Lower John Street, Golden Square, London W1R 4HA

138 Meekness and majesty

This is your God

Words and music: Graham Kendrick
Philippians 2.5, Hebrews 1.3 and 2.8, 2 Peter 1.16
Music arranged Christopher Norton

Thoughtfully

C Am7 Em7 Am7
1 Meek - ness and maj - es - ty, man - hood and de - i - ty,
2 Fath - er's pure ra - di - ance, per - fect in in - no-cence,
3 Wis - dom un - search - a - ble, God the in - vi - si - ble,
C Am7 D9 G7sus G7
in per - fect har - mo - ny – the man who is God:
yet learns o - be - di - ence to death on a cross:
love in - de - struct - i - ble in frail - ty ap - pears:
C C/B♭ F F♯dim
Lord of e - ter - ni - ty dwells in hu - man - i - ty,
suffer - ing to give us life, conquer - ing through sac - ri - fice –
Lord of in - fin - i - ty, stoop - ing so ten - der - ly,
Em7 Am Dm7 C/G G7 C
kneels in hu - mil - i - ty and wash - es our feet.
and, as they cru - ci - fy, prays, 'Fa - ther, for - give'.
lifts our hu - man - i - ty to the heights of his throne.

Words and music: © 1986 Kingsway's Thankyou Music,
PO Box 75, Eastbourne, East Sussex BN23 6NW

Chorus
Dm7 F/G G E7 E/A Am F
Oh what a mys-te-ry – meek-ness and ma-jes-ty:
F♯dim C/G Am Dm7 G7
bow down and wor-ship, for this is your
B♭ F/A G7
God, this is your
1.2.
A♭ Gm7 C G7 F/A G7/B
God!
3.
B♭
God,
F/A G7 A♭ Gm7 C
this is your God!

139 My Lord, you wore no royal crown

Words: Christopher Idle
Matthew 20.28, Mark 10.45, Luke 19.10
Music: English traditional melody
arranged David Peacock

O Waly, Waly 8 8 8 8 (LM)

Flowing

C/D G Am7 Bm7 Em7
Part II 6 So when I stum - ble, set me right;
1 My Lord, you wore no roy - al crown; you did not
2 You ne - ver used a kil - ler's sword to end an
3 You did not live a world a - way in her - mit's
C G Am D7
com - mand my life as you re - quire;
wield the powers of state, nor did you
un - just ty - ran - ny; your on - ly
cell or des - ert cave, but felt our
Bm7 Em Bm/D Em/C♯ Cm6 G/B
let all your gifts be my de - light
need a scho - lar's gown or priest - ly
wea - pon was your word, for truth a -
pain and shared each day with those you

Music arrangement: © David Peacock / Jubilate Hymns †

Words: © Christopher Idle / Jubilate Hymns †

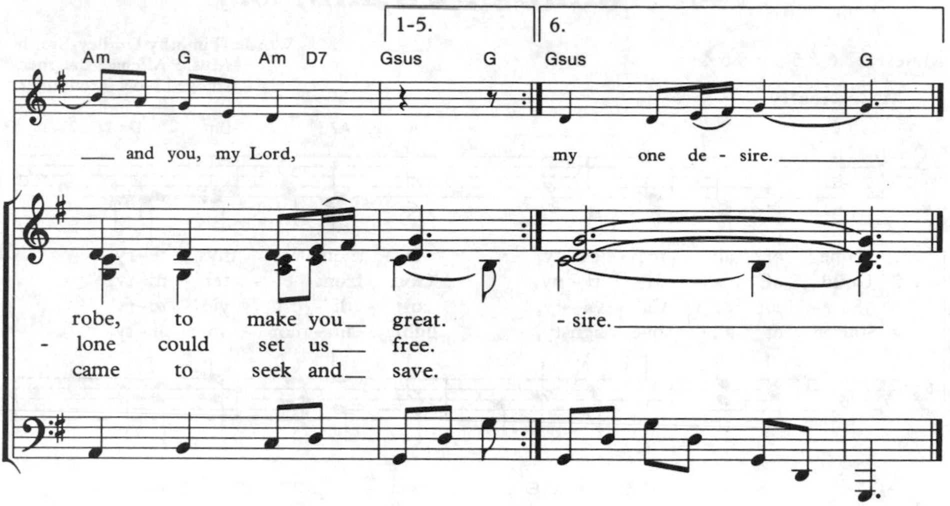
1-5.
6.
Am G Am D7 Gsus G Gsus G
and you, my Lord, my one de - sire.
robe, to make you great. - sire.
- lone could set us free.
came to seek and save.

4 You made no mean or cunning move,
chose no unworthy compromise,
but carved a track of burning love
through tangles of deceit and lies.

5 You came unequalled, undeserved,
to be what we were meant to be:
to serve, instead of being served –
a light for all the world to see.

6 So when I stumble, set me right;
command my life as you require;
let all your gifts be my delight
and you, my Lord, my one desire.

B♭ melody version

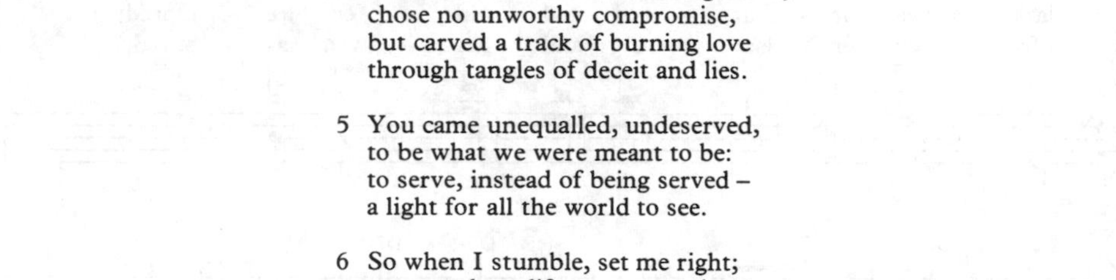

140 Name of all majesty

Words: Timothy Dudley-Smith
Music: Michael Baughen
arranged Noël Tredinnick

Majestas 6 6 5 5 6 6 6 4

Majestically

C A A7 Dm Dm7
1 Name of all ma - jes - ty, fa - thom-less mys - te - ry,
2 Child of our des - ti - ny, God from e - ter - ni - ty,
3 Sav - iour of Cal - va - ry, cost - li - est vic - to - ry,
4 Source of all sove - reign - ty, light, im - mor - ta - li - ty,
G C/E E Am G/D D7 Gsus G
king of the a - ges by an - gels a - dored;
love of the Fa - ther on sin - ners out - poured;
dark - ness de - feat - ed and Ed - en re - stored;
life ev - er - last - ing and hea - ven as - sured;
C C7 F D D7 G
power and au - tho - ri - ty, splen - dour and dig - ni - ty,
see now what God has done send - ing his on - ly Son,
born as a man to die, nailed to a cross on high,
so with the ran - somed, we praise him e - ter - nal - ly,
E E7 Am Dm Dm/G G7 C
bow to his mas - te - ry – Je - sus is Lord!
Christ the be - lov - èd One – Je - sus is Lord!
cold in the grave to lie – Je - sus is Lord!
Christ in his ma - jes - ty – Je - sus is Lord!

Music: © Michael Baughan/Jubilate Hymns †
Music arrangement: © Noël Tredinnick/Jubilate Hymns †
Words: © Timothy Dudley-Smith

141 Now let us learn of Christ

Parkstone 6 6 6 6
Capo 5(C)

Words Christopher Idle
Ephesians 4.16, 4.20, 4.32 and 6.14
Music: David Peacock

Flowing

C7 (G) F (C) Gm (Dm) F (C) C7 (G7)
1 Now let us learn of Christ: he speaks, and
(2) love in Christ as he has
(3) grow in Christ and look to
(4) stand in Christ in ev - ery
F (C) D7 (A7) Gm (Dm) C7 (G7)
we shall find he light-ens our dark mind; so let us
first loved us; as he en - dured the cross, so let us
things a - bove, and speak the truth in love; so let us
trial we meet, in all his strength com - plete; so let us
1-3.
F (C) Gm7 (Dm7) F (C) C7 (G7)
learn of Christ. 2 Now let us
love in Christ. 3 Now let us
grow in Christ. 4 Now let us
4.
F (C)
stand in Christ.

Music: © David Peacock / Jubilate Hymns †
Words: © Christopher Idle / Jubilate Hymns †

142 No more weeping . . .

Paschal Procession

1
No more weep - ing,
2
Do not fear, Je - sus has con - quered –
3
Je - sus lives – the Lord of lords
he has ri - sen from the dead! In joy - ful-ness we
4
The Lord is call - ing his dis - ci - ples to
love him, we be - lieve him, and will
5
Sing him praise all of our days –
sing him praise all of our days, for his
6
'Glo - ry in the
Capo 3(D)
F (D)
Gm (Em)
C (A)
F (D)
Keyboard

The piece works well with any combination of these lines. With small numbers, try singing just two or three. Divide the congregation into groups. . . .

Words and music: © 1983, 1984 Christopher Walker, published by OCP Publications, 5536 NE Hassolo, Portland, Oregon 97213 USA. All rights reserved. Used with permission.

. . . (Easter Procession)

Words and music: Christopher Walker
Matthew 28.5 and 28.19, Mark 16.6, Luke 24.6, John 20.14

joy has come in-to the world – he is ri - sen!
he is ri - sen from the dead!
fills the world with his glo - ry;
greet the ri - sen Lord, sing - ing . . .
send us out in-to the world; for we
fol - low him till we rise with him. The . . .
bless-ings on him for ev - er;
name is Won - der-ful, Coun-sel - lor. So . . .
high - est heaven!
B♭
(G)
Gm
(Em)
C7
(A7)

. . . Each group repeats its line again and again. To start with, establish line 1 firmly, then add others gradually, saving line 6 to the last. Lines 3, 4, and 5 can be sung in canon.

143 O give thanks to the Lord

Words and music: Joanne Pond
Psalm 100.4

With pace

A7 D G D G
O give thanks to the Lord, all you his
D A7 D G D A E7
peo-ple. O give thanks to the Lord, for he is good;
A A7 D G D G
let us praise, let us thank, let us ce - le-brate and
D A7 D G D A7 D
dance: O give thanks to the Lord, for he is good.

Words and music: © 1980 Kingsway's Thankyou Music,
PO Box 75, Eastbourne, East Sussex BN23 6NW

144 O Father, we bless your name

Words: Vanessa Strachan
John 3.7 and 13.34
Music: Guararé (c 1930)
arranged Vanessa Strachan

Panama Praise

Strong rhythmic feel

G C D7 G C D7
G C D7 G C D7
1 O
G C D G C D7
Fa-ther, we bless your name and come now to sing your prais-es;__ O Fa -
(2) - sus, we love you, Lord, and long for your king-dom com - ing; Christ Je -
(3) - rit, we need your power – break in - to our lives and fill__ us;__ O Spi -

Music: copyright controlled
Words and music arrangement: © 1987 'Don't call me Music',
6 Robin Court, 46 Lupus Street, London SW1V 3ED

G C D G C D
- ther, we bless your name and come now to sing your prais-es: we join
- sus, we love you, Lord, and long for your king-dom com - ing: you ask
- rit, we need your power - break in - to our lives and fill us: we long
Am D Am D
in with all cre-a - tion to wor-ship and hon-our you, with thanks
us to love each o - ther as you here on earth have done – no sta -
for your signs and won-ders on earth as it is in heaven, so we
G C D Am D7
that you call us chil - dren and we can be born a-new.
- tus or class or cul - ture shall keep us from be - ing one. Come and
can reach out to o - thers – all glo - ry to you be given!

G C D G C D
sing, come and sing, come and sing, come and sing to the Lord your God; come and
1.2.
G C D G C D
sing, come and sing, come and sing, come and sing to the Lord your God. 2 Christ Je -
3 O Spi -
3.
G C D G
sing to the Lord your God.

145(i) O for a thousand tongues to sing
(FIRST TUNE)

Lyngham 8 6 8 6 extended

Words: C Wesley (1707–1788)
Matthew 11.4 and 28.19, Mark 16.5,
Luke 7.22 and 24.47, Acts 1.8 and 4.12
Music: T Jarman (1782–1862)

G C G/D D7
1 O for a thou - sand tongues to
2 Je - sus, the name that charms our
3 He breaks the pow - er of can - cel - led
G D7/A G D/F♯ A7/E D
sing my great re - deem - er's praise, my
fears and bids our sor - rows cease; and
sin, he sets the pri - soner free; he
G Em D/A A D
great re - deem - er's praise,
bids our sor - rows cease –
sets the pri - soner free;
G D7/A G D/F♯ A7/E
the glo - ries of my God and
this mu - sic in the sin - ner's
his blood can make the foul - est

D G C
king, the tri - umphs of his
ears is life and health and
clean, his blood a - vailed for
the tri - umphs of his grace, the
is life and health and peace. is
his blood a - vailed for me. his
G D D7 G
grace! the tri - umphs of his grace! the
peace. is life and health and peace. is
me. his blood a - vailed for me. his
tri - umphs of his grace, the tri - umphs of his
life and health and peace, is life and health and
blood a - vailed for me, his blood a - vailed for
C G/B D7/A G Dsus D D7 G
tri - umphs of his grace!
life and health and peace.
blood a - vailed for me.
grace, the tri - umphs of his grace!
peace, is life and health and peace.
me, his blood a - vailed for me.

4 He speaks – and, listening to his voice,
new life the dead receive,
the mournful broken hearts rejoice,
the humble poor believe.

5 Hear him, you deaf! his praise, you dumb,
your loosened tongues employ;
you blind, now see your saviour come,
and leap, you lame, for joy!

6 My gracious Master and my God,
assist me to proclaim
and spread through all the earth abroad
the honours of your name.

145(ii) O, for a thousand tongues to sing

(SECOND TUNE)

Azmon 8 6 8 6

Words: C Wesley (1707–1788)
Matthew 11.4 and 28.19, Mark 16.15,
Luke 7.22 and 24.47, Acts 1.8 and 4.12
Music: Carl Gläser (1724–1829)
arranged L Mason (1792–1872)

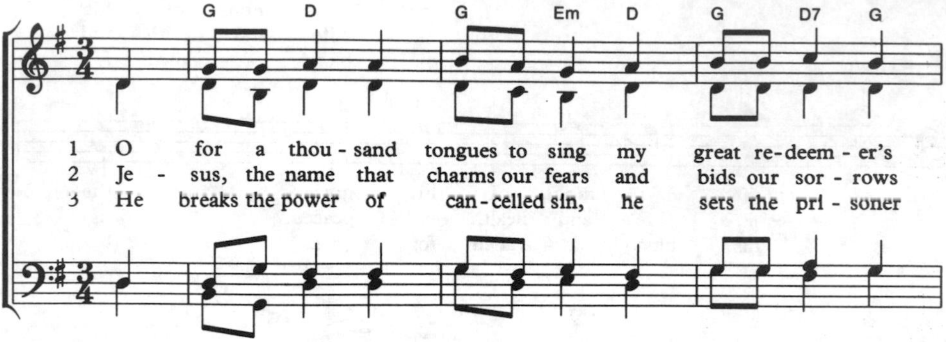
G D G Em D G D7 G
1 O for a thou - sand tongues to sing my great re-deem - er's
2 Je - sus, the name that charms our fears and bids our sor - rows
3 He breaks the power of can - celled sin, he sets the pri - soner

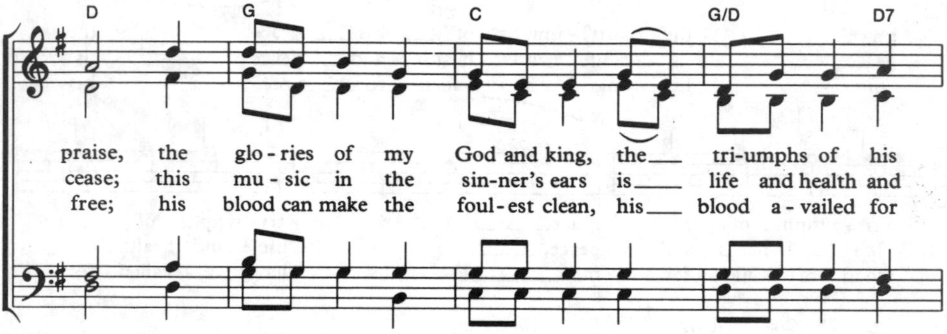
D G C G/D D7
praise, the glo - ries of my God and king, the triumphs of his
cease; this mu - sic in the sin-ner's ears is life and health and
free; his blood can make the foul - est clean, his blood a - vailed for

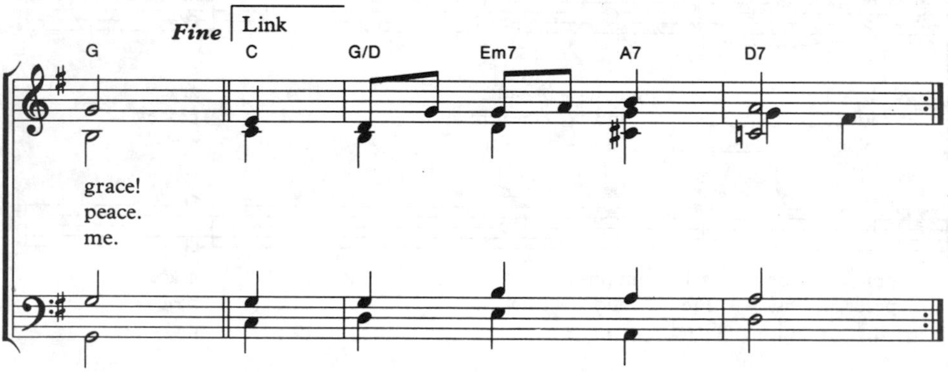
Fine
Link
G C G/D Em7 A7 D7
grace!
peace.
me.

4 He speaks – and, listening to his voice,
new life the dead receive,
the mournful broken hearts rejoice,
the humble poor believe.

5 Hear him, you deaf! his praise, you dumb,
your loosened tongues employ;
you blind, now see your saviour come,
and leap, you lame, for joy!

6 My gracious Master and my God,
assist me to proclaim
and spread through all the earth abroad
the honours of your name.

Perfect harmony

146 Oh, isn't it good

Words and music: Howard Francis
and Wayne Wilson

Acts 2.42

Soul feel

F
Dm
B♭/E♭
B♭/C
F
Dm
B♭/E♭
C7
Chorus
F
C/E
Dm7
F/G
Oh, is-n't it good___ to be as one,___ liv-ing in per - fect har-mo-ny,_
B♭+7
Am7
Dm
Gm9
Gm7
B♭/C
___ shar - ing the good___ things___ God___ has done, God___ has done?___

Words and music: © 1985 Stanmore Music

Solo verse
F9
A
G/B
A7/C♯
Dm7
Am7
Oh, is-n't it beau - ti-ful to be___ shar-ing ev-ery-thing,_
B♭maj7
Am7
Dm7
Gm7
C7
___ the way___ the Lord___ wants___ us to be?___ And I
F9
A
G/B
A7/C♯
Dm7
Am7
feel that we___ should all___ be___ shar-ing ev - ery-thing -_
B♭maj7
Am7
Dm7
B♭/C
B/C♯
___ to-ge - ther we shall stand!___

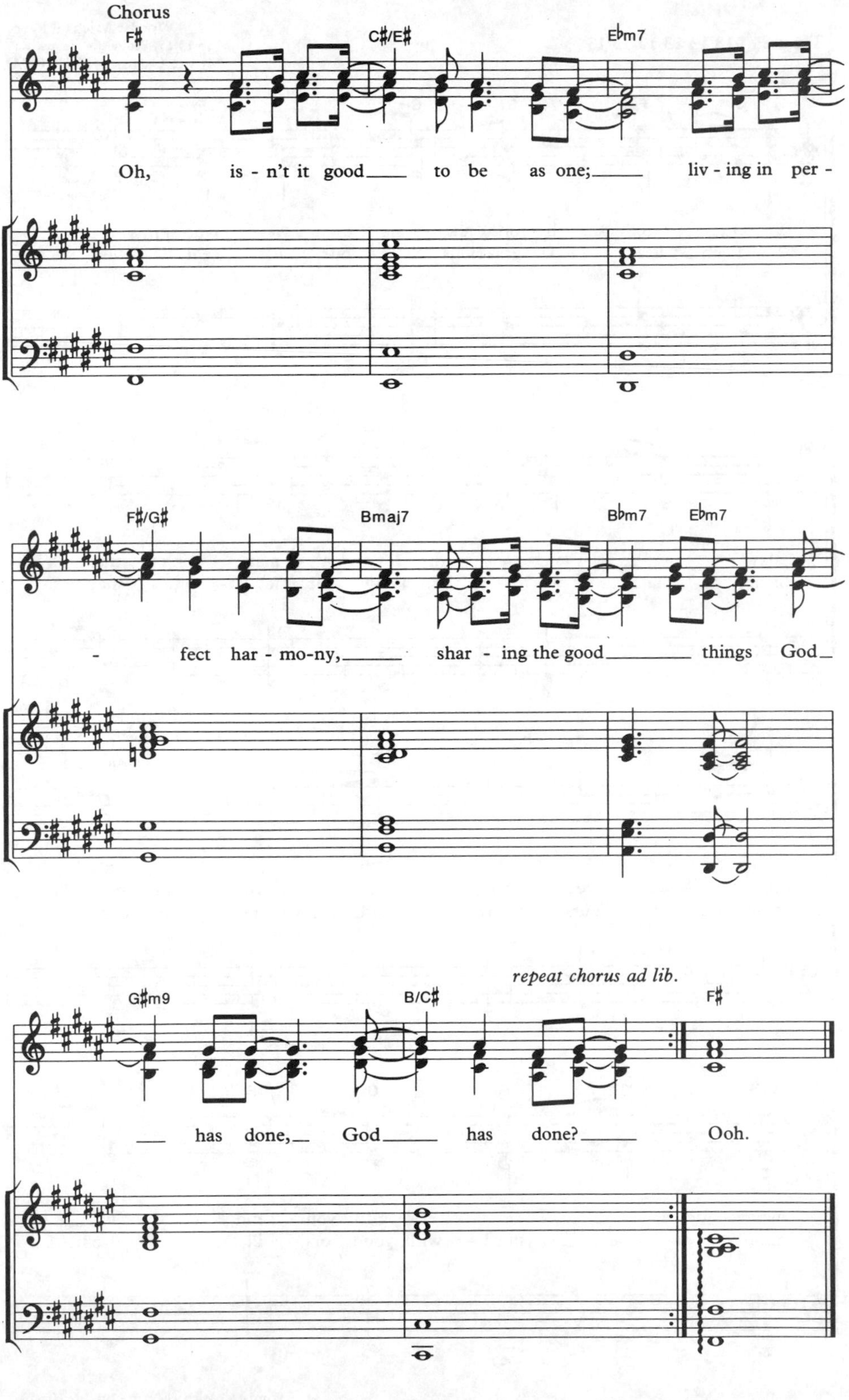
Chorus
F♯
C♯/E♯
E♭m7
Oh, is - n't it good to be as one; liv - ing in per -
F♯/G♯
Bmaj7
B♭m7
E♭m7
- fect har - mo - ny, shar - ing the good things God
G♯m9
B/C♯
repeat chorus ad lib.
F♯
has done, God has done? Ooh.

147 O God beyond all praising

Thaxted 13 13 13 13 13 13

Words: Michael Perry
Job 13.15, Psalm 8.4, James 1.17
Music: G Holst (1874–1934)

C F G7 C F G
1 O___ God be-yond all prais - ing, we wor-ship you to -
2 Then_ hear, O gra-cious Sav - iour, ac - cept the love we
Am Em F G7/D C/E
- day and___ sing the love a - maz - ing that
bring, that___ we who know your fav - our may
F C C/E G Am
songs can - not re - pay; for___ we can on - ly
serve you as our king; and___ whe - ther our to -
G/B C/E G C F Dm
won - der at___ ev - ery gift you send, at___
- mor - rows be___ filled with good or ill, we'll___

Words: © Michael Perry / Jubilate Hymns †

Am F C Dm Am
bless - ings with - out num - ber and mer - cies with - out
tri - umph through our sor - rows and rise to bless you
G F G7 C
end: we lift our hearts be - fore you and
still: to mar - vel at your beau - ty and
F G Am Em F G7/D
wait up - on your word, we hon - our and a -
glo - ry in your ways, and make a joy - ful
C F C
- dore you, our great and migh - ty Lord.
du - ty our sac - ri - fice of praise!

148 O Lord, all the world belongs to you

Words: Patrick Appleford
Matthew 5.44, Luke 22.26, Acts 17.6
Music: Patrick Appleford
arranged David Peacock

With a gentle swing

Cmaj7
C/D
D
G
D/G
1&5 O Lord, all the
2 The world's on - ly
3 The world lives di -
4 The world wants the
G
G7
C
Bm7
E7
world be - longs to you, and
lov - ing to its friends, but
- vi - ded and a - part; you
wealth to live in state, but
Am
E7/A
Am
A7/C♯
D
you are al - ways mak - ing all things new.
your way of lov - ing ne - ver ends –
draw us to - ge - ther, and we start
you show a new way to be great:
C/D
D7
G
B7/F♯
Em
What is wrong you for - give; and the
lov - ing en - em - ies too. And this
in our friend - ship to see that in
like a ser - vant you came and, if

Words and music: © 1965 and arrangement © 1988 Josef Weinberger Ltd,
12–14 Mortimer Street, London W1N 7RD

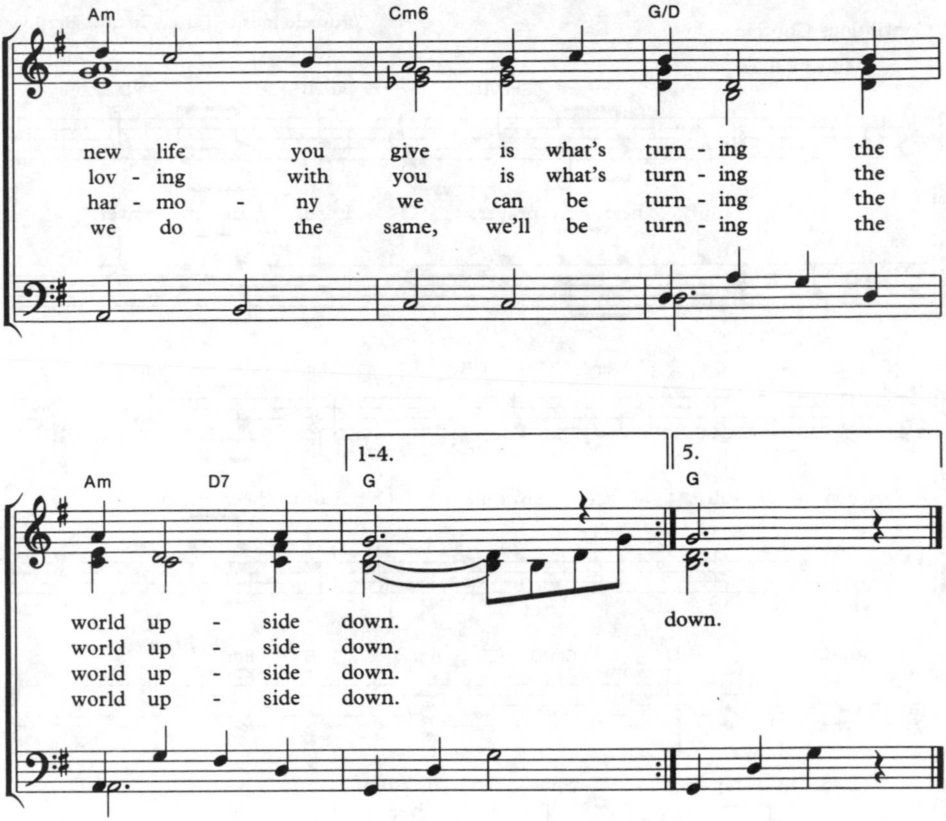
Am
Cm6
G/D
new life you give is what's turn - ing the
lov - ing with you is what's turn - ing the
har - mo - ny we can be turn - ing the
we do the same, we'll be turn - ing the
1-4.
5.
Am
D7
G
G
world up - side down. down.
world up - side down.
world up - side down.
world up - side down.

148A PRAISE SHOUT

LEADER Come, O God, and rule the earth:
ALL **all the nations are yours!**

LEADER Let them know that you are king,
ALL **sovereign over all the world! Amen.**

From Psalms 82, 83

149 O Lord, hear my prayer

Continuous Chorale

Words and music: Taizé – Jacques Berthier
Psalm 130.2

Mixed voices

Em Em7/D Am/C D
O Lord, hear my prayer; O Lord, hear my prayer:
G/B C Am6 B Em Em7/D
when I call, an - swer me – O Lord, hear my prayer; O
Am/C D Em/G Am B Em
Fine
Lord, hear my prayer; come and lis - ten to me. O

Accompaniment

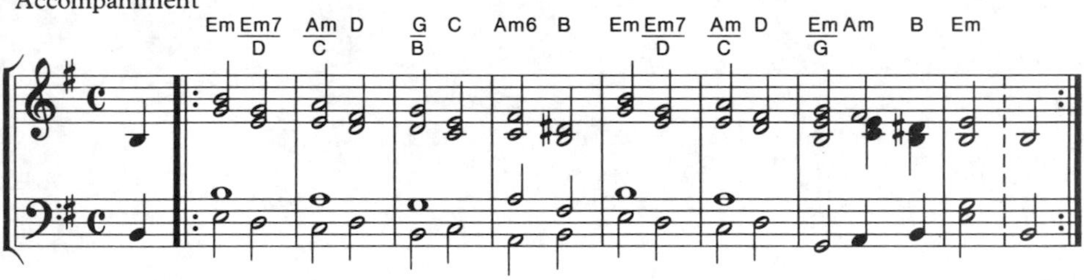
Fine
Em Em7/D Am/C D G/B C Am6 B Em Em7/D Am/C D Em/G Am B Em

Varied Accompaniments and Solos

Simple Melody

(end)

Words and music: © 1982, 1983 and 1984, Les Presses de Taizé (France).
Published by HarperCollins*Religious* and used with permission.

Recorder duo

Flute duo

Oboe

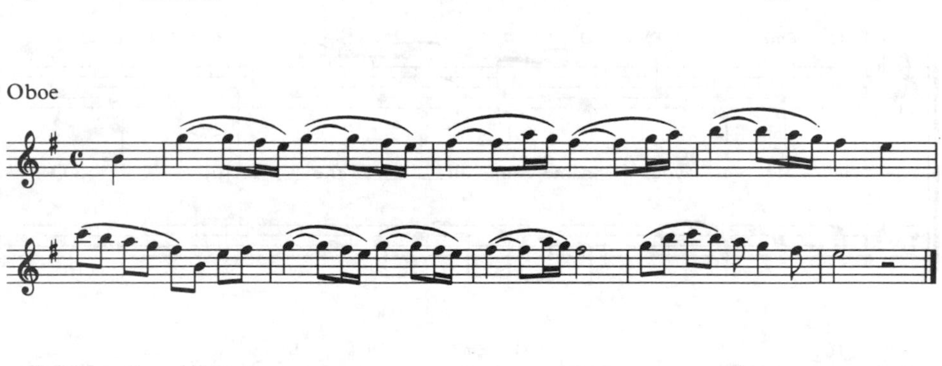

B♭ Clarinet

How majestic is your name

150 O Lord, our Lord

Words and music: Michael Smith
Psalm 8.1, Isaiah 9.8

Joyously
mf
D
G Em7 D/F♯
D
A A9/C♯ D
D
G Em7 D/F♯
D
A A9/C♯ D
O Lord, our Lord, how ma -
G Em7 D/F♯
D
A A9/C♯ D
- jes - tic is your name in all the earth; O
D
G Em7 D/F♯
D
Lord, our Lord, how ma - jes - tic is your name in all the

Words and music: © 1981 Meadowgreen Music

A A9/C♯ D G Em7 A G/B A7/C♯
earth; O — Lord, — we praise your
D G Em7 A G/B A7/C♯
name; O — Lord, — we mag-ni-fy — your
D C♯ F♯m E A A/G D/F♯ G
name. Prince of peace, migh-ty God, O — Lord — God al -
to repeat
Asus A D G Em7 D/F♯
- migh - ty! —
last time
Asus A′ D G Em7 D/F♯ D
migh - ty! —

151 O Lord, the clouds are gathering

Words and music: Graham Kendrick

Amos 5.24

With strength

C G Am Em7
1 O___ Lord,___ the clouds are gath - er - ing, the fire of judge-ment
(2) Lord,___ ov - er the na - tions now, where is the dove of
(3) Lord,___ dark powers are poised to flood our streets with hate and
(4) Lord,___ your glo - rious cross shall tower tri - um - phant in this
Fmaj7 C/G Gsus G C G
burns.___ How we have fal - len! O___ Lord,___ you stand ap -
peace?___ Her wings are bro - ken, O___ Lord,___ while pre - cious
fear.___ We must a - wak - en! O___ Lord,___ let love re -
land,___ e - vil con - found - ing; through the fire,___ your suf-fering
Am Em7 Fmaj7 Dm7 C/G Gsus G
- palled to see your laws of love so scorned.___ and lives so bro - ken.
chil - dren starve, the tools of war in - crease,___ their bread is sto - len.
- claim the lives that sin would sweep a - way,___ and let your king - dom come!
church dis - play the glo - ries of her Christ,___ prais - es re - sound - ing.
Chorus
Am Am/G F C
WOMEN have mer - cy, Lord,___ for - give us, Lord. Re -
MEN
Have mer - cy, Lord,___ For - give us, Lord,___ Re -

Words and music: © 1987 Make Way Music, PO Box 263, Croydon, Surrey CR9 5AP.
International copyright secured. All rights reserved. Used by permission.

B
B7
Esus
E
- store us, Lord; re-vive your church a - gain.
- store us, Lord; re-vive your church a - gain. Let
Am
Am/G
F
C
let jus-tice flow, like ri - vers; and
jus-tice flow, like ri - vers, and
Gsus
D7
Gsus
G
ALL
right-eous-ness like a ne - ver - fail - ing stream.
1.2.3.
4.
F/G
G
F/G
G
C
G/C
F/C
C
2 O
3 O
4 Yet, O
A ne-ver fail-ing stream.

152 O Lord, your tenderness

Words and music: Graham Kendrick
Psalm 103.8, James 5.11

With feelng
C
Dm7
O Lord, your ten - der - ness
G
C
Em7
F
melt-ing all my bit - ter-ness! O Lord, I re -
G
C
G
- ceive your love. O
C
Dm7
G
Lord, your love - li - ness, chang-ing all my

Words and music: © 1986 Kingsway's Thankyou Music,
PO Box 75, Eastbourne, East Sussex BN23 6NW

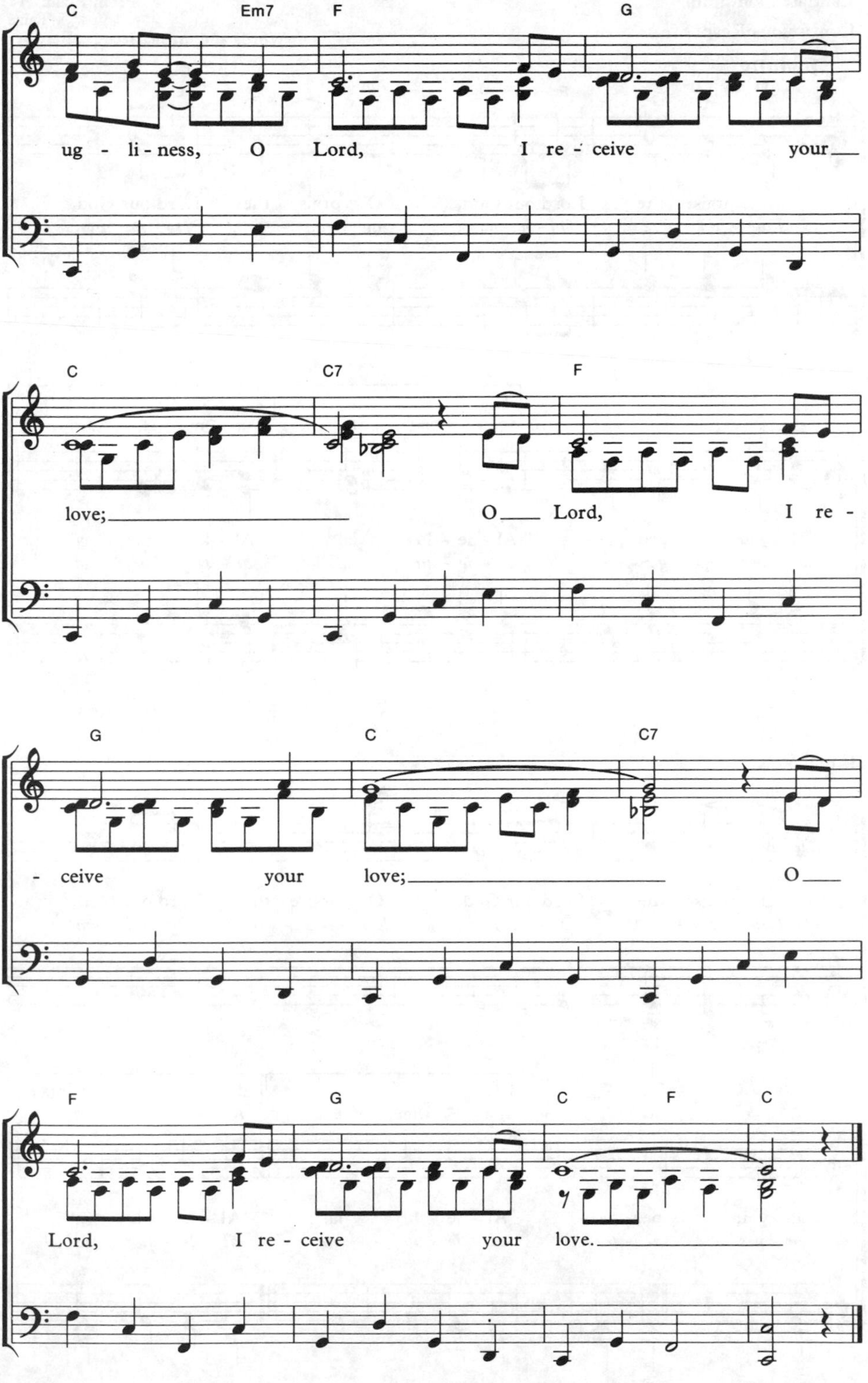
C
Em7
F
G
ug - li - ness, O Lord, I re - ceive your
C
C7
F
love; O Lord, I re -
G
C
C7
- ceive your love; O
F
G
C
F
C
Lord, I re - ceive your love.

153 O praise the Lord God

Laudate Dominum
Continuous Response

From Psalm 117
Taizé
Words and music: Jacques Berthier

Joyfully
Am E Am G
O praise the Lord our God, O praise the Lord our God,
Lau - da - te Do - mi - num, lau - da - te Do - mi - num
C G Am F Dm6 E Am Dm E Am
1. 2. D.C.
all you peo- ple – Al - le - lu - ia! Al - le - lu - ia!
om - nes gen- tes – al - le - lu - ia! al - le - lu - ia!

Equal Voices

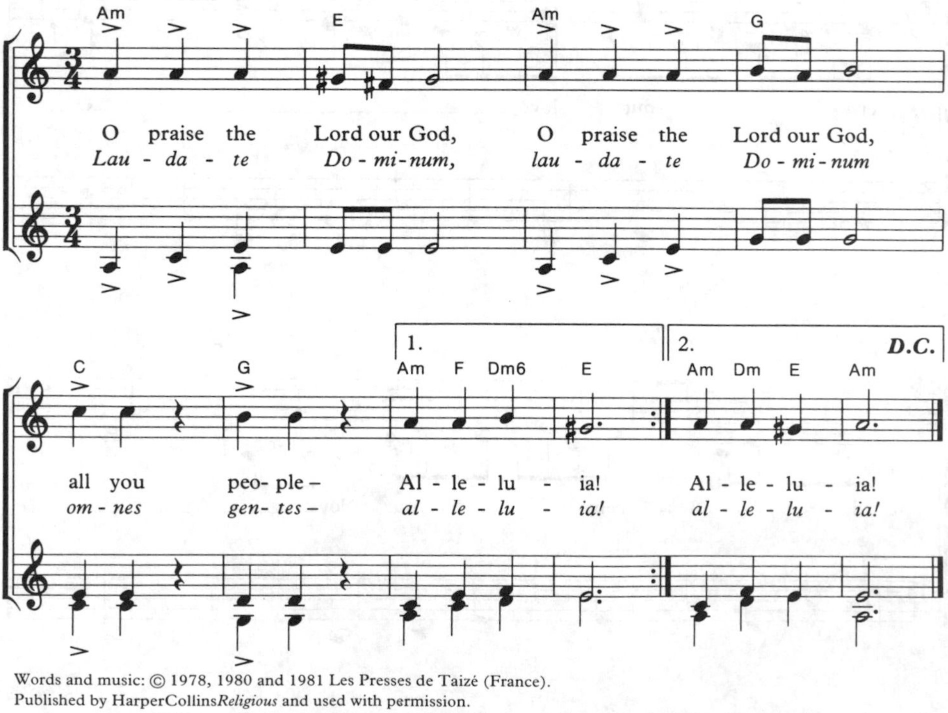
Am E Am G
O praise the Lord our God, O praise the Lord our God,
Lau - da - te Do - mi - num, lau - da - te Do - mi - num
C G Am F Dm6 E Am Dm E Am
1. 2. D.C.
all you peo- ple – Al - le - lu - ia! Al - le - lu - ia!
om - nes gen- tes – al - le - lu - ia! al - le - lu - ia!

Words and music: © 1978, 1980 and 1981 Les Presses de Taizé (France).
Published by HarperCollins*Religious* and used with permission.

Solo verses (sung above continuous response)

Am E Am G
1 Praise___ the Lord, all you na - tions, praise him,
C G Am F Dm6 E
all you___ peo- ples – Al - le - lu - ia.
Am E Am G
2 Strong is his love and mer - cy, he is
C G Am Dm E Am
faith - ful for ev - er – Al - le - lu - ia! 3 Al - le -
Am E Am G
- lu - ia, al - le - lu - ia – let
C G Am F Dm6 E
ev - ery - thing liv - ing give praise to the Lord! 4 Al - le -
Am E Am G
- lu - ia, al - le - lu - ia – let
C G Am Dm E Am
ev - ery - thing liv - ing give praise to the Lord!

154 O shout to the Lord

Jubilate

Words: from Psalm 100
in *The Psalms,*
A New Translation for Worship
David Frost and others
Music: Chris Rolinson
arranged David Peacock

Triumphantly

D
A/D
G/D
A/D
D
A/D
G/D
A/D
GROUP A
1 O
Chorus 1
D
A/D
G/D
A/D
shout to the Lord in tri-umph all the earth,
GROUP B
O
D
A/D
G/D
A/D
shout to the Lord in tri-umph all the earth;

Group A: could be men/soloist/group, Group B: could be women/congregation

Words and music: © 1987 Kingsway's Thankyou Music,
PO Box 75, Eastbourne, East Sussex BN23 6NW

G/A D G/A D
GROUP A
serve the Lord with glad - ness,
GROUP B
serve the Lord with glad - ness, and
GROUP A
G D/F♯ Em7 G/A A7 D G/A D
come be - fore his face with songs of joy,
GROUP B
and
1.
G D/F♯ Em7 G/A A7 D G/A D
come be - fore his face with songs of joy!
GROUP A
O
2.3.
3rd time to Chorus 2
Verse 1
D G/A D B♭/F C/G D/A B♭/F C/G
joy!
ALL
Know that the Lord, he is
D/A G D/F♯ Em7 D/E
God; it is he who has made us and we are

Asus A B♭/F C/G D/A B♭/F C/G D/A
his: we are his peo - ple and the
G D/F♯ Em D/E Asus A
sheep of his pas - ture.
Chorus 2
D A/D G/A A/D
GROUP A
Come in - to his gates with thanks - giv - ing,
D A/D G/A A/D
GROUP B
come in - to his gates with thanks - giv - ing,
G/A D G/A D
GROUP A
and in - to his courts with praise, and in - to his courts with praise; give

G D/F♯ Em7 G/A A7 D G/A D
thanks to him and bless his ho-ly name, GROUP B give
G D/F♯ Em7 G/A A7 D G/A D
Fine
thanks to him and bless his ho-ly name.
Verse 2
B♭/F C/G D/F♯ B♭/F C/G D/F♯ G
ALL
For the Lord, the Lord is good: his lov-ing
D/F♯ Em7 Asus A B♭/F C/G D/A
mer-cy is for ev-er, his faith-ful-ness
B♭/F C/G D/A G G/A
D.𝄋 al Fine
through-out all ge-ne-ra-tions. GROUP A O

155 O worship the King

Hanover 10 10 11 11

Words: from Psalm 104
after W Kethe (died 1594), R Grant (1779–1838)
Music: *A Supplement to the New Version* 1708
probably by W Croft (1678–1727)
Descant A Gray (1855–1935)

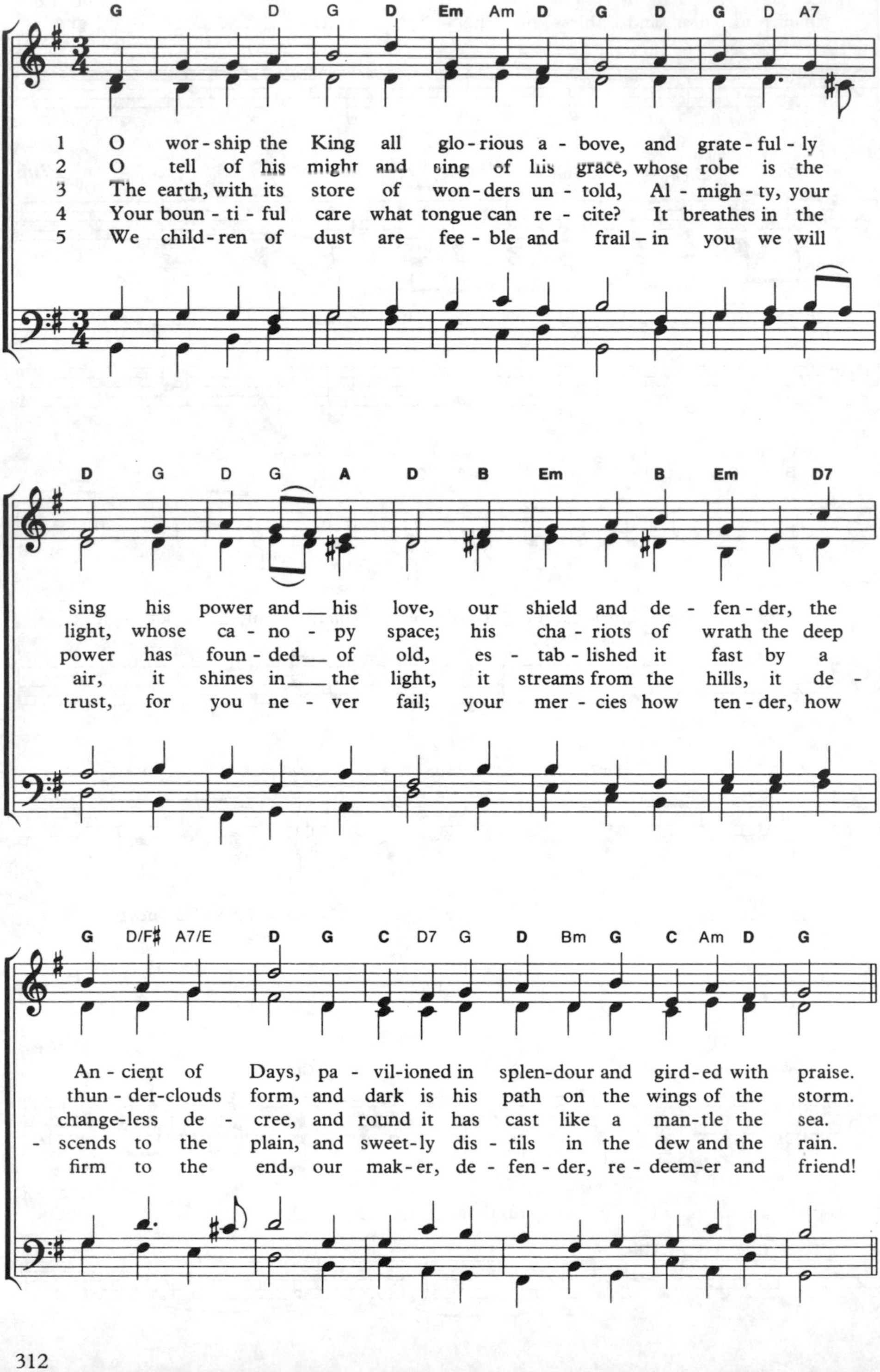
G D G D Em Am D G D G D A7
1 O wor-ship the King all glo-rious a-bove, and grate-ful-ly
2 O tell of his might and sing of his grace, whose robe is the
3 The earth, with its store of won-ders un-told, Al-migh-ty, your
4 Your boun-ti-ful care what tongue can re-cite? It breathes in the
5 We child-ren of dust are fee-ble and frail – in you we will
D G D G A D B Em B Em D7
sing his power and his love, our shield and de-fen-der, the
light, whose ca-no-py space; his cha-riots of wrath the deep
power has foun-ded of old, es-tab-lished it fast by a
air, it shines in the light, it streams from the hills, it de-
trust, for you ne-ver fail; your mer-cies how ten-der, how
G D/F# A7/E D G C D7 G D Bm G C Am D G
An-cient of Days, pa-vil-ioned in splen-dour and gird-ed with praise.
thun-der-clouds form, and dark is his path on the wings of the storm.
change-less de-cree, and round it has cast like a man-tle the sea.
-scends to the plain, and sweet-ly dis-tils in the dew and the rain.
firm to the end, our mak-er, de-fen-der, re-deem-er and friend!

G D G D Em Am D G D G D A7
6 O mea-sure-less Might, un-change-ab-le Love, whom an-gels de-
6 O mea-sure-less Might, un-change-ab-le Love, whom an-gels de-
D G D G A D B Em B Em D7
-light to wor-ship a-bove: your ran-somed cre-a-tion with
-light to wor-ship a-bove: your ran-somed cre-a-tion with
G D/F♯ A7/E D G C D7 G D Bm G C Am D G
glo-ry a-blaze, in true a-dor-a-tion shall sing to your praise!
glo-ry a-blaze, in true a-do-ra-tion shall sing to your praise!

156 Oh, freedom is coming

Freedom is coming

Words: African origin,
collected and edited by Anders Nyberg
Romans 8.23, Revelation 22.20
Music: African melody scored by
Notman KB, Ljungsbro and Lars Parkman

African style

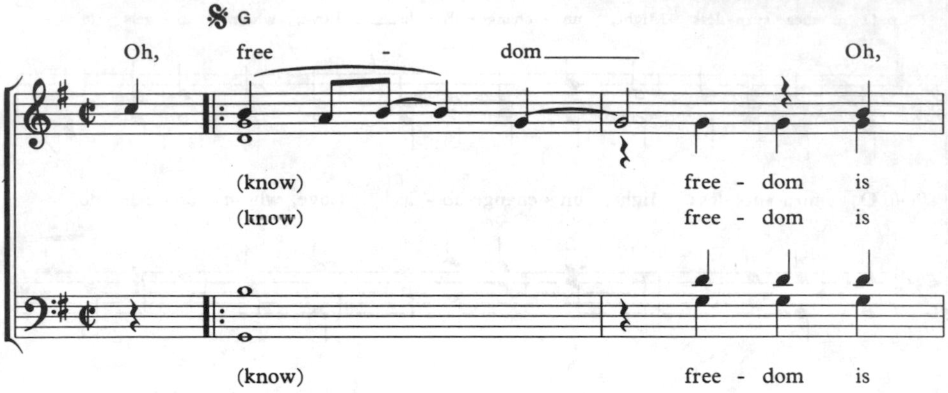

G
Oh, free - dom Oh,
(know) free - dom is
(know) free - dom is
(know) free - dom is

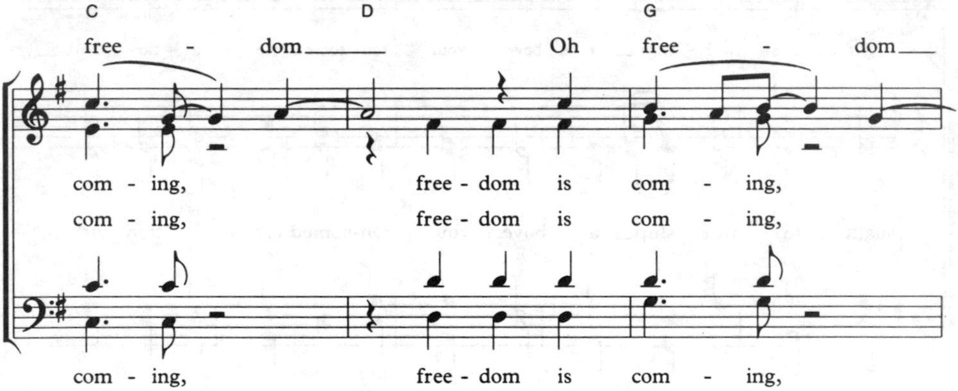

C D G
free - dom Oh free - dom
com - ing, free - dom is com - ing,
com - ing, free - dom is com - ing,
com - ing, free - dom is com - ing,

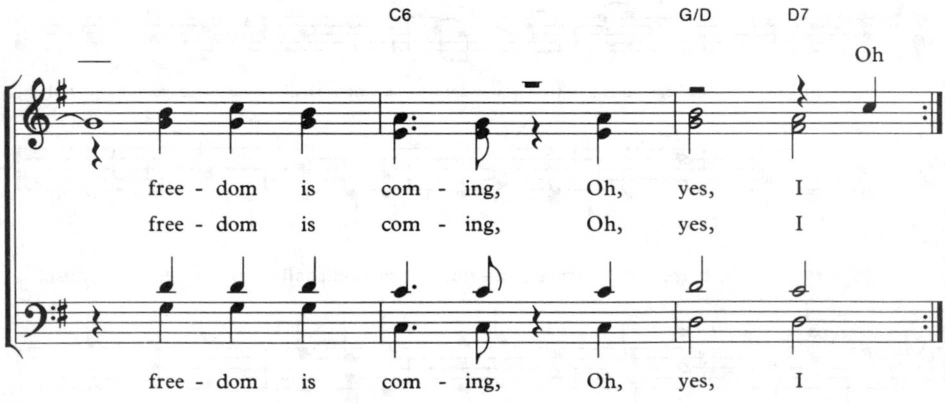

C6 G/D D7
Oh
free - dom is com - ing, Oh, yes, I
free - dom is com - ing, Oh, yes, I
free - dom is com - ing, Oh, yes, I

© The Iona Community / Wild Goose Publications

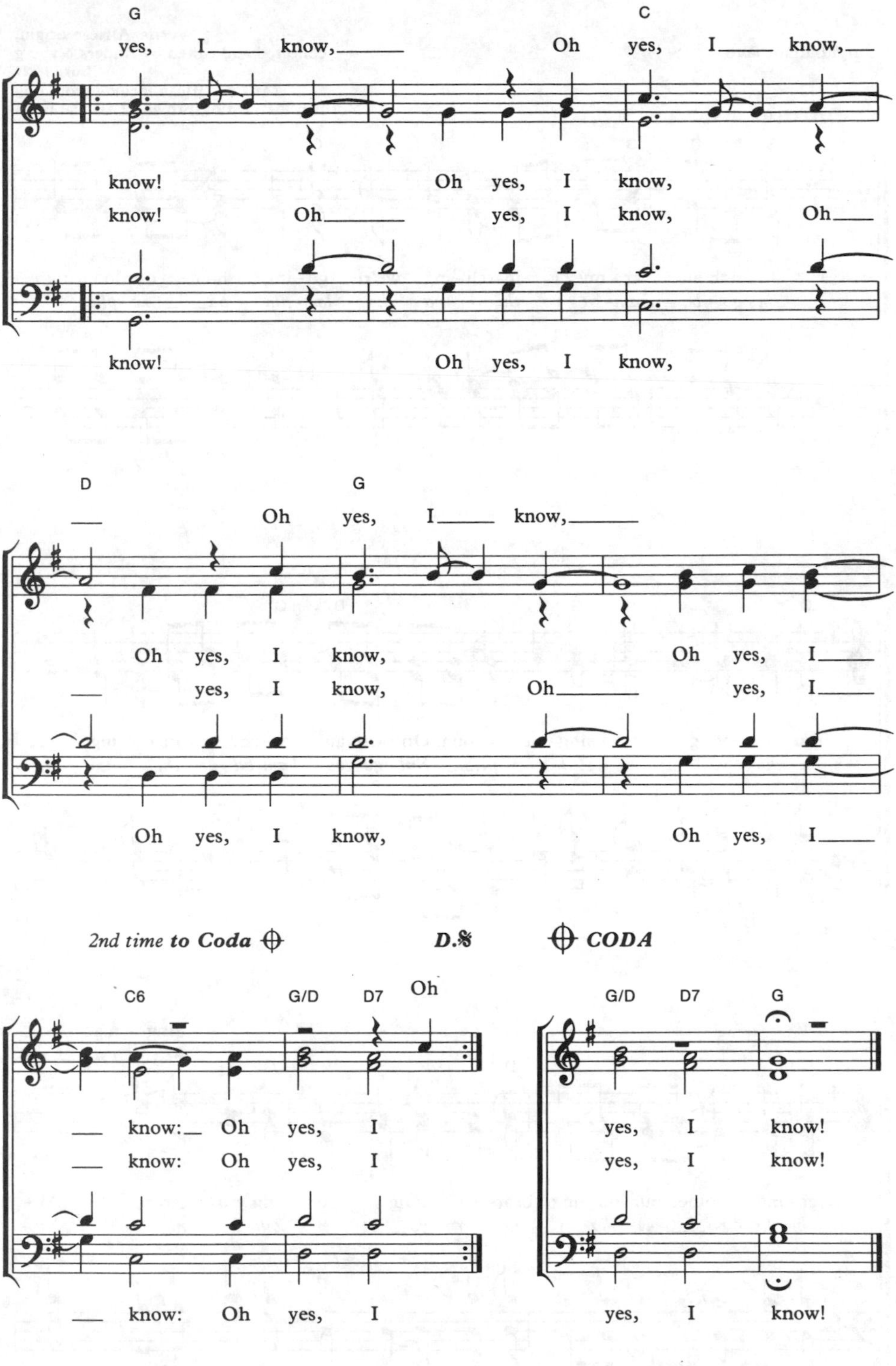
G
C
yes, I___ know,___
Oh yes, I___ know,___
know!
Oh yes, I know,
know!
Oh___
yes, I know,
Oh___
know!
Oh yes, I know,
D
G
___
Oh yes, I___ know,___
Oh yes, I know,
Oh yes, I___
___ yes, I know,
Oh___
yes, I___
Oh yes, I know,
Oh yes, I___
2nd time to Coda
D.S.
CODA
C6
G/D
D7
Oh
G/D
D7
G
___ know:___ Oh yes, I
yes, I know!
___ know: Oh yes, I
yes, I know!
___ know: Oh yes, I
yes, I know!

Verse 2: Oh Jesus (Jesus is coming) . . .

157 On earth an army is marching

Singabahambayo

Words: African origin,
collected and edited by Anders Nyberg
Luke 13.29
Music: African melody scored by
Notman KB, Ljungsbro and Lars Parkman

African style
G D7 G C
1 On earth an ar - my is march - ing: we're go - ing home, our long - ing
1 Sin - ga - ba - ham - ba - yo thi - na ku - lom hla - ba ke - pha si -
D G D7 G
bears a song, so sing out strong. On earth an ar - my is march - ing: we're
- ne - kha - ya e - Zul - wi - ni. Sin - ga - ba ham - ba - yo thi - na ku -
C D G
Sing - ing
Si - thi
go - ing home, our long - ing bears a song, so sing out strong. (Al -
- lom - hla - ba ke - pha si - ne kha - ya e - Zul - wi - ni. (ha -

© The Iona Community / Wild Goose Publications

Am D G
— sing - ing ___ sing - ing
— si - thi ___ si - thi
D
- le - lu - ia), ___ (Al - le - lu - ia), ___ Al - le - lu - ia, al - le - lu - ia, al -
- le - lu - ya), ___ (ha - le - lu - ya), ___ ha - le - lu-ya, ha - le - lu-ya, ha -
Am D G
sing - ing ___ sing - ing ___ sing - ing
si - thi ___ si - thi ___ si - thi
G
- le - lu - ia! ___ (Al - le - lu - ia), ___ (Al - le - lu - ia), ___ Al -
- le - lu - ya! (ha - le - lu - ya), ___ (ha - le - lu - ya), ___ ha -
D G
- le - lu - ia, Al - le - lu - ia, al - le - lu - ia,
- le - lu - ya, ha - le - lu - ya, ha - le - lu - ya!

2 With love our hearts are ablazing
for those who roam
and wander far away,
yet long for home.
With love . . .
Singing (Alleluia) . . .

3 Each day our friendship is growing,
and with all speed;
we share our wine and bread,
a hasty meal.
Each day . . .
Singing (Alleluia) . . .

African verse *Singabahambayo thina*
kulomhlaba
kepha sinekhaya
eZulwini.
Singabahambayo . . .
Sithi (haleluya),
sithi (haleluya),
sithi haleluya,
haleluya, haleluya!
Sithi (haleluya) . . .

158 Open our eyes

Words and music: Robert Cull
John 12.20
Music arranged David Peacock

Prayerfully
D G A7 G6
O - pen our eyes, Lord, we want to see Je -
D Bm Bm7 G G6 A7
- sus to reach out and touch him and
G6 D B7 Em
say that we love him; o - pen our ears,
A7 G6 D Bm Bm7
Lord, and help us to lis - ten: O o - pen our
G G6 A7 Dsus D
eyes, Lord, we want to see Je - sus!

Words and music: © 1976 Maranatha! Music/CopyCare Ltd,
PO Box 77, Hailsham, East Sussex BN27 3EF

159 Open your eyes

Words and music: Carl Tuttle

Worshipfully
C G/C F G C F/C
O - pen your — eyes, see the glo - ry of the King;
C G/C F G C
lift up your — voice, and his prais - es —— sing!
F G C F G C
I love you, Lord, I will pro - claim:
F G Am7 F Dm7 G C
Al - le - lu - ia! I bless your name.

Words and music: © 1982 Mercy Publishing/Kingsway's Thankyou Music,
PO Box 75, Eastbourne, East Sussex BN23 6NW

160 Praise and adoration

Words and music: Lance Lincoln
Music arranged David Peacock

Jazz swing style
G
Bm7
C
Praise and a - dor - a - tion! I sing an
D
G
Bm7
ac - clam - a - tion all for the ex - alt - a - tion
C
D
G
of the King: I love a
Bm7
C
D
ce - le - bra - tion and loud ju - bi - la - tion;

Words and music: © Copyright controlled
Music arrangement: © David Peacock / Jubilate Hymns †

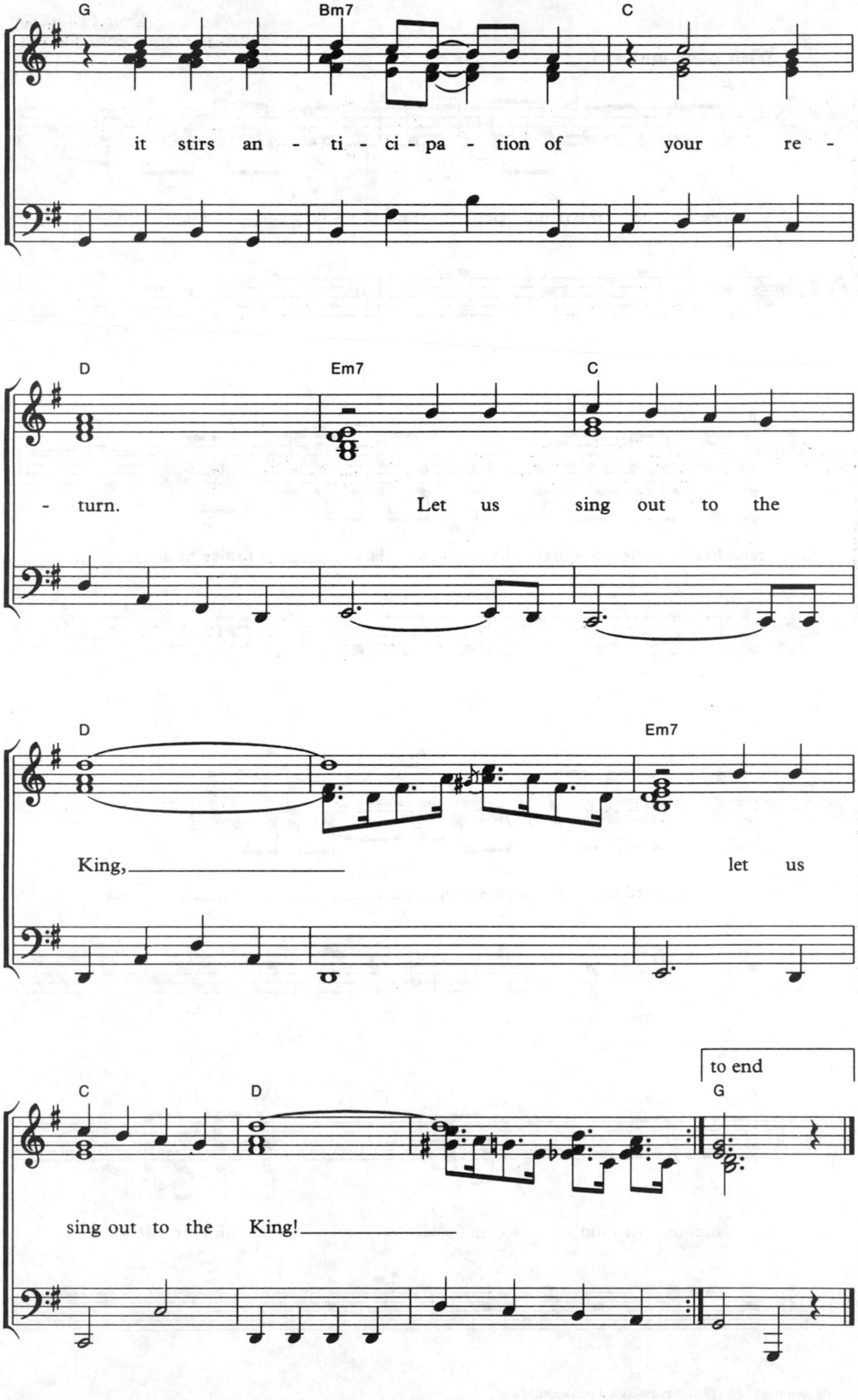
G
Bm7
C
it stirs an - ti - ci - pa - tion of your re -
D
Em7
C
- turn. Let us sing out to the
D
Em7
King,
let us
to end
C
D
G
sing out to the King!

161 Praise him on the trumpet

From Psalm 150
Words and music: John Kennett

With pace and swing
E
Praise him on the trum - pet, the psal - tery and harp;
A
E
praise him on the tim - brel and the dance; praise him
B7
with stringed in - stru-ments too;
E
E7
A
praise him on the loud cym - bals,
praise him on the loud

Words and music: © 1981 Kingsway's Thankyou Music,
PO Box 75, Eastbourne, East Sussex BN23 6NW

Am E B7
cym - bals: let ev - ery - thing that has breath praise the
E B7 E
Lord! Al - le - lu - ia - praise the Lord;
A E
al - le - lu - ia - praise the Lord: let ev - ery - thing that has
1.
B7
breath praise the Lord!
2.
B7 E
breath praise the Lord!

162 Praise the Lord

From Psalm 148
Words and music: Bill Batstone
and Tom Howard

In four, with a beat ♩= 96

E B/E E
A
Praise the Lord, praise the Lord from the
E
A E/G♯ F♯m7 B7sus
hea - vens; all the an - gels sing: Praise the Lord!
E
E B/E E
Praise the Lord from the

Words and music: © 1982 Maranatha! Music/CopyCare Ltd,
PO Box 77, Hailsham, East Sussex BN27 3EF

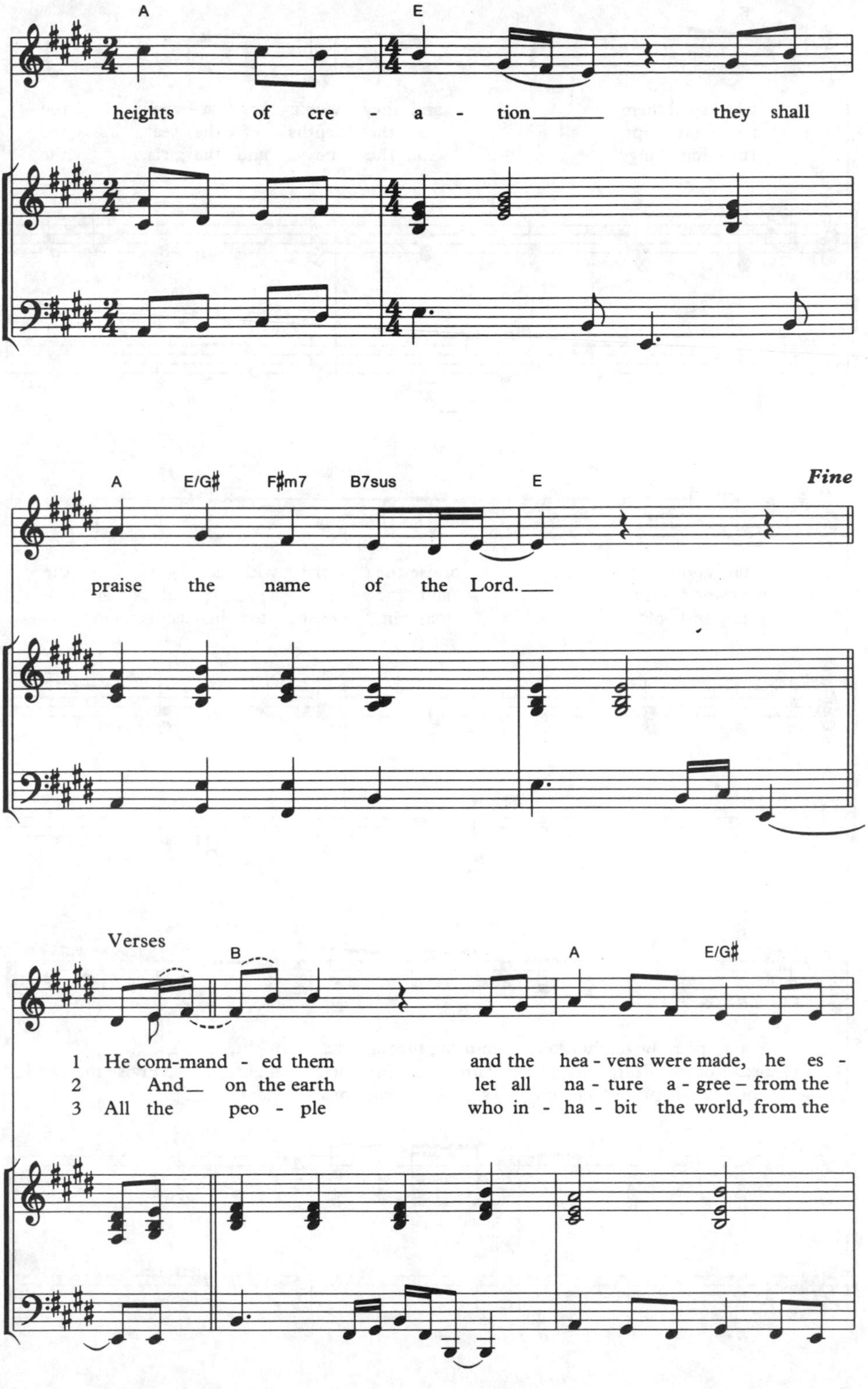
A
E
heights of cre - a - tion___ they shall
A
E/G♯
F♯m7
B7sus
E
Fine
praise the name of the Lord.___
Verses
B
A
E/G♯
1 He com-mand - ed them and the hea - vens were made, he es -
2 And__ on the earth let all na - ture a - gree – from the
3 All the peo - ple who in - ha - bit the world, from the

B
A
E
- tab-lished them and they won't pass a - way: the
mountain - tops to the depths of the sea: the
rul - ing kings to the boys and the girls; the
B
C♯m7
F♯
sun and moon praise the Lord with their light; all the
winds and rain and the fie - ry___ light, all the
young and old join in praise to his name: God a -
B
F♯m7
A/B
B
stars up a - bove, they keep shin-ing through the night.___
beasts of the field, all the birds___ in their flight.___ Praise the Lord__
- lone is su-preme let cre - a - tion pro - claim!___

163 Praise, my soul, the king of heaven

Praise my soul 8 7 8 7 8 7

Words: from Psalm 103
H F Lyte (1793–1847)
Music: J Goss (1800–1880)
descant: Robin Sheldon

Unison
D A7/E D/F♯ G D G D
1 Praise, my soul, the king of hea - ven! to his
G A Bm Em A F♯ Bm E7
feet your tri - bute bring: ran-somed, healed, re - stored, for - gi - ven,
A E A D Bm E7 A Bm A7/C♯
who like me his praise should sing? Al - le - lu - ia,
D A7/E B7 Em A7 D
al - le - lu - ia! praise the ev - er - last - ing king!

Descant: © Robin Sheldon

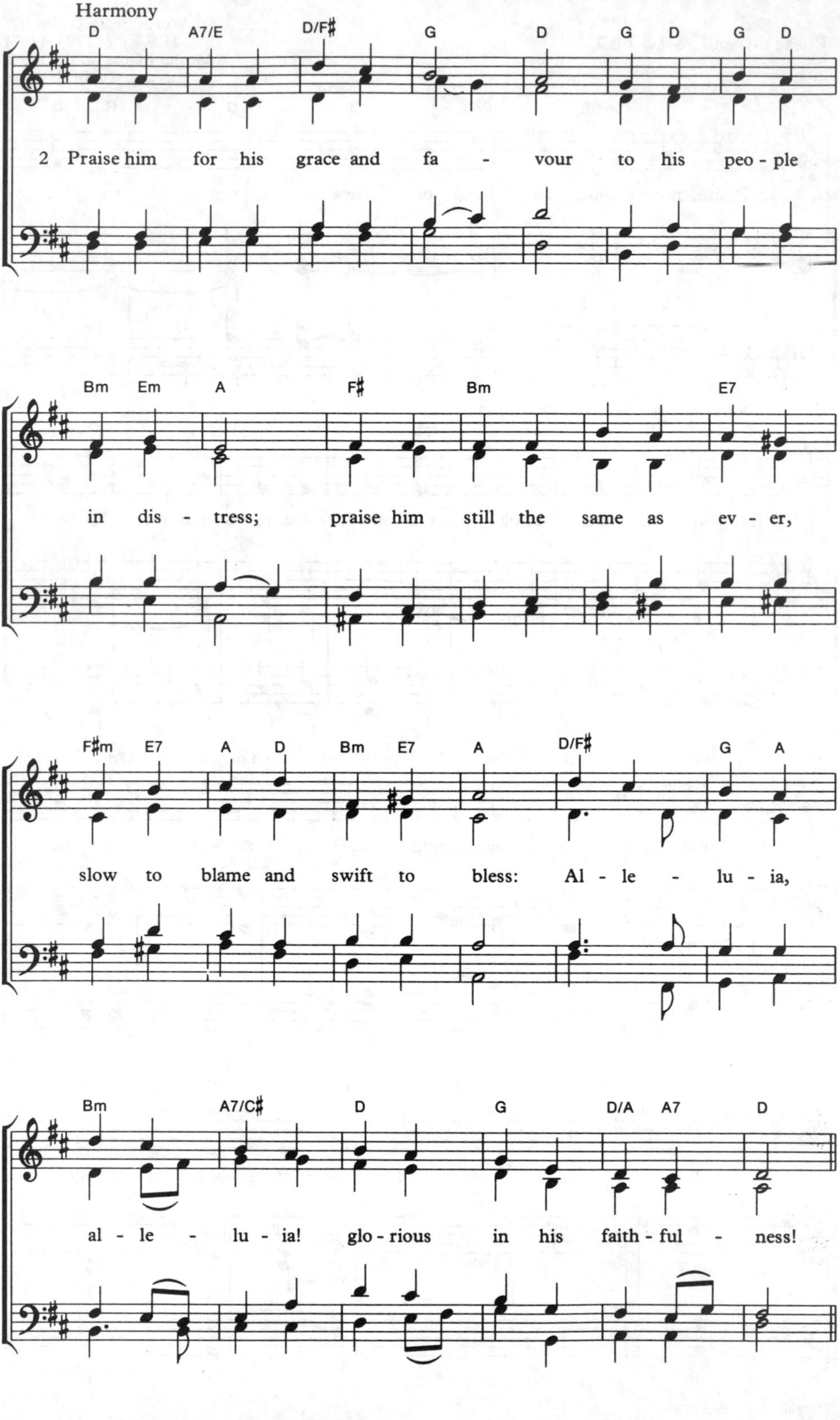
Harmony
D A7/E D/F♯ G D G D G D
2 Praise him for his grace and fa - vour to his peo - ple
Bm Em A F♯ Bm E7
in dis - tress; praise him still the same as ev - er,
F♯m E7 A D Bm E7 A D/F♯ G A
slow to blame and swift to bless: Al - le - lu - ia,
Bm A7/C♯ D G D/A A7 D
al - le - lu - ia! glo - rious in his faith - ful - ness!

D D/C♯ Bm♯6 C♯ F♯m B Em B7
3 Fa - ther - like, he tends and spares us; all our
Em Am B7 Em A D F♯7/C♯ Bm
hopes and fears he knows, in his hands he gen - tly
E F♯m E7 A D Bm E7 A D/A
bears us, res - cues us from all our foes, Al - le -
A7 Bm A7/C♯ B7 Em D/A A7 D
- lu - ia, al - le - lu - ia! wide - ly as his mer - cy flows.

Descant
D F♯m Bm7 E7
4 An - gels help us to a - dore
4 An - gels help us to a - dore
A G D Bm Em A
him you be - hold him face to face;
him – you be - hold him face to face;
F♯7 Bm E7
sun and moon, bow down be - fore him –
sun and moon, bow down be - fore him –

A E A D Bm E7 A A7
praise him, all in time and space:
praise him, all in time and space:
D A7/D D G/D
Al - le - lu - ia, al - le - lu - ia!
Al - le - lu - ia, al - le - lu - ia!
D G D/A A7 D
praise with us the God of grace!
praise with us the God of grace!

164 Praise the Father

Gabi, gabi

Capo 1(G)

Words: African origin,
collected and edited by Anders Nyberg
Isaiah 61.1, Ezekiel 18.7 and 18.16, Luke 4.18
Music: African melody scored by
Notman KB, Ljungsbro and Lars Parkman

African style

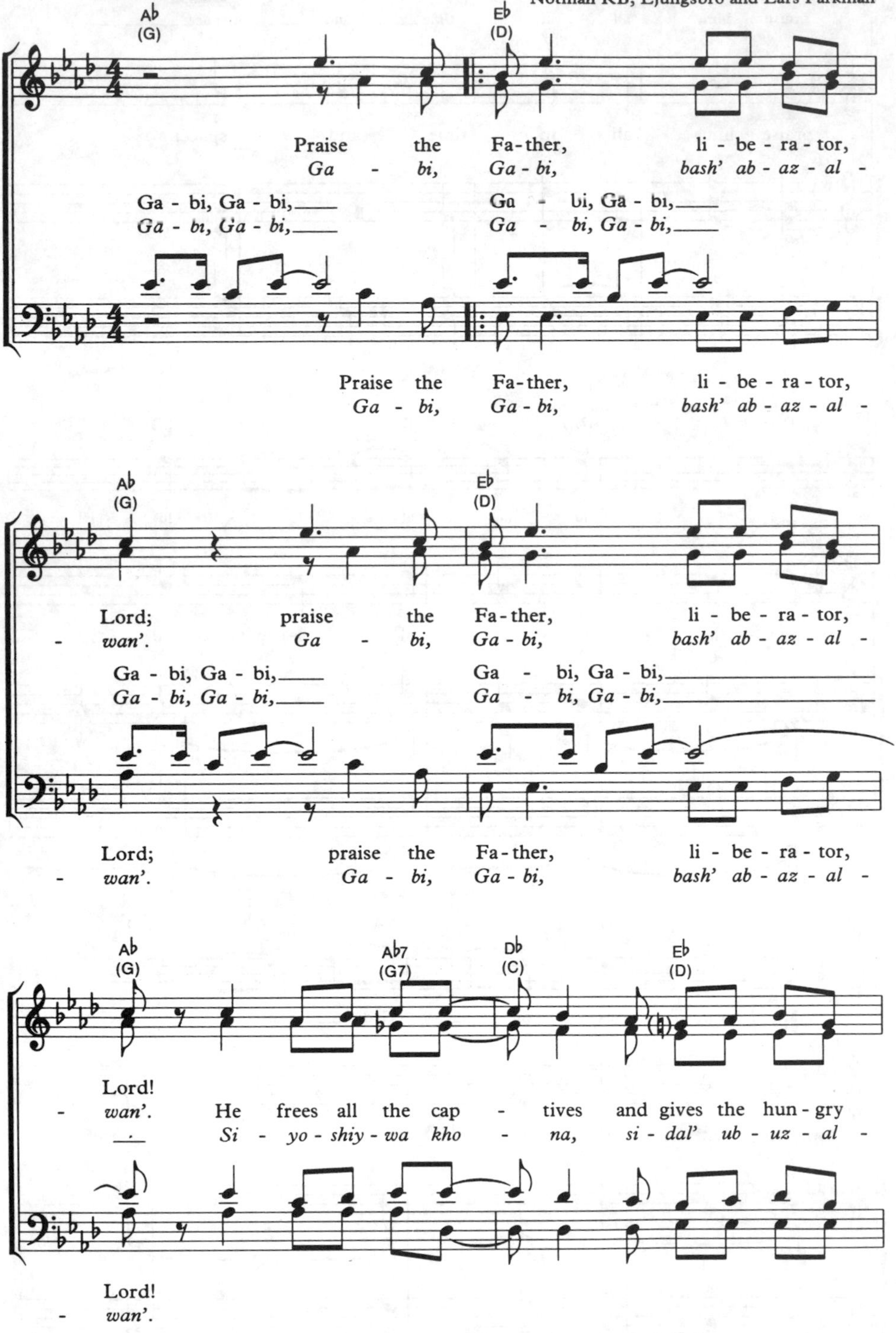
Ab (G)
Eb (D)
Praise the Father, liberator,
Gabi, Gabi, bash' abazal-
Gabi, Gabi,
Gabi, Gabi,
Lord; praise the Father, liberator,
-wan'. Gabi, Gabi, bash' abazal-
Ab7 (G7)
Db (C)
Lord!
-wan'. He frees all the captives and gives the hungry
Siyoshiywa khona, sidal' ubuzal-

© The Iona Community / Wild Goose Publications

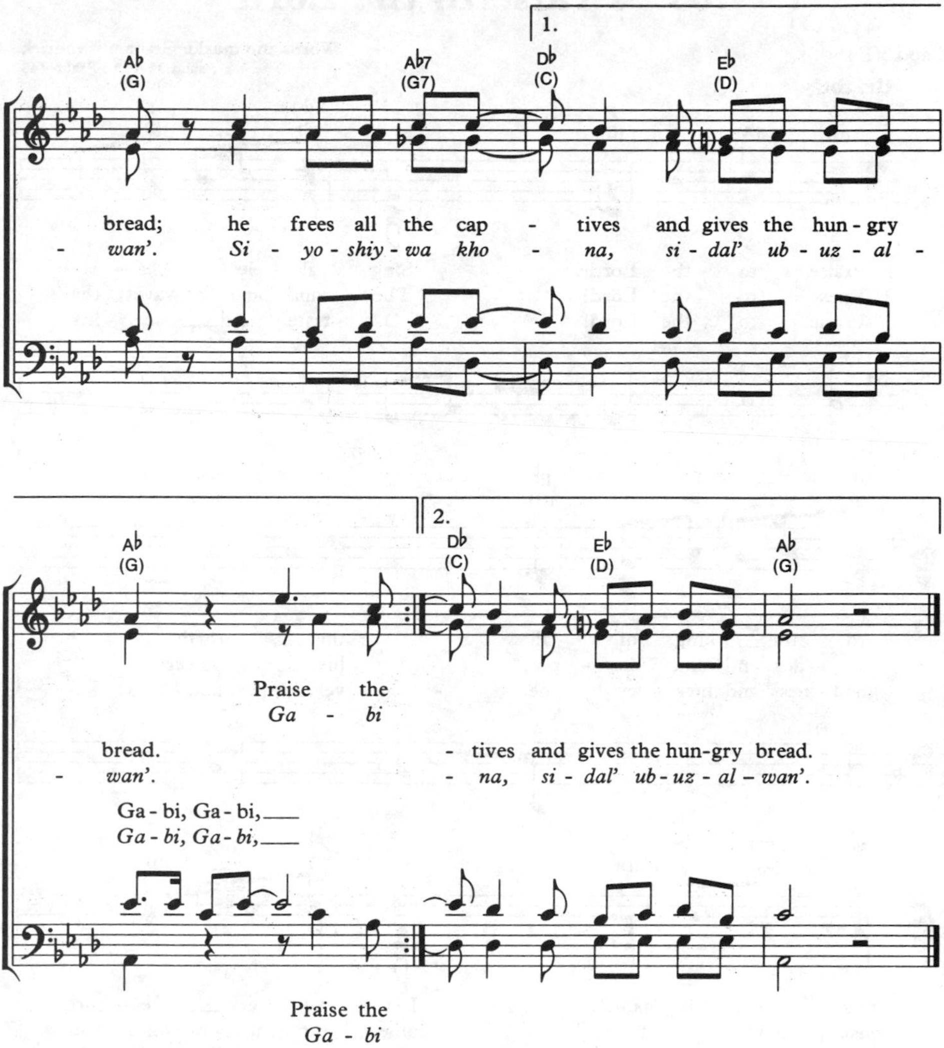
1.
A♭ (G)
A♭7 (G7)
D♭ (C)
E♭ (D)
bread; he frees all the cap - tives and gives the hun - gry
- wan'. Si - yo - shiy - wa kho - na, si - dal' ub - uz - al -
2.
A♭ (G)
D♭ (C)
E♭ (D)
A♭ (G)
Praise the
Ga - bi
bread.
- wan'.
- tives and gives the hun-gry bread.
- na, si - dal' ub - uz - al – wan'.
Ga - bi, Ga - bi,
Ga - bi, Ga - bi,
Praise the
Ga - bi

164A PRAISE SHOUT

LEADER Let us give thanks to the Lord for his unfailing love
ALL **and the wonders he has done for us.**

LEADER He satisfies the thirsty
ALL **and fills the hungry with good things.**

From Psalm 107

165 Praise to the Lord

Capo 3(D)

Words and music: Graham Kendrick
Psalm 34.8 and Psalm 148

Brightly
Bb (G) C (A) F (D) Bb (G) F (D)
1 Praise to the Lord! Sing al - le - lu - ias
2 Praise to the Lord! The wind and the waves, the
3 Praise to the Lord! O taste and__ see his
Gm (Em) F (D) Bb (G) Csus (Asus) C (A)
to the__ king of all the__ earth.
thun - der and rain, dis - play his__ power:
good - ness and mer - cy ne - ver__ fail.
Bb (G) C (A) F (D) Bb (G) F (D)
Praise to his name! Let ev - ery__ crea - ture
raise now the shout; come, lift up your voice and
Praise to his name, who gives to his chil - dren
Gm (Em) F (D) Csus (Asus) C (A)
join in the joy - ful song.
join with all na - ture's song.
gifts from his gen - erous hand.

Words and music: © 1983 Kingsway's Thankyou Music,
PO Box 75, Eastbourne, East Sussex BN23 6NW

Chorus
F (D) C (A) F (D) C (A)
MEN
I will praise him,
WOMEN
I will praise him;
Dm (Bm) G (E) Dm (Bm) G (E)
MEN
I will ex - alt him,
WOMEN
I will ex - alt him –
Dm (Bm) G (E) Dm (Bm) G (E) Dm (Bm) Dm7/C (Bm7)
MEN
for his love,
WOMEN
for his love,
ALL
for his
last time
G7/B (E7) G7 (E7) Csus (Asus) C (A) F (D)
love en - dures for ev - er.

166 Prince of peace, counsellor

Prince of peace

Words and music: Jennifer Randolph
Isaiah 9.6
Music arranged David Peacock

Gently

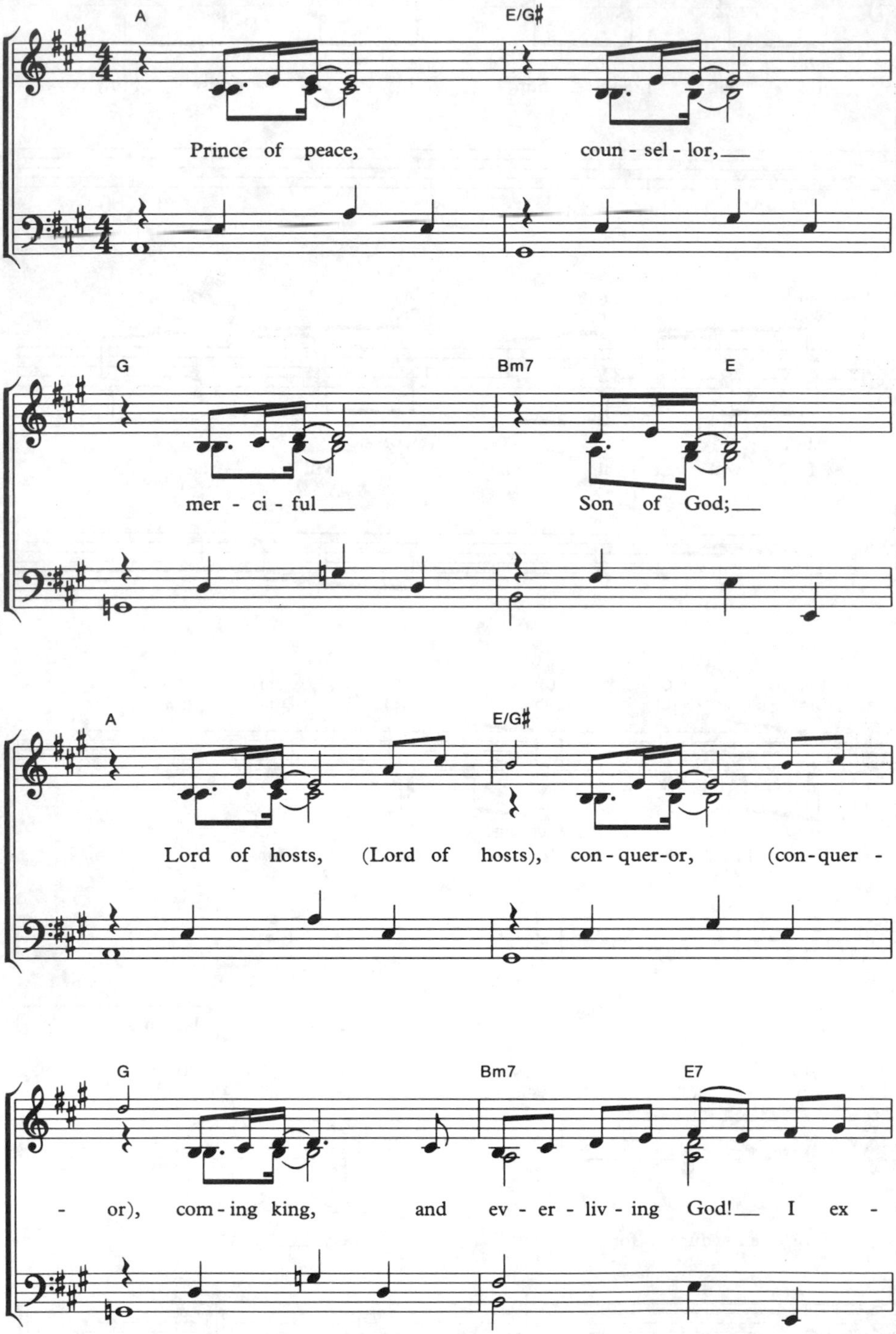
A
E/G♯
Prince of peace, coun - sel - lor,
G
Bm7
E
mer - ci - ful Son of God;
A
E/G♯
Lord of hosts, (Lord of hosts), con - quer-or, (con-quer -
G
Bm7
E7
- or), com - ing king, and ev - er - liv - ing God! I ex -

Words and music: © 1985 Integrity's Hosanna! Music, administered in Europe (excl. German speaking countries) by Kingsway's Thankyou Music, PO Box 75, Eastbourne, East Sussex BN23 6NW

A
E/G♯
- tol you, Lord, I ex - tol you: you are
D
Bm
E7
high a - bove the earth all cre - a - tion shouts your worth – I ex -
A
E/G♯
- tol you, Lord, I ex - tol you, my Je -
Bm
A/C♯
D
E7
D/A
A
- ho - vah, I ex - tol you.

167 Raise the shout

Words and music: Graham Kendrick
1 Corinthians 15.20

Triumphantly ♩ = 86

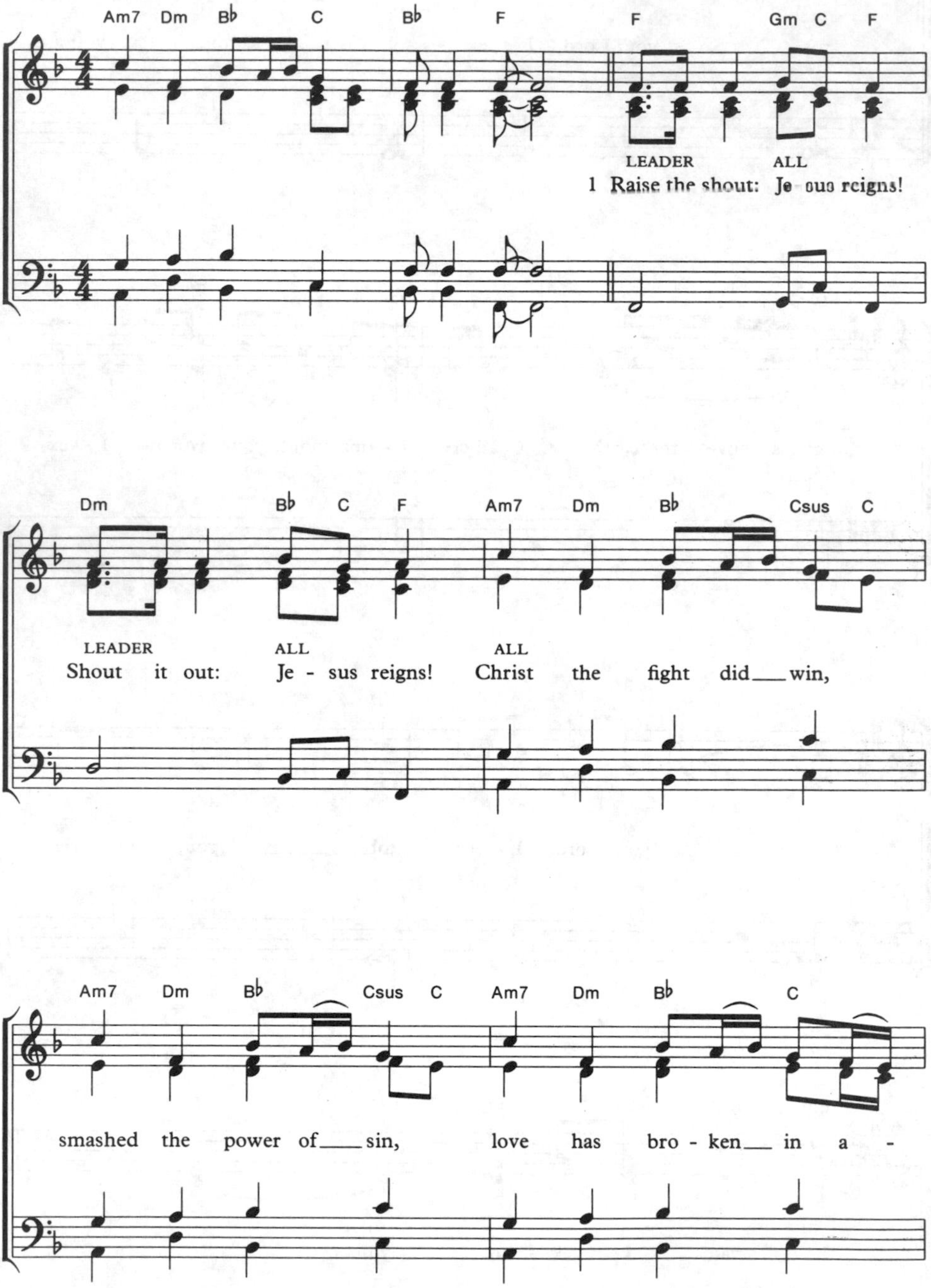
Am7 Dm B♭ C B♭ F F Gm C F
LEADER
ALL
1 Raise the shout: Je - sus reigns!
Dm B♭ C F Am7 Dm B♭ Csus C
LEADER
ALL
ALL
Shout it out: Je - sus reigns! Christ the fight did win,
Am7 Dm B♭ Csus C Am7 Dm B♭ C
smashed the power of sin, love has bro - ken in a -

Words and music: © 1988 Make Way Music,
PO Box 263, Croydon, Surrey CR9 5AP.
International copyright secured. All rights reserved. Used by permission.

B♭ F B♭ F D7 G Am D G
- mong us.
LEADER ALL
2 Raise the shout: Je - sus lives!
Em C D G Bm7 Em C Dsus D Bm7 Em C Dsus D
LEADER ALL ALL
Shout it out: Je - sus lives! He burst from the grave, now has power to save
Bm7 Em C D C G C G
all who put their trust in him.

168 Reigning in all splendour

Capo 5(Am)

Words and music: Dave Bilborough
Philippians 2.9

Majestically

Dm (Am) C (G) Bb (F) F (C) Dm (Am) C (G) Gm (Dm) C (G)
Reign-ing in all splen - dour - vic-tor-i-ous love; __
Dm (Am) C (G) Bb (F) F (C) Dm (Am) C (G) Gm (Dm) C (G)
Christ Je-sus the sav - iour, tran-scen-dent a-bove. __
Bb (F) C (G) Dm (Am) C (G) Bb (F) C (G) Dm (Am) C (G)
All earth-ly dom-in - ions and king-doms shall fall, __
Bb (F) Dm (Am) C (G) Bb (F) C (G)
for his name is Je - sus __ and he is the Lord. _

Words and music: © 1984 Kingsway's Thankyou Music,
PO Box 75, Eastbourne, East Sussex BN23 6NW

A
(E)
Dm
(Am)
Am7/C
(Em)
He is Lord,
B♭
(F)
C
(G)
he is Lord,
he is
1.
Lord,
he is Lord.
2.
he is Lord.

169 Rejoice, rejoice! Christ is in you

Rejoice

Words and music: Graham Kendrick
2 Corinthians 12.9. Colossians 1.27

Triumphantly

Chorus
D G D A7 D Bm7
Re - joice, re-joice! Christ_ is in you – the hope of glo - ry in_
Em7 A D G D A7 D
_ our_ hearts. He lives, he lives! his breath_ is in you. A -
Bm7 Em7 A D Dmaj7
- rise! A might - y ar - my_ we a - rise!
Fine
Em7 Dmaj7 D Dmaj7 Em7 Dmaj7 D

Words and music: © 1983 Kingsway's Thankyou Music,
PO Box 75, Eastbourne, East Sussex BN23 6NW

Verse
A
Bm
1 Now is the time for us ___ to march up - on the land ___ in - to our
2 God is at work in us ___ his pur-pose to per-form ___ build - ing a
3 Though we are weak, his grace is ev - ery-thing we need ___ we're made of
G
A
D
hands he will give the ground we claim; ___
king - dom of pow - er not ___ of words; ___
clay, but this trea - sure is ___ with - in; ___
A
Bm
he rides in ma - jes - ty ___ to lead us in - to vic - to - ry, ___
where things im - poss - i - ble ___ by faith shall be made poss - i - ble: ___
he turns our weak-ness-es ___ in - to his op - por - tun - i - ties, ___
G
Bm
Em7
Asus
A
the world shall see that Christ is Lord. ___ Re -
let's give the glo - ry to him now. ___ Re -
so that the glo - ry goes to him. ___ Re -

170 Rejoice, rejoice, rejoice

Words and music: Chris Bowater
Luke 1.46
Music arranged C Henderson

Lively
D
Dsus
D
Dsus
Re - joice, re - joice, re - joice, re-joice,
D
Dsus
D
Dsus
D
re - joice, re - joice; my soul re-joi -
last time to Coda
A7
D
Dsus
D
Dsus
- ces in the Lord.
D7
Gmaj7
A7
My soul mag - ni - fies the Lord,

Words and music: © 1986 Sovereign Lifestyle Music,
PO Box 356, Leighton Buzzard LU7 8WP. Used by permission.

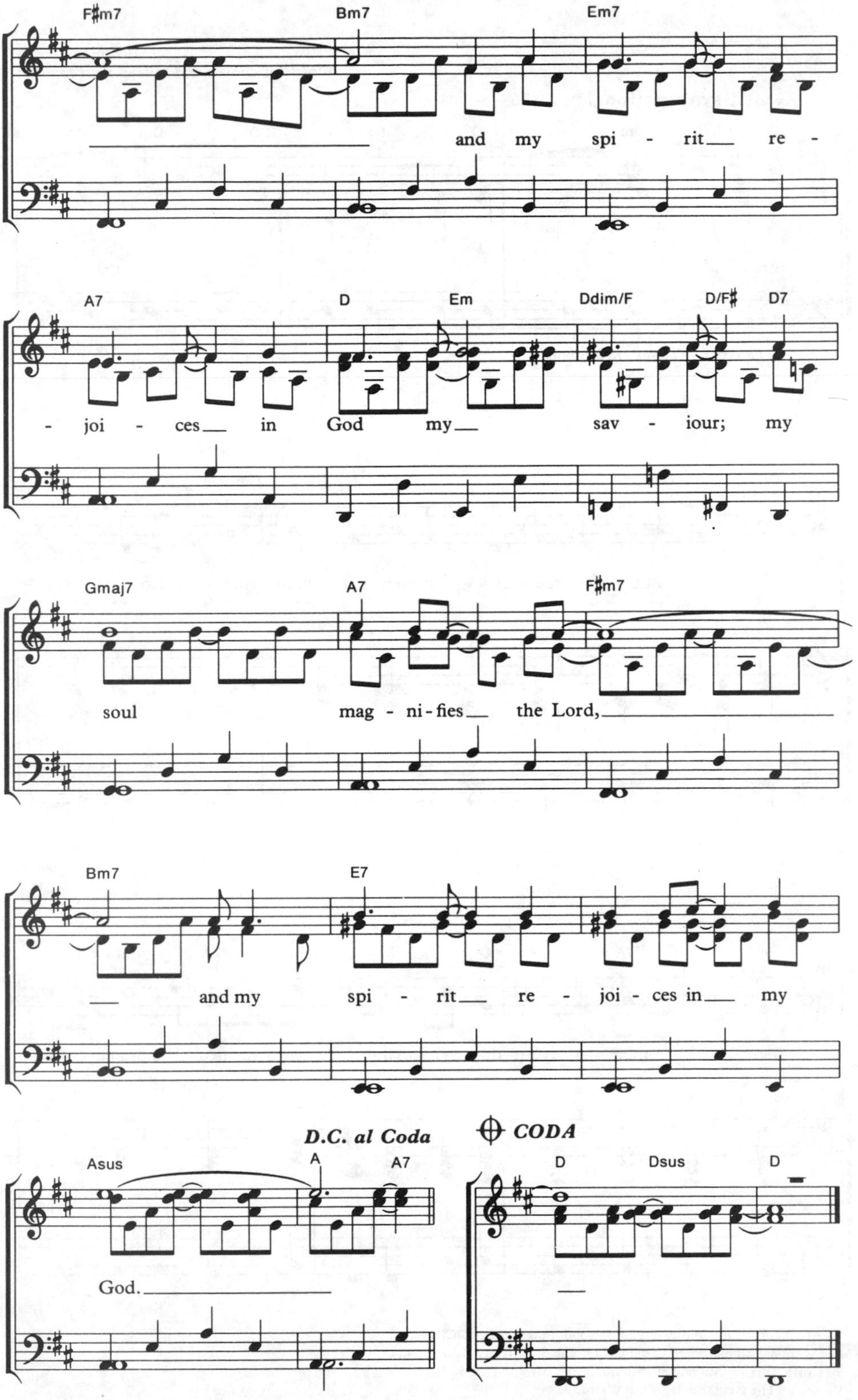
F♯m7 Bm7 Em7
and my spi - rit re -
A7 D Em Ddim/F D/F♯ D7
- joi - ces in God my sav - iour; my
Gmaj7 A7 F♯m7
soul mag - ni - fies the Lord,
Bm7 E7
and my spi - rit re - joi - ces in my
D.C. al Coda
CODA
Asus A A7 D Dsus D
God.

171 Remember, remember your mercy

From Psalm 25
Words of chorus and music: Paul Inwood

Gentle syncopation ♩ = 72–76

C/D Dm C/D Dm C/D Dm
(bass in octaves throughout)
C/D Dm Dm/C Gm7/B♭ Dm7/A
ALL Re - mem-ber, re-mem-ber your mer - cy, Lord; re -
Gm7 F/A C F B♭ Gm Am7 Dm7
- mem-ber, re-mem-ber your mer-cy, Lord: hear your peo-ple's prayer as they

Words of chorus and music: © Paul Inwood. Published by OCP Publications. Administered in the UK by The St Thomas More Group, 30 North Terrace, Mildenhall, Suffolk IP28 7AB
Verses: © The Grail, England/A P Watt Ltd, 20 John Street, London WC1N 2DR

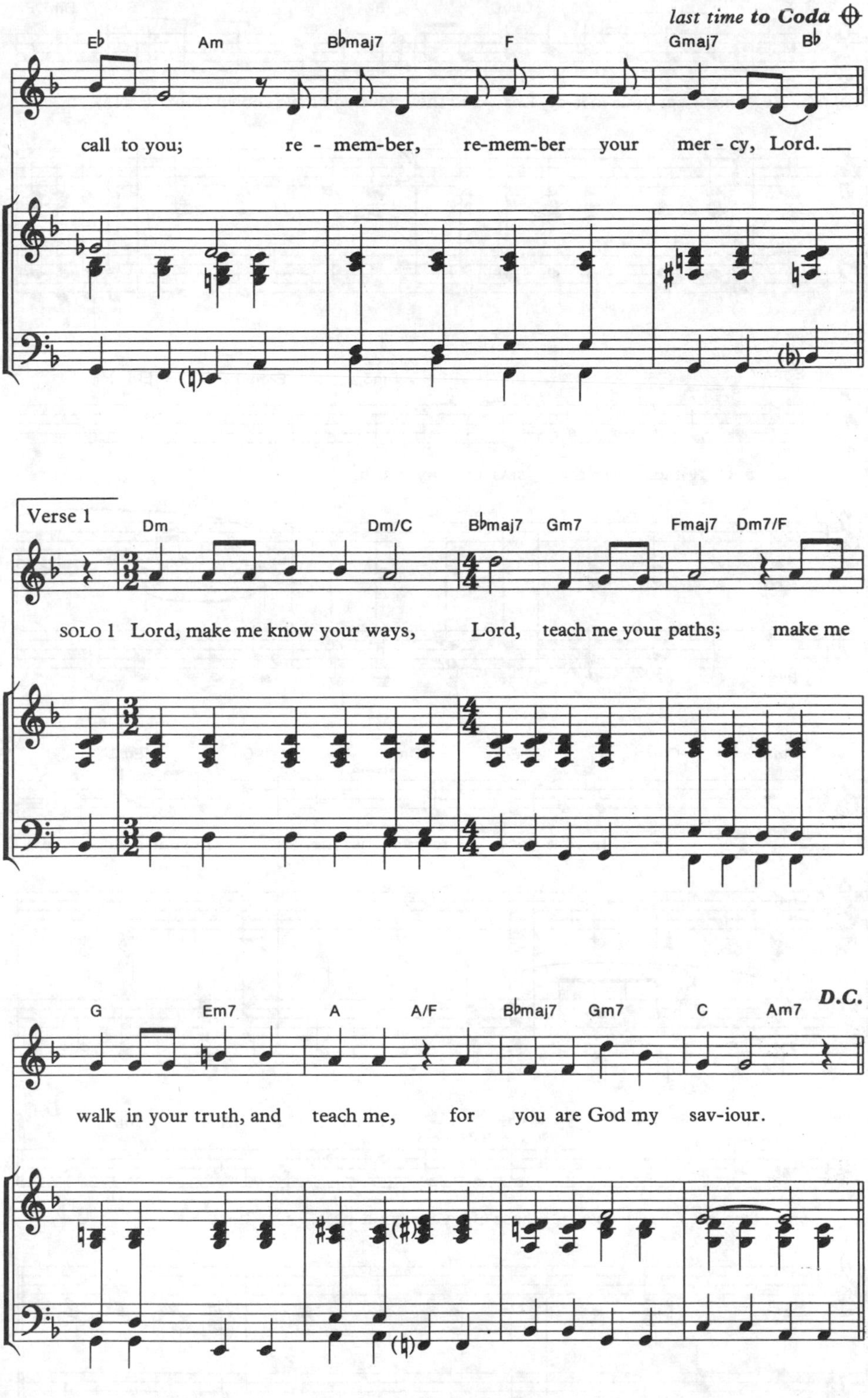
last time to Coda
E♭ Am B♭maj7 F Gmaj7 B♭
call to you; re - mem-ber, re-mem-ber your mer - cy, Lord.
Verse 1
Dm Dm/C B♭maj7 Gm7 Fmaj7 Dm7/F
SOLO 1 Lord, make me know your ways, Lord, teach me your paths; make me
G Em7 A A/F B♭maj7 Gm7 C Am7
D.C.
walk in your truth, and teach me, for you are God my sav-iour.

Verse 2
Dm Dm/C B♭ Gm7 Fmaj7 Dm7/F
SOLO 2 Re - mem-ber your mer-cy, Lord, and the love you have shown from of old;
E♭maj7 E♭6 Dm7 Dm6 E♭maj7 E♭6
do not re-mem-ber the sins of my youth.
E♭maj7 Cm7 F Dm7 G Em7
In your love re-mem-ber me, in your love re -
A A/F B♭ Gm7 C Am7
- mem-ber me be - cause of your good-ness, O Lord.
D.C.

Verse 3
Dm Dm/C B♭maj7 Gm7
SOLO 3 The Lord is good and up-right, he shows the path to all who
Fmaj7 Dm7/F G Em7 A A/F
stray; he guides the hum-ble in the right path, he
B♭maj7 Gm7 C Am7
3
teach-es his way to the poor.
D.C.
CODA
C/D Dm
C/D Dm C/D Dm C/D Asus7/D

172 Restore, O Lord

Steadily, with feeling

Words and music: Graham Kendrick and Chris Rolinson
Isaiah 2.19, Malachi 3.2, 1 Peter 1.6
Music arranged David Peacock

Descant last verse
D Em/D D
1&4 Re - store, O Lord, the hon - our of your
(2) store, O Lord, in all the earth your
(3) us, O Lord, where we are hard and
Em/D Bm A Gmaj7 Asus A
hon - our of your name – works of sov - ereign
name! In works of sov - ereign pow - er come
fame, and in our time re - vive the
cold, in your re - fin - er's fire; come
Bm Gmaj7 F♯sus F♯ Em Asus A
power; shake the earth a - gain
shake the earth a - gain, that all may
Church that bears your name; and in your
pu - ri - fy the gold: though suff - ering

Words and music: © 1981 Kingsway's Thankyou Music,
PO Box 75, Eastbourne, East Sussex BN23 6NW

D F♯7 Bm Bm/A
that all may come with rev - erent fear to the
see, and come with rev - erent fear to the
ang - er, Lord, re - mem - ber mer - cy – O
comes, and ev - il crouch - es near, still our
G F♯m7 Em7 G/A Gmaj9
liv - ing God whose King - dom
liv - ing God whose King - dom
liv - ing God whose mer - cy
liv - ing God is reign - ing –
1.2.3.
4.
Em7 G/A D Em7 D/F♯ Asus A D
shall out - last the years.
shall out - last the years. 2 Re - 4 years.
shall out - last the years. 3 Bend
he is reign - ing here! 4 Re -

173 Risen Lord, whose name we cherish

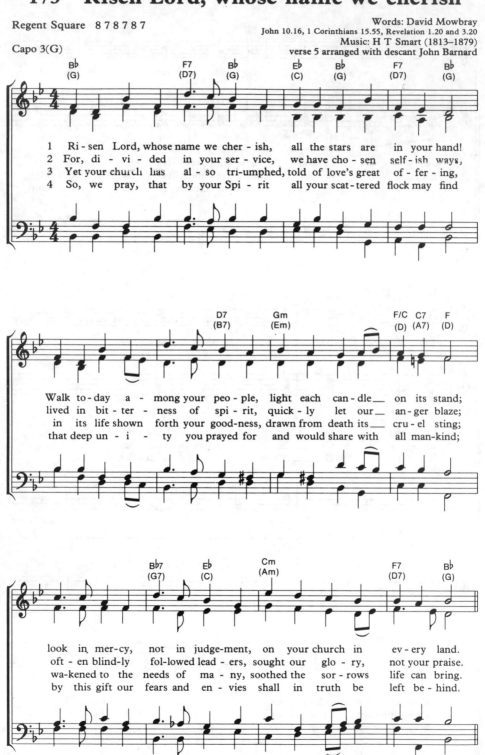

Regent Square 8 7 8 7 8 7

Words: David Mowbray
John 10.16, 1 Corinthians 15.55, Revelation 1.20 and 3.20
Music: H T Smart (1813–1879)
verse 5 arranged with descant John Barnard

Capo 3(G)

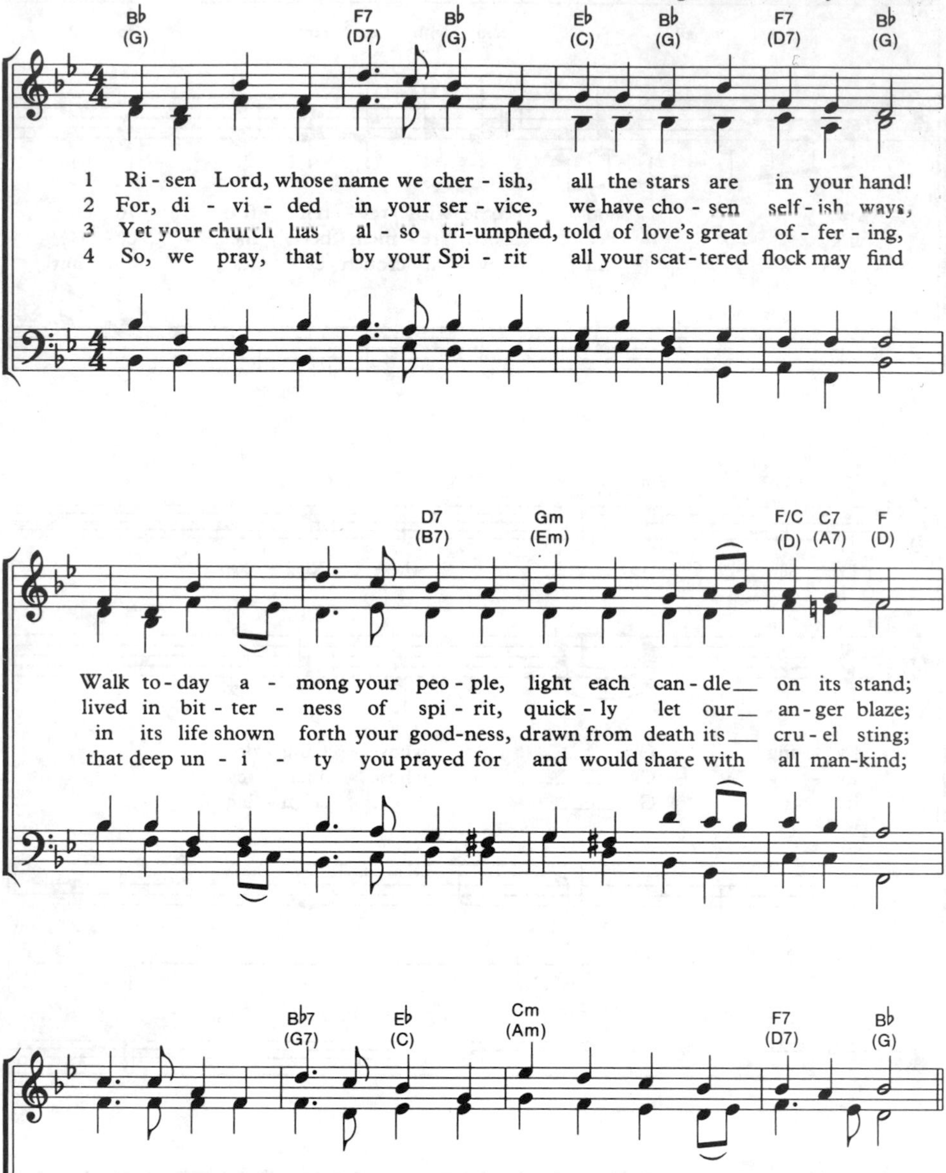

B♭ (G) F7 (D7) B♭ (G) E♭ (C) B♭ (G) F7 (D7) B♭ (G)
1 Ri - sen Lord, whose name we cher - ish, all the stars are in your hand!
2 For, di - vi - ded in your ser - vice, we have cho - sen self - ish ways,
3 Yet your church has al - so tri-umphed, told of love's great of - fer - ing,
4 So, we pray, that by your Spi - rit all your scat - tered flock may find
D7 (B7) Gm (Em) F/C (D) C7 (A7) F (D)
Walk to - day a - mong your peo - ple, light each can - dle on its stand;
lived in bit - ter - ness of spi - rit, quick - ly let our an - ger blaze;
in its life shown forth your good-ness, drawn from death its cru - el sting;
that deep un - i - ty you prayed for and would share with all man-kind;
B♭7 (G7) E♭ (C) Cm (Am) F7 (D7) B♭ (G)
look in mer - cy, not in judge-ment, on your church in ev - ery land.
oft - en blind-ly fol-lowed lead - ers, sought our glo - ry, not your praise.
wa-kened to the needs of ma - ny, soothed the sor - rows life can bring.
by this gift our fears and en - vies shall in truth be left be - hind.

Verse 5 arrangement with descant : © John Barnard / JubilateHymns †
Words: © David Mowbray / Jubilate Hymns †

Descant
B♭ (G) F7 (D7) B♭ (G) E♭ (G) Dm7 (Bm7) Gm (Em) Cm7 (Am7) F7 (D7) B♭ (G)
5 Ri - sen Lord, your hand is knock - ing at each chur - ch's bol - ted door!
5 Ri - sen Lord, your hand is knock - ing at each chur - ch's bol - ted door!
D7 (B7) Gm (Em) B♭/C (G) C7 (A7) F (D)
En - ter now, and dwell with - in us, trust and fel - low - ship re - store;
En - ter now, and dwell with - in us, trust and fel - low - ship re - store;
B♭7 (G7) E♭ (C) G7 (E7) Cm (Am) F7 (D7) B♭ (G)
that your Fa - ther's joys to - ge - ther all may taste for ev - er - more.
that your Fa - ther's joys to - ge - ther all may taste for ev - er - more.

174 River, wash over me

Words and music: Dougie Brown
2 Kings 5.14, Ephesians 3.17, Colossians 3.15

Capo 3(C)
Unhurried with strength

E♭ (C) B♭ (G) A♭ (F) E♭ (C)
1 Ri - ver, wash o - ver me,
2 Spi - rit, watch o - ver me,
3 Je - sus, rule o - ver me,
A♭ (F) B♭7 (G7) E♭ (C) C7 (A7)
cleanse me and make me new;
lead me to Je - sus' feet;
reign o - ver all my heart;
Fm7 (Dm7) B♭7 (G7) E♭ (C) Csus (Asus) C7 (G7)
bathe me, re - fresh me and fill me a - new –
cause me to wor - ship and fill me a - new –
teach me to praise you and fill me a - new –
Fm (Dm) E♭/B♭ (C) B♭7 (G7) A♭/E♭ (F) E♭ (C)
ri - ver, wash o - ver me.
Spi - rit, watch o - ver me.
Je - sus, rule o - ver me.

Words and music: © 1980 Kingsway's Thankyou Music,
PO Box 75, Eastbourne, East Sussex BN23 6NW

175 Reign in me

Words and music: Chris Bowater
Luke 17.21, Ephesians 3.17
Music arranged Geoff Baker

Prayerfully
G Am D7 C/G G
Reign in me, sove-reign Lord, reign in me,
Fine
G Am7 D C/G G
reign in me, sove-reign Lord, reign in me.
E♮9 Am D7 G
Cap-ti-vate my heart, let your king-dom come,
D.C. al Fine
E♮9 Am D7 G C G
es-tab-lish there your throne, let your will be done!

Words and music: © 1985 Sovereign Lifestyle Music,
PO Box 356, Leighton Buzzard LU7 8WP. Used by permission.

176 Send me out from here Lord

Words and music: John Pantry
Matthew 10.9 and 28.19, Mark 6.8, Luke 10.4

With urgency ♩= 138
C Dm7 C/E F C/E G7/D C Gsus G
Send me out from here Lord, to serve a world in need; may I
E/G♯ Am F C/E Am B Em F Gsus G
know no - one by the coat they wear, but the heart that Je - sus sees. And
C Dm7 C/E F C/E G7/D C Gsus G
may the light of your face shine up - on me Lord – You have
last time to Coda
E/G♯ Am F C/E Am B Em F Gsus G
filled my heart with the great-est joy and my cup is ov - er - flow - ing.

Words and music: © 1986 HarperCollins*Religious*/CopyCare Ltd,
PO Box 77, Hailsham, East Sussex BN27 3EF

C G/B Dm A/C♯ F C/E B♭ F/A
1 'Go now, and car - ry the news to all ___ cre - a - tion – ev - ery race and
2 'Go now, bear - ing the light, liv - ing for o - thers, fear - less - ly walk - ing
F/G G C G/B Dm A/C♯ F C/E
ev - ery tongue; take no purse ___ with you, take no - thing to eat for
in - to the night; take no thought for your lives – like lambs a - mong wolves –
B♭ F/A F/G G
1.
F/G G F/G G7
he will sup - ply ___ your ev - er - y need.'
full of the Spi - rit, rea - dy to die.'
2.
D.C. al Coda
F/G G F/G G7
slower
CODA
Em F Dm7 F/G G7
cup is ov - er - flow - ing with
C Dm7 C/E F C/E Dm7 G7 C
joy!

177 Send me, Lord

Thuma Mina

Words: African origin,
collected and edited by Anders Nyberg
Psalm 23.3, Isaiah 6.8
Music: African melody scored by Notman KB,
Ljungsbro and Lars Parkman

African style

E B C♯m B E C♯m E
LEADER
Send me — Lord,
Thu - ma mi - na
ALL
Send me, Je - sus send me, Je - sus send me,
Thu - ma mi - na thu - ma mi - na thu - ma
to repeat
to end
F♯m E/B B E B E
send me, — Lord
thu - ma mi - na
Je - sus send me, Lord Send me, Lord.
mi - na So - man - dla. Thu - ma - dla.

1 LEADER Send me, Lord:
ALL Send me, Jesus
send me, Jesus
send me, Jesus
send me, Lord.

2 LEADER Lead me, Lord:
ALL Lead me, Jesus . . .

3 LEADER Fill me, Lord:
ALL Fill me, Jesus . . .

African verse
Thuma mina,
thuma mina
thuma mina
thuma mina,
Somandla.

© The Iona Community / Wild Goose Publications

178 Send more labourers

Words and music: Graham Kendrick
Matthew 9.38, Luke 10.2, John 4.35

Slowly
F♯m7 B F♯m7
Send, send more la-bour-ers to the har-vest
B F♯m7 B F♯m7
fields; send, send more la-bour-ers, that your love may be re -
B E Emaj7 Amaj7 Bsus B
- vealed, that your name may be known in all the earth – Je-sus'
E Emaj7 Amaj7 Bsus B A E
fame, far and wide in all the earth: Lord of the har - vest, Lord of the
to repeat
last time
A E/G♯ F♯m7 B Amaj7 E
har - vest, we cry to you: you.

Words and music: © 1988 Make Way Music, PO Box 263, Croydon, Surrey CR9 5AP.
International copyright secured. All rights reserved. Used by permission.

179 Shout for joy

Capo 3(C)

From Psalm 100
Words and music: John Daniels

With spirit

E♭ (C)
B♭/E♭ (G)
1 Shout for joy and sing,__ serve the Lord your king,__
2 En - ter in his gates__ and his courts with praise,__
E♭ (C)
__ com - ing be - fore him__
__ giv - ing thanks to him__
Fm/E♭ (Dm)
Gm (Em)
joy - ful - ly - and sing,__ know-ing that the
through-out all our days:__ for the Lord our
Cm7 (Am7)
Gm (Em)
Cm7 (Am7)
Lord is God; he has made us, we are his —
God is good, and his love has ev-er stood;__

Words and music: © 1986 Springtide/Word Music (UK)/CopyCare Ltd,
PO Box 77, Hailsham, East Sussex BN27 3EF

Gm (Em)
Cm7 (Am7)
Fm (Dm)
in his pas - ture we have food and in his pres - ence live
faith - ful - ly he keeps his word; and his love to all
1.3.
B♭9 (G7)
B♭ (G)
D.C.
(repeat verse 1)
(repeat verse 2)
2.
B♭9 (G7)
E♭ (C)
ev - er - more.
B♭/E♭ (G)
E♭ (C)
B♭/E♭ (G)
D.C.
4.
Fm/E♭ (Dm)
E♭ (C)
ge - ne - ra - tions.

180 Shout, shout joyfully

Shout joyfully

Words and music: Tom Brooks
Psalm 100
Music arranged David Peacock

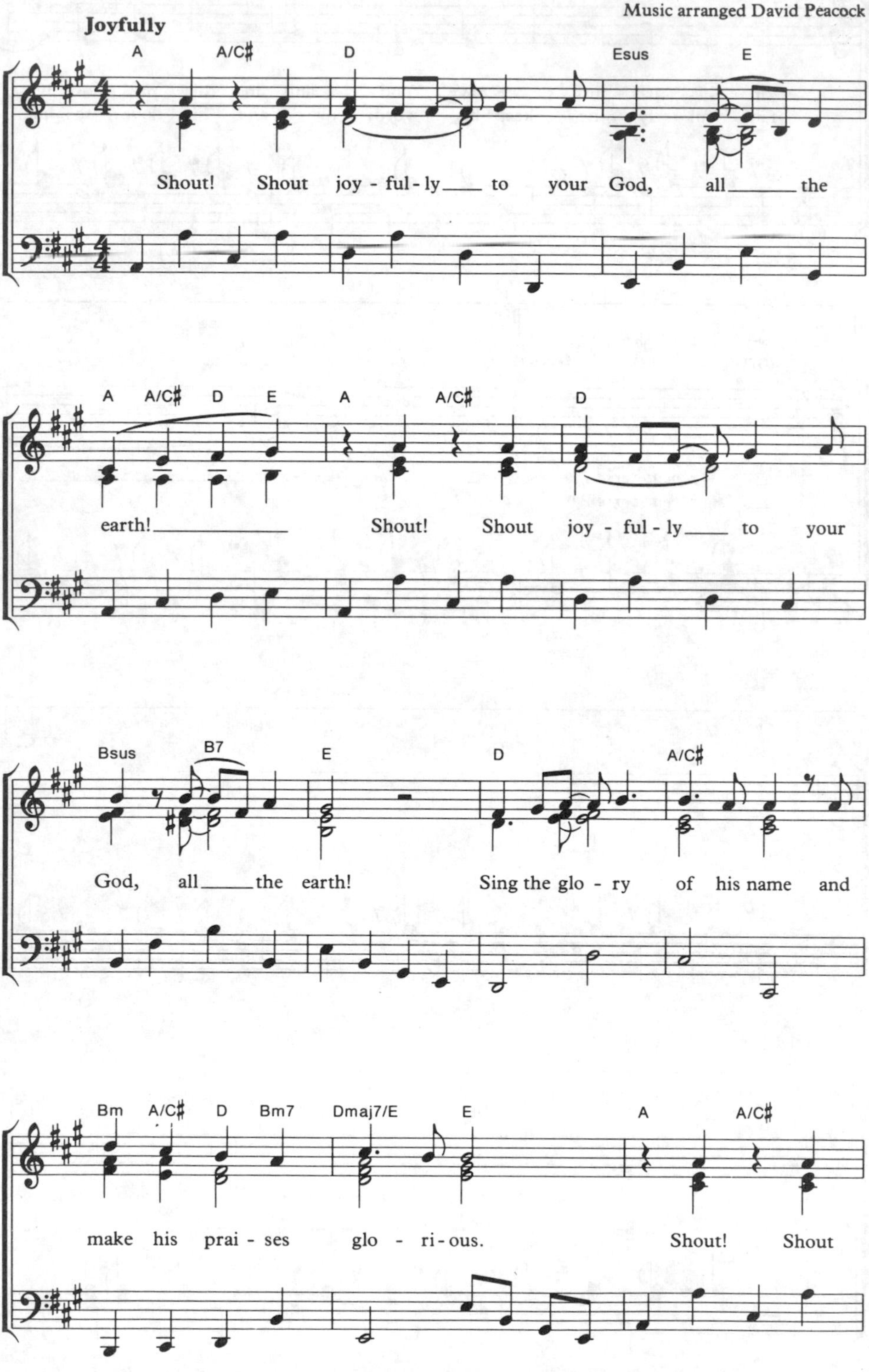
Joyfully
A A/C♯ D Esus E
Shout! Shout joy - ful - ly to your God, all the
A A/C♯ D E A A/C♯ D
earth! Shout! Shout joy - ful - ly to your
Bsus B7 E D A/C♯
God, all the earth! Sing the glo - ry of his name and
Bm A/C♯ D Bm7 Dmaj7/E E A A/C♯
make his prai - ses glo - ri - ous. Shout! Shout

Words and music: © 1985 Integrity's Hosanna! Music, administered in Europe (excl. German speaking countries) by Kingsway's Thankyou Music, PO Box 75, Eastbourne, East Sussex BN23 6NW

Fine
D.C.
D Bm9 Dmaj7/E E7 A
joy - ful - ly to your God, all the earth!
D A/C♯ Bm7 D/E E D/A A
Joy-ful-ly, joy-ful-ly, all the earth shall bow the knee;
D B Bm7 Dmaj7/E E
joy - ful-ly, joy - ful-ly, we will sing in har - mo-ny,
Bm7 A/C♯ D F♯m7 Bm9 D Esus E7
sing - ing prai - ses to your name!

181 Show your power, O Lord

Capo 2(G)

Words and music: Graham Kendrick

With energy ♩ = 143
A (G) D (C) A/E (G) E7 (D7) A (G) Asus (Gsus) A (G) D/A (C)
1 Show your power, O Lord,_ de - mon - strate the just - ice of your king-dom; prove your migh - ty word,_
2 Show your power, O Lord,_ cause your church to rise_ _and take_ ac - tion; let all fear_ be gone,_
C♯m7 (Bm7)
vin - di - cate your name_ be-fore a watch-ing world._
pow-ers of the age_ to come are break-ing through._

Words and music: © 1988 Make Way Music,
PO Box 263, Croydon, Surrey CR9 5AP.
International copyright secured. All rights reserved. Used by permission.

D (C) E/D (D) C♯m7 (Bm7) F♯m7 (Em7)
Awe - some are your deeds, O Lord – re -
We your peo - ple are rea - dy to serve, to a -
B7 (A7) D/E (C) E (D)
- new them for this hour.
- rise and to o - bey.
1.
A (G) D (C) A/E (G) E7 (D7) A (G) Asus (Gsus) A (G)
Show your power, O Lord – a-mong the peo-ple now.
2.
A (G) D (C) A/E (G) E7 (D7) A (G) D (C)
Show your power, O Lord, and set the peo-ple; show your power, O Lord,
A/E (G) E7 (D7) A (G) Asus (Gsus) A (G)
and set the peo - ple free.

182 Sing alleluia to the Lord

Words: verse 1 Linda Stassen,
verses 2–4 anonymous
Matthew 28.6, Mark 16.6, Luke 24.34, John 14.3
Music: Linda Stassen
arranged David Peacock

Capo 3(Am)

Flowing

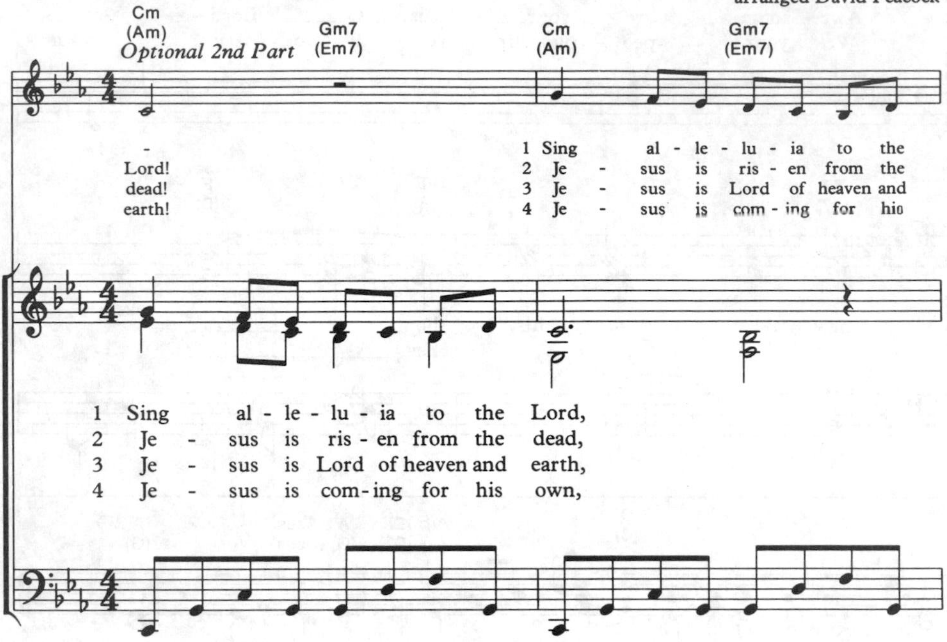

Cm (Am)
Gm7 (Em7)
Optional 2nd Part
Cm (Am)
Gm7 (Em7)
1 Sing al - le - lu - ia to the
Lord! 2 Je - sus is ris - en from the
dead! 3 Je - sus is Lord of heaven and
earth! 4 Je - sus is com - ing for his
1 Sing al - le - lu - ia to the Lord,
2 Je - sus is ris - en from the dead,
3 Je - sus is Lord of heaven and earth,
4 Je - sus is com - ing for his own,

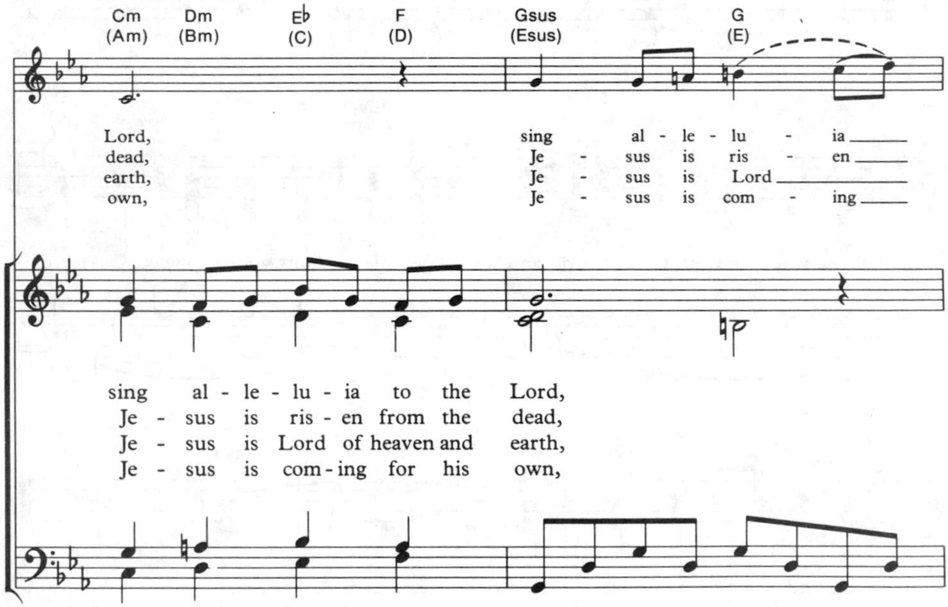

Cm (Am)
Dm (Bm)
E♭ (C)
F (D)
Gsus (Esus)
G (E)
Lord, sing al - le - lu - ia
dead, Je - sus is ris - en
earth, Je - sus is Lord
own, Je - sus is com - ing
sing al - le - lu - ia to the Lord,
Je - sus is ris - en from the dead,
Je - sus is Lord of heaven and earth,
Je - sus is com - ing for his own,

Words (verse 1) and music: © 1974 Linda Stassen/New Song Ministries.
Music arrangement: © David Peacock/Jubilate Hymns †

Cm (Am)
Gm/B♭ (Em)
A♭ (F)
E♭/G (C)
al - le - lu - ia,
sing al - le - lu - ia, sing al - le - lu - ia,
Je - sus is ris - en, Je - sus is ris - en,
Je - sus is Lord, Je - sus is Lord,
Je - sus is com - ing, Je - sus is com - ing,
Fm9 (Dm9)
Gm7 (Em7)
Cm (Am)
Gm7 (Em7)
4.
Cm (Am)
sing al - le - lu - ia to the
Je - sus is ris - en from the
Je - sus is Lord of heaven and
Je - sus is com - ing for his own.
sing al - le - lu - ia to the Lord!
Je - sus is ris - en from the dead!
Je - sus is Lord of heaven and earth!
Je - sus is com - ing for his own.

183 Sing of the Lord's goodness

Words and music: Ernest Sands
descant: Christopher Walker
arranged Paul Inwood

Lively jazz 'feel'

Intro (1st time only)
Em Bm7 Em Bm7 Em Bm7
Verses may be sung by soloist or small group
1 Sing of the Lord's good-ness, Fa - ther of all wis-dom,
2 Pow - er he has wield - ed, hon - our is his gar-ment,
3 Cour - age in our dark-ness, com - fort in our sor-row –
4 Praise him with your sing - ing, praise him with the trum-pet,
Em D G Bm7 Em Bm7
come to him and bless his name. Mer - cy he has shown us,
ri - sen from the snares of death. His word he has spo - ken,
Spi - rit of our God most high! Sol - ace for the wea - ry,
praise God with the lute and harp. Praise him with the cym-bals,
Descant
Em Bm7 Am7 Bm7 Em
You peo - ple
his love is for ev - er, faith - ful to the end of days.
one bread he has bro - ken, new life he now gives to all.
par - don for the sin - ner, splen-dour of the liv - ing God!
praise him with your danc-ing, praise God till the end of days.

Words and music: © Ernest Sands
Music arrangement: © Paul Inwood. Descant: © Christopher Walker
Published by OCP Publications. Administered in the UK by
The St Thomas More Group, 30 North Terrace, Mildenhall, Suffolk IP28 7AB

Am7 D Gmaj7 Am B7
come sing praise sing praise to
Come then all you na-tions, sing of your Lord's good-ness, me-lo-dies of praise and
Em Am7 D Gmaj7
God Come and ring out the Lord's glo - ry praise him with your mu - sic,
thanks to God; ring out the Lord's glo - ry, praise him with your mu - sic,
Am Bm7 Em Bm7 Em Bm7 Em
wor - ship him and bless his name.
wor-ship him and bless his name.

Another rhythm for the keyboard accompaniment:

etc.

184 Sing praise to the Lord

Words: from Psalms 148, 150
H W Baker (1821–1877)
in this version Jubilate Hymns
Music: C H H Parry (1848–1918)

Laudate Dominum 10 10 11 11

Capo 3(G)

1 Sing praise to the Lord! praise him in the
2 Sing praise to the Lord! praise him up - on
3 Sing praise to the Lord! all things that give
height; re - joice in his word you an - gels of
earth in tune - ful ac - cord, you saints of new
sound, each ju - bi - lant chord re - e - cho a -
light: you hea - vens, a - dore him__ by__ whom you were
birth: praise him who has brought you__ his__ grace from a -
- round: loud or - gans, his glo - ry__ proc - laim in deep
made, and wor - ship be - fore__him in bright-ness ar - rayed.
- bove; praise him who has taught you to sing of his love.
tone, and sweet harp, the sto - ry of what he has done.

Words: © in this version Jubilate Hymns †

B♭ (G) Cm (Am) F (D) B♭ (G) E♭ (C) F7 (D7)
4 Sing praise to the Lord! thanks - giv - ing and
B♭ (G) F (D) B♭ (G) F (D) Gm (Em) C7 (A7)
song to him be out - poured all a - ges a -
F (D) B♭ (G) E♭ (C) Cm (Am)
- long; for love in cre - a - tion, for heaven re -
F (D) D (B) Gm (Em) Cm (Am) B♭/F (G) F7 (D7) B♭ (G)
- stored, for grace of sal - va - tion, sing praise to the Lord!

185 Sing to the Lord

Marche Militaire

Capo 5(C)

Words: from Psalm 96
Michael Perry
Music: F Schubert (1797–1928)
arranged Norman Warren

Intro.(1st verse only)
F (C)
f
C (G) F (C) C (G)
1 Sing to the Lord with a
2 Beau - ty and power are the
3 So let the skies sing a -
F (C) C7 (G7) F (C) D (A)
song of pro - found de - light, serve him by day and bring
marks of our Sav - iour's grace, splen - dour and light shine in
- loud and the earth re - joice – beasts of the field and the

Music arrangement: © Norman Warren / Jubilate Hymns †

Words: © Michael Perry / Jubilate Hymns †

Gm (Dm) D7 (A7) Gm (Dm) C (G) F (C)
MEN
prais-es in the night: tell of the bat-tles fought for us,
glo-ry from his face: wor-ship the Lord in ho-li-ness,
for-est lift their voice: firm-ly he set the sol-id ground,
C7 (G7) F (C) C (G) F (C)
ALL – PART I
ALL – PART II
WOMEN
mar-vel-lous, glo-ri-ous; tell of his won-ders done for us,
faith-ful-ness, god-li-ness – judg-ing the world with right-eous-ness
seas a-bound, skies re-sound; all we de-sire in God is found –
1.2.
3.
G7 (D7) C (G) C7 (G7) F (C)
ALL
ALL
wor-thy of ac-claim.
he will come to reign.
glo-ry to his name!

186 Sing to the world

Universa laus

Words: Patrick Lee
Mark 16.15
Music: Ernest Sands
arranged Paul Inwood

Lively

Instrumental Descant (v.5 only)
Instruments
D C/D D Em/D D Em/D D C/D
GROUP (OR SOLO)
1 Sing to the world of Christ our sove - reign
2 Sing to the world of Christ the Prince of
3 Sing to the world of Christ our stead - fast
4 Sing to the world of Christ our Sav - iour
5 Sing to the world of Christ at God's right
D C/D D C7 F Gm/F
Lord, tell of his birth which
peace show - ing to us the
friend, ALL off - ering him-self to
king, born that his death the
hand: praise to the Spi - rit

Music: © Ernest Sands. Music arrangement: © Paul Inwood
Published by OCP Publications. Administered in the UK by The St Thomas More Group, 30 North Terrace, Mildenhall, Suffolk IP28 7AB

Words: © Patrick Lee

F Gm7 A A7 D D7
brought new life___ to all;
Fa - ther's lov - ing care,
live the con - stant sign,
world's re - lease should win:
both have sent from heaven,
GROUP (OR SOLO)
G Em F♯m Bm7 Em7 A7
speak - of his life, his love, his ho - ly
plead - ing that love should reign that wars might
food for our souls un - til we meet life's
hung on a cross, for - give - ness he could
liv - ing in us till earth shall reach its

D G A7 D
word, let ev - ery na - tion
cease, teach - ing we need the
end – ALL gives us his flesh for
bring, bur - ied, he rose to
span, time be no more, and
G/F♯ A D G A Bm C
hear and know his call: sing to the world of
love of God to share: sing to the world of
bread, his blood for wine: sing to the world of
con - quer death and sin – sing to the world of
Christ shall come a - gain: sing to the world of

1-4.
Bm7
Am7
D
C/D
D
C/D
Christ our sove - reign Lord.
Christ the Prince of peace.
Christ our stead - fast friend.
Christ our Sav - iour king.
Christ at God's right
Last time
D
C/D
D
C/D
D
hand.

187 Sing to God new songs of worship

Ode to Joy 8 7 8 7 D
Capo 5(C)

Words: from Psalm 98
Michael Baughen
Music: Ludwig van Beethoven (1770–1827)

F (C) Gm7/F (Dm7) F (C) Dm7 (Am7) F (C) C (G) F (C) C (G) F (C) F/C (C) C (G)
1 Sing to God new songs of wor-ship – all his deeds are mar - vell-ous;
2 Sing to God new songs of wor-ship – earth has seen his vic - to - ry;
3 Sing to God new songs of wor-ship – let the sea now make a noise;
F (C) Gm7/F (Dm7) F (C) Dm7 (Am7) F (C) C (G) F (C) C (G) F (C) Csus (Gsus) C (G) F (C)
he has brought sal - va-tion to us with his hand and ho - ly arm:
let the lands of earth be joy - ful prais - ing him with thank - ful-ness:
all on earth and in the wa-ters sound your prais - es to the Lord:
C (G) F/C (C) Dm7/C (Am7) C7 (G7) F/C (C) Dm7/C (Am7) C (G) A7/C♯ (E7) Dm (Am) G (D) Csus (Gsus) C (G)
he has shown to all the __ na-tions right-eous-ness and sav - ing power;
sound up - on the harp his prais-es, play to __ him with me - lo - dy;
let the hills re - joice to - ge-ther, let the __ ri - vers clap their hands,
F (C) E♭ (B♭) B♭/D (F) F (C) Gm (Dm) B♭ (F) F/A (C) C7/G (G7) F (C) Csus (Gsus) C (G) F (C)
he re-called his truth and mer - cy to his peo-ple Is - ra - el.
let the trum-pets sound his tri-umph, show your joy to God the king!
for with right-eous - ness and jus - tice he will come to judge the earth.

Words: © Michael Baughen / Jubilate Hymns †

188 Soften my heart

Words and music: Graham Kendrick
Romans 12.9, 15; Ephesians 4.32

Prayerfully ♩ = 104
D Em Baug/E Em7 A G/B A/C♯ D
Sof-ten my heart, Lord, sof-ten my heart;
Dmaj7 D6 D Em Baug/E Em7
from all in-dif - ference
A D F♯m/C♯ Cdim Gmaj7
set me a-part to feel your com-pas - sion,
A/G F♯m7 Bm7 B♭maj7
to weep with your tears come sof-ten my
D F♯m/C Bm B♭maj7 D Dsus D
heart, O Lord, sof-ten my heart.

Words and music: © 1988 Make Way Music, PO Box 263, Croydon, Surrey CR9 5AP.
International copyright secured. All rights reserved. Used by permission.

189 So freely flows the endless love

Capo 2(G)

Words and music: Dave Bilbrough
Hosea 14.4

With a sense of mystery

A (G)
E (D)
1 So free - ly___ flows the
(2) -plete - ly -___ that's the
(3) ea - sy,___ I re -
D (C)
E (D)
A (G)
end-less love___ you give___ to me;___ so free - ly,___
way you give___ your love___ to me,___ com - plete - ly,___
- ceive the love___ you give___ to me;___ so ea - sy,___
E (D)
D (C)
E (D)
___ not de - pen-dent on___ my part.___ As I am
___ not de - pen-dent on my part.___ As I am
___ not de - pen-dent on my part.___ Flow-ing

Words and music: © 1983 Kingsway's Thankyou Music,
PO Box 75, Eastbourne, East Sussex BN23 6NW

F♯m (Em)
D (C)
Esus (Dsus)
reach-ing out, re-veal the love with-in your heart;
reach-ing out, re-veal the love with-in your heart;
out to me — the love with-in your heart;
E (D)
F♯m (Em)
D (C)
as I am reach-ing out, re-veal the love with-in your
as I am reach-ing out, re-veal the love with-in your
flow-ing out to me — the love with-in your
1.2.
3.
Esus (Dsus)
E (D)
E (D)
A (G)
heart!
heart!
heart!
2 Com -
3 So

190 Soon – and very soon

Capo 3(D)

Joyfully

Words and music: Andrae Crouch
Revelation 21.4 and 22.20
Music arranged David Peacock

F (D)
Gm7/C (Em7)
F (D)
1&4 Soon – and ve - ry soon –
2 No more cry - ing there, we are go-ing to see the King,
3 No more dy - ing there,
Gm7/C (Em7)
Gm7
C (A)
Gm7/C (Em7)
soon – and ve - ry soon –
No more cry - ing there, we are
No more dy - ing there,
F (D)
C7 (A7)
F (D)
A7/E (F♯7)
go-ing to see the King,
soon – and ve - ry soon –
No more cry - ing there,
No more dy - ing there,
Dm (Bm)
B♭m/D♭ (Gm)
F/C (D)
F
we are go-ing to see the King. Al - le -

Words and music: © 1976 Bud John Songs/Crouch Music

F7 (D7) Gm7/B♭ (Em7) B♭m (Gm) F/C (D)
- lu - ia, al - le - lu - ia, we're go-ing to see the King!
1.2.
F C7 (A7)
3.4.
F (D) Dm7 (Bm7) G7 (E7) C7 (A7) F (D) Dm7 (Bm7)
Al - le - lu - ia, al - le -
G7 (E7) C7 (A7) F (D) Dm7 (Bm7) G7 (E7) C7 (A7)
p
- lu - ia, al - le - lu -
v.3
v.4
F (D) Dm7 (Bm7) G7 (E7) C7 (A7) F (D) D.C. F (D)
f
- ia, al - le - lu - ia! - ia!

191 Spirit of God

Capo 2(C)

Words and music: Chris Bowater

John 16.14

Broadly

Spi - rit of God, show me Je-sus;
re - move the dark - ness, let truth shine through.
Spi - rit of God, show me Je-sus;
re - veal the full - ness of his love to me!

Words and music: © 1978 Sovereign Lifestyle Music,
PO Box 356, Leighton Buzzard LU7 8WP. Used by permission.

192 Such love

Capo 4(C)

Words and music: Graham Kendrick
Ephesians 3.19

Flowing ♩ = 104

B (G) E (C) C♯m7 (Am7) 3 F♯m7 (Dm7)
1 Such love, pure as the whit - est snow,
2 Such love, still - ing my rest - less-ness,
3 Such love springs from e - ter - ni - ty,
B7 (G) F♯m7 (Dm7) B (G) 3 A/E (F) E (C)
such love weeps for the shame I know,
such love, fill - ing my emp - ti-ness,
such love, stream-ing through his - to-ry,
G♯sus (Esus) G♯ (E) C♯m (Am) C♯m/B (Am) 3 Amaj7 (Fmaj7)
such love, pay-ing the debt I owe –
such love, show-ing me ho - li-ness –
such love, foun-tain of life to me:
A♯dim7 (F♯dim7) E/B (C) Amaj7/B (Fmaj7) B6 (G6) E (C) Esus (Csus) E (C)
O Je - sus, such love!
O Je - sus, such love!
O Je - sus, such love!

Words and music: © 1988 Make Way Music,
PO Box 263, Croydon, Surrey CR9 5AP.
International copyright secured. All rights reserved. Used by permission.

193 Take my life and let it be

Nottingham 7777
Capo 5(C)

F R Havergal (1836–1879)
in this version Jubilate Hymns
Romans 12.1
W A Mozart (1756–1791)

F (C)
C (G)
C7 (G7)
F (C)
1 Take my life and let it be all you
2 Take my hands, and let them move at the
3 Take my voice, and let me sing al - ways,
Gm (Dm)
F (C)
C (G)
F (C)
C7 (G7)
pur - pose, Lord, for me; con - se - crate my pass - ing
im - pulse of your love; take my feet, and let them
on - ly, for my King; take my lips, let me pro -
F (C)
Gm (Dm)
C/F (G)
C7 (G7)
F (C)
days, let them flow in cease - less praise.
run with the news of vic - tory won.
- claim all the beau - ty of your name.

4 Take my wealth – all I possess,
make me rich in faithfulness;
take my mind that I may use
every power as you shall choose.

5 Take my motives and my will,
all your purpose to fulfil;
take my heart – it is your own,
it shall be your royal throne.

6 Take my love – my Lord, I pour
at your feet its treasure-store;
take myself, and I will be
yours for all eternity.

Words: © in this version Jubilate Hymns †

194 The Kingdom of God

Words: Bryn Rees (1911–1983)
Matthew 11.4 and Luke 7.22
Music: *A Supplement to the New Version* 1708
probably by W Croft (1678–1727)

Hanover   10 10 11 11

1 The King - dom of God is jus - tice and
2 The king - dom of God is mer - cy and
3 The king - dom of God is chal - lenge and
4 God's king - dom is come, the gift and the

joy; for Je - sus re - stores what sin would des -
grace; the cap - tives are freed, the sin - ners find
choice: be - lieve the good news, re - pent and re -
goal; in Je - sus be - gun, in hea - ven made

- troy. God's pow - er and glo - ry in Je - sus we
place, the out - cast are wel - comed God's ban - quet to
- joice! His love for us sin - ners brought Christ to his
whole. The heirs of the king - dom shall an - swer his

know; and here and here - af - ter the king - dom shall grow.
share; and hope is a - wak - ened in place of des - pair.
cross: our cri - sis of judge - ment for gain or for loss.
call; and all things cry 'Glo - ry!' to God all in all.

Words: © Mrs M Rees

195 Teach me your way

Undivided heart

Words and music: John Daniels
Psalm 86.11

Prayerfully
C B7 D/E A7 Dm7 F/G
Teach me your way, O Lord, and I will walk in
C G/B Am7 B7 D/E A7
your truth; give me an un - di - vi - ded heart
Dm7 F/G C Gm7 Gm7/C C
that I may fear your name. And I will praise you,
Fmaj7 B♭maj7 Gm7 B♭/C C Fsus F♯dim
O Lord my God, with all of my heart;

Words and music: © 1986 Kingsway's Thankyou Music,
PO Box 75, Eastbourne, East Sussex BN23 6NW

Gm7 Gm7/C C Fmaj7 B♭maj7
and I will praise you, O Lord my God,
Gm7 Gm7/C C Fsus F/G G C B7
and I will glo - ri-fy your name for ev - er. Teach me your
D/E A7 Dm7 F/G C G/B
way, O Lord, and I will walk in your truth;
Am7 B7 D/E A7 Dm7 F/G C
give me an un - di - vi - ded heart that I may fear your name.

196 Tell all the world of Jesus

Thornbury 7 6 7 6 D

Words: J E Seddon (1915–1983)
Mark 16.15
Music: B Harwood (1859–1949)

D A Bm G D/F♯ E A
1 Tell all the world of Je - sus, our
2 Tell all the world of Je - sus, that
3 Tell all the world of Je - sus, that
D G Em7 A7 D
sav - iour, Lord and king; and
ev - ery - one may find the
ev - ery - one may know of
A Bm G D/F♯ E A
let the whole cre - a - tion of
joy of his for - give - ness – true
his al - migh - ty tri - umph de -
D G Em A7 Dsus D
his sal - va - tion sing: pro -
peace of heart and mind: pro -
- feat - ing ev - ery foe: pro -

Music: © Executors of the late B Harwood
Words: © Mrs M Seddon / Jubilate Hymns †

F♯m Bm C♯ F♯m
- claim his glo - rious great - ness in
- claim his per - fect good - ness, his
- claim his com - ing glo - ry, when
Bm C♯7 F♯m A7
na - ture and in grace; cre -
deep, un - fail - ing care; his
sin is ov - er - thrown, and
D G E A D A
- a - tor and re - deem - er, the Lord of
love so rich in mer - cy, a love be -
he shall reign in splen - dour – the King up -
Bm G D Em A7 D
time and space.
- yond com - pare.
- on his throne!

197 Tell out, my soul

Woodlands 10 10 10 10

Words: from Luke 1
Timothy Dudley-Smith
Music: W Greatorex (1877–1949)
descant David Iliff

A D G A D
1 Tell out, my soul, the great-ness_ of the Lord!
2 Tell out, my soul, the great-ness_ of his name!
3 Tell out, my soul, the great-ness of his might!
A Bm D A7 D Em Em/G F♯
un - num - bered bless-ings give my spi - rit voice;
make known his might, the deeds his arm has done;
powers and do - min-ions lay their glo - ry by.
B7 Em Em7/D A7
ten - der to me the pro-mise of his word;
his mer - cy sure, from age to age the same;
Proud hearts and stub - born wills are put to flight,
D G D G A D Em7/G A Asus D
in God my sav - iour shall my heart re - joice.
his ho - ly name – the Lord, the migh - ty one.
the hun - gry fed, the hum - ble lift - ed high.

Music: © Oxford University Press
Descant: © David Iliff / Jubilate Hymns †
Words: © Timothy Dudley-Smith

Descant
A D G A D A Bm
4 Tell out, my soul, the glo-ries of his word! firm is his
4 Tell out, my soul, the glo-ries of his word! firm is his
D A7 D Em Em/G F♯ B7 Em Em7/D
pro-mise, and his mer - cy sure. Tell out, my soul, the great - ness
pro-mise, and his mer - cy sure. Tell out, my soul, the great-ness of the
A7 D G D G A D Em7/G A Asus D
of the Lord to child - ren's child - ren and for ev - er - more!
Lord to child-ren's child-ren and for ev - er - more!

198 The earth was dark

(Lights to the world)

Words and music: John Daniels
and Phil Thomson
Genesis 1.3, Matthew 5.14
Music arranged Christopher Norton

Spirited ♩ = 112

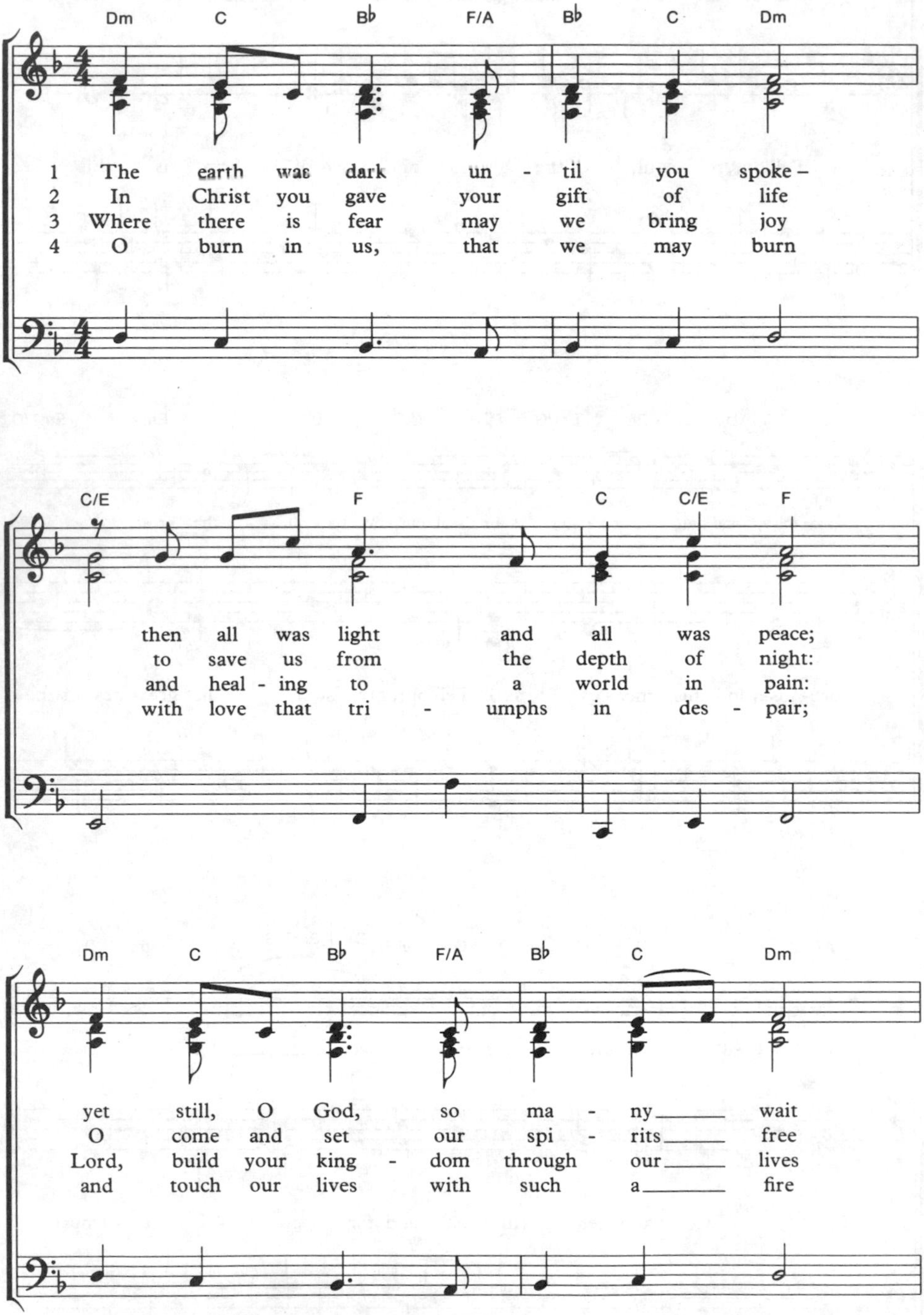
Dm C B♭ F/A B♭ C Dm
1 The earth was dark un - til you spoke –
2 In Christ you gave your gift of life
3 Where there is fear may we bring joy
4 O burn in us, that we may burn
C/E F C C/E F
then all was light and all was peace;
to save us from the depth of night:
and heal - ing to a world in pain:
with love that tri - umphs in des - pair;
Dm C B♭ F/A B♭ C Dm
yet still, O God, so ma - ny wait
O come and set our spi - rits free
Lord, build your king - dom through our lives
and touch our lives with such a fire

Words and music: © HarperCollins*Religious*/CopyCare Ltd,
PO Box 77, Hailsham, East Sussex BN27 3EF

C/E F G C
to see the flame of love re - leased.
and draw us to your per - fect light!
till Je - sus walks this earth a - gain.
that souls may search and find you there.
Am Dm7 Gm7 C Am7 Dm7
Lights to the world! O Light di - vine, kin - dle in us a
Gm7 C A/C♯ Dm C/E Cm/F B♭ F/A
migh-ty flame, till ev-ery heart, con-sumed by love shall rise to
1.2.3.
4.
Gm C7 F F/A Gm7 C7sus C7 F
praise your ho - ly name!

199 The King is among us

Words and music: Graham Kendrick
Joel 2.28, Romans 8.17, Ephesians 1.5
Music arranged David Peacock

Flowing

E
A
1 The King is a - mong
(2) looks down up - on
(3) each child is spe -
B
G♯7/B♯
C♯m
us, his Spi - rit is
us, de - light in his
- cial, ac - cep - ted and
F♯m7
Am6
here: let's draw near and
face, en - joy - ing his
loved – a love - gift from
E
G♯7
C♯m
F♯9
wor - ship, let songs fill the
child - ren's love, en - thralled by our
Je - sus to his Fa - ther a -

Words and music: © 1981 Kingsway's Thankyou Music,
PO Box 75, Eastbourne, East Sussex BN23 6NW

4 And now he is giving
his gifts to us all;
for no-one is worthless
and each one is called.

5 The Spirit's anointing
on all flesh comes down,
and we shall be channels
for works like his own:

6 We come now believing
your promise of power,
for we are your people
and this is your hour.

7 The King is among us,
his Spirit is here:
let's draw near and worship,
let songs fill the air!

199A PRAISE SHOUT

LEADER Praise God in his sanctuary;
ALL **praise him in his mighty heavens.**

LEADER Praise him for his acts of power;
ALL **praise him for his surpassing greatness**

LEADER Let everything that has breath praise the Lord:
ALL **praise the Lord! Amen!**

From Psalm 150

200 The Lord has led forth

Words and music: Chris Bowater
Psalm 105.43
Music arranged David Peacock

Joyfully
D Em7 D/F♯ G
The Lord has led forth his peo - ple with
D Em7 D Em7 D G
joy, and his cho - sen ones with
D/A A D G/D A D Em7
sing - ing, sing - ing; the Lord has led
D/F♯ G D Em7 D/F♯ Em7/G
forth his peo - ple with joy, and his

Words and music: © 1982 Sovereign Lifestyle Music,
PO Box 356, Leighton Buzzard LU7 8WP. Used by permission.

Fine
D/A Bm Em7 D/A A D G/D D
cho - sen ones with sing - ing.
Bm F♯m
He has given to them the lands of the na -
Bm F♯m
- tions, to pos - sess the fruit and keep his laws, and
D.𝄋 al Fine
G G/A A
praise, praise his name. The

201 The Lord is a mighty king

Creation Creed
Capo 2(G)

Words and music: Graham Kendrick
Genesis 1.1, 1.26; Romans 8.19

Strongly ♩ = 86
F♯m (Em) D/F♯ (C) E/F♯ (D)
E (D) Dmaj7 (Cmaj7)
MEN
WOMEN
1 The Lord is a migh-ty king, the mak - er of ev-ery-thing,
2 And yet we were de-ceived, in pride the lie be-lieved;
the Lord, he made the earth; he spoke, and it came at once to
to sin and death's de-cay the whole cre - a - tion fell that
birth. He said, 'Let us make man-kind' – 'The crown of his de-sign.'
day. Now all cre - a - tion yearns for lib-er-a - tion

Words and music: © 1988 Make Way Music, PO Box 263, Croydon, Surrey CR9 5AP.
International copyright secured. All rights reserved. Used by permission.

E (D)
Dmaj7 (Cmaj7)
E (D)
F♯m (Em)
MEN
WOMEN
ALL
'in our own like - ness'. his im - age in ev-ery hu - man face!
all things in Christ re-stored – the pur - chase of his pre-cious blood. And he
Chorus
A (G)
E/A (D)
Bm (Am)
F♯m (Em)
A (G)
E/A (D)
made us for his de-light, gave us the gift of life, cre - a-ted us fa-mi-ly,__ to
Dmaj7 (Cmaj7)
E (D)
F♯sus (Esus)
F♯ (E)
Bm (Am)
Esus (D)
E (D)
1.
D (C)
A (G)
F♯m (Em)
D/F♯ (C)
E/F♯ (D)
be his glo - ry, to be his glo - ry.
2.
last time
F♯m (Em)
D/F♯ (C)
E/F♯ (D)
D (C)
A (G)
D.S.
D (C)
A (G)
D (C)
A (G)
- ry And he - ry

202 The Lord was born

Belize Boogie

Words: Vanessa Strachan
Music: Belize traditional melody
arranged Vanessa Strachan

Lively

C F G7 C F G7
1 The Lord was
C F G7
born a babe in a sta - ble, poor and
(2) sick – it was - n't ex - pect - ed that our
(3) what you do or you don't do that you
(4) lives and gifts as we bring them – may we
C
bare he died on a tree; but by the
God would stand with the weak – be - friend - ed
are ac - cep - ted and loved; but by the
share your love and your word! And as we
F G7
power of love he was a - ble from the
those that o - thers re - ject - ed: may we
grace of God, for he wants to be your
see the signs of your king - dom, we pro -

Words and music arrangement: © 1987 'Don't call me Music',
6 Robin Court, 46 Lupus Street, London SW1V 3ED

C
power of death to be free.
too be hum - ble and meek.
friend in hea - ven a - bove.
-claim that 'Yes, you are Lord!'
Our
F G7 C
Lord, he is the re-deem-er, Je-sus Christ–we wor-ship his name: so
F G7 C F
come, be-lieve in his word, and you will not be search-ing a-gain!
1.2.3.
4.
G C F G C
2 He healed the
3 It's not by
4 We give back

203(i) The Lord my shepherd

(FIRST TUNE)

Crimond 8 6 8 6 (CM)

Words: from Psalm 23
Christopher Idle
Music: J S Irvine (1836–1887)
arranged D Grant (1833–1893)
descant: Norman Warren

Capo 5(C)

Descant
F (C)
B♭ (F)
F/C (C)
C (G)
5 Your good - ness and your gra - cious
6 To Fa - ther, Son, and Spi - rit,
1 The Lord my shep - herd rules my
2 The Lord re - vives my fail - ing
3 Though in a val - ley dark as
4 While all my en - em - ies look
5 Your good - ness and your gra - cious
6 To Fa - ther, Son, and Spi - rit,

F (C)
G7/D (D7)
G7 (D7)
love pur - sue me all my
praise! to God whom we a -
life and gives me all I
strength, he makes my joy com -
death, no e - vil makes me
on you spread a roy - al
love pur - sue me all my
praise! to God whom we a -

Descant: © Norman Warren / Jubilate Hymns †

Words: © Christopher Idle / Jubilate Hymns †

C (G) F (C) F/C C7 (G7) F/A (C) C7 (G7)
days; your house, O Lord, shall be my
- dore be wor - ship, glo - ry, power and
need: he leads me by re - fresh - ing
- plete, and in right paths, for his name's
fear; your shep - herd's staff pro - tects my
feast; you fill my cup, an - oint my
days; your house, O Lord, shall be my
- dore be wor - ship, glo - ry, power and
F (C) Gm/B♭ (Dm) F/C (C) C7 (G7) F (C)
home – your name, my end - less praise.
love both now and ev - er - more.
streams; in pas - tures green I feed.
sake, he guides my fal - tering feet.
way, for you are with me there.
head, and treat me as your guest.
home – your name, my end - less praise.
love both now and ev - er - more.

203(ii) The Lord my shepherd

(SECOND TUNE)

Words: from Psalm 23
Christopher Idle
Music: Merla Watson
arranged Norman Warren

Hebrew style

Em
B7
1 The Lord my shep - herd rules my life and gives me all I
3 Though in a val - ley dark as death, no e - vil makes me
5 Your good-ness and your gra-cious love pur - sue me all my
Em
B7
need: he leads me by re - fresh-ing streams; in pas-tures green I
fear, your shep-herd's staff pro - tects my way, for you are with me
days; your house, O Lord, shall be my home - your name, my end - less
Em
Am
Em
B7
feed. 2 The Lord re - vives my fail-ing strength, he makes my joy com -
there. 4 While all my en - em - ies look on you spread a roy - al
praise. 6 To Fa-ther, Son, and Spi-rit, praise! to God whom we a -
Em
Am
Em
B7
Em
- plete, and in right paths, for his name's sake, he guides my fal-tering feet.
feast; you fill my cup, an - oint my head, and treat me as your guest.
- dore be wor-ship, glo - ry, power and love both now and ev - er - more.

Music: © Catacombs Publications/CopyCare Ltd,
PO Box 77, Hailsham, East Sussex BN27 3EF

Words: © Christopher Idle / Jubilate Hymns †

204 There is a green hill far away

Words: C F Alexander (1818–1895)
Matthew 27.33, Mark 15.22, Luke 23.33, John 19.17
1 Corinthians 6.20, 1 Peter 2.23 and 3.18
Music: W Horsley (1774–1858)

Horsley 8 6 8 6 (CM)

Capo 3(C)

E♭ (C) B♭ (G) E♭ (C) A♭ (F) E♭ (C) A♭ (F) B♭ (G)
1 There is a green hill far a - way,
2 We may not know, we can - not tell
3 He died that we may be for - given,
E♭ (C) B♭ (F) F7 (D7) B♭ (G)
out - side a ci - ty wall,
what pains he had to bear,
he died to make us good;
A♭ (F) B♭7 (G7) E♭ (C) A♭ (F) G (E)
where our dear Lord was cru - ci - fied,
but we be - lieve it was for us
that we might go at last to heaven,
A♭ (F) E♭/B♭ (C) B♭7 (G7) E♭ (C)
who died to save us all.
he hung and suf - fered there.
saved by his pre - cious blood.

4 There was no other good enough
to pay the price of sin;
he, only, could unlock the gate
of heaven – and let us in.

5 Lord Jesus, dearly you have loved;
and we must love you too,
and trust in your redeeming blood
and learn to follow you.

205 The spirit of the Lord

Words and music: Chris Bowater
Isaiah 61.1, Luke 4.18

With strength
G F/G C
1 The Spi - rit of the
2 And he has called on
3 Let right-eous - ness a -
G G/B Am G/D D7
Lord, the sove - reign Lord, is on me
me to bind up all the bro - ken hearts,
- rise and blos - som as a gar - den;
C G Bm7 Am7
be-cause he has a - noin - ted me to preach good news
to min - is - ter re - lease to ev - ery cap - ti - va - ted
let praise be-gin to spring in ev - ery tongue and
D7 C/D D7 G Bm7
to the poor:
soul: Pro-claim-ing Je -
na - tion:

Words and music: © 1985 Sovereign Lifestyle Music,
PO Box 356, Leighton Buzzard LU7 8WP. Used by permission.

Am7 D7 G Bm7 Am7 D7
- sus, on - ly Je - sus – it is
G Em Am D7
Je - sus, sav - iour, heal - er and bap - ti - zer, and the
G Em7 Am7 D7 C
migh - ty king, the vic - tor and de - liv - erer – he is Lord, he is
G/B Am7 Am7/D G
Lord, he is Lord!

206 The price is paid

Words and music: Graham Kendrick
Isaiah 53.5, Romans 8.1, 1 Corinthians 6.20, 1 Peter 2.24
Music arranged Geoff Baker

Triumphantly
G C F C
1 The price is paid: come, let us en - ter in to all that
(2) paid: see Sa-tan flee a - way – for Je-sus,
(3) paid: and by that scourg-ing cruel, he took our
(4) paid: 'Wor-thy the Lamb!' we cry – e - ter - ni -
F C/E G9 C G C F
Je - sus died to make our own. For ev - ery sin more than e-nough he
cru - ci-fied, de-stroys his power. No more to pay! Let ac - cu - sa - tion
sick-nes-ses as if his own. And by his wounds, his bo-dy bro-ken
- ty shall ne-ver cease his praise. The Church of Christ shall rule up - on the
C F C/E G9 C
Chorus
gave, and bought our free-dom from each guil - ty stain.
cease: in Christ there is no con-dem-na-tion now!
there, his heal - ing touch may now by faith be known.
earth: in Je - sus' name we have au - tho - ri - ty!
The price is
F G C F D/F♯
paid, Al - le - lu - ia – a - ma-zing grace, so strong and

Words and music: © 1984 Kingsway's Thankyou Music,
PO Box 75, Eastbourne, East Sussex BN23 6NW

G G7 F C
sure! And so with all my heart,___ my life in
F Am7 D7/F♯ F C/E G9 G
ev - ery___ part,___ I live to thank you for___ the price you paid.___
1-3.
C Dm7 G9 G C G
2 The price is
3 The price is
4 The price is
4.
Am Am/G D9/F♯ F C/E F/G G C F/C C
paid

207 There is a Redeemer

Flowing

Words and music: Melody Green
Music arranged David Peacock

D A/D D G/D D
optional 2nd part
1 There is a Re - deem - er,
2 Je - sus, my Re - deem - er,
3 When I stand in glo - ry
1 There is a Re - deem - er,
2 Je - sus, my Re - deem - er,
3 When I stand in glo - ry
con ped.
Em7 G/A A7 D Asus A7 D A/D D
Je - sus, God's own Son, pre - cious Lamb of
name a - bove all names, pre - cious Son of
I will see his face, and there I'll serve my
Je - sus, God's own Son, pre - cious Lamb of
name a - bove all names, pre - cious Son of
I will see his face, and there I'll serve my
G D/F♯ Em7 Asus A7 D D/F♯ G A7
God, Mes - si - ah, ho - ly One.
God, Mes - si - ah, Lamb for sin - ners slain:
king for ev - er in that ho - ly place.
God, Mes - si - ah, ho - ly One.
God, Mes - si - ah, Lamb for sin - ners slain:
king for ev - er in that ho - ly place.

Words and music: © 1982 Birdwing Music/Cherry Lane Music/EMI Music,
127 Charing Cross Road, London WC2H OEA

Chorus
D D/F♯ G D Em7 G/A A7
Thank you, O my Fa - ther, for giv-ing us your
Thank you, O my Fa - ther, for giv-ing us your
D Em7/G A D Dmaj7/F♯ G D/F♯
Son, and leav - ing your Spi - rit till the
Son, and leav - ing your Spi - rit till the
1.2. 3.
Em7 Asus A7 D D/F♯ G A7 D
work on earth is done. done.
work on earth is done. done.

208 This earth belongs to God

Words: from Psalm 24
Christopher Idle
Music: J Clarke (c.1674–1707)
arranged Noël Tredinnick

Trumpet Voluntary

March style

A E A E
1 This earth be - longs to God, the
2 Lift high your heads, you gates, rise
3 Lift high your heads, you gates, and
4 All glo - ry be to God the
A E A B7 E
world, its wealth, and all its peo - ple;
up, you ev - er - last - ing doors, as
fling wide o - pen the an - cient doors, for
Fa - ther, Son, and Ho - ly Spi - rit;
A E A E
he formed the wa - ters wide and
here now the king of glo - ry
here comes the king of glo - ry
from a - ges past it was, is
A D Esus (tr) E7 A
Fine
fash - ioned ev - ery sea and shore.
en - ters in - to full com - mand.
tak - ing u - ni - ver - sal power.
now, and ev - er - more shall be.

Music arrangement: © Noël Tredinnick/Jubilate Hymns †
Words: © Christopher Idle / Jubilate Hymns †

Chorus
A (G) A (G)
(GROUP A)
Who may go up the hill of the Lord and
Who is the king, this king of glo - ry,
Who is the king, this king of glo - ry,
A E
stand in the place of ho - li - ness?
where is the throne he comes to claim?
what is the power by which he reigns?
(D) E (D)
(GROUP B)
On - ly the one whose heart is pure, whose
Christ is the king, the Lord of glo - ry,
Christ is the king, his cross his glo - ry,
E F♯m Bsus B7 E D.C.
hands and lips are clean.
fresh from his vic - to - ry.
and by love he rules.

The singers may divide at A and B

209 Through our God

Victory Song

Capo 3(Am)

Words and music: Dale Garratt
Psalm 108.13

Resolutely with steady pace
Cm (Am)
G7 (E7)
Descant (2nd time)
Ah
Through our God we shall do val - iant-ly, it is
Ah
Cm (Am)
he who will tread down our e - ne-mies; we'll
G7 (E7)
3rd time to Coda
Ah
sing and shout his vic - to - ry:
Cm (Am)
Bb (G)
Christ is king! For God has won the

Words and music: © 1977 Scripture in Song/CopyCare Ltd,
PO Box 77, Hailsham, East Sussex BN27 3EF

E♭ (C)
Fm (Dm)
B♭7 (G7)
vic - to - ry and set his peo - ple
Cm (Am)
B♭ (G)
E♭ (C)
free; his word has slain the e - ne - my, the
Fm (Dm)
G7 (E7)
Fm (Dm)
F7 (D7)
G7 (E7)
earth shall stand and see that Through our
CODA
G7 (E7)
Cm (Am)
G7 (E7)
Christ is king, Christ is
Cm (Am)
G7 (E7)
Cm (Am)
king, Christ is king!

210 To God be the glory

To God be the glory 11 11 11 11 and refrain

Words: F J van Alstyne (1820–1915)
John 3.16, Romans 3.25, Ephesians 1.7
Colossians 1.14, 1 John 2.2 and 4.10, Revelation 1.5
Music: W H Doane (1832–1916)

Capo 1(G)

Ab (G) Eb7 (D7) Ab (G) Eb (D) Ab (G)
1 To God be the glo - ry! great things he has done;
2 O per - fect re demp - tion, the pur - chase of blood!
3 Great things he has taught us, great things he has done,
Db (C) Ab (G) Bb7 (A7) Eb (D)
so loved he the world that he gave us his Son
to ev - ery be - liev - er the pro - mise of God:
and great our re - joic - ing through Je - sus the Son:
Ab (G) Eb7 (D7) Ab (G) Eb (D) Ab (G)
who yield - ed his life an a - tone - ment for sin,
the vil - est of - fen - der who tru - ly be - lieves,
but pur - er and high - er and great - er will be
Db (C) Ab/Eb (G) Eb7 (D7) Ab (G)
and op - ened the life - gate that all may go in.
that mo - ment from Je - sus a par - don re - ceives.
our won - der, our glad - ness, when Je - sus we see!

Chorus
Ab (G) Eb (D)
Praise the Lord, praise the Lord! let the earth hear his voice;
Eb7 (D7) Ab/C (G) Eb7/Bb (D7) Ab (G)
praise the Lord, praise the Lord! let the peo - ple re - joice:
Eb7 (D7) Ab (G) Eb7 (D7) Ab (G) Eb (D) Ab (G)
O come to the Fa - ther through Je - sus the Son
Db (C) Ab/Eb (G) Eb7 (D7) Ab (G)
and give him the glo - ry – great things he has done.

211 To him we come

Living Lord 9 8 8 8 8 3

Words: J E Seddon (1915–1983)
Isaiah 60.3, Ephesians 2.13, Philippians 3.8
Music: Patrick Appleford

With strength

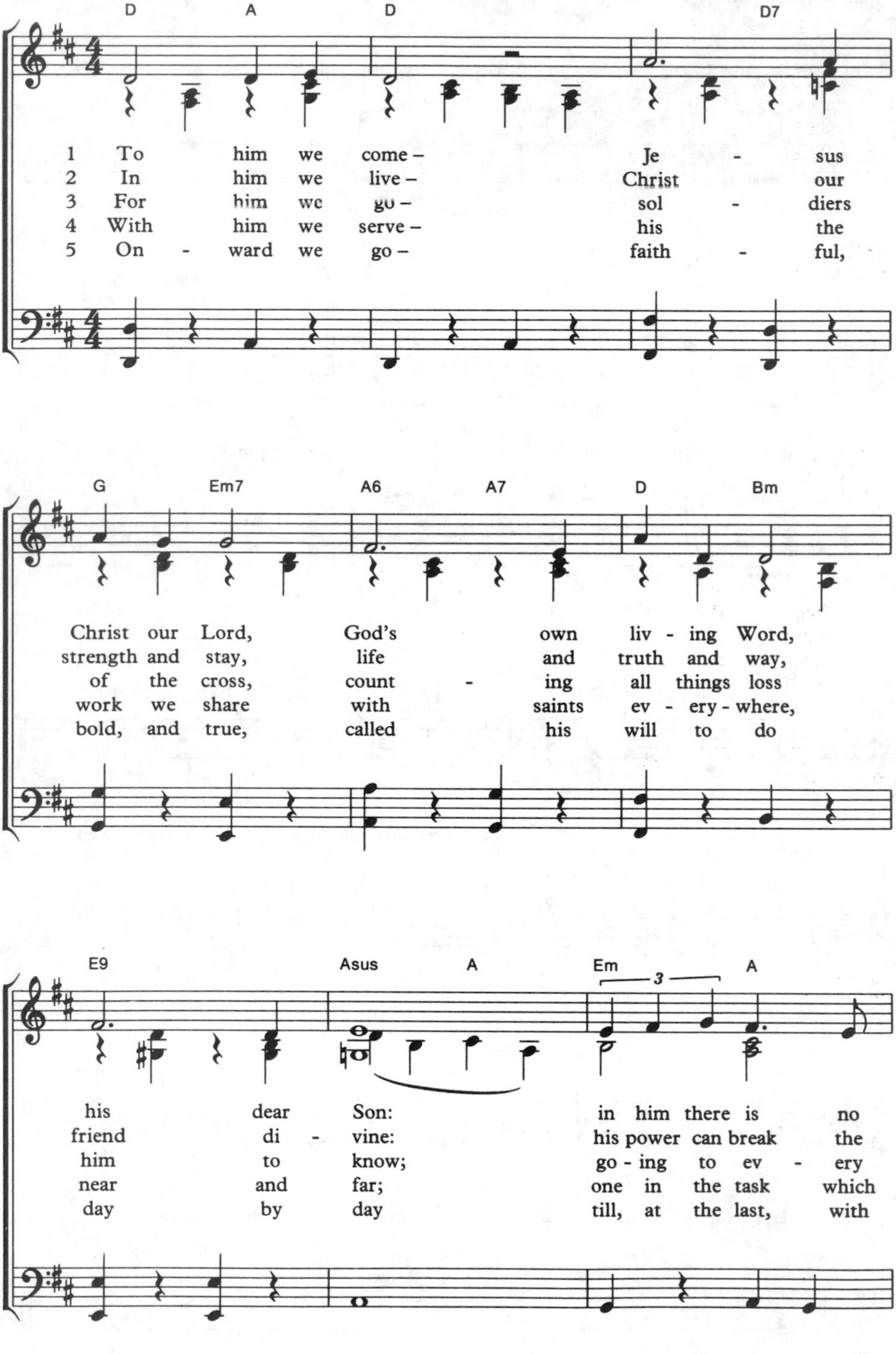
D A D D7
1 To him we come – Je - sus
2 In him we live – Christ our
3 For him we go – sol - diers
4 With him we serve – his the
5 On - ward we go – faith - ful,
G Em7 A6 A7 D Bm
Christ our Lord, God's own liv - ing Word,
strength and stay, life and truth and way,
of the cross, count - ing all things loss
work we share with saints ev - ery - where,
bold, and true, called his will to do
E9 Asus A Em 3 A
his dear Son: in him there is no
friend di - vine: his power can break the
him to know; go - ing to ev - ery
near and far; one in the task which
day by day till, at the last, with

Music: © 1960 Josef Weinberger Ltd,
12–14 Mortimer Street, London W1N 7RD

Words: © Mrs M Seddon / Jubilate Hymns †

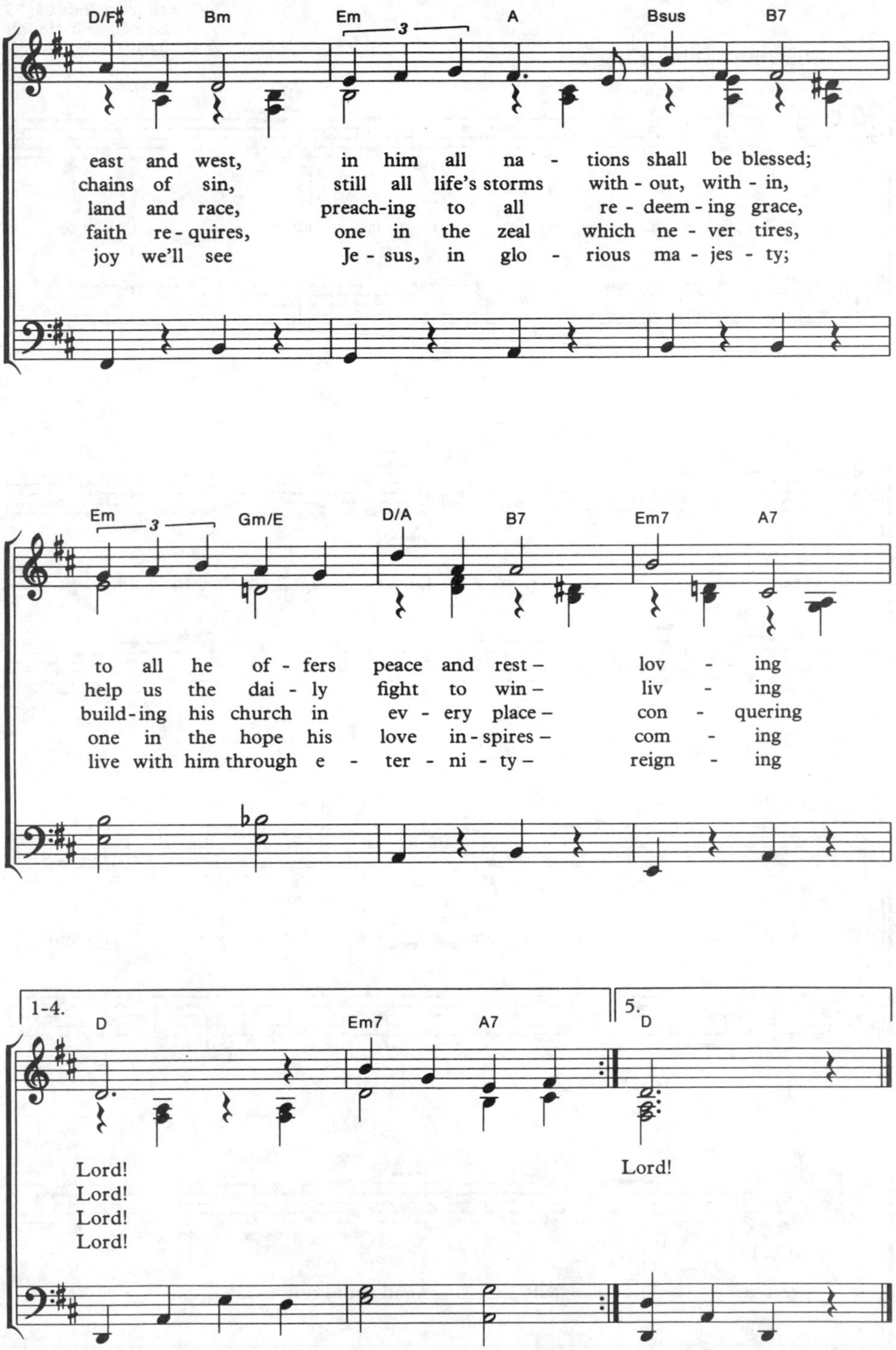
D/F♯ Bm Em 3 A Bsus B7
east and west, in him all na - tions shall be blessed;
chains of sin, still all life's storms with - out, with - in,
land and race, preach-ing to all re - deem - ing grace,
faith re - quires, one in the zeal which ne - ver tires,
joy we'll see Je - sus, in glo - rious ma - jes - ty;
Em 3 Gm/E D/A B7 Em7 A7
to all he of - fers peace and rest – lov - ing
help us the dai - ly fight to win – liv - ing
build-ing his church in ev - ery place – con - quering
one in the hope his love in - spires – com - ing
live with him through e - ter - ni - ty – reign - ing
1-4. D Em7 A7 5. D
Lord! Lord!
Lord!
Lord!
Lord!

212 To him who is able

Words: from Jude 24, 25
Music: Clive Meredith
arranged David Peacock

Flowing and building

A7 Dmaj7 Gmaj7
To him who is ab - le to
Em A7 D
keep us from fall - ing and to pre -
Dmaj7 Gmaj7 C
- sent us be - fore his glo - ri - ous
A Dmaj7 Gmaj7
pre-sence with-out fault and with great joy to the

Music: © Clive Meredith
Music arrangement: © David Peacock / Jubilate Hymns †
Words: © in this version Word & Music / Jubilate Hymns †

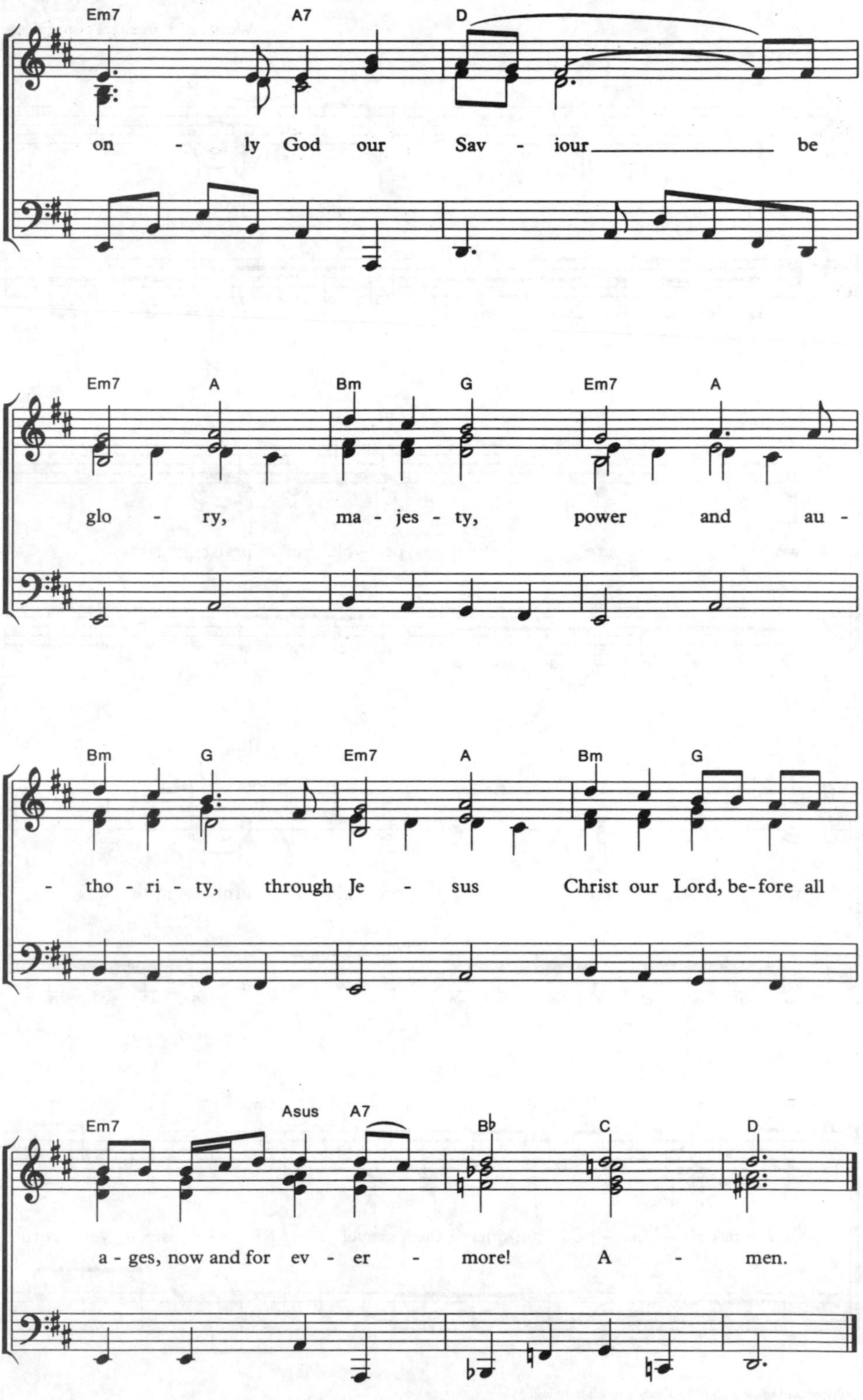
Em7 A7 D
on - ly God our Sav - iour be
Em7 A Bm G Em7 A
glo - ry, ma - jes - ty, power and au -
Bm G Em7 A Bm G
- tho - ri - ty, through Je - sus Christ our Lord, be-fore all
Em7 Asus A7 B♭ C D
a - ges, now and for ev - er - more! A - men.

213 We are a people of power

Words and music: Trevor King

Driving rock

C F C
We are a peo - ple of pow - er,
F G
we are a peo - ple of praise;
C F C
we are a peo - ple of pro - mise:
F C G C Am G
Je-sus has ri - sen – he's con-quered the grave! Ri - sen – yes – born

Words and music: © 1986 Kingsway's Thankyou Music,
PO Box 75, Eastbourne, East Sussex BN23 6NW

F G Am G
— a - gain, we walk — in the pow -
F G Am G
- er of his name; pow - er to be —
F G F
— the sons of God, the sons of God the sons of
G F G F G
God – we are the sons, sons of God!
last time
C

214 We are here to praise you

Words and music: Graham Kendrick
Romans 8.15, Hebrews 13.15

Capo 2(D)

Smoothly
F♯m (Em)
B7 (A7)
E (D)
A/E (G)
E (D)
F♯m (Em)
B (A)
We are here to praise you, lift our hearts and
E (D)
F♯m (Em)
sing; we are here to give you
B (A)
E (D)
the best that we can bring. And it is our

Words and music: © 1985 Kingsway's Thankyou Music,
PO Box 75, Eastbourne, East Sussex BN23 6NW

Amaj7 (Gmaj7) B/A (A) G♯m7 (F♯m7)
love ris-ing from our hearts –
C♯m (Bm) F♯m (Em) B7 (A7)
ev-ery-thing with-in us cries: 'Ab - ba,
A/E (G) E (D) Amaj7 (Gmaj7)
Fa - ther!' Help us now to give you
B/A (A) G♯m7 (F♯m7) C♯m (Bm)
pleа-sure and de-light – heart and mind and
F♯m (Em) B7 (A7) E (D) A/E (G) E (D)
will that say: 'I love you, Lord!'

215 We are marching

Siya hamba

Words: African origin,
collected and edited by Anders Nyberg
Music: African melody scored by
Notman KB, Ljungsbro and Lars Parkman

Lively African style

G C
We are march - ing in the light of God, we are
1. D G
march-ing in the light of God, we are
2. D G
God
march-ing in the light of, the
G7 C
we are march - ing,
light of God, we are march-ing, march-ing, we are
G C D G
Oh, we are
march-ing, march-ing, we are march-ing in the light of God.

Optional further verses:

2 *We are living in the love of God . . .*

3 *We are moving in the power of God . . .*

© The Iona Community / Wild Goose Publications

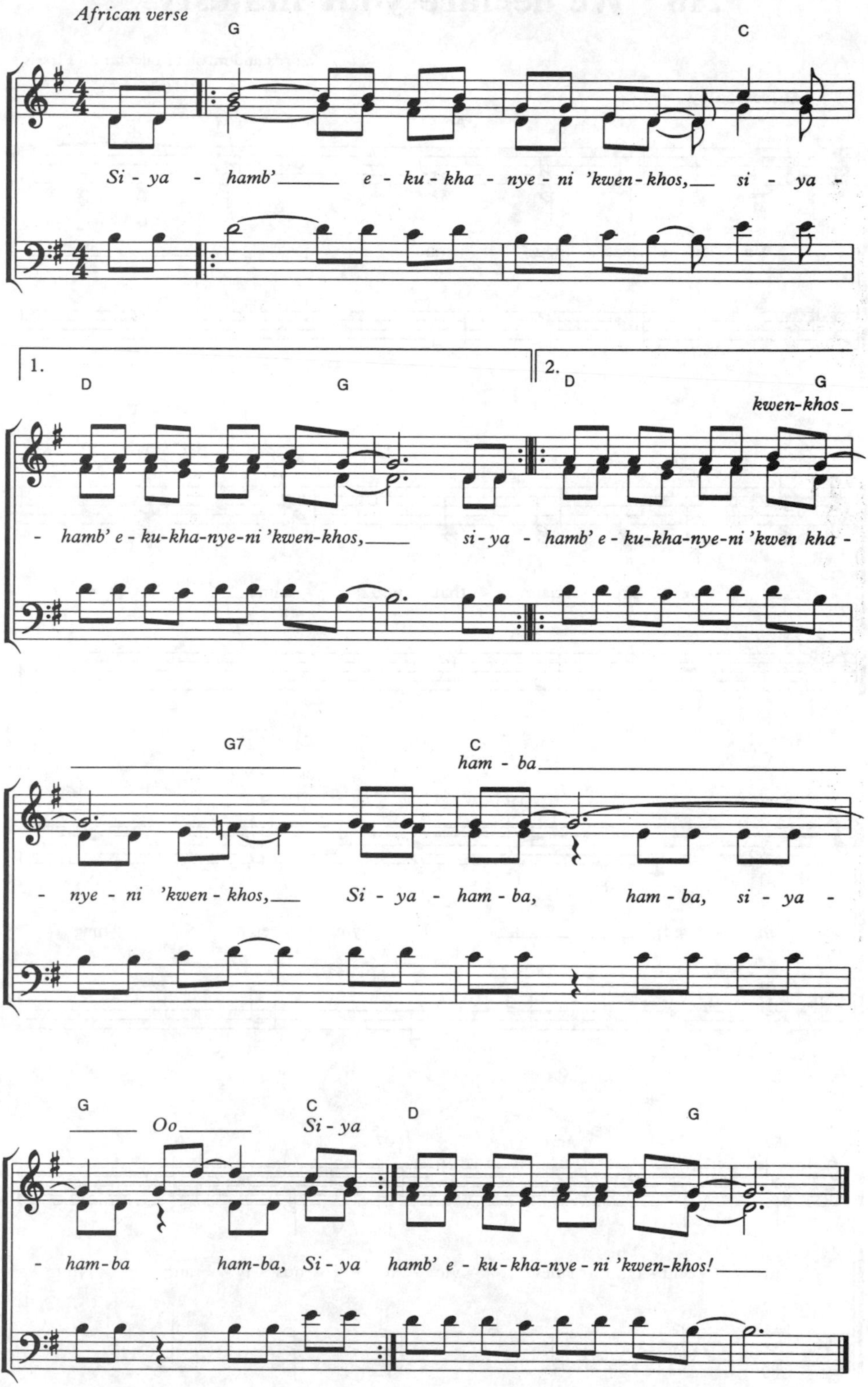
African verse
G C
Si - ya - hamb' e - ku - kha - nye - ni 'kwen - khos, si - ya -
1. D G
2. D G
kwen-khos
- hamb' e - ku-kha-nye-ni 'kwen-khos, si - ya - hamb' e - ku-kha-nye-ni 'kwen kha -
G7 C
ham - ba
- nye - ni 'kwen - khos, Si - ya - ham - ba, ham - ba, si - ya -
G C D G
Oo Si - ya
- ham-ba ham-ba, Si - ya hamb' e - ku - kha-nye - ni 'kwen-khos!

216 We declare your majesty

Words and music: Malcolm du Plessis

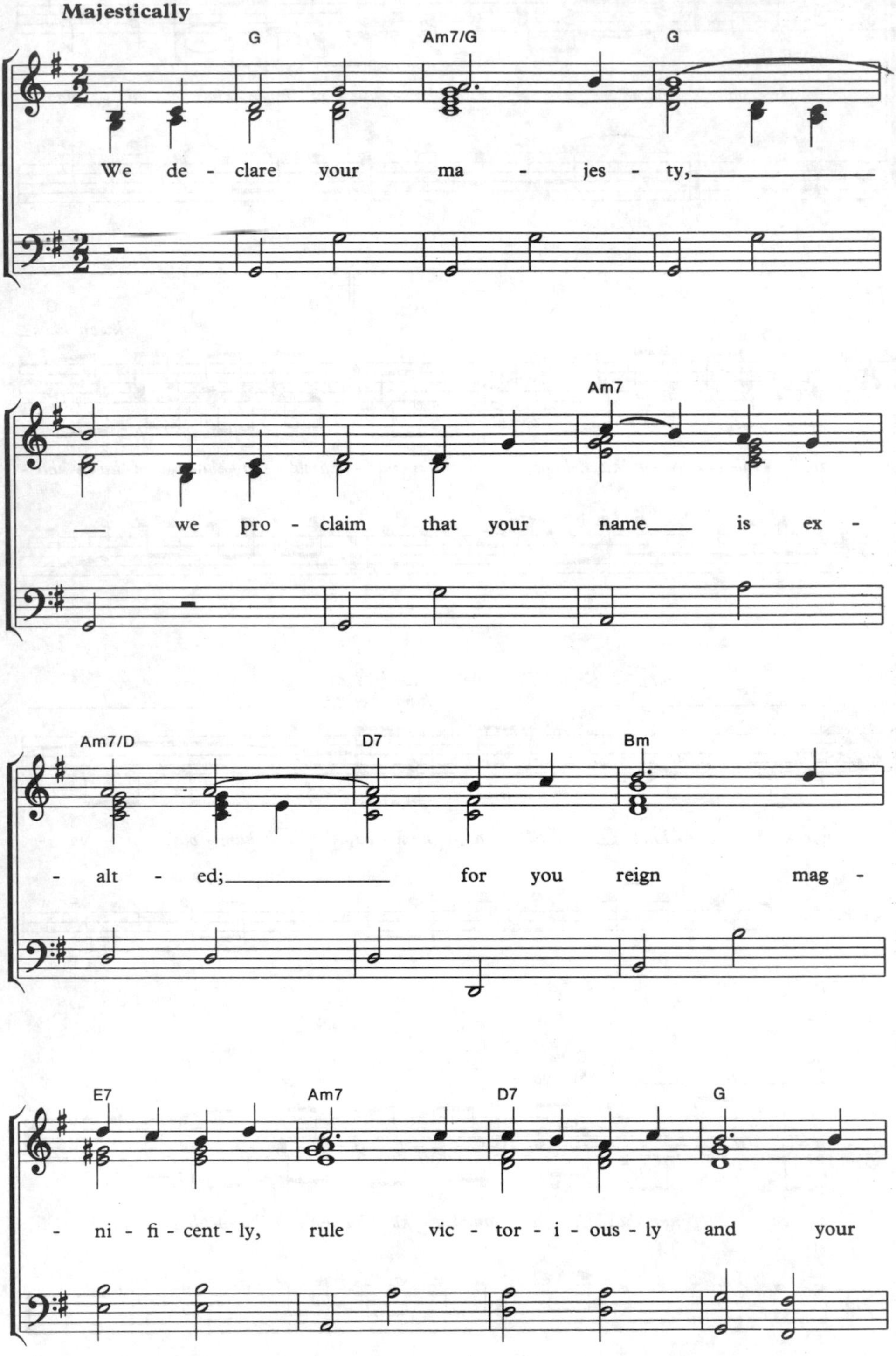
Majestically
G Am7/G G
We de - clare your ma - jes - ty,
Am7
we pro - claim that your name is ex -
Am7/D D7 Bm
- alt - ed; for you reign mag -
E7 Am7 D7 G
- ni - fi - cent - ly, rule vic - tor - i - ous - ly and your

Words and music: © 1984 Kingsway's Thankyou Music,
PO Box 75, Eastbourne, East Sussex BN23 6NW

Em7 Am7 D7 G
power is shown through-out the earth, and we ex-claim
Am7 Am7/D
our God is migh-ty, lift up your name
D7 C/G G
for you are ho-ly. Sing it a-gain,
Am7
all hon-our and glo-ry in a-dor-
Am7/D D7 G
-a-tion we bow be-fore your throne!

217 We shall stand

Capo 3(D)

Words and music: Graham Kendrick
Psalm 40.2, John 15.16, Acts 1.8
Romans 12.2, 2 Corinthians 3.18

Rocky ♩ = 143

Fsus2
(Dsus2)
Dm
(Bm)
We shall stand, ___ with our feet on the Rock; ___
B♭
(G)
B♭/C
F
(D)
___ what-ev-er men ___ may say, ___ we'll lift your name up high – ___
B♭/C
(G)
Fsus2
(Dsus2)
Dm
(Bm)
and we shall walk ___ through the dark - est ___ night; ___
last time to Coda
F/B♭
(D)
B♭
(G)
B♭/C
(G)
Fsus2
(Dsus2)
___ set-ting our fa - ces like flint we'll walk in-to ___ the ___ light! ___

Words and music: © 1988 Make Way Music,
PO Box 263, Croydon, Surrey CR9 5AP.
International copyright secured. All rights reserved. Used by permission.

F (D)
F/A
B♭maj7 (G)
C/F (A)
F (D)
1 Lord, you have cho - sen me for fruit-ful-ness,
2 Lord as your wit - nes-ses you've ap - point-ed us,
F/A
B♭maj7 (G)
F (D)
to be trans-formed in-to your like -
and with your Ho - ly Spi - rit a - noint - ed
C (A)
Dm (Bm)
B♭ (G)
Csus (Asus)
- ness: I'm going to
us: and so I'll
fight on through till I see you face
to face.
C (A)
CODA
F (D)

218 We worship God
(All as one)

Auld Lang Syne

Words: Michael Baughen
Romans 15.5-7, Galatians 3.25-29, Ephesians 4.1-7, Philippians 2.1-11, 1 Thessalonians 4.17-18
Music: Scots traditional melody
arranged Noël Tredinnick

Capo 3(C)

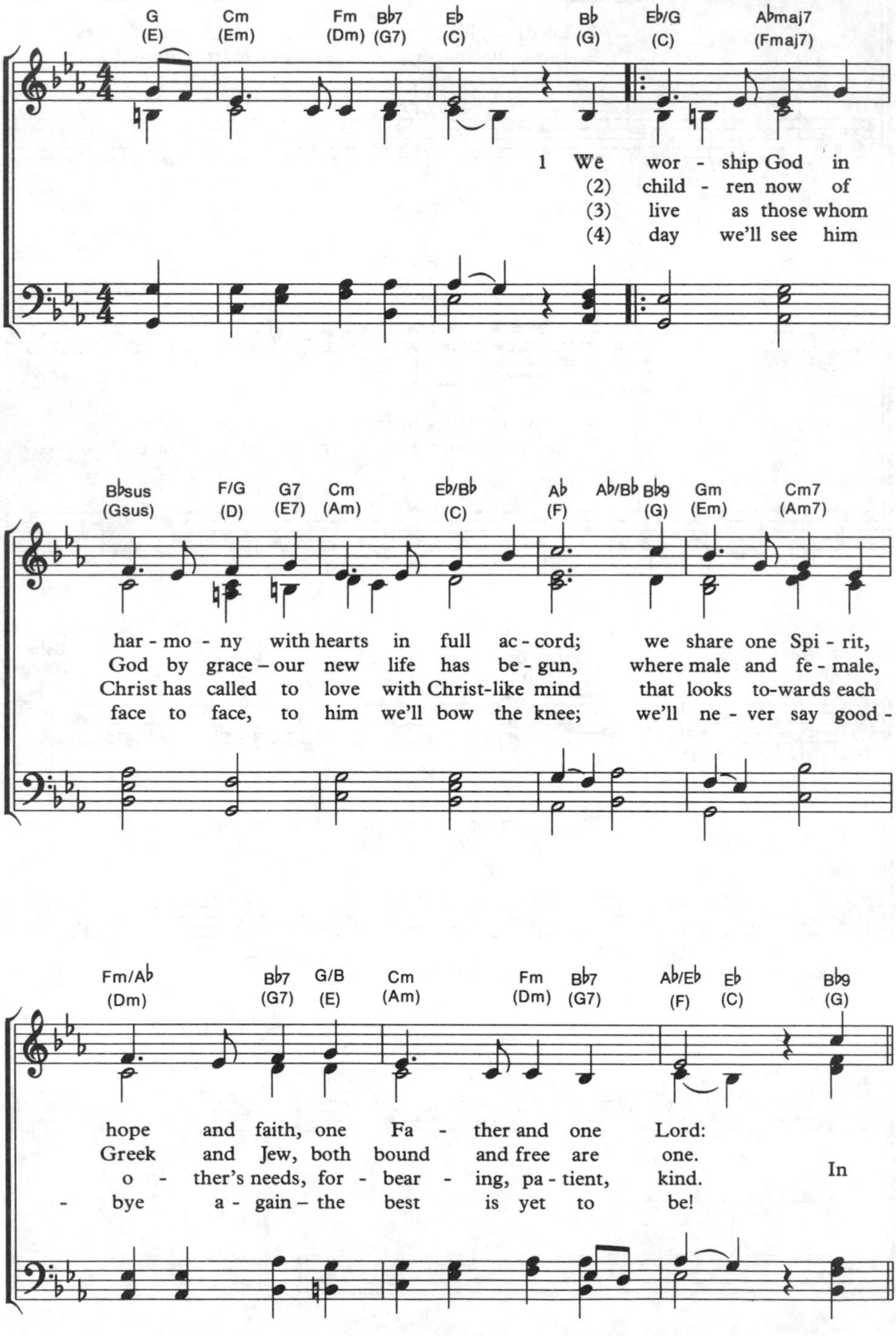
G (E) Cm (Em) Fm (Dm) B♭7 (G7) E♭ (C) B♭ (G) E♭/G (C) A♭maj7 (Fmaj7)
1 We wor - ship God in
(2) child - ren now of
(3) live as those whom
(4) day we'll see him
B♭sus (Gsus) F/G (D) G7 (E7) Cm (Am) E♭/B♭ (C) A♭ (F) A♭/B♭ B♭9 (G) Gm (Em) Cm7 (Am7)
har - mo - ny with hearts in full ac - cord; we share one Spi - rit,
God by grace – our new life has be - gun, where male and fe - male,
Christ has called to love with Christ-like mind that looks to-wards each
face to face, to him we'll bow the knee; we'll ne - ver say good -
Fm/A♭ (Dm) B♭7 (G7) G/B (E) Cm (Am) Fm (Dm) B♭7 (G7) A♭/E♭ (F) E♭ (C) B♭9 (G)
hope and faith, one Fa - ther and one Lord:
Greek and Jew, both bound and free are one.
o - ther's needs, for - bear - ing, pa - tient, kind.
- bye a - gain – the best is yet to be!
In

Music arrangement: © Noël Tredinnick/Jubilate Hymns †
Words: © Michael Baughen / Jubilate Hymns †

Eb9 (C)
Abmaj7 (Fmaj7)
Bbsus (Gsus)
Fm/Ab (Dm)
Eb/G (C)
Eb7 (C7)
Je - sus Christ our Lord and king, in Je - sus Christ our
Ab (F)
Cm/A (Am)
F7/A (D7)
Eb9/Bb (C)
Cm (Am)
Fm (Dm)
F/G (D)
G7 (E7)
Lord, the Spi - rit makes us all as one in
1-3.
Link
Cm7 (Am7)
Fm7 (Dm7)
Bb (G)
Ab/Eb (F)
Eb (C)
G7/D (E7)
Cm (Am)
Ebmaj7/Bb (Cmaj7)
Je - sus Christ our Lord.
Abmaj7 (Fmaj7)
Cm7/Bb (Am7)
Bb7 (G7)
Ab/Eb (F)
Eb (C)
Bb (G)
4.
Ab/Eb (F)
Eb (C)
2 We're
3 We
4 One
Lord.

219 We your people

Words and music: Adrian Snell
Daniel 9.5

Moderato

1 We your peo - ple bow be - fore — you bro - ken and a - shamed; we have turned on your cre - a - tion crushed the life you free - ly — gave.
3 Fa - ther, in this hour of dan - ger we will turn to you: O for - give us, Lord, for - give us and our lives and faith re - new.
2 Lord, have mer - cy on your chil - dren
4 Pour your Ho - ly Spi - rit on — us,

Words and music: © 1986 Serious Music UK,
11 Junction Road, Oldfield Park, Bath BA2 3NQ

Dm7 Dm/C G/B A/C♯ Dm7 Em7
weep - ing and in fear: for you are our
set our hearts a - flame: all shall see your
Fmaj7 Em7 Dm7 C/E Dm/F
1.
G7 C
God and sav - iour – Fa - ther in your love draw near.
power in the na - tions – may we bring glo - ry
Am7 F/A Em/G G C F/A G7
2.
G7
to your
Am Dm7 C/E Dm/F C/G G7 C
name, may we bring glo - ry to your name!

220 We have a gospel

Fulda 8 8 8 8 (LM)

Capo 3(G)

Words: Edward Burns
Mark 16.20, Luke 9.6, John 1.14, Acts 8.4
Music: W Gardiner's *Sacred Melodies* 1815

Bb (G) F7 (D7) Gm (Em) Cm (Am) Bb (G) F7 (D7) Bb (G)
1 We have a gos - pel to pro - claim,
2 Tell of his birth at Beth - le - hem,
3 Tell of his death at Cal - va - ry,
C (A) F (D) Dm (Bm) Dm/Bb F/C (D) C (A) F (D) F7 (D7)
good news for all through - out the earth; the
not in a roy - al house or hall but
ha - ted by those he came to save; in
Bb (G) F7/C (D7) Bb/D (G) Eb (C) C7/E (A7)
gos - pel of a sav - iour's name: we
in a sta - ble dark and dim: the
lone - ly suf - fering on the cross for
F (D) Gm (Em) Cm (Am) Bb/F (G) F7 (D7) Bb (G)
sing his glo - ry, tell his worth.
Word made flesh, a light for all.
all he loved, his life he gave.

4 Tell of that glorious Easter morn:
empty the tomb, for he was free;
he broke the power of death and hell
that we might share his victory.

5 Tell of his reign at God's right hand,
by all creation glorified;
he sends his Spirit on his church
to live for him, the Lamb who died.

6 Now we rejoice to name him king:
Jesus is Lord of all the earth;
this gospel-message we proclaim:
we sing his glory, tell his worth.

Words: © Edward Burns

221(i) When I survey the wondrous cross

(FIRST TUNE)

Rockingham 8 8 8 8 (LM)

Capo 1(D)

Words: I Watts (1674–1748)
Matthew 27.29, Mark 15.17, John 19.2
1Corinthians 2.2, Philippians 3.7
Music adapted by E Miller (1735–1807)

E♭ (D) B♭ (A) E♭ (D) A♭ (G) E♭ (D)
1 When I sur - vey the wond - rous cross
2 For - bid it, Lord, that I should boast
3 See from his head, his hands, his feet,
4 Were the whole realm of na - ture mine,
A♭ (G) B♭7 (A7) E♭ (D) E♭/B♭ B♭ (A)
on which the prince of glo - ry died,
save in the cross of Christ my God:
sor - row and love flow ming - led down:
that were an of - fering far too small;
F (E) B♭ (A) B♭/A♭ E♭/G (D) E♭ F7 (E7) B♭ (A)
my rich - est gain I count as loss
the ve - ry things that charm me most –
when did such love and sor - row meet
love so a - maz - ing, so di - vine,
E♭ (D) B♭ (A) E♭ (D) Fm (Em) E♭ (D) E♭/B♭ B♭7 (A7) E♭ (D)
and pour con - tempt on all my pride.
I sac - ri - fice them to his blood.
or thorns com - pose so rich a crown?
de - mands my soul, my life, my all!

221(ii) When I survey the wondrous cross

(SECOND TUNE)

Words: I Watts (1674–1748)
Matthew 27.29, Mark 15.17, John 19.2
1 Corinthians 2.2, Philippians 3.7
Music: English traditional melody
arranged David Peacock

O Waly, Waly 8 8 8 8 (LM)

Flowing

C/D G Am7 Bm7 Em7
Part II 4 Were the whole realm of na - ture mine,
1 When I sur - vey the won-drous cross on which the
2 For - bid it, Lord, that I should boast save in the
3 See from his head, his hands, his feet, sor - row and
4 Were the whole realm of na - ture mine, that were an
C G Am D7
that were an of - fering far too small;
prince of glo - ry died, my rich - est
cross of Christ my God: the ve - ry
love flow ming - led down: when did such
of - fering far too small; love so a -
Bm7 Em Bm/D Em/C♯ Cm6 G/B
love so a - maz - ing, so di - vine,
gain I count as loss and pour con -
things that charm me most – I sac - ri -
love and sor - row meet or thorns com -
- maz - ing, so di - vine, de - mands my

Music arrangement: © David Peacock / Jubilate Hymns †

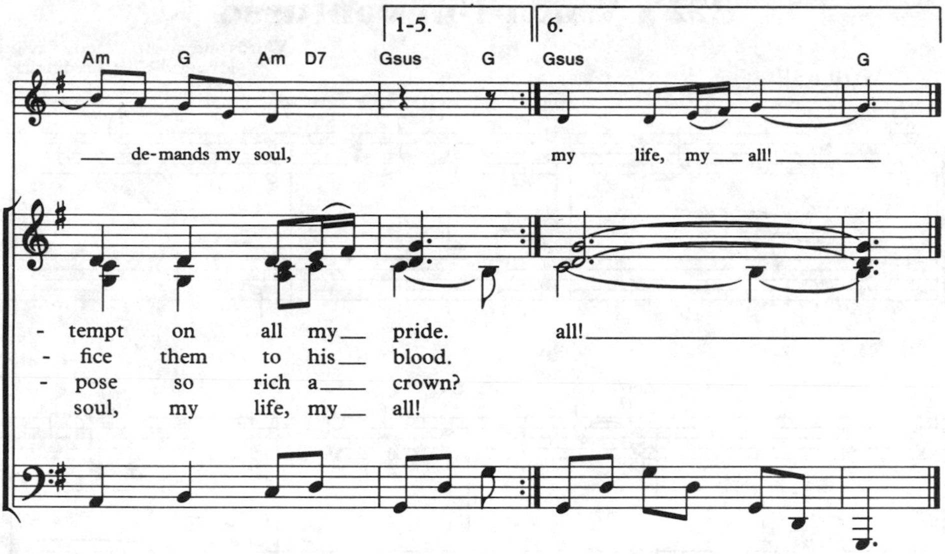
1-5.
6.
Am G Am D7 Gsus G Gsus G
— de-mands my soul, my life, my — all! —
- tempt on all my — pride. all! —
- fice them to his — blood.
- pose so rich a — crown?
soul, my life, my — all!

B♭ melody version

221A PRAISE SHOUT

LEADER Give thanks to God, for he is good;
ALL **his love endures for ever.**

LEADER Let those whom the Lord has redeemed
repeat these words of praise:
ALL **O thank the Lord for his love**
and the wonderful things he has done!

From Psalm 107

Show me the way
222 When I'm confused

Words and music: Wendy Craig
arranged Noël Tredinnick

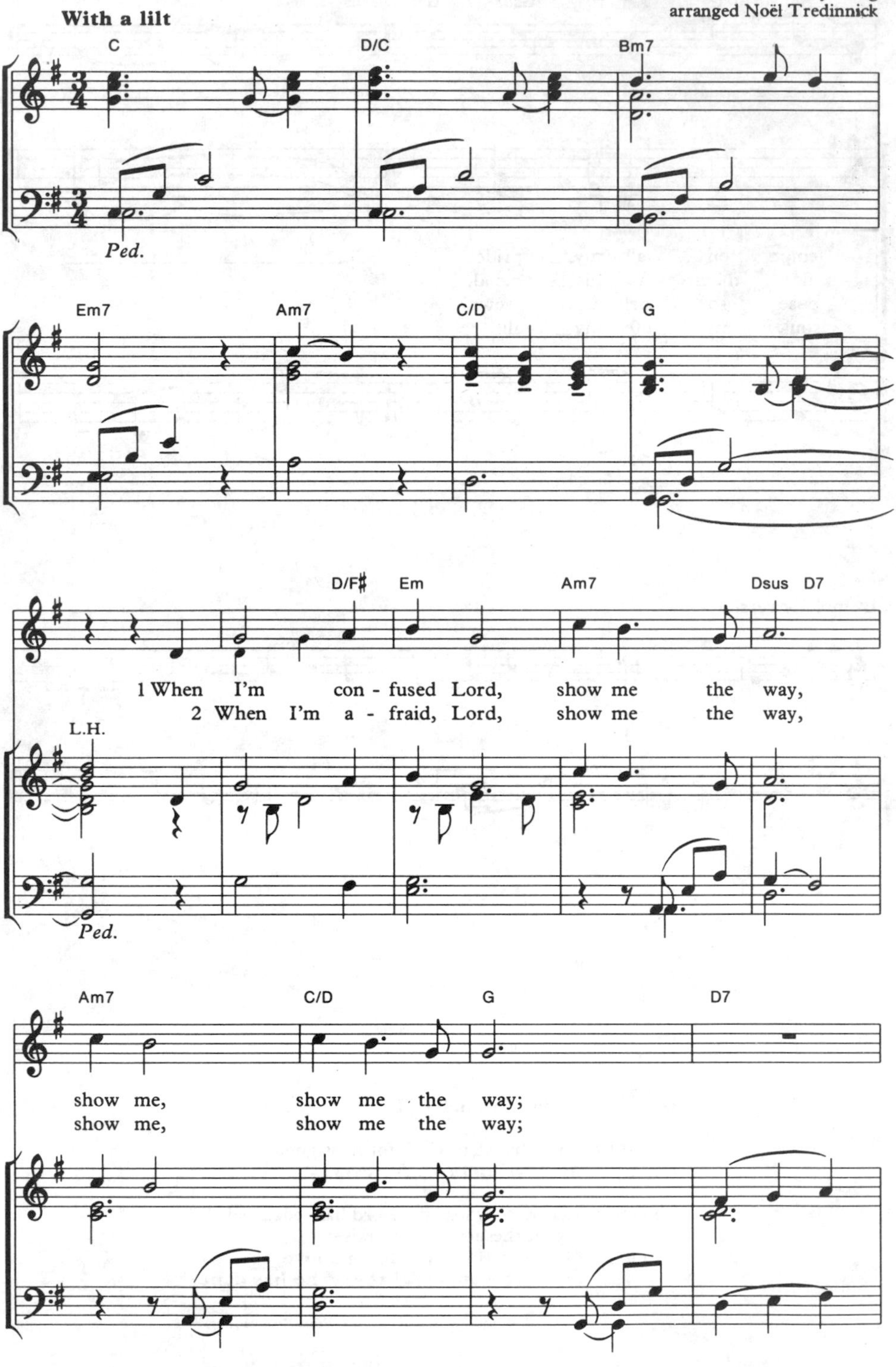
With a lilt
C
D/C
Bm7
Ped.
Em7
Am7
C/D
G
D/F♯
Em
Am7
Dsus D7
1 When I'm con - fused Lord, show me the way,
2 When I'm a - fraid, Lord, show me the way,
L.H.
Ped.
Am7
C/D
G
D7
show me, show me the way;
show me, show me the way;

Words and music: © 1987 BMG Music Publishing Ltd,
Bedford House, 69–79 Fulham High Street, London SW6 3JW

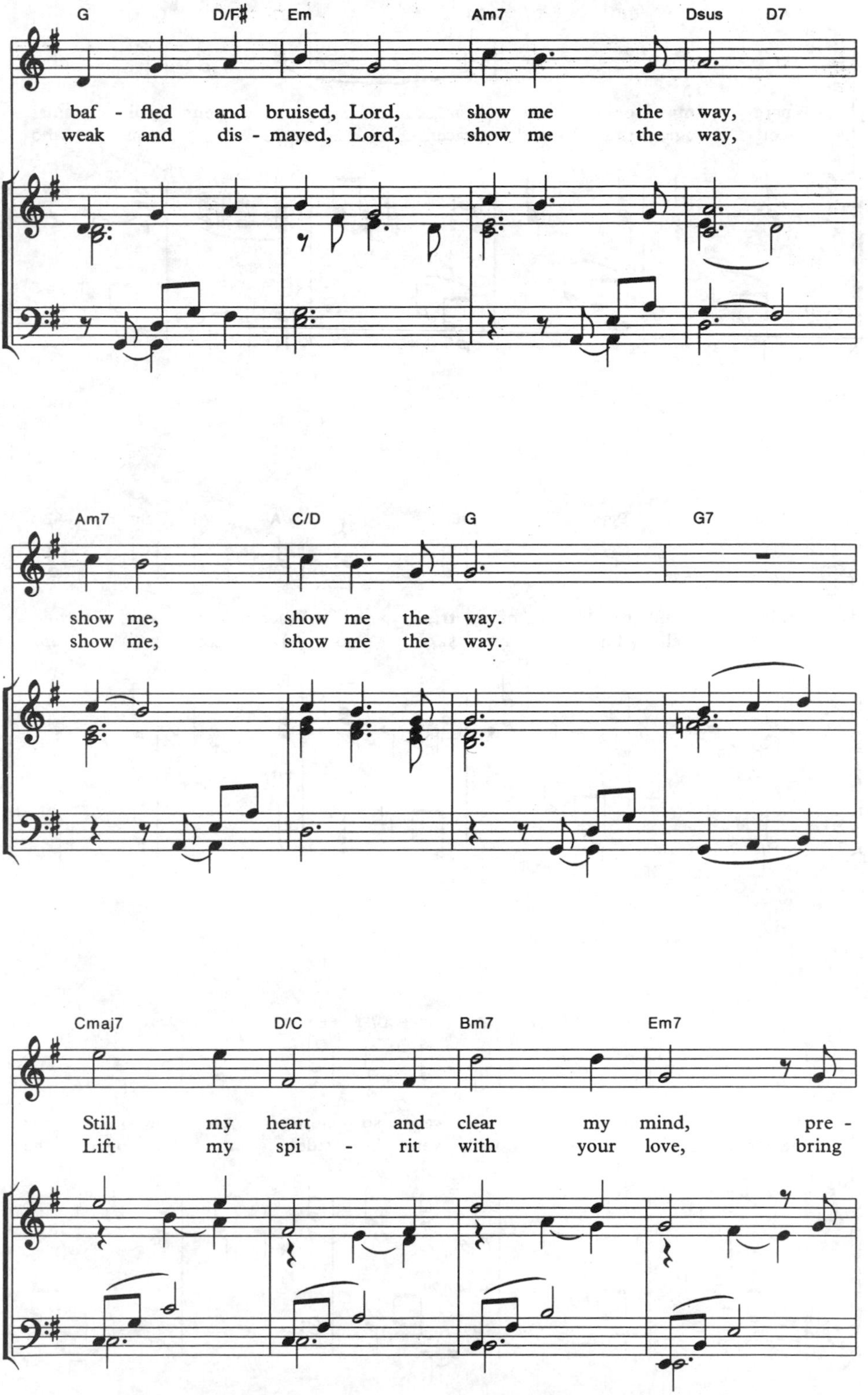
G D/F♯ Em Am7 Dsus D7
baf - fled and bruised, Lord, show me the way,
weak and dis - mayed, Lord, show me the way,
Am7 C/D G G7
show me, show me the way.
show me, show me the way.
Cmaj7 D/C Bm7 Em7
Still my heart and clear my mind, pre -
Lift my spi - rit with your love, bring

Am7 C/D D7 G9 G7 Cmaj7
-pare my soul to hear your still, small
cou - rage, calm and peace: you who
Am6 Bm6 Em G/A A7 Bm A7
voice, your word of truth: Peace be still! your
bore all for my sake so I could walk from
rit.
D Dsus D7 G D/F♯ Em Am
Lord is near; al - ways so close to show you the
fear re - leased – with you be - side me show-ing the
a tempo

1.
Dsus D7 Am C/D G G7
way, show you, show you the way.
way, show-ing, show-ing the
2.
G D/F♯ Em Am Dsus D7
way,
Am7 C/D G Am/G G
show-ing, show-ing the way.
rit.
Slow
a tempo

223 What a mighty God

Words: Unknown
Music: Zulu working song
arranged P Sandwall

With strength and joy

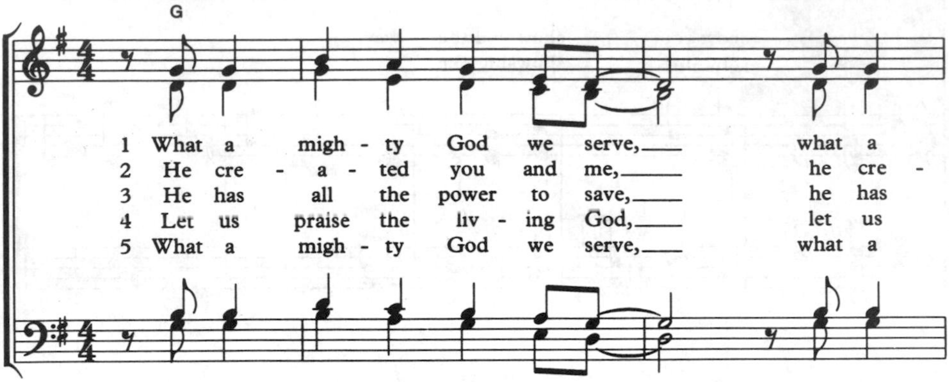
G
1 What a migh - ty God we serve, what a
2 He cre - a - ted you and me, he cre -
3 He has all the power to save, he has
4 Let us praise the liv - ing God, let us
5 What a migh - ty God we serve, what a

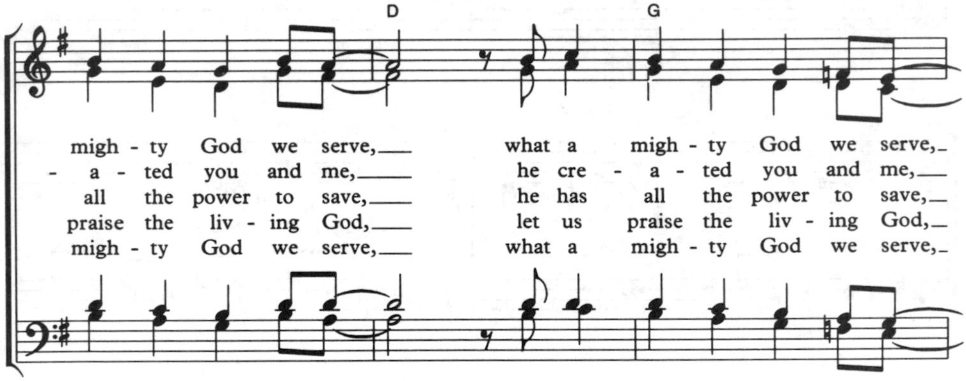
D
G
migh - ty God we serve, what a migh - ty God we serve,
- a - ted you and me, he cre - a - ted you and me,
all the power to save, he has all the power to save,
praise the liv - ing God, let us praise the liv - ing God,
migh - ty God we serve, what a migh - ty God we serve,

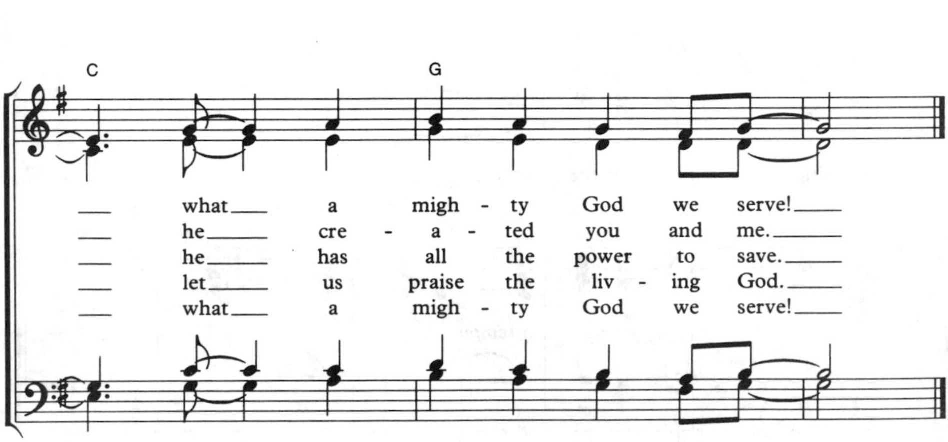
C
G
what a migh - ty God we serve!
he cre - a - ted you and me.
he has all the power to save.
let us praise the liv - ing God.
what a migh - ty God we serve!

Music arrangement: © 1986 Peter Sandwall, Dalskog 57022, Forsenum, Sweden

224 When the Spirit of the Lord

Words and music: Unknown
2 Samuel 6.14
Music arranged David Peacock

With increasing pace

Em
1 When the Spi - rit of the Lord is with - in my heart, I will
2 When the Spi - rit of the Lord is with - in my heart, I will
3 When the Spi - rit of the Lord is with - in my heart, I will
4 When the Spi - rit of the Lord is with - in my heart, I will
B7
1.
Em
2.
Em
sing as Da - vid sang; When the sang; I will
clap as Da - vid clapped; When the clapped; I will
dance as Da - vid danced; When the danced; I will
praise as Da - vid praised; When the praised; I will
Am
Em
1.
B7
sing, I will sing: I will sing as Da - vid
clap, I will clap: I will clap as Da - vid
dance, I will dance: I will dance as Da - vid
praise, I will praise: I will praise as Da - vid
Em
2.
B7
Em
sang; I will sing as Da - vid sang;
clapped; I will clap as Da - vid clapped;
danced; I will dance as Da - vid danced;
praised; I will praise as Da - vid praised;

Words and music: © copyright controlled
Music arrangement: © David Peacock / Jubilate Hymns †

225 Who can sound the depths of sorrow

Capo 1(A)

Words and music: Graham Kendrick
Psalm 12, Psalm 82 etc.

With feeling ♩ = 106

G♭ (F) Cdim/E♭ (Bdim) G♭/D♭ (F) B♭ (A) Cm7 (Bm7) Cm7/F F (E)
1 Who can
B♭ (A) F/B♭ (E) E♭/B♭ (D) B♭ (A) Gm (F♯m) Gm/F E♭ (D)
sound the depths of sor-row in the Fa-ther heart of God, for the
(2) scorned the truth you gave us, we have bowed to o - ther lords, we have
MEN (3) stand be - fore your an-ger; who can face your pier-cing eyes? for you
F/E♭ (E) B♭/D (A) Gm7 (F♯m7) C9 (B) Cm7 (Bm7) F (E)
child-ren we've re - ject - ed, for the lives so deep - ly scarred? And each
sac - ri - ficed the child-ren on the alt - ars of our gods. O let
love the weak and help-less, and you hear the vic-tims' cries. ALL Yes, you
B♭ (A) F/B♭ (E) E♭/B♭ (D) B♭ (A) Gm (F♯m) Gm/F E♭ (D)
light that we've ex - tin-guished has brought dark - ness to our land:
truth a - gain shine on us, let your ho - ly fear de - scend:
are a God of jus - tice, and your judgement sure-ly comes:

Words and music: © 1988 Make Way Music, PO Box 263, Croydon, Surrey CR9 5AP.
International copyright secured. All rights reserved. Used by permission.

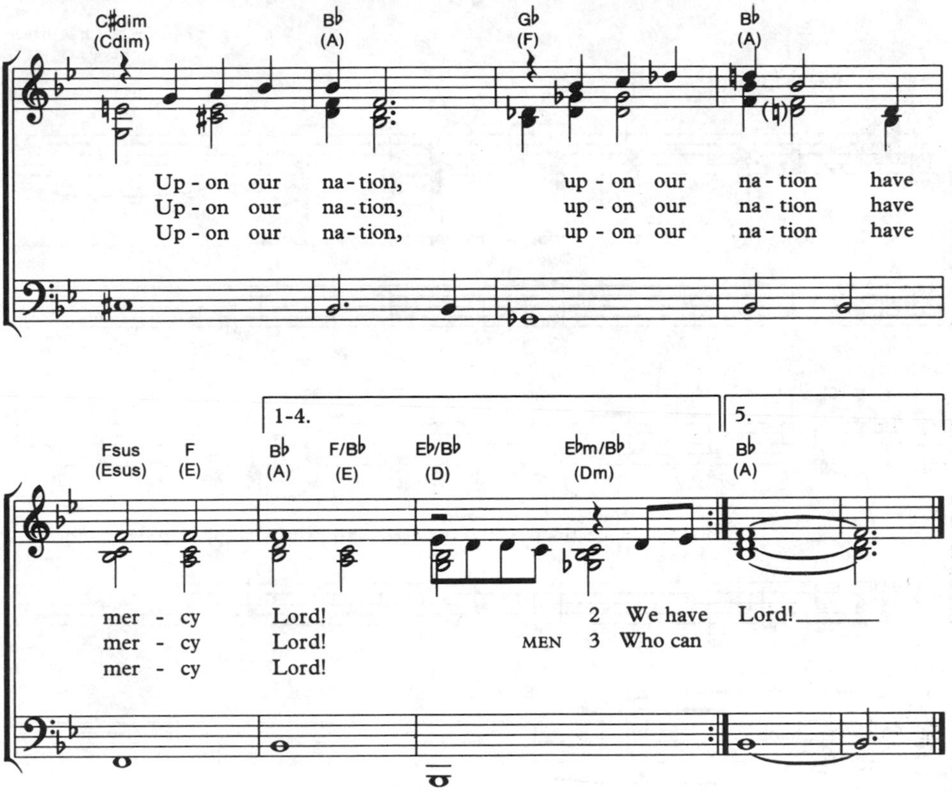
C♯dim (Cdim) B♭ (A) G♭ (F) B♭ (A)
Up - on our na - tion, up - on our na - tion have
Up - on our na - tion, up - on our na - tion have
Up - on our na - tion, up - on our na - tion have
1-4.
5.
Fsus (Esus) F (E) B♭ (A) F/B♭ (E) E♭/B♭ (D) E♭m/B♭ (Dm) B♭ (A)
mer - cy Lord! 2 We have Lord!
mer - cy Lord! MEN 3 Who can
mer - cy Lord!

4 WOMEN
Who will stand against the violence?
Who will comfort those who mourn?
In an age of cruel rejection,
who will build for love a home?
ALL
Come and shake us into action,
come and melt our hearts of stone:
Upon your people, upon your people,
have mercy Lord!

5 Who can sound the depths of mercy
in the Father heart of God?
For there is a Man of sorrows
who for sinners shed his blood.
He can heal the wounds of nations,
he can wash the guilty clean:
Because of Jesus, because of Jesus
have mercy Lord!

225A PRAISE SHOUT

LEADER Turn to us, almighty God;
ALL **look down from heaven and see!**

LEADER Renew us, O Lord God almighty;
ALL **show us your mercy**
that we may be saved!

From Psalm 80

226 Worthy, O worthy

Words and Music: Mark Kinzer
Revelation 4.11

Worshipfully
E F♯m B7 E
Wor - thy, O wor - thy are you Lord,
C♯m F♯m B7
worthy to be thanked and praised and wor - shipped and a-dored;
E Bsus B E
wor - thy, O
F♯m B7 E C♯m
wor - thy are you Lord, wor-thy to be
F♯m B7 E A/E
thanked and praised and wor - shipped and a - dored.

Words and music: © 1976, 1980 Word of God Music/CopyCare Ltd,
PO Box 77, Hailsham, East Sussex BN27 3EF

E7 A Bsus B E B7
— Sing-ing al - le-lu - ia, Lamb up-on — the
C♯m F♯m B
throne, — we wor-ship and a - dore — you,
E B E E7 A Bsus B
make your glo - ry known. Al - le-lu - ia,
E B7 C♯m F♯m B
glo-ry to — the King: — you're more than a con - quer-or, you're
F♯m A/B B7 E A/E E
Lord of ev - ery - thing! —

227 You are the light of the world

Light of the world
Capo 5(G)

Words and music: Michael Card
John 1.9, 6.35 and 16.33

F (C) F/G G (D) C (G) F (C)
1 You are the Light of the world,
2 You are the Bread of life,
G (D) C (G) F (C) G (D) C (G)
O Lord, and you make your ser - vants shine: so
O Lord, and bro - ken to set us free: so
Dm7 (Am7) G (D) E/G♯ (B) Am (Em) F (C) F/G G (D)
how can there be a-ny dark-ness in me if you are the light of the world?
how can there be a-ny hun - ger in me if you are the Bread of life?

Words and music: © Whole Armor Publishing for the World excluding North, Central and South America.
Whole Armor Publishing, c/o TKO Publishing Ltd, PO Box 130, Hove, East Sussex BN3 6QU

1.
E/G♯ (B)
Am (Em)
F (C)
F/G
G (D)
C (G)
You are the light of the world!
2.
Dm7 (Am7)
F/G (C)
You are the Bread of life!
G (D)
F (C)
3 You've ov-er-come the world,

G (D) C (G) F (C) G (D) C (G)
O Lord and giv-en us vic - to-ry: so
F (C) G (D) E/G♯ (B) Am Am/G (Em) F (C) Gsus G (Dsus) (D)
why should I fear when trou-ble is near, if you've ov-er-come the world?
E7/G♯ (B7) Am Am/G (Em) F (C) Gsus G (Dsus) (D) C (G)
You've ov-er-come the world! So

F (C) G (D) E/G♯ (B) Am Am/G (Em) F (C) Gsus G (Dsus) (D)
why should I fear when trou-ble is near, if you've ov-er-come the world?
E7/G♯ (B7) Am Am/G (Em) F (C) Gsus (Dsus) G (D) E7/G♯ (B7) Am Am/G (Em)
You've ov-er-come the world!
F (C) G9sus (D9sus) C (G) F/C (C) C (G)
You've ov-er-come the world!

228 Who is the rock

Words and music: Unknown
1 Corinthians 10.4

Mwamba ni Yesu

African style

F
B♭
C
SOLO 1 Who is the Rock?
Mwam-ba, Mwam-ba?
(only on repeat)
ALL The Rock is Je - sus, the Rock.
Mwam-ba ni Je - su, Mwam-ba.
D.C.
F
B♭
C
F
Who is the Rock?
Mwam-ba, Mwam-ba?
The Rock is Je - sus, the Rock.
Mwam-ba ni Je - su, Mwam-ba.

2 SOLO He blesses us:
ALL the Rock is Jesus, the Rock.
SOLO He blesses us:
ALL the Rock is Jesus, the Rock.

3 SOLO He heals from sin:
ALL the Rock is Jesus, the Rock.
SOLO He heals from sin:
ALL the Rock is Jesus, the Rock.

4 SOLO The Rock protects:
ALL the Rock is Jesus, the Rock.
SOLO The Rock protects:
ALL the Rock is Jesus, the Rock.

5 SOLO He rescues us:
ALL the Rock is Jesus, the Rock.
SOLO He rescues us:
ALL the Rock is Jesus, the Rock.

6 SOLO Who is the Rock . . .

7 SOLO Who is the Rock . . .

2 *Abariki:*
Mwamba ni Jesu, Mwamba.
Abariki:
Mwamba ni Jesu, Mwamba.

3 *Anaponya:*
Mwamba ni Jesu, Mwamba.
Anaponya:
Mwamba ni Jesu, Mwamba.

4 *Analinda:*
Mwamba ni Jesu, Mwamba.
Analinda:
Mwamba ni Jesu, Mwamba.

5 *Aokoa:*
Mwamba ni Jesu, Mwamba.
Aokoa:
Mwamba ni Jesu, Mwamba.

6 *Mwamba . . .*

7 *Mwamba . . .*

Words and music: © copyright controlled.

229 You are the mighty King

Capo 3(C)
Words and music: Eddie Espinosa
Isaiah 9.6 and John 1.4

Stately
Ab (F) Bb (G) Ebmaj7 (Cmaj7) Cm7 (Am7) Ab (F) Bb (G)
1 You are the migh - ty king, the liv - ing
2 You are al - migh - ty God, sav - iour and
3 You are the Prince of peace, Em - ma - nu -
4 You are the migh - ty king, the liv - ing
Ebmaj7 (Cmaj7) Ab (F) Bb (G) Gm7 (Em7) Cm7 (Am7)
Word; mas - ter of ev - ery-thing –
Lord; won - der - ful coun - sel - lor,
- el; Ev-er-last - ing Fa - ther,
Word; mas - ter of ev - ery - thing,
Fm7 (Dm7) Bb (G) Ab/Eb (F/C) Eb (C) Fine Fm7 (Dm7)
you are the Lord. And we praise your
you are the Lord. And we praise your
you are the Lord. And we love your
you are the Lord.
Bb (G) Fm7 (Dm7) Bb (G) D.C. al Fine
name, and we praise your name.
name, and we praise your name.
name, and we love your name.

Words and music: © 1982 Mercy Publishing/Kingsway's Thankyou Music,
PO Box 75, Eastbourne, East Sussex BN23 6NW

230 You laid aside your majesty

Words and music: Noël Richards
Isiah 53.4, Philippians 2.6

I really want to worship you

Majestically

G D Em Bm C
You laid a - side your ma-jes - ty, gave up ev-ery-thing for me, suf-fered
G Am7 D G D
at the hands of those you had cre - a - ted; you took all my guilt and
Em Bm C G
shame, when you died and rose a - gain – now to-day you reign in
Am7 D G D
heaven and earth ex - alt - ed. I real-ly want to wor-ship you, my

Words and music: © 1985 Kingsway's Thankyou Music,
PO Box 75, Eastbourne, East Sussex BN23 6NW

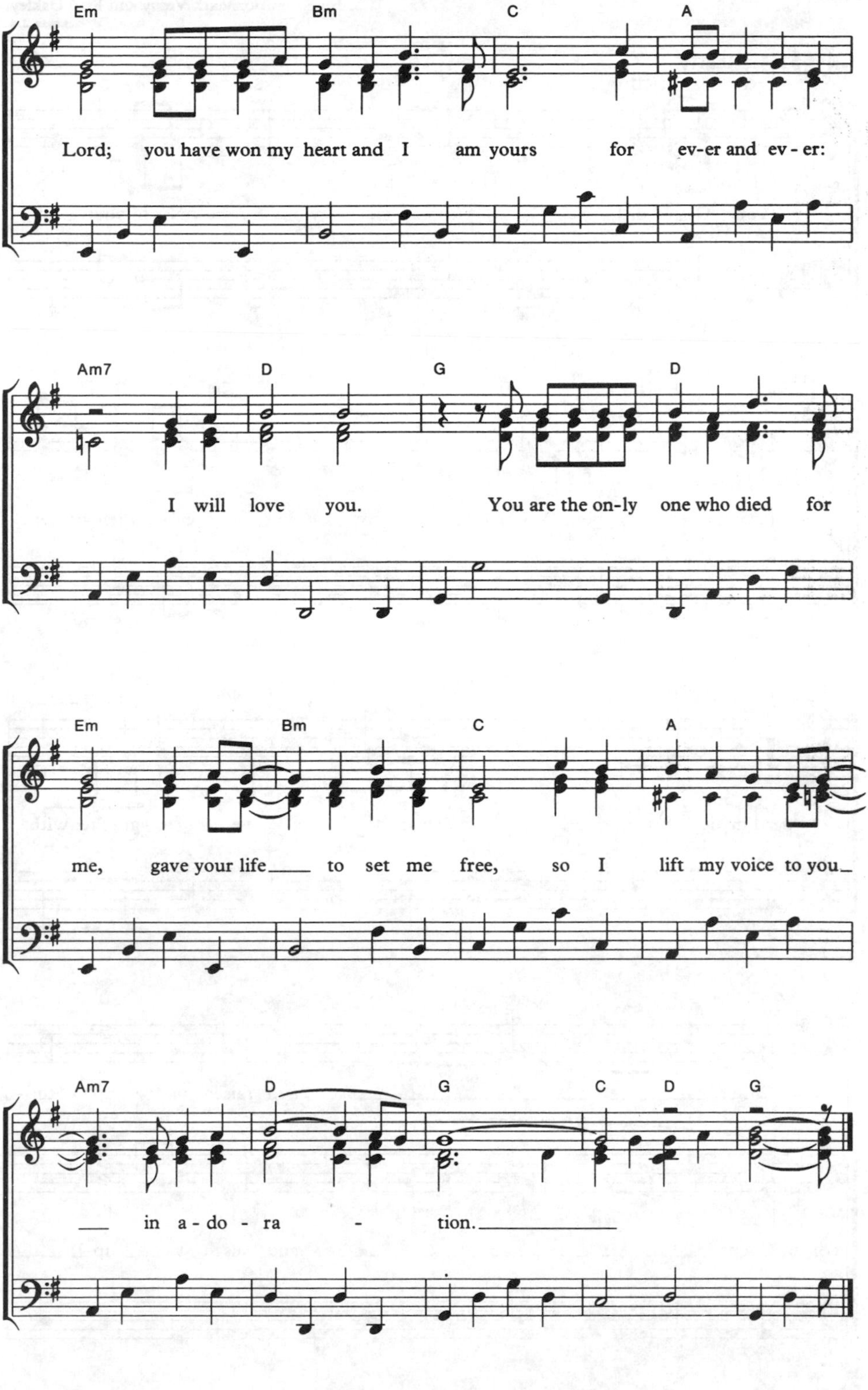
Em Bm C A
Lord; you have won my heart and I am yours for ev-er and ev - er:
Am7 D G D
I will love you. You are the on-ly one who died for
Em Bm C A
me, gave your life to set me free, so I lift my voice to you
Am7 D G C D G
in a - do - ra - tion.

231 You, O Lord

Words and music: Mark Veasy and Paul Oakley
Ephesians 2.4

Majestically
G D C D Em C
You, O Lord, rich in mer - cy, be-cause of your great
Dsus D G D C D Em C
love; you, O Lord, so loved us, ev-en when we were
Am D Bm7 Cmaj7
dead in our sins. You made us a - live to - ge - ther with
Am7 Dsus D7 G D
MEN Christ, and raised us up to -
WOMEN Christ, and raised us up

Words and music: © 1986 Kingsway's Thankyou Music,
PO Box 75, Eastbourne, East Sussex BN23 6NW

C D7 G D C D7
- ge - ther with him, and seat - ed us with him in heaven-ly pla - ces; and
and seat - ed us and
G D C D7 G D
raised us up to - ge - ther with him, and seat - ed us with
raised us up and seat - ed us
last time
C D7 G D C D G
him in heaven-ly pla - ces in Christ.
in Christ.

232 Your word is a lamp

Thy word is a lamp

Words: Amy Grant
Psalm 119.105
Music: Michael Smith
arranged Geoff Baker

Smoothly
G D9 D G
Your word is a lamp un-to my feet and a
C D G G
light un-to my path; your word is a lamp
D9 D G C D G
un-to my feet and a light un-to my path.
D/F# Am Em Bm C D
1 When I feel a-fraid, think I've lost my way, still you're there right be-side
2 I will not for-get your love for me – and yet my heart for ev-er is wan-

Words: © 1983 Bug and Bear Music/BMG Music Publishing Ltd,
Bedford House, 69–79 Fulham High Street, London SW6 3JW

Music: © 1983 Meadowgreen Music

C/G G D/F# Am Em Bm
me: and no-thing will I fear as long as you are near.
-dering: Je-sus, be my guide and hold me to your side. And
C D D/E Em D9 D
Please be near me to the end.
I will love you to the end.
G D9 D G
Your word is a lamp un-to my feet and a
C D G G
light un-to my path; your word is a lamp
D9 D G C D G
un-to my feet and a light un-to my path.

233 Yours be the glory

Maccabaeus 10 11 11 11 and refrain

Words: after E Budry (1854–1932)
R B Hoyle (1875–1939)
in this version Jubilate Hymns
Matthew 28.2, John 20.24, Romans, 8.37
Music: adapted from G F Handel (1685–1759)

Capo 3(C)

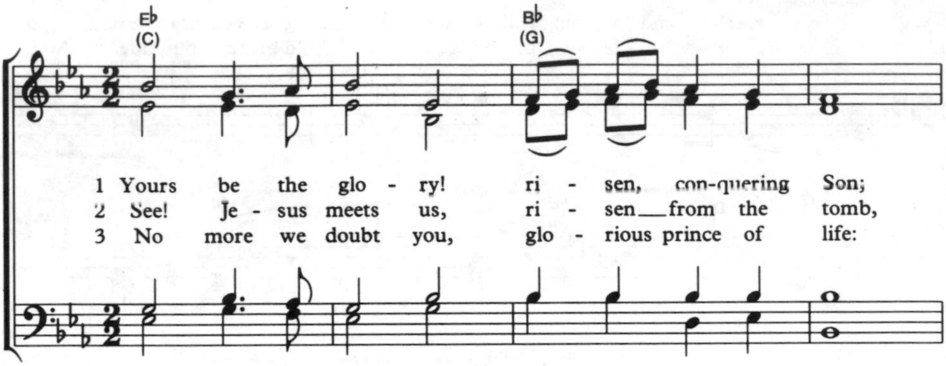
E♭ (C)
B♭ (G)
1 Yours be the glo - ry! ri - sen, con-quering Son;
2 See! Je - sus meets us, ri - sen from the tomb,
3 No more we doubt you, glo - rious prince of life:

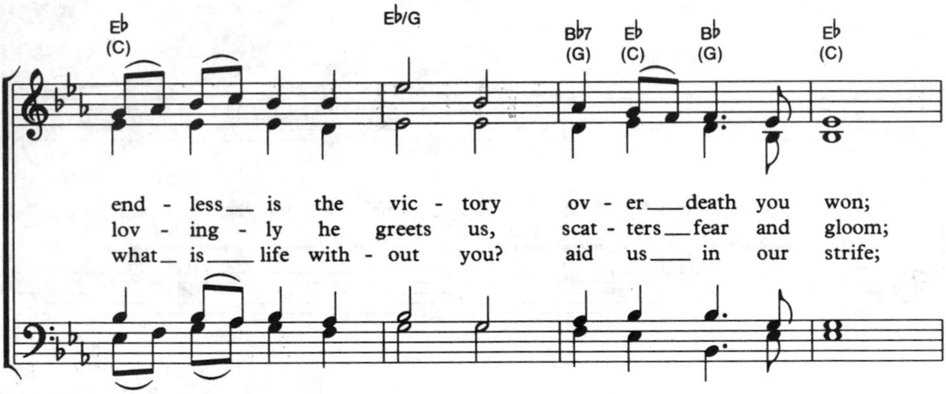
E♭ (C)
E♭/G
B♭7 (G) E♭ (C) B♭ (G) E♭ (C)
end - less is the vic - tory ov - er death you won;
lov - ing - ly he greets us, scat - ters fear and gloom;
what is life with - out you? aid us in our strife;

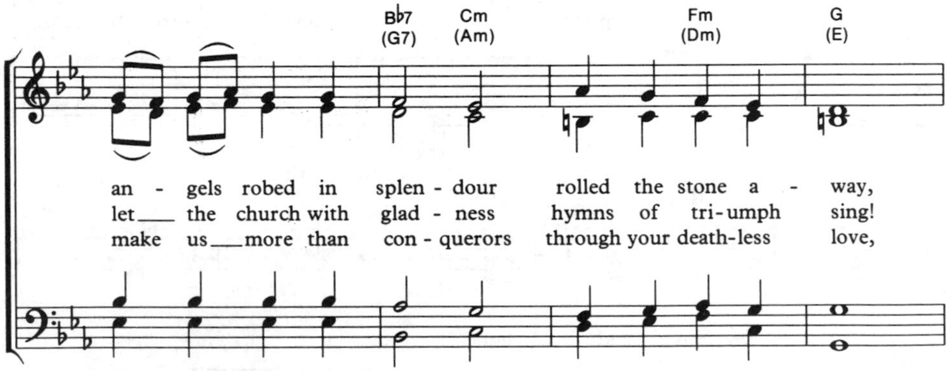
B♭7 (G7) Cm (Am) Fm (Dm) G (E)
an - gels robed in splen - dour rolled the stone a - way,
let the church with glad - ness hymns of tri - umph sing!
make us more than con - querors through your death-less love,

Words: © in this version Jubilate Hymns †

Cm (Am) F7 (D7) Gm (Em) Cm (Am) F (D) B♭ (G)
kept_ the_ fold - ed grave clothes where your bo - dy lay:
for_ her_ Lord is liv - ing, death has_ lost its sting:
bring us_ safe through Jor - dan to your home a - bove:
E♭ (C) B♭ (G)
Yours be the glo - ry! ri - sen,_ con-quering Son;
E♭ (C) E♭/G B♭7 (G7) E♭ (C) B♭ (G) E♭ (C)
end - less_ is the vic - tory ov - er_ death you won.

LEGAL INFORMATION

Those seeking to reproduce outside North America works in this book which are the property of Jubilate Hymns or associated authors (attributed '. . / Jubilate Hymns') may write to The Copyright Manager, Jubilate Hymns Ltd, 61 Chessel Avenue, Southampton SO2 4DY (telephone 0703 630038). In the United States of America, these same copyrights, along with those of Timothy Dudley-Smith, are administered by Hope Publishing Company, Carol Stream, IL 60188.

A number of publishers of UK Christian music have uniform concessions and rates. There is normally no charge for 'once off' use of an item provided that permission is obtained and proper acknowledgement made in print. Reproduction for permanent use, or re-sale, does attract a small charge in most cases. Details are available from The Copyright Manager, Jubilate Hymns Ltd.

Most of these publishers also combine to offer a licencing scheme for limited term reproduction. Where this is felt to be an advantage, application should be made to the Christian Music Association, Glyndley Manor, Stone Cross, Pevensey, East Sussex BN24 5BS (telephone 0323 440440).

Items copyrighted Stainer & Bell may not be photocopied or reprinted under any blanket licencing scheme, and should be cleared individually with Stainer & Bell.

As with all the major copyright holders represented in this collection, Jubilate Hymns with their associated authors and composers, and Word & Music, are members of the Mechanical Copyright Protection, and Performing Rights Societies. Appropriate application should be made to these bodies as follows: The Mechanical Copyright Protection Society, Elgar House, 41 Streatham High Road, London SW16 1ER (081 769 4400); The Perfoming Rights Society, 29–33 Berners Street, London W1P 4AA (071 580 5544).

NOTES ABOUT THE MUSIC

● It will be understood that many of the keyboard arrangements give only an outline of the accompaniment. Consequently, enterprising keyboard players will want to improvise and elaborate upon the given arrangements, in a style appropriate to the nature of the song or hymn.

● The chords given in *Let's Praise!* have been chosen with the average guitarist in mind. With many of the arrangements, capo markings are given to make the songs more accessible. '**Capo 5(C)**' means place the capo at the fifth fret and play the chords in brackets, which will be found to be in the key of **C**, rather than **F**.

● For chords marked '. . **sus**' assume they are sustained 4th chords.

● '**N.C.**' indicates no chords are to be played.

● For chords marked '. . +' play the equivalent augmented chord. For example '**C+**' = C aug. 5th.

● A guitarist may find it easier to dispense with the 'extras' of a chord – for example, instead of **C9** play C; instead of **Csus** play C; instead of **Cm7** play Cm.

● Bass notes are given where appropriate. Bass players are encouraged to follow these where possible.

● Certain hymns have a fast harmonic rhythm, and a guitarist may have problems keeping up with the change of chords! These may be best left to the keyboard player.

● On a number of items, certain chords are in bold type. By playing these chords only, the average guitarist will be able to accompany the songs with greater ease. However, these chords are not consistent with the keyboard harmony and are more suited to 'guitar-only' accompaniment.

CHORD CHART

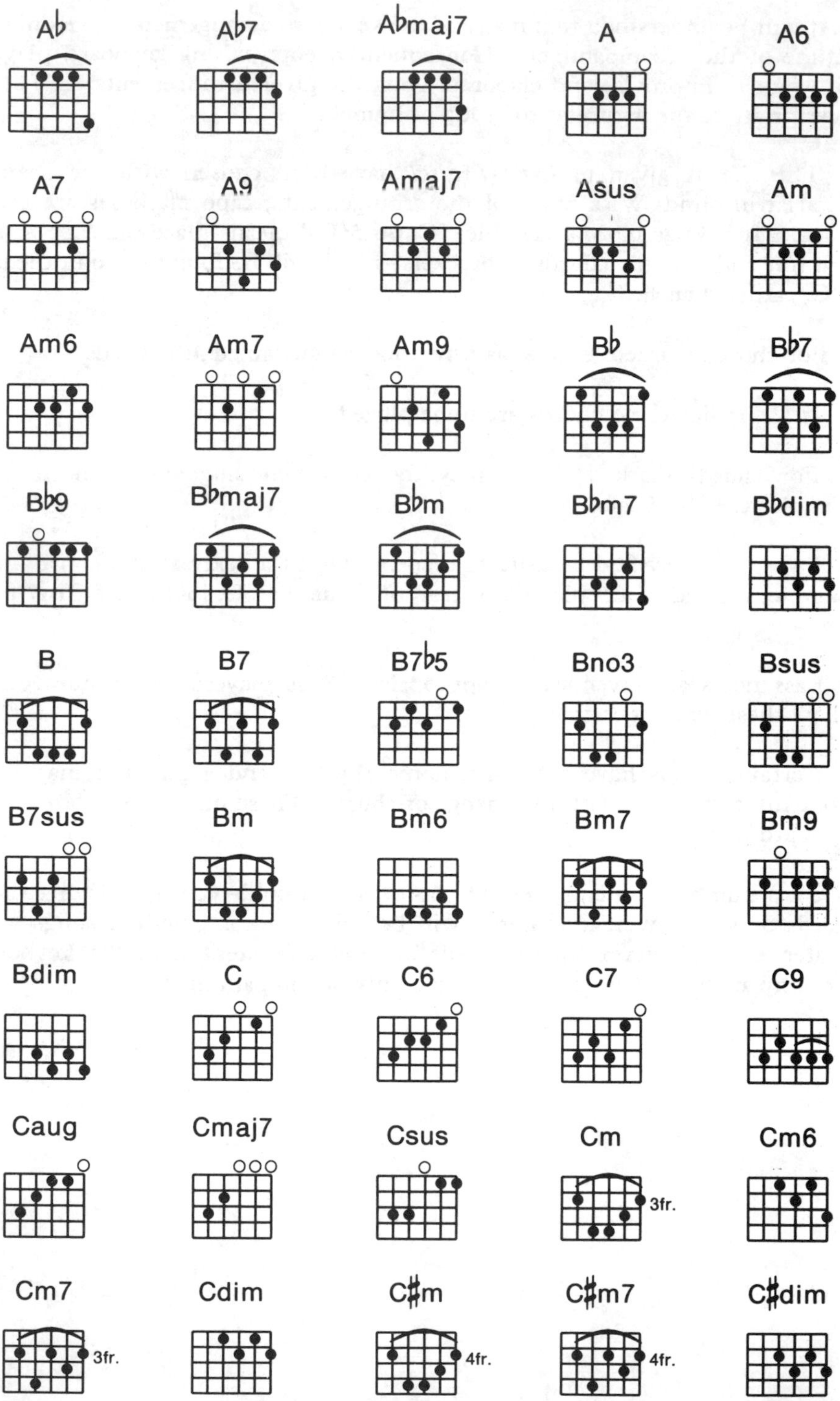

A♭
A♭7
A♭maj7
A
A6
A7
A9
Amaj7
Asus
Am
Am6
Am7
Am9
B♭
B♭7
B♭9
B♭maj7
B♭m
B♭m7
B♭dim
B
B7
B7♭5
Bno3
Bsus
B7sus
Bm
Bm6
Bm7
Bm9
Bdim
C
C6
C7
C9
Caug
Cmaj7
Csus
Cm
3fr.
Cm6
Cm7
3fr.
Cdim
C♯m
4fr.
C♯m7
4fr.
C♯dim

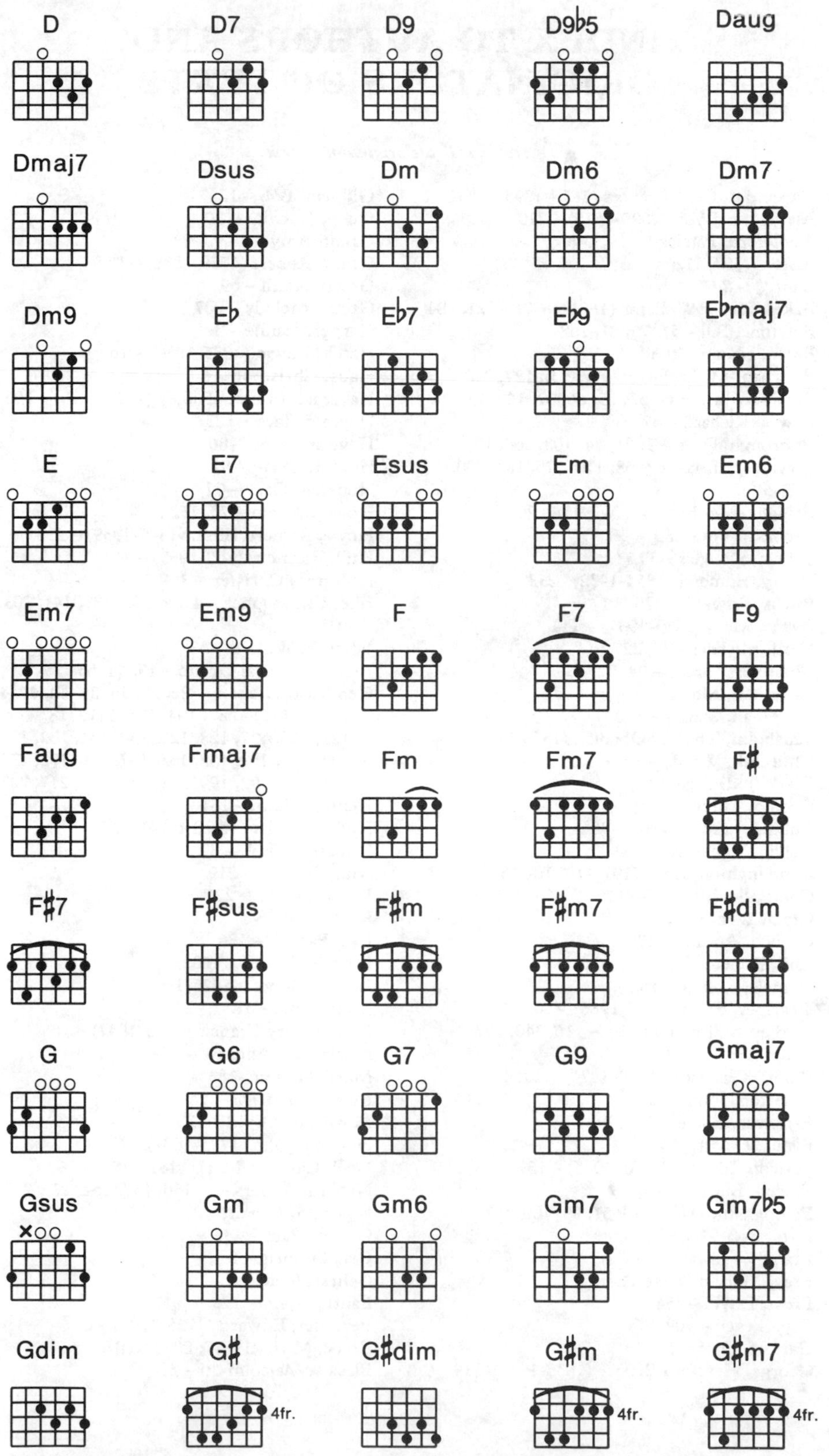
D
D7
D9
D9♭5
Daug
Dmaj7
Dsus
Dm
Dm6
Dm7
Dm9
E♭
E♭7
E♭9
E♭maj7
E
E7
Esus
Em
Em6
Em7
Em9
F
F7
F9
Faug
Fmaj7
Fm
Fm7
F♯
F♯7
F♯sus
F♯m
F♯m7
F♯dim
G
G6
G7
G9
Gmaj7
Gsus
Gm
Gm6
Gm7
Gm7♭5
Gdim
G♯
4fr.
G♯dim
G♯m
4fr.
G♯m7
4fr.

INDEX TO AUTHORS AND ORIGINATORS OF TEXTS

Italics indicate originator of text

INDEX TO COMPOSERS, ARRANGERS AND SOURCES OF MUSIC

Italics indicate arrangements

INDEX TO BIBLE REFERENCES

INDEX TO THEMES

JESUS CHRIST RULES

Jesus Christ rules all

Jesus Christ rules the world

Jesus Christ rules the church

Jesus Christ rules the individual

Jesus Christ rules for ever

INDEX TO MUSICAL STYLES

Some examples of distinctive musical styles found in the book

African

Black Gospel

Hebrew

Jazz

Latin American

Solo performance songs

Taizé

Response-style songs

'Make Way 1 – A Carnival of Praise' street procession songs

'Make Way 2 – Shine, Jesus, Shine' (selected) street procession songs

Comtemporary words to existing tunes

INDEX TO HYMNS (WITH TUNES)

Italics indicate titles and earlier first lines

PRAISE INDEX

Songs and hymns
suitable for 'Praise' sections of meetings –
more exhuberant material

See also index to Praise-Shouts

WORSHIP INDEX

Songs and hymns
suitable for Worship sections of meetings –
usually more reflective material

RESPONSE INDEX

Songs and hymns
suitable for 'Response' sections of meetings

INDEX TO VOCAL ARRANGEMENTS

INDEX TO INSTRUMENTAL ARRANGEMENTS

INDEX TO COMMUNION SONGS AND HYMNS

INDEX TO PRAISE-SHOUTS

MAIN INDEX

Italics indicate other names
by which the songs and hymns are known,
and also the Praise-Shouts.